KEEPING THE FAITH

KEEPING THE FAITH

Essays to Mark the Centenary of Lux Mundi

Edited by
GEOFFREY WAINWRIGHT

Fortress Press
Philadelphia

Pickwick Publications
Allison Park, Pennsylvania

Library of Congress Cataloging-in-Publication Data

Keeping the faith.

    1. Theology, Doctrinal. I. Wainwright, Geoffrey,
1939–   . II. Lux mundi.
BT80.K44 1988   230   87–46096
ISBN 0–8006–0876–3
ISBN 1–55635–001–5 (Pickwick Publications)

1451C88   Printed in the United States of America   1–876

In memory of Michael Ramsey,
valiant for
the gospel and the catholic church

CONTENTS

CONTENTS

CONTENTS

CONTENTS

CONTRIBUTORS

PAUL AVIS, a priest of the Church of England, is vicar of Stoke Canon in the diocese of Exeter. After studies at Cambridge and London, he received a Ph.D. from the University of London in 1976. He is the author of *The Church in the Theology of the Reformers* (1982), *Ecumenical Theology and the Elusiveness of Doctrine* (1986, U.S. title: *Truth Beyond Words*), *The Methods of Modern Theology* (1986), *Foundations of Modern Historical Thought: From Machiavelli to Vico* (1986), and *Gore: Construction and Conflict* (1988).

DUNCAN B. FORRESTER, a minister of the Church of Scotland, is Principal of New College and Professor of Christian Ethics and Practical Theology at the University of Edinburgh. He served as a missionary teacher at Madras College in India and as a chaplain and lecturer at the University of Sussex, England. His books include *Caste and Christianity* (1980), *Christianity and the Future of Welfare* (1985), and *Theology and Politics* (1988). Dr. Forrester is a member of the Faith and Order Commission of the World Council of Churches.

DIKRAN Y. HADIDIAN, a member of the United Church of Christ, served as librarian at the Hartford Seminary Foundation and at Pittsburgh Theological Seminary. He initiated the yearly "Ex Auditu" symposium on the theological interpretation of Scripture. He is the founder and general editor of Pickwick Publications.

DANIEL HARDY was ordained a priest in the Episcopal Church, U.S.A. Having taught theology at the University of Birmingham, England from 1965 to 1986, he is now Van Mildert Professor of Divinity at the University of Durham and a residentiary canon of Durham Cathedral. He coauthored *Jubilate: Theology in Praise* (1984, U.S. title: *Praising and Knowing God,* 1985) and wrote *Education for the Church's Ministry* (1987). Professor Hardy is president of the Society for the Study of Theology (United Kingdom).

BRIAN HEBBLETHWAITE, a priest of the Church of England, is Dean of Chapel at Queens' College and Lecturer in Divinity at the University of Cambridge. He is the author of *Evil, Suffering and Religion* (1976), *The Problems of Theology* (1980), *The Adequacy of Christian Ethics* (1981, U.S. title: *Christian Ethics in the Modern Age,* 1982), *The Christian Hope* (1984), *The Incarnation: Collected Essays in Christology* (1987), and *The Ocean of Truth* (1988). He is a canon theologian of Leicester.

ALASDAIR HERON is a minister of the Church of Scotland and of the Reformed Church of Bavaria, being a member of the Moderamen of the Reformed Alliance in West Germany. A Dr.Theol. of the University of Tübingen, he taught at the Irish School of Ecumenics and at the University of Edinburgh before becoming Professor of Reformed Theology at the University of Erlangen in 1981. Dr. Heron is an editor of the Scottish Journal of Theology. He is the author of *A Century of Protestant Theology* (1980), *The Holy Spirit* (1983), and *Table and Tradition* (1983). He has participated in the bilateral dialogues of the World Alliance of Reformed Churches with the Roman Catholic Church and the Disciples of Christ.

ROBERT W. JENSON, a Dr.Theol. of the University of Heidelberg, is Professor of Religion at St. Olaf College, Northfield, Minnesota. His books include *God After God: The God of the Past and the God of the Future* (1969), *The Knowledge of Things Hoped For: The Sense of Theological Discourse* (1969), *Visible Words: The Interpretation and Practice of Christian Sacraments* (1978), *The Triune Identity: God according to the Gospel* (1982), and *America's Theologian: A Recommendation of Jonathan Edwards* (1988). An ordained presbyter in the Evangelical Lutheran Church in America, Dr. Jenson was for twenty years Professor of Systematic Theology at Gettysburg Lutheran Seminary.

GEORGE LINDBECK, a member of the Evangelical Lutheran Church in America, is Pitkin Professor of Historical Theology in the Department of Religious Studies and the Divinity School, Yale University. An observer at the Second Vatican Council, he wrote *Challenge and Response: A Protestant Perspective on the Vatican Council* (1966) and *The Future of Roman Catholic Theology: Vatican II, Catalyst for Change* (1970). For ten years Dr. Lindbeck acted as Lutheran co-chair of the International Lutheran/Roman Catholic Study Commission. His most recent book is *The Nature of Doctrine: Religion and Theology in a Postliberal Age* (1984).

LESSLIE NEWBIGIN was a bishop of the Church of South India from its founding in 1947 and also served in the general secretariat of the International Missionary Council and the World Council of Churches. His many books include *A South India Diary* (1951), *The Household of God* (1953), *A Faith for this One World?* (1961), *The Finality of Christ* (1969), *The Open Secret* (1979), *Unfinished Agenda: An Autobiography* (1985), and *Foolishness to the Greeks* (1986). Bishop Newbigin, who now ministers to a local congregation in the United Reformed Church of England and Wales, holds honorary doctorates from the Universities of Chicago, St. Andrews, Hamburg, Basel, Hull, and Newcastle.

RICHARD NORRIS is Professor of Church History at the Union Theological Seminary, New York, and priest associate at St. Ignatius' Episcopal Church, Manhattan. An Oxford D.Phil., Father Norris previously taught at the Philadelphia Divinity School and at the General Theological Seminary in New York. He is the author of *Manhood and Christ* (1962) and *Understanding the Faith of the Church* (1978). He has served on the theological commission of the Consultation on Church Union in the United States and on the Anglican–Reformed International Commission. He was the president of the American Theological Society for 1986–87.

DAVID N. POWER, a Roman Catholic presbyter who previously taught at the Gregorian University in Rome, is now Professor of Systematic Theology and Liturgy at the Catholic University of America in Washington, D.C. He is the author of *Ministers of Christ and His Church* (1969), *Christian Priest: Elder and Prophet* (1973), *Gifts That Differ: Lay Ministries Established and Unestablished* (1980; 2d ed., 1985), *Unsearchable Riches: The Symbolic Nature of Liturgy* (1984), and *The Sacrifice We Offer: The Tridentine Dogma and Its Reinterpretation* (1987). A member of the editorial board of Concilium since 1970, Dr. Power was for 1987–88 the president of the North American Academy of Liturgy.

THEODORE RUNYON, an elder in the United Methodist Church, is Professor of Systematic Theology at the Candler School of Theology, Emory University. A Dr.Theol. of the University of Göttingen, he has been active in the Oxford Institute of Methodist Theological Studies. He edited *Hope for the Church* (1979), *Sanctification and Liberation* (1981), and *Wesleyan Theology Today* (1985). In 1988 he chaired an international consultation on "Theology, Politics and Peace."

STEPHEN SYKES, ordained in the Church of England, is Regius Professor of Divinity at the University of Cambridge. He is an assistant priest at St. John's Church, Cambridge, and an honorary canon of Ely Cathedral. He has given the Edward Cadbury Lectures at the University of Birmingham (1977–78) and the Hensley Henson Lectures at the University of Oxford (1982–83). His books include *Friedrich Schleiermacher* (1971), *Christian Theology Today* (1971; 2d ed., 1983), *The Integrity of Anglicanism* (1978), and *The Identity of Christianity* (1984). He is also coeditor of *The Study of Anglicanism* (1988).

GEOFFREY WAINWRIGHT, a British Methodist minister, taught in Cameroon and England before becoming Professor of Systematic Theology at the Union Theological Seminary in New York and then, in 1983, at Duke University. He holds the Dr.Theol. of the University of Geneva and the D.D. of the University of Cambridge. His books include *Christian Initiation* (1969), *Eucharist and Eschatology* (1971; 2d ed., 1981), *Doxology* (1980), and *The Ecumenical Moment* (1983). He is coeditor of *The Study of Liturgy* (1978) and *The Study of Spirituality* (1986). He presided over the final redaction of the Faith and Order text, *Baptism, Eucharist and Ministry* at Lima in 1982 and currently co-chairs the Joint Commission between the World Methodist Council and the Roman Catholic Church.

KEITH WARD, an Anglican priest, was Dean of Trinity Hall, Cambridge, before moving to the University of London, where he was first Professor of Moral Theology and is now Professor of the History and Philosophy of Religion at King's College. His chief publications are

Ethics and Christianity (1970), *Kant's View of Ethics* (1972), *The Concept of God* (1974), *Rational Theology and the Creativity of God* (1982), and *Images of Eternity* (1987). He is a member of the Church of England's Board for Social Responsibility.

PREFACE

In 1889, eleven Oxford dons wrote a book "to put the Catholic faith into its right relation to modern intellectual and moral problems," or, lest that formulation imply a reversal of priorities, to expound "the Christian Creed" which they believed to be "as adequate as ever to interpret life and knowledge in its several departments." The hundred years that have elapsed since the publication of *Lux Mundi* constitute a dynamic and agitated period in the history of humankind, marked by an explosion of knowledge (in the natural sciences in particular), of communications, and of bombs. The church of Christ soldiers on, a source of light and strength to many, yet still needing to confront what Charles Gore called "the claims, intellectual and practical, made upon us from outside" and, we must add, from within. The time is again ripe, as perhaps it always is, for "interpreting the faith we have received," for a "restatement of its claim and meaning," to "present positively the central ideas and principles" of the Christian faith under the stimulus of "contemporary thought" and in an effort to meet "current problems." The book in hand is intended as a contribution to that task.

The witness can emerge only from a wrestling with internal and external challenges, even if the challengers cannot be allowed simply to set the terms of the debate and the rules of the discussion.

In intellectual and cultural history, our century has been dominated, directly or indirectly, by the assumptions, methods and achievements of the natural sciences. At a popular, practical and sometimes philosophical level, these have been taken to exclude a transcendent and gracious Mystery who would be source, sustenance and goal of the world. But the sociology of knowledge has now begun to teach us the

PREFACE

extent to which science itself is culturally conditioned and, to put it more personally, remind us that our acquisition of knowledge is governed by our "interests." Now, Christianity has long known that our intellect is affected by our will, which is itself both perpetrator and victim of our "fallen" condition. But while there is today an incipient human disillusionment at the failure of morality to progress at the pace of modern Western science and technology, that does not mean that Christian thinkers should join the bandwagon of "postmodern" irrationalisms. Rather, we need to relocate rationality, as Daniel Hardy argues in chapter 12, in an altogether deeper and denser Wisdom that bears intellectual, moral and practical aspects. Mental and technical disciplines require discipleship to the Word made flesh. The contributors to this book do not characteristically rush for "models" either to the natural or human sciences or to literary or philosophical theory, autonomously understood. They tend, rather, to suggest that the Christian story or vision offers a comprehensive context or perspective in which particular knowledge can be illuminatingly and effectively pursued and applied.

Our century's rapid increase in worldwide communications has been accompanied by an increased awareness of the various stories and visions that lay claim to interpret and perhaps change the world. The several *Weltanschauungen* develop in competition. An irenic pluralism is no guarantee of peace, and, at its worst, it sacrifices the question of truth to indifferentism. That is quite inadequate to people looking for meaning and well-being, whether in a present or an ultimate sense. Lesslie Newbigin, in chapter 13, points once more to the judgment and hope that constitute the universal horizon for those who see in Jesus the very particular revelation of the loving purposes of God. His contribution springs from commending Christ to the peoples of India during four tumultuous decades.

At the geopolitical level, our century has been the first to experience two "world wars", which are not unconnected with an unprecedented degree of economic interdependence. War, even genocide, is the drastic communal expression of the pride, greed and hatred that mark our sinful condition, the wages of which is death. It is Christian teaching that humankind is made for a life of mutual society in communion with God. The former cannot be had without the latter. Political arrangements, always imperfect, are at least a means of mitigating the worst ravages of sin; at best, the social order may begin to approach, in a way appropriate to the present history of God with the world, the freedom, justice and peace in which the final reign of God will consist. In chapter 11, Duncan Forrester argues that a sober, critical, encouraging political theology will be rooted in a trinitarian faith, illumined by an eschatological hope, and inspired by a prophetic love for people. In his chapter on Christian ethics (chapter 10), Keith Ward shows how Jesus, as the human form taken by the divine power, wisdom and love in our broken world, becomes the sovereign exemplar for a personal transformation that participation in the Holy Spirit can bring to human beings made for communal bliss in God. In chapter 4, Richard Norris underlines how constitutive, in the Christian way of talking, are relationships, both internal and transcendent, and the implied dialectic of limitation and freedom, to the being of human individuals and communities; finally our personhood depends on our answerability before God, the divine Trinity. In chapter 3, Brian Hebblethwaite sets the problem of evil in the perspective of the conditions that are intrinsically necessary for the formation of creaturely personality, while indicating the length and depth of God's engagement to achieve the final good of humankind.

If the epistemological, ideological and moral factors that I have mentioned characterize the shifting global circumstances since *Lux Mundi,* it must also be noted that the immediate context of Christianity has also changed. Old Christendom has undergone an ever increasing secularization. To draw on the original use of that term, it may be said that the church has lost much of its property, in every sphere of life. Throughout Europe, including Poland, and even in the United States, the liturgical assembly has shrunk. Christian considerations are no longer so present to the institutions of society. Literature and the arts find other patrons and other inspirations. Perhaps in this last realm it would have been interesting to include a chapter on signs of continuing or renewed Christian vitality in the broader Western culture. My impression, however, is that more exciting things are to be found among the Christian storytellers, dramatists, sculptors and painters of Africa, Asia and the Pacific; and it is from those regions that a more general revival in the fortunes of Christianity is likely to come. That does not mean that as older Christians we may sit back and wait. We still have our responsibilities to our nearer neighbors and as a continuing part of the universal church.

It was in fact evangelistic and missionary motives that launched the ecumenical movement of the twentieth century. Whereas all eleven contributors to *Lux Mundi* were clergymen of the Church of England, their four most direct successors in that respect have here been joined by two from the Episcopal Church in the United States, and all of them together have been outnumbered by a combination of two Lutherans, three in the Reformed tradition, two Methodists, and a Roman Catholic. That such cooperation in the theological task seems normal is a measure of the progress made in the century since, for example, the entire Universities of Oxford and Cambridge ceased to be virtually Anglican preserves. Nevertheless there is still far to go before the historic churches—and the divisions they exported in their missionary endeavours—will have been reconciled. In chapter 8, George Lindbeck proposes an ecclesiology of the people of God which is both theologically responsible and (therewith) offers a framework for continuing rapprochement in matters of faith and order.

In its authentic self-understanding, the twentieth-century ecumenical movement has never sought either a reductive or a cumulative unity, limited to a highest common factor or reaching for a lowest common denominator. It is, rather, a qualitative matter of embodying simultaneously the purity and richness of the gospel. That requires criteria for discernment. Hence the importance of the hermeneutical explorations made by David Power in his pneumatological chapter on Scripture, tradition and interpretation (chapter 7). Hence also the dogmatic centrality of the "cruciform" chapters by Alasdair Heron and Paul Avis on the person of Christ (chapter 5) and the atonement (chapter 6). Hence, finally, Theodore Runyon's exposition, in chapter 9, of the dominical sacraments as the gracious conveyance and ritual celebration of a redemption that is total in scope.

It is the proper centrality of Christ which justifies the subtitle of *Lux Mundi:* "Studies in the Religion of the Incarnation". As I have read and reread the chapters of the present volume, I have become increasingly convinced that it could be subtitled "Essays from Within a Trinitarian Faith". This is most obviously the case with Robert Jenson's bold contribution, deeply indebted to the Cappadocians, on "the Christian doctrine of God" (chapter 2). But Stephen Sykes, in chapter 1, shows that it is not only the content of the Christian faith, the *fides quae creditur,* but also the act of faith, the *fides qua creditur,* which bears a trinitarian structure. And my own chapter on eschatology (chapter 14) recognizes a trinitarian pattern in final salvation and in the way towards it. Attentive readers will not only observe such and other obvious passages but also detect a trinitarian watermark running through much else in the book.

The emphasis placed by *Lux Mundi* on the incarnation may have been an attempt to capture from the inside—and reclaim for Christ—the immanentist mood and the turn to the human that had increasingly characterized Western thought and culture since the Renaissance and the Enlightenment. Certainly a stress on the incarnation was and remains a valuable counter to the deistic retreat endemic to much English-language theology and lately typified by *The Myth of God Incarnate*. But if Christocentrism ever tends to Christomonism, it can then come dangerously close to a Feuerbachian reduction of theology to anthropology—or *sub specie crucis* to the "death of God" proclaimed by "Christian atheism" in naive dependence on Jean-Paul and Nietzsche. With varying degrees of explicitness, either singly or in combination, the authors of this present volume move in a comprehensively trinitarian way. By attending to the diversity-in-unity exhibited in the life of the three-personed God, it may be possible, as a byproduct if not as a direct apology, to capture from the inside the current cultural mood of "pluralism"—and thereby give a coherent shape to an otherwise amorphous secular ideology that lacks center and edges, while also letting appear the substantial Christian answer to the crying human need of community. However that may be, I personally am convinced that historic Christianity stands or falls with a trinitarian faith.

How does our present book relate more particularly to the chapters of the original *Lux Mundi,* with whose authors we are engaged in theological fellowship within the communion of the saints? As editor, Charles Gore claimed that their studies "will be seen to cover, more or less, the area of the Christian faith in its natural order and sequence of parts, but the intention is not to offer complete theological treatises, or controversial defences of religious truths: it is rather to present positively the central ideas and principles of religion, in the light of contemporary thought and current problems". We have followed roughly the same general plan, although we have thought it necessary, on account of both their intrinsic importance and their prominence in twentieth-century scholarly reflection, to devote entire chapters to the dogmatic topics of anthropology and eschatology; and we have likewise added special chapters on the relations of the Christian faith to the natural sciences and the world religions. Even in chapters that correspond directly to the titles of those in *Lux Mundi,* we have filled in some of the gaps left by the original, while leaving many new ones of our own. Where possible, we have picked up valuable impulses from the original, but we have not hesitated to criticize certain features or follow other approaches. This volume, *Keeping the Faith*, is not, then, a "revision" of *Lux Mundi*. It honors the original and its authors by attempting in our own time, as they did in theirs, that clarification of faith's apprehension of the everlasting gospel which is always needed for the gospel's transmission to contemporaries and to the future. If our witness is faithful, it will be owned by the Faithful Witness, who is the Light of the World.

The Oxford Eleven had enjoyed more than a decade of "happy companionship" in close physical proximity and as members of a common institution. The difference in the production of *Keeping the Faith* is a sign of both the problems and the opportunities in our changed circumstances. The present book has been in the making since 1982. In 1985 most of the eventual contributors managed to gather for a week of intensive discussion at Hawarden in North Wales. In that connection we are grateful for the financial support of Mrs. Frederick Neumann and of our publishers, and for the hospitality of St. Deiniol's Library offered by Dr. Peter Jagger. Since that time, we have had to proceed by correspondence and casual encounters. Our contributors live on both sides of Hadrian's Wall, the English Channel, and the Atlantic Ocean. We include an Englishman resident in Durham, North Carolina; an Irishman teaching in Washington, D.C.; and a Scotsman living in Erlangen, Bavaria—not to mention an American canon of Durham, England. Our English associations, by the way, lie rather more with Cambridge than with Oxford, though we have an American who was a curate at the University Church of St. Mary the Virgin and another who was a tutor at Mansfield College. Our ecumenical range has already been indicated. Most of us belong to what I suppose must be called the middle generation of active theologians, but we are proud to have as a senior partner a bishop of the Church of South India who has served as moderator of the United Reformed Church of England and Wales.

Mutual debate and discussion have led to refinement and correction, though not as much as we would have liked had circumstances permitted. Each remains responsible for his own contribution, while grateful for the help of colleagues. Within a far-reaching commonality of outlook, there remain differences of emphasis, and even substantive ten-

sions. Perhaps the most striking is that between Hebblethwaite and
Jenson on freedom. But, as Sykes points out, that is a classic one in the
history of theology, and it may therefore be expecting too much that
it should be resolved here; there are perhaps signs in the contributions
of Norris, Ward and myself that the opposition need not be as strong
as Jenson and Hebblethwaite make out.

The idea for the book came from the Armenian-American Congre-
gationalist Dikran Hadidian, librarian, historical theologian, and
publisher at Pickwick Publications, who has himself added a biblio-
graphical epilogue. Our thanks are due to first Norman Hjelm and
then Harold Rast, at Fortress Press, and to Judith Longman at SPCK,
for their editorial acceptance of the project; and to Stephanie Eg-
notovich and her technical associates at Fortress for expertise in production. My special gratitude goes to my assistant Paul Burgess, not
only for help with the manuscripts and proofs but also for reading the
whole with an outside eye for thematic coherence.

The Divinity School   GEOFFREY WAINWRIGHT
Duke University
25 January 1988

KEEPING THE FAITH

1

FAITH

I. VARIETY OF USAGE

"Faith", in the words of the memorable translation of Heb. 11:1 offered in the King James (Authorized) Version, "is the substance of things hoped for, the evidence of things not seen." It would be more than ordinarily convenient if we could simply say that this verse provides us with a clear and authoritative definition of faith. But it does not. As Calvin succinctly explained, what we have here is the description of an aspect of faith important for the purposes of a larger argument. "The apostle is not discussing the nature of faith as a whole but he selects that part which fits his purpose, namely that it is always joined to patience."[1] The need for patience or endurance is the real subject of the whole section, and the previous verse draws a vivid contrast between a fearful shrinking from the task and a bold grasp upon life by faith. "And what is faith?"—the New English Bible inserts a rhetorical question—"Faith gives substance to our hopes, and makes us certain of realities we do not see." Here, then, is no definition but the elucidation of one important facet of faith, significant for this argument in this context. The proposition is perfectly compatible with other sentences giving other descriptions, and all are compatible with a much more general definition of faith, if such a definition exists.

It is a matter of some importance that we grasp the fact that the history of theology presents us with nothing like a standard definition of faith. It is not just the case that there is a long-standing disagreement between post-Reformation Roman Catholic and Protestant understandings of faith; it is also apparent that there are a whole variety of dimensions, facets or aspects of faith that need to be taken into account.

1

Without attempting any kind of organization, we can simply inspect a catalogue of phrases in which we are accustomed to finding the word "faith". For example: faith (as in the text from Hebrews) as confidence; faith as the human response to divine revelation; faith as a gift of God; faith as grasp upon the prevenient justifying grace of God; faith as intellectual assent; faith as obedience; the shared faith of a community; faith as *the* faith, signifying the totality of the content of Christian belief; faith exemplified in works of love; faith as contrasted with knowledge; faith as personal knowledge, of God and of oneself. Concerning each of these examples, somewhat in the manner of the writer to the Hebrews, one would not be surprised to find a Christian pausing to ask, "And what is faith?" and proceeding to give, not a definition, but another aspect of the description of faith—for example, "Faith is unquestioning trust in the power of God." Once having encountered a number of such pronouncements, a critical reader might be forgiven for wondering whether this all too malleable of words in the Christian's vocabulary is so imprecise and so elusive that a systematic introduction to its meaning and significance is impossible.

The matter is scarcely improved when we turn to the biblical words corresponding to the English "faith" or "belief". Here too we are confronted by a variety of usages. First, there are, as one would expect, a number of different Hebrew words that might be translated by "to have faith" or "to believe". Second, the New Testament contains a variety of contexts in which the noun, *pistis* ("faith"), or the verb, *pisteuō* ("to believe"), is used.[2] Again without any attempt at classification, we may catalogue them as follows: faith in God; faith in God's saving deed in Christ, that is, belief that God has sent his Son for human salvation; believing in Jesus Christ; faith in the power of God to perform a miracle; faith as obedience and fidelity; faith as confidence in God; faith as the cognitive content, or knowledge, truthfully communicated by a Christian preacher; faith as hope in a certain future; faith as union with Christ in his death and resurrection; faith, seen in relation to love and thus to a particular way of living. Again the question presses, Why is there so much variety, and why does no biblical writer appear to provide a comprehensive definition?

To be sure, there are certain important historical turning points in the development of Christian attitudes towards faith that can be observed within the New Testament period itself. Among them is the fact that at a critical moment in arguments with Jews or Judaizing Christians

2

St. Paul cited two Old Testament passages, one from the Greek translation of Gen. 15:6, "Abraham believed God, and it was counted to him for righteousness" (Gal. 3:6; Rom. 4:3; also quoted for a different purpose in the Letter of James 2:23), and the second from Hab. 2:4, "He who through faith is righteous shall live" (Gal. 3:11; cf. Rom. 1:17; the passage is also quoted in full in Heb. 10:38). These are clear instances of a not uncommon New Testament pattern, where the core meaning of a term is given new content by its altered context and associations.[3] In the case of the reference to Abraham, what St. Paul is emphasising is his response of trust to God's prior initiative of grace. But because the Christian is now living in the new covenantal context of Christ's death and resurrection, the precise meaning of the word "faith" is changed, specifically so as to make it impossible any longer to believe that works of obedience to the divinely given law could constitute what is in mind. The new covenant embraces both Jews and Gentiles; faith, therefore, cannot be by the works of the law.

A second observation of importance in the interpretation of faith in the New Testament is the fact that *pistis* as a religious term was a catchword used by those religions which engaged in propagandist missionary activity. Origen (ca. 185–ca. A.D. 254) cited Celsus, a second-century pagan philosopher, as complaining that Christians were indistinguishable from other groups in continually exhorting people to believe if they wanted to be saved—or else they would perish.[4] "Having faith" meant, inevitably, giving credence to the propaganda and behaving accordingly by enlisting in the mission; and this would have been as true of the doctrines of the hermetic movement of the second and later centuries, of the Isis mystery religion, and of Pythagoreanism as of Christianity.

A third historical turning point is the evident fact that, in what appears to be an inevitable development, faith came to be objectified as right doctrine or "orthodoxy".[5] Here is to be observed the same process of "routinization" (to use Weber's term) that produced the rituals of Christianity with their recollection of the mighty works of God. The repetition of the authentic message thus came to be expressed in a formula, which was regarded as a sacred deposit to be handed on by authorised preachers, and itself the object of credence. The process was already well advanced within the period covered by the New Testament documents. It is exemplified in the formula, "This is a true saying" or "Here are words you may trust," used in the pastoral

3

epistles and nowhere else in the New Testament. No attempt at a synthetic overview of the New Testament usage of *pistis* or *pisteuō* can afford to neglect the fact that the sociological conditions of Christianity changed markedly within the New Testament period and that this change is reflected in the central vocabulary of the religion.

II. FAITH AND ITS CORRELATES

In order, therefore, to get an account of faith off the ground, some plausible explanation will need to be offered for the astonishing variety exhibited in the history of the use of the word "faith" from the start of the Christian movement. What we do not need, evidently enough, is yet another partisan or a priori definition. We may also have to eschew the temptation, vividly exemplified in the history of theology, to use one understanding of faith (e.g., that of St. Paul) as a criterion for all others, after which there could only be inadequacy, decline and fall. On the available evidence there is no reason to suppose that St. Paul himself used the word in only one way; and given the history of Pauline interpretation, there would be even less reason to imagine that the quest for "St. Paul's profoundest insight into the nature of faith" would ever arrive at a final conclusion. Too much of the very apparatus of scholarship is itself the product of particular historical conditions for us to have any confidence that we could eliminate the interest of the reader from the account of the supposed content of the term, even if that were thought to be a desirable objective.

To start, then, by answering the question why it should be that there are a variety of aspects of faith reflected in the history of theology is to acknowledge that what we deem to *be* Christianity is itself inextricable from our construal of its history. The very term "Christianity" itself is one about which there are a series of chronic disagreements, and one could come to an informed understanding of how to use the word only if one had some acquaintance with the history of Christianity.[6] Precisely the same is true of the word "faith". Simply in order to understand the word, one must have a notion of the reasons for the variety of usages with which Christian history confronts us, and for a practising contemporary Christian it is also necessary to offer, at least in outline, a theory of why that variety contributes to, and does not undermine, the witness which the church offers in the world. This last task will concern us in section IV of this essay; in the present and following parts, we shall attempt to explain why faith necessarily wears a plurality of aspects.

4

We may begin by asking how, as a matter of common contemporary usage, the word "faith" is deployed in speaking of Christianity. We deploy it, it seems, as *the synoptic or comprehensive term to signify the response of an individual believer or of a community of believers to what is said to be God's self-revelation.* Because faith is a term related to another variable, namely, revelation, the word contains implicitly within itself the impact of all the multifarious aspects of God's self-revelation. If God reveals knowledge about himself, then faith will bear the aspect of knowledge; if God demands obedience to his will, then faith will imply assent; if God makes promises about the human future, then faith will signify confidence in those promises. The word "faith", therefore, is drawn by the many-sidedness of God's activity in relation to humankind into a context of usage that *must* include a variety of aspects. Faith and revelation are correlative terms.

But that is by no means the only source of pluralism and variety. Precisely because the new Christian movement both inherited and transformed the notion of faith from Judaism, the word acquired its new connotations precisely by being brought into creative association with other terms and concepts. A good example of this process is the association-by-denial contained in the Pauline slogan, "through faith in Jesus Christ, . . . not by works of the law" (Gal. 2:16). Here the content of what is meant by "faith in Jesus Christ" is partially conveyed by what is denied; but at the same time sufficient ambiguity remains about the positive connotations for it to be possible in another context to present the notion of faith in a formula reversing the slogan—faith without works is dead (James 2:17). In the one case (St. Paul's), we are confronted with faith as an entailment of the concept of justification; in the other (James's) with works, that is, acting in a particular way, as an entailment of the concept of faith.[7] The type of association between the different concepts will determine the way in which the term "faith" is to be understood. Precisely because of its fundamental quality, that is, its being located at the starting point of any Christian's public profession of his or her belief, the term "faith" comes to be drawn into conceptual contact with a plurality of other terms that are also aspects of Christian living.

This thought can briefly be developed somewhat further in relation to the various forms of *competitive* relation in which faith in its Christian sense is bound to stand. It has recently been argued that a particular belief has always to be interpreted as relative to its alternatives, that to say one believes in God is implicitly to hold that belief to be more probable than, say, the belief that there is no God.[8] Applied to the history of Christianity, this proposal seems to be supported by the plain fact that early Christian writers formulated their understanding of the gospel in the context of a wide variety of alternatives, some of which are difficult to make vivid to the contemporary imagination. Thus, for example, for many modern Christians the implied negations of aspects of Judaism contained in the presentation of faith in the New Testament are by no means self-explanatory; it may take a very substantial act of historical imagination to recover the precise point of the contrasts that St. Paul is drawing, or on the basis of which Jesus himself fell foul of the Jewish authorities of his day.

But a moment's thought makes it apparent that the New Testament provides us with evidence of a considerable range of competitive relationships. Not merely is Christian faith a "new covenant", the rites of baptism and eucharist are seen by contrast to similar initiatory or participatory rituals in the cults of the day, and the teachings of Christ are presented as a true wisdom and knowledge *(gnōsis)*. The content of the notion of faith, which is always presented as *sui generis,* because it is faith in Christ the unique and final revelation of God, is conceptually impregnated by that with which it is contrasted. No one, for example, would go to the trouble of contrasting faith with myths and godless speculations who did not sense that there was a mythological or speculative aspect to "the true faith" or who was not drawn to a presentation of Christianity that might give rise to that kind of error. One does not deny relationships where no question of their existence would occur to anyone.

Of nothing is this more certainly the case than the denial of doubt and the contrast between faith and disbelief. It has often been observed that the New Testament provides an extraordinarily full picture of those who were unpersuaded by Jesus and the apostles. Written though these documents are from the standpoint of faith and for believers, their insistence on the miraculous, especially on the miracle of the resurrection, is accompanied by open acknowledgement that there were those who doubted. When Mary Magdalene, Joanna, Mary the mother of James, and other women first told the apostles of the empty tomb and the vision of two angels, their words "seemed to them an idle tale" (Luke 24:11). Seen in contrast to doubt, faith has already come to be specifically resurrection faith. For St. Paul, that was the sine qua non of any Christian believing whatsoever (1 Cor. 15:14); and the narrative activity around the story of the resurrection, so evident in the versions that we have in the Gospels and works of St. Paul, is sufficient evidence of its centrality. Believing in the resurrection of Jesus was an element of enormous importance in the diverse construals of the story of Jesus with which these documents supply us.[9] The process of correlating the resurrection with the substance of Christianity as a whole was continued into the patristic period. For the unknown author of a treatise *On the Resurrection* (perhaps of the early third century), the resurrection was a general test case for what God is both able and willing to do, citing in this connection the biblical maxim that what is impossible for human beings is possible for God (Mark 10:27).[10] For St. Augustine, discussing in the remarkable twenty-second chapter of the *City of God* cases of authentic contemporary miracles, these events are the direct corollary of the physical resurrection and ascension of Christ to heaven. With each affirmation the frontier of doubt or scepticism recedes. Christian living is the actualisation of resurrection faith.

Variety in the very notion of faith is, then, the product of a whole series of attractions to neighboring concepts or competition with alternative possibilities. There is no standard definition of faith, because the meaning of the term is shaped by other parts of any given form of the Christian tradition and by the ways in which that tradition is challenged from time to time by the prevalence of doubt or other foci of allegiance.

III. THEOLOGICAL AND ANTHROPOLOGICAL APPROACHES

But there is one further complication of major importance, if we are to understand the history of the various ways in which faith has been conceptualised. One important strand of thinking in the New Testament is that which attributes the occurrence of Christian discipleship to the agency of God himself, who draws or calls the disciple. "No one", said Jesus (in the Fourth Gospel), "can come to me unless the Father who sent me draws him" (John 6:44). Faith, therefore, is not one's own doing; it is not a work; it is, rather, the gift of God (Eph. 2:8). The history of Christian theology demonstrates with clarity that this line of thinking can be developed in such a way as to provide a challenge to a more common-sense viewpoint which sees faith as the humanly possible response of an individual to God's gracious invitation. On a "common-sense" view, God calls and we obey; thus the response of faith is an exercise of an initially God-given but now humanly exercised freedom. Faith in St. Paul is predominantly used in relation to decision, but he turns to the language of grace and predestination when wanting to emphasise the assurance of salvation.[11]

At once we are in the midst of a discussion that has constantly recurred since the days of St. Augustine, whether and to what extent one can rely on common-sense notions of human freedom. Augustine mounted the most persistent and at the same time the most disturbing denials of everyday assumptions about free choice. For him, freedom could never simply be the ability to weigh up and decide between alternatives. Being truly free is always a greater or lesser achievement, the result of an interiorly transformed will. God works upon the will, providing both inducements and invitations and kindling the love of or desire for God, without which mere acts of choice are taken within the context of an overarching slavery.[12] In time, Augustine's thought moved strongly into predestinarian channels, stopping short only of bluntly affirming that God foreordains certain persons to damnation. Further discussion of the issue of free will will be found to concern both Robert Jenson, writing in this volume on the Christian doctrine of God, and Brian Hebblethwaite on the problem of evil.

The tension between theologies that emphasise divine grace and those that seek adequately to do justice to human freedom has a perennial character, and the content of the idea of faith has swung uneasily between them. As a result, the Christian tradition taken as a whole can be seen to have promoted both of two lines of enquiry. On the one hand, there is a line of thinking that has sought to relate the human capacity to respond to God to contemporary philosophical anthropologies; and on the other hand, there is a history of theological enquiry strongly affirming the uniqueness of the divine revelation and the irreducibility of the categories of divine grace, invitation and summons. Thus we can find without difficulty evidence of a long-standing investment in rational analysis of the act of faith or religious self-commitment and at the same time numerous examples of primarily theocentric accounts of the phenomenon of faith. Many of the most sophisticated modern authors have attempted to combine both strands in their theological syntheses.

A striking example of this dual commitment is to be found in the work of the classic German theologian, Friedrich Schleiermacher (1768–1834). Educated as a pietist, Schleiermacher was at an early stage of his adult life "converted" to the task of providing a philosophical anthropology as a conversation partner for his theology. In due course he developed an understanding of the divinity of Christ embodying this dual focus. On the one hand, it spoke of Christ's "God-consciousness" in terms that connected it to the "God-consciousness" of every human being; on the other hand, he insisted that in Christ we have something unique. In a letter to a contemporary he wrote:

> If my Christian feeling is conscious of a Son of God who is different from the best of us in another way than by being still better, so will I never cease to search out the genesis of this Son of God in the deepest depths of nature and to say to myself that in all likelihood I shall comprehend that other Adam just as soon as I do the first Adam or Adams, whom I must also accept without comprehending.[13]

The reference to searching out the genesis of the Son of God is still significant, since, of course, it is perfectly possible to address questions to the New Testament about the "faith of Jesus". What did he believe, and how? Is his believing analogous to our own? What is to be learnt from the New Testament reports of his attitudes to God—for example, his address to God as Father, Abba? The moment we seek to make comprehensible to ourselves Jesus' own trust and confidence in God, we are engaged in one part of this dual enquiry, and we implicitly raise complex questions about the relationship between Christ and ourselves. As Richard Norris shows in his chapter on human being in this volume, changes in philosophical anthropology plainly have had an impact upon Christian theology. In our own century we may instance the "discovery" of the unconscious and its consequences both for human self-understanding and for ethical reasoning. The whole enterprise of *Lux Mundi* itself had earlier been concerned not just with developments in biology or palaeontology but specifically with the way in which philosophical anthropology had sought to respond to new ideas in the social and physical sciences.

From this point of view we may examine Henry Scott Holland's essay on "Faith", the opening contribution to *Lux Mundi,* with some interest. Scott Holland defined the crisis for the theology of his day as the apparent destruction by modern science of the "evidences for God", which had been deployed classically by William Paley (1743–1805) and had formed the backbone of Christian apologetic in British university education.[14] The recently advanced theory of evolution had apparently provided, without any reference to God's supposed design for creation, an account of how humankind had developed. In response to this challenge, Scott Holland strove to disentangle the notion of faith from an obsolete natural theology and at the same time to challenge the assumption that scientific reasoning would make faith itself redundant. Faith, as he presented it, is an integrating, person-constituting energy of the moral will, inaccessible as such to the empirical procedures of scientific enquiry. In effect, Scott Holland's refuge, faced with the challenge of the new scientific enquiry, was to develop (or, in his case, to import) a Christianly appropriate philosophical anthropology. Philosophy became for him the common middle ground between scientific empiricism and Christian theology, and he hoped to reassure the believer by the assertion that this philosophy was as necessary to the scientist, if he or she were to make sense of the world, as it might be to a Christian theologian.

Correlative to this philosophical position, Scott Holland strongly insisted on a personalistic account of the Christian religion as communion with God and thus of faith as personal trust in God. In the light of this understanding of faith he was at pains to show how the human being is intrinsically shaped for such fellowship. Thus he pursued what we have identified as the dual strategy, combining on the one hand a theological account of Christian revelation with, on the other, a philosophical account of human nature in general. "Faith" for him is the mid-term, alike for communion with God and for the possibility of scientific knowledge of the natural environment. Accordingly, faith, on this account, is the elemental, primal confidence that the world genuinely *is* as we experience it. "Our secular and scientific life is an immense experiment in faith", justified by continuous successes but dependent for its reality upon the constant reference to the divine-human relationship which is "the key to all its capacities, the justification of all its confidence, and the security of all its advance".

Scott Holland's attempt to deploy to the advantage of Christian theology a philosophical understanding of faith has a modern analogue in philosophy of religion after Ludwig Wittgenstein. Developing some of Wittgenstein's enigmatic remarks about frameworks, foundations, frames of reference, substratum or scaffolding, certain contemporary philosophers have suggested that religion is not alone in not needing to have evidences or grounds.

10

Religion is a form of life; it is language embedded in action—what Wittgenstein calls a "language game". Science is another. Neither stands in need of justification, the one no more than the other.[15]

Here again the intention is to neutralise the possibility of conflict between science and religion by associating religious faith with the same "groundlessness" as characterises the enterprise of natural science. Whether this proposal carries conviction—and it has serious consequences for any attempt to discriminate between true and false doctrines within any given religion—is not the task of this contribution to decide. The point is, rather, to draw attention to the continued attraction of a double reference in Christian theology, on the one hand to basal conditions of human cognitional activity and on the other to the requirements of fully articulated Christian theology.

Contemporary theology knows of a similar duality in one of its most prominent and characteristic developments, its concern for the phenomenon of narrative. Thus on the one hand it is observed (and has been incidentally observed by many theologians for many centuries) that the biblical revelation of God is in the form of a narrative.[16] God has "storied himself forth", and the narratives of God's self-revelation constitute a logically primary and unsubstitutable identity description of himself. The unique story of Jesus has both preface, in the story of Israel, and postlude, in the story of the church, the pilgrim people of God. On this account, "faith" is the comprehensive term signalling the difference between living in *that* story (as a member of the church) and living in any of its alternatives and competitors.

On the other hand, it makes perfectly good sense to argue that a theory of narrative is fundamental to *any* human identity, especially, as has been argued, to human moral identity. "Narrative history of a certain kind turns out to be the basic and essential genre for the characterisation of human actions."[17] At another level it has even been suggested that analysis of the capacity to recall a story is inherent in human cognitive processes.[18] Certainly it is appropriate to ask whether there is any relationship between the notion of "framework" or "schema" as it has been used in psychology since the pioneering work of Sir Frederick Bartlett and the idea of faith being a single comprehensive story. On Bartlett's classic account, a schema is "an active organization of past reactions, or of past experiences, which must always be supposed to be operating in any well-adapted organic response".[19] The structuring of knowledge derived from the past helps the learner to assimilate new information, which may progressively transform the original schema. Bartlett believed that as well as functioning on a relatively low level by processing information from visual, auditory or cutaneous impulses, schemata applied at a higher level to all experiences connected by a common interest, including art, science and philosophy.

It is a short step from such reflections in the realm of cognitional theory to suppose that the Christian story—say, in its ritually familiar form as creed—is a schema of a comprehensive kind supposed to function as *the* most general framework of any knowledge whatsoever, an overarching narrative in which all other schemata are to be contained. Whether in fact it functions in this way for all Christian believers is another question entirely. One may imagine it possible for a person to entertain two quite contradictory schemata unawares. It would not be difficult to suppose that one of the tasks for a Christian is to ensure that the Christian story becomes in reality the most comprehensive framework for all other schemata; that one's Christian life is not dominated de facto by a plurality of gods ("as a rule men are polytheists", according to H. Richard Niebuhr).[20]

Whatever the case may be in practice, the consideration of the theme of story demonstrates the same kind of duality as that on which we earlier commented. The Christian tradition appears to sponsor both the activity of self-understanding from within the tradition and the activity of analysing faith as a psychologically comprehensible type of human behavior. "Story" lends itself, on the one hand, to the idea of God uniquely "storying himself forth" and, on the other, to comparison with a schema or framework. The response of faith may be seen either as the continuation of God's own story, in the community of faith, or as the would-be comprehensive schema for the organisation of every aspect of a person's life story.

IV. COMPLEXITY AND COMMITMENT

All that has been said hitherto has confirmed our initial observation that we deploy the word "faith" as a comprehensive term, to signify the response of a believer or a community of believers to God's self-revelation. Whether the response is to be understood as prompted by God or is within the scope of human abilities has been variously evaluated. In either case, the comprehensiveness of the term is not in doubt, nor the fact that it is a term responsive to a variety of aspects of God's self-revelation and to competitive alternatives. Moreover, it has been suggested that the complexity of the term has to do with factors in its prehistory in Judaism and its history in Christianity. To be a person of faith is to inherit both the comprehensiveness and the complexity.

But there is a serious and too often unacknowledged problem with living with complexity. If faith is so complex a term, how can the occurrence of faith yield joy in the heart of the believer? How can he or she be confident in the claim to know and to love God, by faith? The issue is serious because those whose business it is to study the complexity of the past, that is, professional theologians and the clergy trained by them, too often fail to recognise the difference in the social settings in which various groups of Christians live their respective lives. Theologians and the clergy can, at least in the West, derive a certain measure of psychological support from the prestige attaching to their institutions and the stock of ideas that these institutions exist to promote. Thus their context enables them to tolerate complexity and ambiguity because it is seen to derive from a culturally valued study of the past. Professional theological educators occupy positions of status in the community as scholars and train their students to adapt to the knowledge of complexity and ambiguity by encouraging them to value appreciation for differing sides of an argument and to be critical of premature (and ignorant) resolutions of difficulties.

It is, however, apparent that professional theologians have so far shown inadequate sensitivity to the specific differences between their and the *layperson's* dilemmas. Reassured by their own ability to survive complexity and ambiguity, they have unjustifiably assumed that a suitably dilute version of the same problems can be communicated *de haut en bas.* But the puzzlement bred by complexity and ambiguity has a different significance for the layperson. Since laypersons are unable by reasons of time to give themselves to study of the past and are unprotected by close association with the prestige of the professional institution, their involvement in religious activities is evaluated by a secularised culture simply as the private choice of a life style. Differences inside a religious tradition are supposed to be of no greater significance than any other kind of option. In a pluralistic culture no one is expected to have to justify personal preference, and choices between differing life-style enclaves are made without depth of commitment.[21] If lay Christians simply adopt this secular evaluation of their response to the internal variety of Christianity, the consequences are religiously devastating, for the institution which they "join" no less than for themselves. The very consciousness of Christian pluralism, even if it consists of nothing more profound than awareness of the existence of differing denominations, can undermine the possibility of that single-minded commitment of which the gospel speaks. To this danger a layperson is more exposed than are clergy; and this helps to explain the fact that many newly converted laypeople will at once consider a "call" to the ministry, misperceiving it as an heroic volunteering for the front line.

The power of contemporary fundamentalism lies precisely in its realisation that the threat of pluralism is felt most acutely by the laity. It meets the dilemma of the diminished prestige of the institution by constantly reassuring the believer that he or she has joined the most successful available religious option, as proved by miracles, physical and financial, and by evidence of ever-expanding numerical growth. It resolves the dilemma of Christianity's ambiguous and complex past by ignoring it completely, except where it can be communicated in rigorously controlled packets of information, an exercise to which the modern media lend themselves with unfortunate ease. "Modernist" theologians, who are too prone to turn from fundamentalism with cultural distaste, have much to learn from it about the acute "dilemma of commitment" into which the lay Christian falls in the modern world. Fundamentalism is the major form of religious commitment in which the complexity of Christianity can be so simplified as to resolve (or apparently to resolve) the threat to Christian confidence which historical knowledge of the past involves.

Two other movements characteristic of modern times supply us with somewhat similar evidence. The notorious theological happening of the 1960s, the so-called "death of God" or "secular theology" movement, had a programme whose explicit intention was to abandon unnecessary dogma and ritual from the past and to attempt to survive on some few maxims, often of a nontheistic or ethical character. In its way this response was itself a form of fundamentalism, not least in its programmatic dismissal of Christianity's supposedly superstitious and authoritarian past, and it took pride in the radicalism of its "reduction to fundamentals", seeing itself as a veritable new reformation. The 1960s also saw another major movement, the Pentecostal phenomenon, which unsurprisingly made little headway in academic circles because of its frequent association with forms of fundamentalism. Interestingly, however, it penetrated into the mainstream denominations and continues strongly in Roman Catholicism, Anglicanism, Methodism, and the Reformed and Lutheran churches. Pentecostalism is nothing if not confident and joyous, and its significance for the dilemma of specifically lay Christianity in the churches of the West also deserves to be taken more seriously by their intellectual élites.[22]

A contemporary Christian understanding of faith has, therefore, both to resolve the "dilemma of commitment" for the modern layperson and simultaneously to give at least the beginning of an adequate answer to the problem of Christianity's complexity and ambiguity. The heart of the matter lies, I shall argue, in how the church itself is understood. Any informed person today will be aware that contemporary Christianity presents itself not in one guise but in many—sometimes in a plurality of ways within one denomination. For such a person to have confidence that what he or she hears is in truth the Word of God, there must exist confidence that the proclaimer of the message is also able to give a consistent account of that pluralism. In other words, for faith to be capable of being a matter of joy and confidence, the church itself as a proclaimer of the faith must be simultaneously interpreted.

V. THE LIFE STORY OF THE CHRISTIAN AND THE CHURCH

This possibility is offered to us in consequence of a renewed grasp upon the narrative character of the identity of the church, the people of God, a theme taken up and expanded in George Lindbeck's contribution to this volume. At baptism a believer enters the narrative of the church. The story of Christianity from that moment onwards cannot be fully told without the life story of that believer. But, of course, any given believer knows perfectly well the complexity and the ambiguity of his or her own life. How, then, can the complexity and the ambiguity of the life of the church be any special matter of difficulty? Only, I suggest, on one of two mistaken assumptions: first, that the believer supposes that his or her life is exempt from ambiguities (as fundamentalism frequently suggests), or, alternatively, that the believer is led to think that the life of the church exists independently of his or her own failures and difficulties (as clericalised institutionalism would seem to imply). The answer to both of these errors is a theology of the church which fully embraces and interprets the life of every member of the same in his or her vocation and ministry.

For a Christian instructed from the first in such a way, although God's story with humanity is the story of the church, the church itself is transcended by the reality of faith, the name for which is the Holy Spirit. That is why, for the New Testament, there is no gift of faith which is not, in and at the same time a gift of the Holy Spirit, leading to a life of prayer. The Holy Spirit is the co-present agent transcending and interpreting the response of the individual Christian in the initial, and every subsequent, movement into fellowship with God. Furthermore, for this reason the gift of the Holy Spirit is to be seen eschatologically and in relation to the life of prayer, as the promise of a movement begun in God but to be continued and ended in him likewise. Although Calvin rightly said of the classic text on faith in Hebrews (11:1) that it does not present "the nature of faith as a whole", nonetheless what it does teach, that faith "is always joined to patience", is of exceptional importance. The story of faith, which is inextricable from the story of the church, has an anticipated ending in the very narrative which the church rehearses and the prayer of longing which it offers. The eschatology of the narrative guarantees, or should guarantee, that what is enjoyed here and now of the reality of faith is also seen to be transcended by what is rightly longed for.

The modern "dilemma of commitment" can be resolved by an historically instructed layperson only if such a person is able to keep a critical distance between his or her account of faith and the actual experience of living within the church. Such critical distance affirms the absolute necessity of the church and of life in its context, but at the same time assesses the inevitable failures of the church (and of every member of it, including oneself) with an objectivity akin to humour. Why humour? The reason appears to lie with what has been identified by many writers as the "paradox of humility", the fact that one is forbidden to congratulate oneself on being successfully humble, precisely in relation to the approach to God in worship. The poet George Herbert (1593–1633) observed the analogous dilemma inherent in the self-examination required by the Church of England's *Book of Common Prayer* as the normal preparation for coming to the Lord's Table. In the poem "Love III", a guest too insistently protests unworthiness in a "courtesy-contest" with his host—a contest which has, as have so many of Herbert's poems, humorous overtones—and is eventually "put in his place" by Love. "You must sit down, says Love, and taste my meat." This half-exasperated command is the last resort of a Love that has up until then been gentle, sweet and smiling. Love has, one might say, perceived the cancer of pride in the protestations of humility.[23] As a Christian writer, of course, Herbert is inviting his readers to perform for themselves what he lays out in the poetic dialogue. We are both guest and loving host in our administration of the discipline of self-examination. It is we who have to treat our own protestations of unworthiness with exasperated humour. We simply cannot achieve the required state of humility as a precondition of being a worthy guest at the Lord's Supper. We have no other resort than an objectivity about our failures akin to humour.

It is this same objectivity, I believe, which alone can restore to the Christian that sense of joy which is the fruit of genuine faith, a joy which is not striven for but given in and with the love which creates its object (Luther).[24] It is a joy which continuously makes the Christian conscious of the phenomenon of interior disorder, even of warfare, of which the spiritual writings of the Christian tradition are so eloquent. At this point we move in our argument from the requirements of Christian self-understanding faced with the modern dilemma of commitment, to the basic terms on which an instructed Christian can come to an understanding of the pluralism and ambiguity of the church's performance in time and history.

The metaphor of "interior warfare", used above to describe the self-consciousness of the Christian, might lead one to suppose that forces of good are observably ranged against forces of evil; that indeed is how much of the military language of the New Testament and subsequent spiritual writing apparently presents the matter. Scholarship, however, has led us to see that the background to these metaphors is Jewish apocalyptic, in which the *true* or *ultimate* order of things is being laid bare, with a view to reassuring the believer that he or she is secure, despite what his or her experience of the historical course of events might suggest.[25] "Interior warfare" is, therefore, the result of importing an apocalyptic metaphor into the elucidation of conflicting self-perceptions. But the self is inextricable from history, and history by no means displays the clarity and finality of apocalyptic. The metaphor of warfare applied to the self-consciousness of the Christian is supposed to display the true or ultimate order of things in the midst of historic ambiguity. But the ambiguity itself needs explanation in terms other than those which simply range good against evil.

Just as the individual Christian understands his or her life as displaying elements of sheer ambiguity, so also does the life of Israel and the

17

church; indeed, there are good grounds for arguing that the interior ambiguity is the mirror of the exterior rather than that the exterior reflects the interior. The position may be put in simplified form, as follows. All individual Christians are dependent for their understanding of their religion, and of themselves as believers, upon the content of "the Christian tradition" passed on to them by their respective churches. There are different versions of this "Christian tradition", and because modern Christians are relatively conscious of this diversity they have to distinguish between "lower" and "upper" versions of this tradition, the "lower" being relatively more mundane, fallible, and historically enmeshed and the "upper" being more divine, authoritative, and transcendent. The "lower" is not purely "earthly", because the incarnation affirms earth and human history; the "upper" is not purely "heavenly", because of unavoidable mundane conceptual entanglements. But how the "lower" and "upper" elements have been conceptually formulated in the public history of the Christian tradition has led to the dialectic driving the complexity of the church's life.

VI. THE INSTITUTIONAL-SACRAMENTAL AND THE EXPERIENTIAL MODELS

One may identify, accordingly, two major models of faith, both of which at different times and places have been accorded the lower or upper roles in the dialectic. The first of these has been the institutional-sacramental model of faith; and the second, the experiential. At the reformation of the sixteenth century these two models separated to become rival hermeneutical keys, whose fundamental incompatibility still receives recurrent support. The institutional-sacramental model is sociohistorical in character. It has its roots in affirmations about the divine foundation of the church and in the development of a mystery ecclesiology by which ideal and actual in the life of the historic body may be distinguished. The church becomes, on this model, the necessary presupposition of faith. The first charge upon the capital of faith, the first doubt to be overcome, is the doubt that there exists a divinely instituted society with the authority to declare with finality what the content of the faith is. Although historically this (Tridentine) understanding has been associated with a strongly intellectualist, content-oriented notion of faith, it is, in modern Roman Catholic thought, capable of also being advanced in personalist or communitarian terms. The reason for this is that it is held, as the presupposition for all further

18

reflection, that God has brought into being the church of Jesus Christ in which alone real community and personal encounter are possibilities. This is the "upper", transcendent level of conceptual ordering, and "below" it exists the experiential, frequently linguistically rejected as "individualistic". Onto this lower level are projected much of the weakness, fallibility and culpable lack of balance exhibited in the historic disorders of Christendom.

But the position is equally capable of being reversed, and the reversal is often strongly theological (even trinitarian) in character. On this account of the matter, it is the faithful act of preaching the good news of Jesus Christ which is brought home to the believer by the power of the Holy Spirit. Where such experiences occur, there God is present; this is the "upper" level of conceptual ordering, and "below" it is the fallible human institution whose ministrations and rituals are constantly in danger of being merely cultic or legalistic in character (both terms being the corresponding code words signifying the relative ordering of upper and lower spheres). At the Reformation, the experience of justification by faith—which is not to be reduced to an "emotional" experience—was made the hermeneutical key for the systematic transformation of an inherited ecclesiology and sacramental theology.

The above simplified presentation of "models of faith" goes a certain way to satisfy the legitimate demand from a contemporary instructed lay Christian for an account of how and why the denominational Christianity with which he or she is familiar led to separated versions which have maintained themselves, and thus acquired the right to be taken seriously, over many centuries. The argument is that each Christian believer, in assimilating from his or her denomination "the Christian tradition", absorbs at the same time an ordering of the dialectic driving the Christian religion. It is not that Roman Catholics reject the life-transforming experience of justification, nor, on the other hand, that Protestants reject the church and sacraments. Rather, both constitute "upper" and "lower" levels differently and thus conceive of their power mutually to correct each other in different ways. The impact of these differences reaches right into the marrow of the believer's self-understanding if, as was suggested above, the ambiguity and complexity of any single believer's self-consciousness is a mirror of the terms on which the exterior dialectic is conceived. Thus Roman Catholics may come to see the diviner part of their lives as their enmeshment in the given sacramental and communal life of the church, with the more mundane and fallible element constituted by inadequately interpreted experiences; and Protestants, conversely, may prize the experience of conversion and a sense of interior peace above everything, associating fallibility and discord with the all-too-human life of the institution.

It is to be remarked that the project of ecumenism, on this analysis, is likely to prove attractively possible in theory (for neither side need actively *deny* what is affirmed by the other) and acutely frustrating in practice (for the differing perceptions are a matter of self-understandings communicated over many centuries by the separated bodies).

But we should obviously face the question whether it need be the case that the dialectic, so identified, should persist as an ordering of differently identified "upper" and "lower" conceptualities. Plainly there is nothing inevitable or strictly unmendable about the Reformation or, indeed, the Great Schism of earlier centuries. Provided that the churches do not attempt to construct and return to a mirage of primitive agreement and uniformity, it ought again to be possible to live with a dialectic that neither involves the permanent adoption of a single hermeneutical key to the whole edifice of Christian living and thinking nor perpetuates the dominance of one level over another. The requisite dialectic could once again become internal to a united but not uniform church, and the issue of which level should predominate could be decided by the needs of a given culture at a specific time. To unthink ourselves out of the habits of centuries of established patterns of Christian discipleship will be no mean feat. It is possible that in the long run nothing will be achieved until the separated churches begin to acknowledge their own internal discord and cease to perpetuate mythologies of their historical consistency. Needless to say, matters of prestige and power play a substantial role in all efforts at self-presentation made by denominational apologists.

VII. AND WHAT IS FAITH?

And what is faith? It is perfectly appropriate to ask ourselves the same rhetorical question as the New English Bible inserts into the translation of Hebrews. For despite the claim to a comprehensive appraisal of problems in the definition of faith, the answer we have given here is doubtless similarly partial and will consist in that aspect which is believed to meet the challenges of the present. Faith, as we have presented it, is the intention and passion which move a believer's self-understanding into the narrative of the people of God and sustain it there. Faith is, therefore, a recollection, an *anamnesis,* of what God has done, which must always be a thanksgiving, a *eucharistia.* It is the setting of a whole life story in the context of God's dealings with humanity through his particular people; and from the multifaceted character of that history faith derives its diversity of aspects, its complexity, and also its ambiguities.

But the life of faith, membership of the household of faith (Gal. 6:10; cf. Eph. 2:19), involves a journey which can be entered upon wholeheartedly and without reservation because there is no contingency in it that could separate us from the love of God. The promise of faith rests on a God who has created humanity out of a consistent and undeviating benevolence, who draws humanity into fellowship with himself, and is their redeemer. Faith thus is the expression of ultimate confidence in God and enables a believer to be also an utterly realistic observer of human folly and failure and a compassionate participator in sorrow and tragedy. Faith opens the possibility of liberation from obsessive self-regard for a life of love and generosity, supported by the knowledge that one is oneself generously and undeservingly forgiven. It is a rejection of the service of the false gods of the culture, among which one might mention stoicism, epicureanism, cynicism and envious self-regard. The life of faith is, therefore, always a struggle for right perceptions, of oneself, of the church, and of the wider community of which both we and it are inseparable parts; it is a struggle for right perceptions leading to right actions, the achievement of coherence in the complex and ambiguous story in which we are inevitably agents of one kind or another.

Finally we have found Christian faith, in the very context of complexity and ambiguity, to be necessarily and characteristically resurrection faith, always participating in the baptismal movement from death to new life through the power of the Holy Spirit. It is the fact of this movement which should enable the believer to live a life of confidence and joy without any denial of human weakness, pain and tragedy. St. Paul used the vivid metaphor of "inarticulate groaning" to render the quality of this Spirit-inspired longing for the realisation of resurrection. Faith is, therefore, always to be characterized as prayer, when it is truly resurrection faith; and the apostle sees God's Holy Spirit as making articulate and intelligible the longings of the believing community, "pleading for God's own people in God's own way" (Rom. 8:28–29, New English Bible). The intention of the prayer of faith is thus transposed, groans become speech, inarticulacy is turned into communicative skill. The life of prayer is itself participation in the resurrection, in which sorrow is turned into joy. For, as George Herbert wrote in one of his many vivid deployments of St. Paul's metaphor,

> Grones are quick, and full of wings,
> And all their motions upward be;
> And ever as they mount, like larks they sing;
> The note is sad, yet musick for a King.
>
> ("Sion," in *The Church*, published 1633)

NOTES

1. *Epistle to the Hebrews,* trans. W. B. Johnson, in Calvin's New Testament Commentaries, vol. 12 (Grand Rapids: Wm. B. Eerdmans, 1963), 12:157. There are still modern authors who assert that Heb. 11:1 offers a definition of faith.

2. See the analysis of the *pisteuō* group of words in the New Testament by Rudolf Bultmann in G. Friedrich, ed., *Theological Dictionary of the New Testament* (Grand Rapids: Wm. B. Eerdmans, 1968), 6:174–82 and 197–228. Care, however, needs to be taken with Bultmann's overemphatic insistence on the distinction between conceptual inheritance from the Old Testament and supposedly "specifically Christian" usages, which is closely linked to the theological proposals of existentialist hermeneutics.

3. This process is nicely analysed in relation to the teaching of Jesus by John Riches, *Jesus and the Transformation of Judaism* (London: Darton, Longman & Todd, 1980), chap. 2.

4. Origen, *Contra Celsum* 6.11, trans. Henry Chadwick (Cambridge: Cambridge University Press, 1980), 324.

5. See Rudolf Bultmann, *Theology of the New Testament* (London: SCM Press, 1955), 2:135 and 211.

6. On the necessity of so-called "essentially contested concepts" in the history of ideas, see W. B. Gallie, *Philosophy and the Historical Understanding* (London: Chatto & Windus, 1964). I have discussed the theological implications of this proposal in Stephen Sykes, *The Identity of Christianity* (London: SPCK, 1984), esp. chap. 10.

7. See the discussion of the relation between these two usages in A. Thistleton, *The Two Horizons* (Exeter, Eng.: Paternoster Press, 1980), 422–27.

8. Richard Swinburne, *Faith and Reason* (Oxford: Clarendon Press, 1981), 3ff.

9. On this variety, see the neglected but conceptually impressive work of Christopher Evans, *Resurrection and the New Testament* (London: SCM Press, 1970), who shows how the resurrection narratives of each of the main writers

serves "as a proper conclusion for an evangelist of his own particular version of the gospel" (p.128).

10. In Athenagoras, *Legatio and de Resurrectione,* ed. and trans. W. R. Schoedel (Oxford: Clarendon Press, 1972), 109. The authorship of the text, traditionally ascribed to Athenagoras, a late-second-century Christian apologist, is uncertain.

11. E. P. Sanders, *Paul and Palestinian Judaism* (London: SCM Press, 1977), 447.

12. See Peter Brown, *Augustine of Hippo* (London: Faber & Faber, 1967), 373ff.

13. In *The Life of Schleiermacher as Unfolded in His Autobiography and Letters* (London, 1860), 2:281.

14. In Cambridge it was not finally dropped from university syllabuses until 1920. From the first publication of *A View of the Evidences of Christianity* (1794), a book written specifically for religious instruction in universities, there was plenty of vigorous dissent from its tone and contents. See M. L. Clarke, *Paley, Evidences for the Man* (London: SPCK, 1974), chap. 10.

15. N. Malcolm, *Thought and Language* (Ithaca, N.Y.: Cornell University Press, 1977); also in "The Groundlessness of Belief", in *Reason and Religion,* ed. S. C. Brown (Ithaca, N.Y.: Cornell University Press, 1977), 156, in which publication the proposal is discussed by Colin Lyas. There seems little doubt that Wittgenstein has been seriously misrepresented by Malcolm, as Fergus Kerr has shown in *Theology After Wittgenstein* (Oxford: Basil Blackwell, 1986), 30–31 and passim.

16. Scott Holland, we should notice, makes use of the idea of story in order to emphasise the antiquity and complexity of the inheritance of faith: "Faith appeals to its own story to justify its career; it bears about that history with it as its explanation, why, and how it has arrived at its present condition."

17. Alasdair Macintyre, *After Virtue* (London: Gerald Duckworth & Co., 1981), 194. For an earlier account, see Stanley Hauerwas (with David B. Burrell), "From System to Story: An Alternative Pattern for Rationality in Ethics", in Stanley Hauerwas and others, *Truthfulness and Tragedy: Further Investigations in Christian Ethics* (Notre Dame, Ind.: University of Notre Dame Press, 1977), 15–39.

18. See Gordon H. Bower, "Experiments on Story Understanding and Recall", *Quarterly Journal of Experimental Psychology* 28 (1976):511–34, and the literature cited.

19. Frederick Bartlett, *Remembering* (Cambridge: Cambridge University Press, 1932), 201.

20. H. Richard Niebuhr, *The Meaning of Revelation* (New York: Macmillan Paperback edition, 1960), 77. The chapter in which this sentence occurs is entitled "The Story of Our Life".

21. On the "dilemma of commitment", see Hans Mol, *Identity and the Sacred: Sketch for a New Social Scientific Theory of Religion* (Oxford: Basil Blackwell, 1976), chap. 15; and, specifically in relation to American culture and the

phenomenon of a "life-style enclave", Robert N. Bellah and others, *Habits of the Heart: Individualism and Commitment in American Life* (Berkeley and Los Angeles: University of California Press, 1985), 71ff.

22. D. W. Hardy and D. F. Ford's *Jubilate: Theology in Praise* (London: Darton, Longman & Todd, 1984) is a significant exception to this general rule.

23. See the interpretation of this poem by Richard Strier in his study of Herbert's Protestant doctrinal antecedents, *Love Known: Theology and Experience in George Herbert's Poetry* (Chicago: University of Chicago Press, 1983), 80.

24. Thesis 28 for the Heidelberg Disputation of 1518: "The love of God does not find its object, but rather creates it. Human Love starts with the object." Trans. in J. Dillenberger, *Martin Luther: Selections from His Writings* (New York: Doubleday & Co., Anchor Books, 1961), 503.

25. See the fine account of the way in which the biblical employment of the narrative mode is designed to secure "a house of being" against the threat of chaos and unreason given by Amos Wilder, *Jesus' Parables and the War of Myths* (London: SPCK, 1982), 55.

2

THE CHRISTIAN
DOCTRINE OF GOD

ROBERT W. JENSON

I. THE PROBLEM OF GOD

It is often said that the cultural and spiritual crises that characterized the nineteenth century remain mostly unresolved, that it is precisely their intransigence which makes our succeeding century so terrifying. Perhaps it is evidence for the truth of such observations that the present essay must begin so very much as did that which it celebrates. Aubrey Moore's admirable contribution to *Lux Mundi,* "The Christian Doctrine of God", argued that Western Christendom's inherited interpretation of God is not viable over against changed "views of the world and man". I agree. Moore attributed theology's failure before the challenge of modernity to a clash between two equally peremptory currents in our spiritual history. So will I. He adduced the "philosophical or scientific" and the "religious" doctrines of God as the contending currents. I will not distinguish quite in that way, but my analysis will not be unrelated to his.

Plainly, Western Christendom is now baffled by its God. The church's own confusion could be quickly documented from the surface of theology: a few years ago it was possible to create a stir in the English-speaking church on the odd supposition that the Christian God's being "incarnate" is a problem,[1] whereas, of course, the real problem has always been how at all to identify the Christian God *apart* from incarnation, how to maintain the gratuity of Christ's death and resurrection. But it will at this stage be better to point to the chaos of the church's primary religious life. Let me instance phenomena ecumenically observable and germane to my purpose: pervasive antinomianism and the accompanying decay of prayer.

25

A superficial observer might think that the Reformation had suddenly triumphed: in all churchly quarters, "legalism" is the one sin to be avoided and "faith", glossed as sincerity, is taken as omnicompetent justification. It takes only a little more penetrating observation, however, to see that this antilegalism is atheism, and quite opposite to the Reformers' passionate proclamation of God. As Moore insisted, a proper God must be both personal and encompassing. But personhood is constituted by specific moral character; to be a person is to will some things and so reject their contraries. And an encompassing moral intention must be peremptory for all and in all cases. Thus the God in whose congregation everything goes is disqualified as God. As to prayer, it is the address of created persons to the personal God; if the object of our religiosity is not thought to have specifiable moral intentions for us, prayer must cease, just as it is doing.

In the larger community, utter bewilderment about God reigns. Our communities can neither affirm nor do without a shared apprehension of God, a civil organ for the "mandate of heaven". There is no election in Britain or the United States in which religion does not somehow become an "issue"; nor is there one in which those who raise the issue fail to deny that they do so.

Why communities cannot endure politically without civil faith is not obscure. A community's polity is the arena in which it deliberates ethically, in which it decides what sort of community it shall be in the future. The polity is the forum, whether this is an assembly of the citizens, a club of optimi, or a prince's bedchamber, in which such questions are argued and decided as: What shall we teach our children? What exercise of force against enemies shall we allow ourselves? For long periods, such deliberation may proceed unprophetically. But time ensures that existing moral consensus will sometimes require expansion from the sources of moral creativity: unlike communities may encroach on one another's schools, or the available force may come to include communicidal weapons. Then the community spins in the void of its future and can be directed only by a call from beyond itself. Who but heaven can answer the questions just cited—if they become genuine questions?

Our two English-speaking nations have adopted twin solutions to the antinomy of religion's intrinsic public necessity and modern public impossibility. In Britain, there is an establishment of religion, which purchases its public position by promising to meddle inoffensively. In the United States, there is a disestablishment of religion, which purchases its freedom by agreeing not to meddle. Neither settlement can much longer be satisfactory. But with what are we to replace them?

II. GOD'S DISABILITIES IN OUR AGE

It is the conviction of this essay that bewilderment about God, whether in the church or the polity, is not accidental to our civilization in this time. Rather, the ideologies that constitute late Western modernity are necessary and sufficient contexts of God's obfuscation. God suffers three disabilities in our age. In order of the following discussions: God is *useless* in the context of a community that interprets itself and its world mechanically; God is *offensive* in the context of our pragmatism of historical liberation; and God is *particular* in the context of universal acquaintance.

If mechanism, liberalism and universalism make God's problem in our time, then God's problem is the European-American Enlightenment. That Aubrey Moore and the present essayist start from much the same place is but one case of what is generally common to the authors of *Lux Mundi* and of this volume in its celebration: we are together engaged in the long labor to "overcome the Enlightenment." One needs to "overcome" only what one affirms. There has been theology that simply capitulates to the standard Enlightenment and seeks whatever Christian-influenced religion can be salvaged; what passes for "radical" in Britain and the United States is often of this sort. There has also been theology that wants to repeal the Enlightenment. The authors of *Lux Mundi* and of these essays regard both alternatives with equal horror; on the Continent, they and we would once have been called "mediating" theologians. If the analyses conducted in the present essay are less mediating—or even less civilized—than Moore's, it is only, I may plead, that the crisis has endured another hundred years.

a. God's Uselessness in a Mechanistic World

God's first debility in the Enlightened West is that he has become *useless.* It might be thought this should be no problem. The Western church and civil community are made of St. Augustine's disciples, and he notoriously taught that God is always to be enjoyed and never to be used. But Augustine's heirs have never fully appreciated the suppositions of this doctrine; nor, perhaps, did he. With rare hesitations, we have continued to interpret the gospel as its earliest gentile hearers

27

inevitably did: as an offer of divine assistance in satisfying antecedently defined religious needs.

Not every need is for God. It is the future's unpredictability that creates our need for God. All living personal acts are done in the faith that somehow the future's onrush will not sweep us away from ourselves, that I may venture upon tomorrow without losing the identity already realized. We live and cannot help living by trust that past and future somehow rhyme in the present, that the sequence of events which makes our lives is somehow held together, that the days of our lives make a story and are not merely one thing—and then surely one damned thing—after another. Those who, like Jean-Paul Sartre, deny the truth of this trust may have the right opinion, but they too do not live by it.

Religion is the cultivation of eternity, of whatever it is thought to be that brackets past and future. There are many and very different putative eternities. Western civilization has sought eternity in a still mathematical point at the center of empirically whirling time. With equal profundity, others have sought eternity in the wisdom of tribal ancients, visible or invisible, who have such long past experience that the future can no longer disconcert them. It has been sought in sheer absence, in which all things past and future are together nothing. Perhaps yet unthought eternities will be proclaimed tomorrow. Insofar as we do not merely rely on some putative eternity but intend and cultivate it, we practice "religion". And if the eternity we intend can plausibly be *addressed,* if prayer is possible, we worship a God or pantheon.

The Enlightened West has been engaged in a titanic experiment; of domesticating time, of so construing reality that religion becomes either unnecessary or itself domesticated, depending on taste. A chief means of this effort has been a metaphysical root metaphor, suggested by the new technology. We have understood our worlds, both material and social, as *mechanisms,* as constraining systems of moving masses which though they contain and use great dynamisms are themselves unchanged thereby. The metaphor was first applied to the material world; its subsequent application to the human community has been the more devastating, and I will begin there.

The initial elaboration of mechanistic theories of the polity and economy was the work of writers in the English language. And it was in Britain's extension into the Americas that Enlightened political theorists found opportunity to devise a state according to their new maxims,

28

according to the "improvements" that the science of politics had "lately received".[2]

I have just quoted *The Federalist,* the great ideological defense of the American Constitution. Those who crafted the Constitution were convinced that for the first time in history a right polity could be constructed on known principles. The new wisdom was a technology, based on extrapolation of Newton's laws of motion. James Madison and his fellows, for polity-designing purposes, treated persons and groups of persons as inertial masses and their interests as inertial vectors. Thus they thought they could, by balancing these within a stable system of constraints, create a sort of mill, reliably to ground out political blessings.

Amazingly, the American polity engineers largely succeeded; the American federal machine grinds along yet and has only occasionally failed to provide sufficient life, liberty and happiness to satisfy. In consequence, Madisonian political engineering has been the ideal of the Western world. Whether Madison's apparent success has been, in general, bane or blessing is arguable; certainly it has left no communal use for God.

It was thought necessary to adduce a past-tense Creator as warrant for the goodness of the polity's designed product, but God's efficacy in the present tense could only have been a spanner in the communal works. For what should an Enlightened polity *pray?* Not for life, liberty and happiness; the machine is designed to produce these without intervention even by the moral will of the human agents involved, never mind by God. About other goods, the machine wants no consensus, for were we to deliberate to achieve such consensus we would thereby drop our roles as pure carriers of inertial interests, and the polity machine would suddenly be afflicted with freely determining levers and cogs. Where politics are practiced by the guidance of modernity's "improvements" of political wisdom, actual religion is a menace and walls are built to separate it from public life.

The world *in* which communities assemble was the initial object of mechanistic interpretation. Isaac Newton did not envision the world as a machine, but his epigoni have. Scientific developments in this century seem incompatible with continued use of a mechanistic root metaphor, but these have yet had little effect on the world view assumed in the schools. If one day the physicists come forward as believers' allies, we will rejoice. In the meantime, the general society still obeys the mechanistic metaphor. What may one day come of contemporary physics, whether it may undercut the notion of an impersonal world system, we must wait to see. In the meantime, popular understanding continues to think of the world as a congeries of masses. And over against the world so interpreted, the freethinker's questions are as unanswerable as ever: If God built a perfect machine, why would he need now to meddle in its operations? Or if he built a rickety or dangerous machine, what is to be expected of so incompetent or hostile an engineer? Either way, why worry about God?

b. God's Offensiveness in an Emancipated World

God is not only useless for us, he is actively *offensive*. Modernity has had one value: the freedom of individuals, to be achieved by the historical efficacy of those same individuals, that is, by their freedom. The supposition of modern virtue is thus the foundation of human freedom in itself. In the tradition, the phrase "the free will" has often denoted this antecedent entitive freedom in which free action has been supposed to be founded. I will here adopt the term in that use and no other.

This notion of "the free will" is not, of course, a modern notion. And throughout the history of the Western church it has been troublesome; our theology has been able to live neither with nor without the attribution of "the free will" to human creatures. That we in fact act freely is not the disputed point and is theologically unchallengeable. But we have thought we also needed an *explanation* of this fact. "The free will" is the explanation the tradition has mostly made available.

We have been thought not only to act freely, determined by our own choices, but to be able to do so because we *possess* freedom prior to all free practice. This explanation has, to be sure, been used with uneasy conscience; Martin Luther only blurted—as was his wont—what many have suspected, when he said that "the free will" is "simply a divine name".[3]

In this, surely Luther was right. The self-founding of freedom is a divine attribute; and the human free will is that attribute slipped down the chain of being. But if that is so, then the Nicene recognition that there are no almost-gods, that all reality is either created or of one being with the Father, must eventually compel us either to deny "the free will" to creatures or to deny that there is God to monopolize it. Moder-

30

nity's pragmatism of freedom is willy-nilly a choice for the second possibility, an atheistic choice whether or not noted as such.

Theology's inability to demythologize the human free will has all along caused trouble. But the atheism of the conception did not strongly assert itself, or escape into the larger community's grasp of reality, until it entered the new context of modernity's historical consciousness. When we understand ourselves as historical beings, for whom freedom is a defining predicate, and then continue to understand our freedom as founded in its own prior reality, a God in our way can only be an intolerable impediment. If we are essentially free, and if our freedom starts with itself, than we are *a se,* absolute; and two absolutes are one too many.

It is helpful to notice the connection between modernity's conception and practice of historical agency and the mechanism discussed under the previous heading. The general metaphor by which we interpret our agency over against one another is that of inertial masses moving one another by effective causation. In a world of which this metaphor can hold, the very occurrence of free actions, unproblematic for the most ruthless theological predestinarian, does indeed become dubious; our need for explanation becomes acute. And the externality which the mechanistic metaphor attributes to historical agents' effects on one another leaves room only for the kind of explanation offered by posit of "the free will", for "the free will" can be interpreted as a something in each separate mass, a factor of its inertia.

c. God's Particularity in a World of Universal Acquaintance

Finally in this sequence, God is disappointingly *particular* in our world. We began the discovery with the Crusades and have not ceased to make it: the world is filled with all sorts of people. Vedic sages and Shiite self-immolators and Marxist cadres are there and are clearly our human sisters and brothers. Yet all are different, most notably about God. Is God the void? Or the principle of concretion? Or the distant Creator in whose occasional actions the ancestors' wisdom was founded? Or the Father of Jesus? Or who? Or what?

The primal church, located in the cultural and religious stew of late Mediterranean antiquity, knew all about pluralism. But in the ages of Christendom, the knowledge became disembodied. Scholars, of

31

course, knew that there were other sorts of folk and that they had their different religions, but acquaintance was lacking. It is, however, acquaintance that makes all the difference, and it is *universal* acquaintance that characterizes modernity. We have all met shamans and bonzes and the self-invented religions of our nieces and nephews; and the sorts we have not met we have watched on the tube. The hardest thing in the world is to look an acquaintance in the eye and tell him or her that he or she is wrong about religion.

The reuniversalizing of acquaintance began centuries ago but is now being perfected by instantaneous and world-spanning communication. The pressure is all but irresistible for each to say to all: Theologically, I'm OK and you're OK. That is, the pressure is great to repristinate the solution of late pagan antiquity, to deny that the concept of specific identity can apply to God.

Even though, say, Isis had that proper name and was descriptively identified as the corn's Fertility, and Marduch had that other proper name and was descriptively identified as the primal Hydroengineer, both these and all other gods, it was said as paganism declined to its decadence, are really the same, avatars of identity-free Deity-as-such. As the West now repristinates this dogma, an irony emerges: the pressure to do so is strongest upon those who have *least* emerged from Christendom's religious shelter and who are therefore most provincially assured that "Of course, everyone must worship the same God"—that is, the same God we do.

The doctrine of late paganism and sheltered modernity possesses little intrinsic plausibility. Actual gods always have proper names and identifying descriptions, and the varying descriptions regularly are such as not to be ascribable to the same subject without plain contradiction. If "the Lord" is "he who delivered Israel from Egypt", what of the gods who tried to keep her there?

Yet the reasons for relativistic reduction are powerful. In a context of universal acquaintance, we seem to have only two possibilities. We may accept plurality in its own terms, and so simultaneously accept ghettoization and claim to be right while the others are wrong; or we may proclaim unidentifiable Deity as the "real" being of the many divine contenders. Were the second way otherwise attractive, we would surely take it. But some may think the price too high.

The price is, first, abandonment of the faith found in Scripture. The

32

biblical God is essentially "jealous": it is fundamental in the Hebrew Scriptures that not to *choose* between the gods and the Lord is to choose the gods. As for the gospel, it was precisely from the gods that its proclamation was to rescue us. It may be that we now wish to be religious without impediment by the Scriptures, but if we do, we should acknowledge it.

The price is, second, the increasing distance of God. All the great religious predicates of God share an odd logical feature: they are vacuous apart from attribution to an identified subject. Thus "X redeems" tells us about X only that X restores whatever state X regards as good, which is little enough. Only when, for example, "Isis" replaces "X" does the sentence acquire the force "Isis is the seed's rebirth". If the god remains unidentified, the god's character remains religiously indeterminate. And exactly the utter abstraction of deity was in fact the outcome of late antiquity's amalgamizing; the one soteriological labor of all its sects had to be the overcoming of sheer *distance* to deity. With Nicaea's decision that God is not abstracted from our world in the first place, that God is eternally and in himself the Father of a particular one of us, Christianity broke out of late antiquity's bondage. It may seem unwise to reenter it.

We seem to be left with an uncomfortable result. Where the biblical God is still affirmed in his particularity as the Father of Jesus Christ, he retains his religious reality but becomes implausible in the exchanges of our universal acquaintance. Where antiquity's alternative is adopted, God vanishes into the distant timelessness in which antiquity lost him and from which the gospel once recovered him.

III. GOD'S FAITHFULNESS VS. DIVINE IMPASSIBILITY

If our confusion about God is not accidental to modernity's ideologies, neither are these accidental to Western Christendom's traditional discourse about God. Christians have prepared our own confusion.

Western Christendom's talk about God has been constituted in the historical interplay of two founding impulses: Greece's quest for true deity and the gospel's proclamation of the one who raised Jesus from the dead.[4] At no time have we abandoned, or should we have been able to abandon, either enterprise. Once Greece's question was raised, it could not be denied: How shall we know true Deity when we encounter it? If the church is to proclaim to all that Jesus' Father is true God, we cannot refuse Greece's challenge.

But Greece stated its challenge in its own terms, which the main line of Christian theology accepted with too little critical awareness. From the origins of Greek piety and reflection, divine eternity was understood as *immunity* to time, as timelessness, as—to use the word that became so fateful for Christian theology—"impassibility", incapacity to be acted upon. From the vantage of eighteen centuries' hindsight, we can see—though in practice just barely—how this understanding is antagonistic to that of Scripture.

Israel understood God's eternity not as abstraction *from* time but as God's "faithfulness" to his promises, achieved *through* time.[5] The New Testament's message of the Son's death and resurrection fulfills this understanding: finally, the biblical God is eternal by overcoming death, not by immunity to it. But in the first meeting between Athens and Jerusalem, Jerusalem's theology fell victim to the supposition that Athens' interpretation of its own question was identical with the question itself, that "How shall we recognize true Deity?" was equivalent with "How shall we describe timelessness?" Thus Christian theology begged the very question at issue, and to its own disadvantage.[6] Materially, it established the task of joining divine impassibility with divine crucifixion. The task is hopeless.

"How can the Logos be God," Arius demanded, "who sleeps like a man and weeps and suffers?"[7] And if deity is impassibility, then Jesus the Logos in fact cannot be God. It was therefore an unimaginable defiance of religious common sense when Nicene theologians and liturgy insisted not only that the Logos can be God but that his being sent to suffer and his obeying as the Son codetermine what it means to be God. As the final Nicene victory formula has it, *"Unus ex trinitate mortuus est."*

But although this victory was won, and within the doctrine of Trinity thereafter maintained, in other theological topics the pagan interpretation of deity continued to assert itself. So the Antiochene Christology merely shifted the attack one notch and demanded, "How can the Logos be this man, who sleeps and weeps and suffers like other men?" Notably, the Western church's usual Christology has always leaned toward Antioch. "What sort of God", complained Huldreich Zwingli from the other side, "would let himself be handled and divided on earthly altars?" "Only the metaphysical saves, and surely not the historical," said Gotthold Lessing, establishing the axiom for all the European continent's nineteenth-century mild left-wing theology and for much English-language theology to this day.

The task is not to exorcise "Greek thought". The task is to face the challenge of the metaphysical question, "What is true deity like?" and give the *gospel's* answer. The task is to assert and clarify the reality of Israel's God, the God identified as he who brought Israel from Egypt and Jesus from the dead. It is alike the successes and failures of this continuing work that determine our present confusions and possibilities.

a. The Perichoresis of God

Again to follow my three-step program, the appearance of physics, of "modern science", was contemporaneously seen by the most discerning as a providential opportunity for Christian insight. Thus Jonathan Edwards, the English-speaking church's most comprehensive modern thinker, building on the work of the Cambridge Platonists, seized on Isaac Newton's universal harmony as a *musical* harmony perfectly coordinate to the musically perichoretic being of its triune Creator.[8] Nor is there in physics itself, then or now, anything to suggest interpretation by the machine metaphor, and surely nothing to suggest the metaphor's extension to the phenomena of human life. To account for these blunders, which have so hexed Western Christianity, we must look again to the history of our interpretation of God.

If the understanding of deity as impassibility is allowed to stand, then all being must be understood analogously, as each thing's security within its own self-possession, that is, as the being of what Aristotle called a "first substance". When the emergence of physics did not, as it well might have, break the rule of this category, and when it was then generally and uncritically supposed that also physics' inertial masses must be "first substances", the machine metaphor resulted. As Edwards saw from the first, the Enlightenment's mechanistic understanding of creation made the biblical God implausible because mechanism itself was initially a theological error.[9] God's uselessness in our time is conditioned by the appearance of "modern science" *and* by the adventitious and slothful interpretation of inertial masses as self-possessed entities, as beings by analogy to the Being of Greece's God.

b. God as the Giver of Freedom

As to the imbroglio by which God has become—of all things!—offensive to our freedom, we have already noted its components. One is historical consciousness and the other is the posit of "the free will" as our defining possession; the mischief lies in their combination.

Western modernity's historical consciousness is itself a complex historical phenomenon, as is its own historical relation to our interacting interpretations of God. It will suffice to note two aspects of historical consciousness. First, we experience distance in past time as separating rather than connecting. In traditional societies, that it has been a long time since an event means that we are elaborately joined to it; among us it means that we must go far to appropriate it. Second, we experience the wholeness of life—if at all—as the completion of a story, as a narrative wholeness.

So far there can be no problem. To inhabit reality as history is to be free, unbound from the past yet called to reclaim it by narrative coherence with the surprising future. Therefore, to inhabit reality as history is to live with the very God identified by the gospel: "See," says that God, "I am doing a new thing. Forget the former things."[10] How can this God have come to seem an offense to freedom, an obstacle to historical enterprise?

The first reason, I think one must say, is our sin. To live in history with God is to be freed, but we refuse to be thus gifted in the ground of our freedom; we insist on being ourselves the ground of our freedom. Our passion is not to be liberated but to be liberators; indeed, we do not want so much to be free as to be the sources—and so manipulators—of others' freedom. Yet we must still ask: How can so patent a capitulation to the tempter have become more than simple unbelief? How can it have come inwardly to inhibit belief? Again, we find a misstep in Western Christendom's delicately poised discourse about God.

If we once suppose that both God and we are real because we are self-contained, that we are "primary substances", then we must experience our relation to God as competitive, precisely with respect to freedom. God and I then stand as separate agents over against each other, and I can choose only what God does not choose for me. Nor will any degree of conceptual sophistication evade these dialectics. If God is free by his self-containment, and if I am only insofar free as I

36

am self-contained, then I can be free only insofar as I am free of God. God's grace must within such thinking be understood as the impetus he exerts on me to alter my behavior, to mold my "habits"; and the search for my freedom can only be the search for some moment of choice not fully determined by this molding.

The God identified by Scripture could very well be *named* "The Free Will"; he is the Creator, the choice by which all things occur. But just so, he is *not* self-contained, for to be Creator is to be involved with others. To be Creator is to be very differently the world's ground than was, for contrary instance, Aristotle's impassible Mover. The *Creator's* freedom envelops and enables us. We do need an explanation of our actual freedom of action; God's own freedom, his reality and presence to us, is the explanation.

It is the identification of divine freedom with divine impassibility that has made God seem a threat to others' freedom and has justified our rebellion against him. Western liberalism's grasp of freedom as freedom from constraint reflects a particular—erroneous—interpretation of God; and in turn it has made the real God seem intolerable. God's offensiveness in our time is conditioned by the appearance of historical consciousness *paired with* the standard Enlightenment's interpretation of our free historical agency.

c. A Jealous God

Finally in this section, I must account for the ideology that makes us *generalize* God away. This can be more quickly done. For the fear that it does my neighbor wrong to impugn his or her theology results from simple displacement of Jerusalem by Athens as arbiter of right. The theological misstep behind the ideology is simply the fragility of the synthesis once achieved. Jerusalem and Athens have gone each its own way; and after the marriage and divorce, we are in Athens' custody.

Pagan antiquity's solution to pluralism was proper to it. In time, each thing is itself and not another. Insofar as putative gods appear in time, they must have identities, with proper names and definite descriptions; and the latter will certainly sometimes be incompatible. But late antiquity could regard these identities as ultimately deceptive accommodations, since its God is God by timelessness, by abstraction from time. A God committed to and in his temporal creation, on the other hand, must merely so be a jealous God.

In late modernity, after the meeting and parting of Athens and

Jerusalem, the repristination of late antiquity's mode of pluralism is the recourse of tired spirits, of those who despair of our theology's historic task. Therefore it is so attractive to us all. That God's particularity is disappointing to us is conditioned by the appearance of universal acquaintance *and* by relapse into late antiquity's interpretation of universality.

IV. THE REVOLUTIONARY RESOURCES OF TRADITION

It is the habit of mind by which these present essays are conceived, as were those of *Lux Mundi* itself, to suppose that the tradition is not without resource for the creative mastering of modernity's problems. I will go through my triple program yet one more time. Let me announce the principal resources I will summon: the Cappadocians for the ancient Catholic Church, Martin Luther for the Reformation, Jonathan Edwards as the English-speaking church's—and perhaps the entire Western church's—most successful grappler with the Enlightenment, and Karl Barth for the turn to the contemporary world.

a. The Cappadocians and the Holy Trinity

We now find God useless. That is or can be progress, for in fact God is *salvifically* useless. God is no use to us, because we are much use to him. What role does God play in our lives? It is an inevitable but wrong question. We shall be freed from it only by captivation to the right question: What role do we play in God's life? In the history we live, that question cannot but raise another: How can we play *any* role in God's life?

To both questions, only the full and unabashed doctrine of Trinity, in its original Cappadocian radicality, can answer. Jonathan Edwards, writing in America in the closest correspondence with Britain, reinvented the Cappadocian wheel, with what was already a true "second naiveté". In piety toward our theology's once achieved and then forgotten overcoming of the Enlightenment, I will cite him: "There was, (as) it were, an eternal society or family in the Godhead, in the Trinity of persons. It seems to be God's design to admit the church into the divine family as his Son's wife."[11]

The thought of the Cappadocian fathers is ecumenically celebrated for making possible the victory of Nicene trinitarianism. Just as ecumenically, it is forgotten what their intellectual achievement in fact was. From the gospel's first penetration of the Hellenistic religious world, it had been presumed that Greece's interpretation of eternity was unchallengeable. Deity, said late Mediterranean antiquity, is immunity to time; God is the Rock of Ages who ignores time's river and in whose cover we too may hide. The Cappadocians, by an almost unimaginable break with their world's self-evidencies, trusted in an opposite eternity, thereby first conceptualizing the specific Christian identification of God.[12]

God's being, said Gregory of Nyssa, is a "life (that) has neither interior measure nor compass, for no temporal ruler can keep up with it". Gregory invoked eternity not as the motionless center of revolving time but as a *movement* that infinitely outruns and *so* envelops laggard time, that is "infinite over against the past and infinite over against the future".[13] He was aware of the break; he mocked the Arians for attributing the perfection of timelessness to the Father, thereby making him "inactive".[14] If the old conception of eternity located God's transcendence of time in the insurpassability of his past, in his status as the "Unoriginate", Gregory challenged the Arians to "reverse their doctrine and see infinite futurity as the mark of deity . . . , finding their warrants in what is to come and is real in hope, rather than in what is past and old".[15]

A first Being who is real by perfect stability, and who is stable by perfect self-possession, can only exclude or absorb other beings that are real by relatively stable self-possession. If God is eternal by immunity to time, by perfect exemplification of primary substantiality, and if we therefore exist by relative resistance to time, by imperfect exemplification of substantiality, only two conceptions of our relationship to God are possible. We can stand over against God as separate and finally competing agents or we can vanish into him. A personal life, on the contrary, can receive other lives without absorbing them; indeed, this possibility belongs to the very notion of personhood.

I have introduced the concept of personhood. Before we dare to speak of our lives as lived in God, we must ask *whose* liveliness it is that the Cappadocian idea of eternity fits, whose liveliness it is that outstrips time.

To that question, the Cappadocians[16] did not answer as mitigated Western trinitarianism would: eternity is the property of God *simplicter,* who then is also three persons. They held back the word "God" and answered directly: time-outstripping Liveliness is the property of Jesus

Christ and of the One he called Father and of their Spirit among us. *Then* they said: and these three are one God because this predicate of infinite futurity belongs mutually to all three.

This last must provoke the question: Why in that case are there not three Gods? Since the predicate of deity belongs equally to three something-or-others? The Cappadocians' answer to this question established the original doctrine of Trinity, the specifically Christian interpretation of God.

The name "God", as Gregory of Nyssa said most bluntly, does not attach to sheer deity at all; a plurality of instances of deity does not, therefore, make a plurality of gods. "God" is a word for the joint *dynamism* of the Father, the Son and the Spirit. Jesus Christ and his Father and their Spirit, precisely *by* the narrative differences and interactions that the Gospels recount, bear on us together. They achieve always one joint deed, by their mutual roles. And the one action is the supreme reality rightly adored and named as the one God.[17] "All action which comes upon the creature . . . begins from the Father and is present through the Son and is perfected in the Holy Spirit. Therefore the name of the action ('God') is not divided among the several actors."[18] God, we may say, is what happens between Jesus and the Transcendence he called Father, and their Power who inhabits our future. He is the infinite life within which all created events are embraced and whose story is told by the trinitarian discourse about divine "proceedings".

This doctrine of Trinity is Christian history's principal victory to date, in its continuing task of identifying the gospel's God. It is this doctrine with which we must press on if we are to apprehend the true God's blessed uselessness. And it is this doctrine which the Western church never quite grasped, thus setting itself up for the crisis of Enlightenment mechanism. The Latin-speaking church's failure to grasp the heart of trinitarianism can be displayed on many technical points; one is appropriate to my need.[19]

The maxim that the "externally directed works of the Trinity are indivisible" could rightly have meant that the Trinity's *opera ad extra* are insurpassably the mutual achievement of Father, Son and Spirit and that this lively mutuality is real in God himself. In Western theology, to the exact contrary, the slogan has meant that the *opera ad extra* are *indifferently* attributable to any of the Three or to the Trinity as such. Thus God is again reduced to stability, his triune life pulled back into the interior of a monadic deity from which it can mean little to our religious life—as St. Augustine himself, after all twistings and turnings, admitted.[20]

The gospel's promise is not that we shall be worked on by a monadic God's agency until we achieve some satisfactory state but that we shall rule with and in him. We will overcome the churchly and civil uselessness of God only by claiming our use for him, in the unmitigated audacity of the promise. We will be, as the Eastern church has always said, "deified"; we will be taken into the Life as participants, obeying and loving the Father with the Son in their Spirit. The Christian God, the triune God, has room in himself for us, in our full communal and individual personhood as the spouse of the Son, the respondents of the Logos. And when now the Word is spoken not only about us but to us, and when we are not merely addressed but commanded to answer, to say "Our Father . . .", then the triune Conversation opens already to include us.

I had next almost written, "To do what we can do we do not need God, but to do what only he can do—live—God uses us". But it is already too late in my argument for the penultimate truth of the first clause. To do what we truly can do we need God. But we will find what we truly can do only when we confess God as he is: the Triune *in* whom we live and move and have our being. Then we will see through the world's false metaphors, to the real human community and the real universe, in which there is much to be done and none of it but with prayer and praise.

A polity is no machine, and in no interesting way does it resemble one. A polity is the forum in which a moral community of persons deliberates its good. That we seek the mandate of heaven when it is needed, and are provided with organs of civil theology and liturgy by which to hear and respond in prayer and praise, but accords with the reality and destiny of human community.

Nor is the cosmos a machine, nor does it in any interesting way resemble one. Newton himself suggested that space is God's sensorium; and relativity theory makes the suggestion plausible. Perhaps the truth is to be sought on lines suggested by Edwards: the material cosmos allows the intersubjectivity of the uncreated and created community of persons. It is the "between" by which we may be there for one another without absorbing one another.[21] I must break with these speculations and move on.

b. Luther and the Liberating Word

We now find God offensive. That is or can be progress, for only when our assertion of freedom founded in ourselves is mortally offended can cracks of real freedom open.

What is it not to be free? Common-sensically, I am unfree when I choose and am prevented from doing or receiving what I have chosen. If it is another's choice that prevents me, I experience not merely unfreedom but subservience. Thus in most, common-sensical, contexts, the extent of our freedom is an empirical problem. Sometimes we are free and sometimes not, and the occasions are sorted out only by experience. The religious context poses a more principled question: Can we *ever* be free if there is God?

We experience God as an offense to freedom when we experience him as "another" in the sense of the previous paragraph, and then necessarily as an *all*-choosing other. We experience God as an offense to freedom when we take his creating will as an interposing will athwart our choices. Precisely this experience is what the Scriptures mean by "sin". Its circular tyranny can be described as follows. First, we freely choose to put God at a distance, in order, we think, to be free. But if there is in fact God, just by this choice we become unfree with him. Then, to be free, we must deny him. "Did God say . . . ?"

Reflective clarifications can help only so much. Western scholasticism did what could be done, with beautiful precision. Precisely *because* we are no competition for God in the matter of choosing, the greatest scholastics argued, his choosings do not cross ours. What God chooses to happen, happens. And if he chooses some things to happen because of creatures' free choices, that is how they will happen.[22] But such distinctions could not by themselves rescue their devisers from falling back into unfreedom with God, so soon as they turned to actual religious life and its explication. What was and is needed is speech in the church that actually liberates, that effectively offends our false freedom. The needed reflection is reflection that prepares such speech.

The choice that Christian thought must soon make clearly has been nowhere more drastically posed than by Martin Luther. Luther's theological impetus was, above all, a passion to plumb the ecumenical correlation of God and faith. Faith, he found, is the liberty to which God offends us.

Luther set out his program in the nineteenth and twentieth theses of

the set prepared for the 1518 convention of Augustinians, at Heidelberg. The pair is built around a rather elegant chiasmus on *intellegere*
and *conspicere;* the published translations ignore this. Let me try my
hand.

> The true theologian does not come to see the invisible things of God by
> reflecting on the creation. The true theologian reflects on the visible and
> hinder parts of God, having seen them in sufferings and the cross.[23]

The theology rejected by the first thesis is what Luther took to be
usual in the West. Provoked by the unsatisfactory character of the
merely "visible" creation, the theologian is launched on a reflective
quest for its invisible Ground and Perfection. Insofar as we succeed, we
arrive at a place from which we can "see"—the sense now is mystic—
God as this Ground. To the exact contrary, "true" theology *begins* with
seeing God, in that God intrudes himself as one of our objects, as a
"visible" event in our world, summed up as "the cross". This event is
anything but the Perfection we seek beyond—or behind or below or
be-whatever—this world; it is "sufferings" *in* our world. The experience of God is thus not the end of a reflective enterprise; it is the
beginning of one. Nor does the theologian make any journey away
from this vision; in it he or she has an eternity's food for reflection, on
the mystery that God makes himself our object, and that in cross and
sufferings.

The reversal is precise. As the dogma of Nicaea laid it down: the
incarnation does not, like the cult figures of antiquity, satisfy our need
for a path to God; it obviates it. God was never abstracted from our
temporal reality; he is eternally and self-definingly the Father of one of
us. The religious quest is empty because God was not missing. He is
all too present, for what could God present in our world be but cross
and sufferings?

Luther evoked the offense along two lines. First, the God known in
the way of "true" theology is impenetrably *hidden.* That God is hidden,
all Christendom has known. The usual interpretation has regarded
God's hiddenness as the shimmer introduced by great metaphysical
distance. Therefore God's hiddenness is thought to be amenable to
degree; revelation is God's lessening of the distance, and religion is our
reciprocal movement. In truth, however, what hides God is precisely
the offense that and how he makes himself a worldly object. That God
presents his *posteriora* to us is both the event of revelation and what

43

hides him from us. Therefore we never get past God's visible and hinder reality; his hiddenness cannot be ameliorated. And since God not revealed is anyway hidden, hiddenness is coextensive with deity.[24]

Second, the God known in the way of true theology preempts and obviates the attribution of "the free will" to creatures. Over against him, we are free because we are freed. For the true God is, *Luthero referente*, first of all the God of promises.

All theology has said that God makes promises, but usually this has been taken for a contingent fact about a God initially interpreted otherwise. For Luther, that God makes promises is the fundamental proposition.[25] God is by platitudinous and materially empty definition somehow "absolute"; the question is how. With Luther, the starting point of all understanding is that God makes absolutely reliable promises.

The God who is a promiser, and whose promises are reliable, must be an utterly free will, who allows for no contingencies in his intention. "If you doubt . . . that God foreknows and wills all things . . . immutably . . . , how can you believe his promises?"[26] A promise liberates its hearer from what would otherwise be the conditions of the intended future: "I will see to the financing." To make a promise is to claim to be free to do this. To say there is a promise-making *God,* and that he is God by making promises, is to say there is a promise-maker whose freedom encompasses *all* contingencies. If any created contingency can intrude between God's knowledge and his will, if there is ever a "Yes, but . . ." with which we must answer a promise of God, it is over with faith and faith's God.

This God is therefore a will who *"omnia in omnibus movet et agit",* [27] a Will in which the good and the bad, life and death, are equally if very differently swept forward,[28] who "kills and makes alive". A promiser drives to a future; the promiser who is God "moves" and "agitates" all things. The root metaphor of more normal religious identifications of God is of a Governor who holds back a creation that threatens to get out of hand; Luther thinks rather of an Agitator who impels a creation that threatens to sink back into quiescence.

We return to the theme of God's hiddenness by noting the anguished question these last paragraphs must provoke. If all things are impelled by the will of God, then, given what actually happens, it looks bad for God's character. The point was starkly clear to Luther: "For God so governs this corporal world in external matters, that if you follow the judgment of human reason . . . , you must conclude that God is not or that he is malicious."[29] And externalities are the least of it. In God's specific relation to personal creatures, the offense of his freedom is the offense of predestination: "By his will he makes us . . . damnable" and then "saves so few and damns so many . . ." that "he seems to delight in torturing his wretched creatures."[30]

The offenses of experienced history and predestination are inescapable if we suppose the Bible's God; what is helpful about Luther is that he eschews every attempt to avoid them. Only in the kingdom will we see how God's majesty and love are one. Now we honor God by withdrawing from the religious attempt to get closer and mitigate his hiddenness, by leaving to him that "hidden and fearsome will" of God's mere unresisted impetus.[31]

If this were the whole story, I would just have described Satan, not God. But we were brought to the interpretation of God as absolute freedom by consideration of his *promises.* To turn away from God as he appears at the end of the religious quest is to turn back to God as he has already addressed us and taken us into community with himself, antecedently to all these torments. To turn away from God's incalculable mere will is to hearken to God as he has defined his will by the gospel.[32]

The gospel, to be sure, does not mitigate God's hiddenness; it redoubles it. If God in the world is hidden in inexplicability, in Christ he is hidden in sufferings and cross. But this redoubled hiddenness is just so a *speaking* hiddenness. The redoubling *defines* the mystery, as the mystery of love. That finally is faith: that we trust the loving word that God speaks, as the very God whose wrath repels us.

Can we believe the word of love, the word of God's hiding for us in the cross? Can we accept this word, from the God of this world's terrors? It is anyway clear that about this God, the real God, there is nothing else to do but believe him.

Christendom must finally come clean. The God we proclaim is irremediably offensive to "the free will" of human religiosity. The offense can be overcome as faith, as a clinging to things not seen, but there are no milder options. God has identified himself by the crucifixion of Jesus. We have been fecund of theories about why this horrific event was necessary in terms of our self-chosen historical agency. All such theory now exposes itself as mythic. As to God's general rule of history, Christendom's mighty effort of theodicy has played out its moves. There is nothing to be done about God's hiddenness. That is always true, but surely we of all generations, indeed "after Auschwitz", have no more excuse not to face it. The only alternative to the abandonment of theodicy would be worship of a God himself subject to contingency; such a God would be another God than the one praised and feared in Israel and the gospel.

Since we have nothing to lose but our faith, we can in fact believe. We are free to trust the real God, freed by his utter freedom and the offense it is to us. We are free to live in history just because we do not rule it—or rather, because we rule in God.

c. Karl Barth and Our Role in Christ's History

And what, at last, is to be done about God's *particularity?* The Christian God has an identity, and his identity is established by a historical particular: our God is whoever raised Jesus from the dead. Just so, as Karl Barth should have taught us if none did before, this God is truly encompassing, the God of all his creation. To see this requires a metaphysical wrench, which Barth accomplished, thereby dividing the theology of this century from that of the nineteenth.

Friedrich Schleiermacher had few imitators, but he pioneered the general way in which the nineteenth century tried to overcome the mechanism and historical pragmatism of the normal Enlightenment.[33] Specifically religious consciousness, he taught, is our unity with the whole of reality; indeed, only in religious consciousness is reality a whole, since only in it are we one with the rest. Thus Schleiermacher identified an encompassing whole that transcends mechanism, and so located us within it that religion is secured in its worth and necessity, and a clash between God's freedom and ours is made inconceivable. It was an ingenious and profound move. Only one cavil presents itself, but some may think it sizable: Schleiermacher's teaching makes matters worse for our present problem.

Wholeness is constituted, according to Schleiermacher, in "religion" sheerly as such. The theological question then becomes: What is Christ's role in our religion? The nineteenth century had many and various answers; none proved satisfactory, running out at last to Ernst Troeltsch's proposal that Christ is the religious inspiration we Westerners happen to be stuck with. As has been lamentably customary since about 1800, the English-speaking church has anachronistically imported also this German counsel of despair, discovering in it nothing less than "Copernican" new insight. It is the question itself that makes the mischief, and against it that Barth protested.

In a confluence of pastoral responsibility, biblical study, and political outrage, young Barth, a great hope of liberal Christianity, was theologically and politically radicalized. We need not trace the steps, only record the outcome: Barth found his way by turning liberalism inside out. The question according to Barth is not what role Christ plays in our religious life and the totality constituted in it but what role we and our religion play in the totality constituted as Christ's history.[34] This reversal is very like that made by original trinitarianism; and one effect of Barth's work was to renew the doctrine of Trinity for our century.

The story is not our story with a role for Christ. The story is Christ's story with roles for us. To state the most audacious of Barth's propositions straightway: the God-man, Jesus Christ, as a historical event, is the ontological foundation in God of all reality other than God.[35]

Therewith Barth only said of Christ what all theology has said of "the Logos". His purpose in saying it, moreover, was the same purpose that made the traditional Logos doctrine so central for the authors of *Lux Mundi:* determination that the world and human history not be abandoned to secularity but be understood as moved and shaped by the same eternal Logos that is in Christ. But the circle of *Lux Mundi* also shared what must now be seen as classical theology's great capitulation: we have been intimidated by uncriticized metaphysical dogma into detaching "the Word" from its original role as a title of the man Jesus Christ and into making the *Logos asarkos,* a *not* yet incarnate extra metaphysical entity, be the inner-triune Ground of creation. We have taken it to be obvious that a historical particular cannot be ontologically foundational. But this axiom seems obvious only so long as we remain bound to Mediterranean antiquity's primal dogma, that eternity is immunity to time. Barth's achievement was to break this bondage. There never, he says, is actually a *Logos asarkos;* what is eternally actual as the Ground of creation is Jesus the Christ.

I must barbarously summarize Barth's elegant teaching. In all eternity, God chose to be one with us in the existence of Jesus Christ. This act of choice made covenant with us; and since the existence of Christ and the reality of this covenant are the same thing, God's eternal act of choice and the existence of Jesus Christ are the same event.[36] Thus what happened in Palestine between Jesus and the one he called "Fa-

47

ther" *is* God's self-determination. And that is, with this God, to say it is God's life, his eternity.[37] With that, metaphysics is stood on its head. Even the creation must be understood as an act of God-determined-in-Christ. To recite the famous doctrine: the covenant, established in the fact of Christ's existence, is the inner possibility and reason of creation; the creation is the outer ground, the stage and supporting players, of the covenant.[38]

God in and of himself is thus a historical being; in all eternity there occurs in him a meeting and a decision, and indeed a meeting and a decision between the Father and one of us.[39] Barth recovers the ability to play the full Cappadocian dialectic. History, as Barth analyzes it, involves self-transcendence, confrontation, and the possession of time in which to accomplish both.[40] Of the triune God it is therefore far from true that he is immune to history; it must, rather, be said that only he is fully historical and that we become historical by participation in his life.[41]

The system by which Barth carried out his insight is full of difficulties, and English-speaking theology has been mostly content to lament them. In my judgment, the difficulties reduce to one—which is shared by his critics. Barth did not fully overcome definition of God's eternity by the past tense. It continued to be an automatic epexegesis: "in eternity, before all time". We may ask, Why not "in eternity, after all time"? It is a common outcome of all the theological openings I have pursued in this essay that the triune God's eternity is to be found in his infinite futurity, in the reality of "hope, rather than in what is past and old". We have still to catch up with Gregory.

Our theological times demand revisionary metaphysics. In this perspective, the real God is not the securely persisting Beginning; he is the triumphing End. God is Spirit, and Spirit in the Scriptures is the power of the last future, the anticipatory presence of the coming Christ, the "down payment" on the kingdom. God—any God—somehow rhymes past and future to create our present; both religious evocations and metaphysical interpretations of God must do so from one or the other of the temporal poles. The one possibility presents no greater logical difficulty than does the other; we suppose that an eschatological understanding of God's eternity is exotic only because we *pre*suppose the protological interpretation, because our thinking is precritically shaped by the metaphysics of Olympian religion, because it is unconverted by that very different discourse about God which derives from Israel's exodus and Jesus' resurrection.

If we take the plunge with Barth, and in this last respect past Barth, we shall be able to honor both Christ's particularity and the truth of humanity's total religious history.[42] For we shall then understand that the truth of all religions is to be established in the particular reality of Jesus Christ. Because Christ's story is the encompassing story, all history and, at history's center, all religious history belong *inside* the story of Christ. And since the encompassing story is impelled and shaped by its End, it is to Christ that the religions are carried.

The point, therefore, is not that all or some religions are, as historical phenomena, right or not right. Comparative study of religions is informative in many connections but tells us nothing about their truth. The religions are variously and truly apprehensions of God as and only as currents in God's universal history, as God creates it to be finally appropriated by Christ. Religious proclamations and rites are not justified as ahistorical items; it is by a word's or an action's place in religious history, by its temporally unique response to previous words and rites and enabling of future speech and practice that it is opened to the coming of the Truth. It is the *outcome* of humanity's religious history that will justify that history, when all our struggles will present a manifold object for Christ to interpret in and by that final address of love which will summon his eternal community.

If we keep it firmly in mind that the Spirit is Christ's spirit, and is never without that identity, we can even say that all religions are evoked by the Spirit. For we may then risk the dangerous proposition that the reality of God's Spirit and the fact that we live in time, that my achieved self is always threatened by I know not what, are the same. Since religion is our creaturely attempt to deal with the future's onrush, to evoke the continuity of achieved selfhood with the uncontrollable future, all religion is response to the Spirit. Or, what is the same, all religion is eschatological vision.

Apart from the gospel, of course, the way we deal with the Spirit's futurity is by erecting barriers against him, by building barns and burying talents. We posit gods whose deity is precisely their timelessness, resistance to the future more reliable than any we can muster on our own; we posit gods to protect us from God the Spirit. But the barriers cannot hold. They crumble before the impact of the future, and precisely in crumbling fulfill their Spirit-given reality. "Thou fool" is said to us all, by and against all our religions; and each time a barrier falls, there is a flash of the Spirit.

The religions' direction to Christ does not occur over our temporal heads. The gospel about Christ, in all its specificity, is now spoken in the world of the religions and is now a power at work historically, urging all religions to their destined outcome. Thus religious history is innerhistorically directed to its final End; its relation to its coming Christ is an internal relation.

Because the gospel is a missionary message, the Christian religion is essentially syncretistic. Each time the gospel crosses a new cultural or epochal boundary it of course finds the ground already religiously occupied. Each time the pattern is the same: the religion of a time or of a people is invaded by the gospel, and a Christianity is created that is neither identical with the antecedent missionary Christianity nor a mere baptizing of the invaded religion. Each such Christianity, as a historical emergent, is fragile, wracked by incomplete syntheses. Its theological life will be spent sorting these out.

We need not go far for an example. It is the specific Christianity bred by the gospel on the soil of Olympian and Socratic religion which sets all the problems with which this essay and its many predecessors have struggled. If we can break through to an eschatological interpretation of God's eternity, we shall understand that our syncretism and its problems are not merely inevitable but are christologically ordained, instances of the gospel's transforming impetus amid the religions. There is a nice irony in our situation: what binds us to a static and comparative understanding of the religions, within which they must appear either as "really" all the same or as merely competitive, is just that historyless interpretation of God which is the chief unresolved item of our particular syncretic task.

If God has history and is Lord from the future, our appropriate policy to other religions can be very simple: we should assert Jesus' resurrection and trust the Spirit. Christianity will be a syncretistic phenomenon with or without our consent; we should relax with this, not because all religion is equally right but because Christ lives to triumph. We need not regret the meeting of Athens and Jerusalem, for all its pitfalls into which we have fallen and from which we struggle to extricate ourselves. And we cannot and do not need to predict what will now come of

Western Christianity's new confrontation with the resurgent religions.

When we speak with other religions, we should ask: What difference do *you* think it would make if Jesus Christ, this particular human being, defined by his particular life and death, should in fact have risen? Should the discussion become religiously creative, we need not determine in advance that the result will be congenial to either partner. We will indeed seek converts, but to the mission of Jesus' resurrection.

It is another difference between the situation of the present essayists and that of those we honor that we have become even more hasty than were those enterprising Victorians. My essay lacks even such leisure and ripeness as were still left to Aubrey Moore. There is more to be said than there is time to say it in, and thought becomes harshly systematic. We can hardly take another hundred years to deal with the Enlightenment.

If God intends European-American Christianity to die, as other Christianities have before it, perhaps to make way for a world mission of African or South Asian Christianity, his pleasure is good. If he intends the Lord to return before anything of the sort can happen, his pleasure is good. But of such decrees we know nothing; we must continue to take responsibility for our church's future. If that future is not to be desperate, it is time and past time to let the tradition and our necessities teach us of God's triune uselessness, of his freeing offensiveness, and of his eschatologically encompassing particularity. What Aubrey Moore would think of such formulations is past supposing. They are offered in this time as faithful to the faith and insight of his time.

NOTES

1. John Hick, ed., *The Myth of God Incarnate* (Philadelphia: Westminster Press, 1977).

2. Alexander Hamilton, *The Federalist* no. 9, in *American State Papers,* ed. Robert M. Hutchins, vol. 43 (Chicago: Encyclopaedia Britannica, 1952), 47. Continuing the citation: "The efficacy of various principles is now well understood, which were either not known at all, or imperfectly known to the ancients."

3. Martin Luther, *De servo arbitrio,* Weimarer Ausgabe (WA) 18:636.

4. For the single most powerful analysis of this matter, see Wolfhart Pannen-

berg, "Die Aufnahme des philosophischen Gottesbegriffs als dogmatisches Problem der frühchristlichen Theologie," in his *Grundfragen systematischer Theologie* 1:296–346.

5. In one passage, this is almost a metaphysical definition: Isa. 55:3.

6. A fuller and documented account of this story is in Carl E. Braaten and Robert W. Jenson, eds., *Christian Dogmatics,* 2 vols. (Philadelphia: Fortress Press, 1984), 1:115–27.

7. Arius, as cited by Athanasius(?), *Discourses Against the Arians* 3:28, Patrologia Graeca, 26:321–407.

8. Perhaps I may refer to my forthcoming study: Robert W. Jenson, *America's Theologian: A Recommendation of Jonathan Edwards* (New York: Oxford University Press, 1988), chap. 2.

9. E.g., Jonathan Edwards, "Of Atoms", in *The Works of Jonathan Edwards,* ed. P. Miller and J. E. Smith (New Haven: Yale University Press, 1957–), 6:208–18.

10. Isa. 43:18–19.

11. Jonathan Edwards, *Miscellanies* (ms. collection containing the drafts of Edwards's planned major work, at Beinecke Library, Yale University), 741.

12. Robert W. Jenson, *The Triune Identity: God According to the Gospel* (Philadelphia: Fortress Press, 1982), 162–68.

13. Gregory of Nyssa, *Against Eunomius,* in his *Opera,* vols. 1–2, ed. W. Jaeger (Leiden: E. J. Brill, 1960), book 1:366.

14. Ibid., 3/10:36.

15. Ibid., 1:666–72.

16. To the following, Jenson, *Triune Identity,* 111–14.

17. Gregory of Nyssa, *Against Eunomius* 2.34; *To Ablabius: That There Are Not Three Gods,* in *Opera,* vol. 3/1, ed. F. Müller (Leiden: E. J. Brill, 1958), §124.

18. Ibid., 125.

19. To the following, Jenson, *Triune Identity,* 118–21, 125–30.

20. E.g., Augustine, *On the Trinity* 6.12; 5.10; 7.7–11.

21. Jenson, *America's Theologian,* chap. 3.

22. Thomas Aquinas, *Summa theologiae* i.22.4: "The efficacy of divine providence is not merely that something shall *somehow* happen; but that it shall happen either contingently or necessarily. And so that happens infallibly and necessarily which divine providence ordains to happen infallibly and necessarily; and that happens contingently whose reason in divine providence is such that it must happen contingently." For a very useful compressed presentation of Aquinas on the whole matter, see Harry J. McSorley, *Luther: Right or Wrong?* (New York: Paulist/Newman Press, 1969), 138–61.

23. Martin Luther, *Disputatio Heidelbergae habita,* WA 1:361–62.

24. See the splendid article by Eberhard Jüngel, "Quae supra nos nihil ad nos", *Evangelische Theologie* 32:219–22. The one side of the matter is in the cited passage from the disputation; the other side is in *De servo arbitrio,* WA 18:685.

25. Luther, *De servo arbitrio,* 614–21.

26. Ibid., 619.

27. Ibid., 709.

28. Ibid., 709–10, 585.

29. Ibid., 784.

30. Ibid., 633.

31. Ibid., 684–85.

32. Ibid., 685–86.

33. It is, of course, the great *Speeches* that had this force: *Über die Religion: Reden an die Gebildeten unter ihren Verächtern* (Berlin, 1799).

34. For the formal dogmatic presentation, see Karl Barth, *Kirchliche Dogmatik* (Zollikon: Evangelischer Verlag, 1932–), III/2:64–82, 158–241.

35. Ibid., II/2:86, 109–214; III/1:44–103; 258–377; IV/1:54.

36. Ibid., II/2:109–18.

37. Ibid., II/1:294–305.

38. Ibid., III/1:103, 258.

39. Ibid., II/2:192–202.

40. Ibid., III/2:189.

41. E.g., ibid., II/2:201: the divine life "is the principle and being of all events whatsoever."

42. Instead of picking through Barth, see Robert W. Jenson, "Religious Pluralism, Christology, and Barth", *dialog* 20:31–38.

3
THE PROBLEM OF
EVIL

BRIAN HEBBLETHWAITE

I. A REAL PROBLEM AND SOME
UNSATISFACTORY SOLUTIONS

There can be little doubt that the problem of evil provides the gravest threat to the intellectual and moral credibility of Christianity. It is of course true that Christianity has supplied, for countless men and women, a refuge and a consolation in the face of the world's ills and a hope for an ultimate future where there will be no more grief, loss or pain. Christianity has also inspired and sustained heroic dedication to the relief of suffering and a way of redemptive suffering and self-sacrificial love, patterned on the way of the cross, that, at times, have brought good out of evil to a quite astonishing degree. But the problem of why God permits so much evil and suffering in his world remains as baffling as ever. It represents the most common charge of unintelligibility brought by critics of Christian belief, it is the most frequent ground advanced to explain the loss of faith, and it is deeply felt as a nagging worry or at best an impenetrable mystery by very many Christian minds. It is J. R. Illingworth's failure to get to grips with this basic question of theodicy in his short essay on "The Problem of Pain" in *Lux Mundi* that accounts for the feeling of inadequacy with which that chapter strikes the contemporary reader.

The task of theodicy—of trying to find out why God allows so much evil in his creation—is no different now, for twentieth-century Christians, from what it has always been. But in some respects it looks and feels different in the light of modern scientific knowledge about the world and in the light of modern moral sensibility. Curiously enough, it is modern moral sensibility rather than modern scientific knowledge

54

that has accentuated the problem. Many of the old explanations fail to convince us, morally speaking. The idea that suffering is punishment for sin or divine discipline or testing of faith, even when expressed with Illingworth's sensitivity, is usually found morally offensive not only by unbelievers but by believers too. Scientific knowledge, on the other hand, as I hope to show below, may help the Christian theologian to explain why some, indeed much, suffering *cannot* be avoided, if the world is to fulfill its intended function in God's creative plan. Moreover, one of the great advantages for Christian theology of the attempt to integrate scientific knowledge into Christian theodicy is that it enables us to develop a much more careful and mature conception of divine providence and of the way God acts in the world. This too I hope to show in the course of this essay.

Before we address the theodicy problem directly, something must be said about objections to the whole enterprise from within the worlds of religion and theology themselves. I assume here the context of belief in God, in an objective, realist, sense, for the presentation and attempted resolution of the problem of evil. Objections to this on the grounds that evil and suffering constitute just as terrible a problem for the unbeliever as they do for the believer miss the point. The problem of evil as considered in Christian theodicy is not simply the practical problem of what is to be done, nor even what special resources Christianity provides towards the overcoming of evil. It is first and foremost a problem for the understanding. The believer wants to know why God permits so much evil and suffering. The unbeliever wants to know how believers can possibly reconcile their belief in the love and power of God with the fact and extent of evil. That is the problem of evil for Christian theism.

Much more telling religious objections to theodicy, understood in this way, come from such writers as D. Z. Phillips, for whom the life of Christian faith has already begun to be abandoned where the theodicy question is felt and pressed. Phillips finds those people religiously impressive who hold to their faith irrespective of the way things go and who confront evil with an unshakable trust in God.[1] I do not think, however, that this succeeds in capturing either the religious quality of the believer's self-questioning or the moral quality of the unbeliever's attack. Neither Job nor Ivan Karamazov can be so easily dismissed. There is nothing essentially irreligious in seeking consistency of belief, still less in trying to give an answer both to agonising religious doubt and to deeply felt moral incredulity. I do not propose here to examine the charge of noncognitivism that has been brought against Phillips's analysis of religious language. But one can see that where theological realism in talk of God is eroded, the theodicy question as formulated above loses its bite and the problem of evil can then be treated only in practical terms. Moreover, such erosion, one feels, is subtly assisted by allegedly religious objections to pressing the theodicy question at the level of understanding. A more persuasive form of this religious objection, one that remains within the framework of realist theistic belief, will be considered in a moment.

Another approach altogether is essayed by Stewart Sutherland in a recent book.[2] Sutherland calls in question the assumption of traditional Christian writers on the problem of evil that Christianity's conception of a personal, loving, all-powerful creator God provides the unquestionable framework for the examination of the theoretical problem of evil. Why, he asks, must it always be the apparent incompatibility of the fact and extent of evil with the existence of such a God that has to yield to the arguments of theodicy? The factor in the equation most incontrovertibly known to us is the fact and extent of evil. Is it not therefore more plausible to revise the concept of God that leads to the theoretical problem rather than attempt the impossible task of theodicy? And so Sutherland offers a revisionary theology of impersonal transcendence in place of the traditional Christian personal God of love. On that basis, the theoretical problem of evil does not arise. I cannot see that this is a possible or fruitful path for Christian theology to take. In fact, Sutherland's starting point is not the unquestioned fact of evil but the unquestioned assumption that the problem of evil is insoluble. But this is no more and no less unassailable an assumption than the traditional Christian belief in a personal God; and, in any case, Sutherland gravely underestimates the effect on Christianity as a religion of the revisionary theology which he advocates. It is clear that his agnosticism is in fact fuelled by purely secular philosophical difficulties with the concept of a personal God, which, like the alleged incompatibility with evil, require resolution, not endorsement, from the Christian theologian. I see no point in abandoning the project of theodicy before it has begun.

Less radical than Sutherland's proposal, yet in the end even less morally and religiously tenable, is a way of evading the problem of evil espoused by two Dominican authors, Herbert McCabe[3] and Brian Davies.[4] McCabe's treatment contains acceptable material on the explanation of suffering as inextricably bound up with a material creation. This element will find its place in our own treatment of natural evil below. But on moral evil, McCabe advances the extraordinary view that God cannot be blamed for failing to prevent it, since there is no sense in which God is under any obligation. Similarly, Davies argues that the God of classical theism cannot be blamed for permitting moral evil, since God cannot be thought of as a moral agent, with duties and obligations. As the changeless cause of all positive being, God just does what he does. Davies's and McCabe's rejection of the "free-will defence", a rejection which presupposes this interpretation of classical theism, will also be considered below. Here I simply note the damage done by this understanding of theism to the notions of God's goodness and God's love. It is morally and religiously quite implausible to suppose that the God revealed in Christ has not, by his very nature, obligations to the personal creatures he has made. If God permits evil, it can be only because he has a good reason, morally speaking, for doing so. It will further be argued that, given the inevitable cost in suffering and evil of the creation of a world of persons, God is, in a sense to be further clarified, morally bound to raise the dead. Such obligations are not imposed on God from outside. They are a matter of moral consistency in one who reveals himself as in essence perfect love. If classical theism's conception of divine unchangeability prevents us from ascribing such obligations to God, consequent upon his free creation of persons other than himself, it equally prevents us from speaking of a God of love. Again if, as Davies avers, the changelessness of God entails that "the notion of his being able to do something or refrain from doing it makes no sense", then personal theism is at an end. Is not Sutherland's recourse to impersonal transcendence the more consistent path?

Much more persuasive than Phillips, Sutherland or the Dominicans is recent work on the problem of evil by Diogenes Allen.[5] Allen criticises contemporary theodicists and contemporary antitheodicists for their failure to understand the religious possibility for human beings of coming to accept our vulnerability to nature's workings as itself God's will. The religious power of Christianity lies, rather, in finding the presence and the love of God precisely in suffering, pain and even dereliction. This, Allen points out, was already a possibility recognised by Stoics such as Epictetus as far as our vulnerability to nature is concerned. In Christian writers such as Simon Weil, Allen finds the further existential recognition of "the most perfect contact with the love of God that is possible for a human being in this life" precisely in the deepest affliction, just as the Christian mind has always discerned it in Christ's cry of dereliction on the cross. This paradoxical experience of the Father's love *in* suffering and affliction is simply not recognised by critics of theodicy such as Antony Flew[6] and J. L. Mackie[7] nor by defenders of it such as John Hick.[8] Hick does recognise the contribution of suffering to character and growth in virtue, but he does not seem aware of the unique and central capacity of Christianity to enable us "to conceive of all suffering as the presence of God to us through the world". How much more inappropriate is Flew's presupposition that a perfect God of love could only have the creature's physical and mental ease and happiness in mind. The austere but deeply religious sense of the possibility not only of encountering God but of encountering the love of God in the depths of suffering and affliction must certainly be reckoned with in any treatment of the problem of evil that is to do justice to the actual context of faith and practice within which the problem arises. It certainly shows up as shallow and irrelevant the kind of utilitarian, even hedonistic, presuppositions that characterise much secular antitheodicy. And we shall have to come back to these religious possibilities of insight, growth and experience when, at the end, we return to the practical resources of Christianity for the overcoming of evil.

It must, however, be said that even Allen's profoundly religious repudiation of theodicy is too paradoxical to satisfy the moral and religious sensibility. Whatever the possibility of that kind of experience of the love of God in pain and dereliction, it remains morally incoherent to suppose that the purpose behind a world order that can bring such affliction upon human beings is the realisation of such spiritual states. For one thing, the rarity of experience of the love of God in affliction such as that described by Simone Weil fails to reconcile us to the fact of vast tracts of unredeemed suffering undergone by human beings in the history of the world. There must be some other reason for the world's evil than this rare possibility of bringing good out of evil, profound though it be. Both christological and eschatological considerations reinforce this point. The incarnate Son of God's endurance of dereliction on the cross and the experience and expression of the love of God precisely in and through that endurance were not undertaken for their own sake but for the sake of the redemption of humankind from a state of embroilment in evil and suffering to be accounted for on other grounds. Equally, the perfect experience of the love of God in the life of heaven, as indeed the trinitarian love of God—Father, Son and Holy Spirit—in all eternity, is unquestionably a state beyond all suffering and evil. We cannot so exalt the experience of God's love in affliction as to make pain the sine qua non of perfect love. The kind of experience of the love of God in dereliction, described by Weil and Allen, must be thought of as contingent upon facts whose explanation is other than divine teleology behind a system specifically designed to produce such states.

The need for a theodicy, therefore, remains. It is not inappropriate for the believer, whatever further possibilities for the experience of God's love may mercifully be present in (and despite) suffering and evil, to look for some explanation of why God permits it in the first place and why God creates a world so structured as to be productive of so much pain. Nor are the critics of Christianity to be answered simply by pointing to the positive possibilities of such religious experience and growth. Their attack may in part reflect superficial and inappropriate conceptions of the meaning and purpose of human life. But it remains a moral objection to Christian belief for all that. Ivan Karamazov's refusal to accept the cost of creation in suffering and evil cries out for an answer to the question why.

II. MORAL EVIL AND NATURAL EVIL

The nature of the problem must now be explored in more detail and set in the context of modern scientific knowledge and moral sensibility before an attempt is made to sketch and defend a possible theodicy. It is customary to distinguish and treat differently the problem of moral evil and that of natural evil or suffering. This distinction certainly reflects the age-old Judaeo-Christian discernment of the significance of moral personality and of the apparent injustice in the fate of many individual persons. But it is reinforced by the more modern recognition of the uniqueness of moral personality in a natural world regarded as a law-governed system of interacting systems, admittedly capable of producing and sustaining life, but also, by its very *im*personality, capable of harming and destroying countless individuals.

Moral evil is the evil of the evil will—human wickedness in all its forms. The Judaeo-Christian tradition, from at least postexilic times, has stressed, taught and indeed enhanced human freedom and responsibility. The contrary strand in Christianity, stressing divine sovereignty to the exclusion of the human being's free will, will be discussed in the next section. But for the most part, Christians have been conscious of men's and women's own responsibility for their inordinately wicked acts and for the harm they can do both to themselves and to others out of selfishness, arrogance, malice, cruelty and pride. The question at once arises why God permits such wickedness and its catastrophic effects in the human world.

Natural evil is the evil of accidents, plagues, the mutual destructiveness of nature "red in tooth and claw", and natural disasters of every kind. It is the whole sphere of suffering and evil which, on a modern, science-based view of the world, is no one's fault, unless it be the fault of the creator God who has posited this law-governed world in being. To put the matter in these terms is already to advert to the peculiarly modern way in which the problem of natural evil is felt. We do not see the problem of natural evil in terms of malevolent spiritual forces behind the harsher operations of nature. As will be argued in a later section, ascription of natural disasters to the devil's agency has lost whatever plausibility it had in earlier Christian centuries in the light of our scientific understanding of the elements and powers of physical nature and the universality of natural laws. Such knowledge only reinforces our moral unwillingness to read divine teleology of a punitive or even of a directly educative kind into the innumerable cases of what we increasingly and inevitably recognise as innocent suffering. Something will be said at a later stage in qualification of the somewhat deistic picture of the relationship between God and the world that has replaced the older more personalised conception of the cosmos, but we can readily see that it is acceptance of the natural world as a system of interacting systems in accordance with general laws that has led to current formulations of the problem of natural evil as the problem of why God creates us in and through a physical cosmos that, as well as providing the conditions of organic life, can also do us such untold harm. It is interesting to note that the problem of natural evil, thus expressed, has marked links both with ancient Stoic conceptions (as observed by Allen in the article mentioned above) and with nontheistic conceptions of the world such as that of early Buddhism.

If it is the modern world that has reinforced the separation of the problem of natural evil from that of moral evil, in many ways it has also brought out their interconnection. This is not only a matter of recognising how the actual structure of the physical world subserves the ends of wickedness as in torture, terrorism and war, so that increased scientific knowledge makes new, much larger-scale destructive capacities available to evil men and women. The interconnection is also seen at a much deeper level, though in diametrically opposite ways, by both critics and defenders of theodicy. Thus we shall find Mackie, in the course of his attempted rebuttal of the freewill defence, arguing that even the worst manifestations of moral evil—he explicitly mentions the Nazis' murder of six million Jews at this point—arise in part from *circumstances* of injustice, in which people get entrapped without deliberate intention. On the other hand, we shall find exponents of the freewill defence, such as Hick, arguing that embeddedness in a law-governed, physical environment both provides the necessary conditions for the emergence and growth of free personhood and at the same time explains the susceptibility of such "souls in the making" to temptation. We shall note how greatly this way of relating the problems of moral and natural evil differs from that of ascribing natural evil to the devil's agency.

In recent discussions of the problem of evil, it is the Nazis' treatment of the Jews that has provided the most insistent and nagging example of the magnitude of the task of theodicy and its constant danger of slipping into a morally outrageous stance of trying to justify the unjustifiable.[9] Sensitivity to Jewish theology—always less theoretically inclined than Christian philosophy of religion—leads some Christian writers to abandon the task of theodicy at this point as morally indefensible. It can indeed seem outrageous even to try to justify the creation of a world in which something so unimaginably evil as this can happen and be allowed to happen.

There are difficult questions of balance and perspective at stake here. A morally and religiously sensitive treatment of the problem of evil must certainly not involve any playing down of or shutting one's eyes to the magnitude of examples such as that of Hitler's genocide. But equally it cannot allow the sense of horror at the wickedness of what was done by the Nazis to overwhelm its attempt to see the world and human life as a whole in the creative intention of God. Such things can be done by human beings in the grip of perverse ideas and fears. In other contexts other examples indeed might seem more pressing. Indian and Japanese Christians, for instance, have sometimes expressed surprise at European and American preoccupation with the fate of the

Jews in the twentieth century. A knowledge of history refutes the claim that what the Nazis did represents a completely new and unparalleled dimension of human wickedness. Yet it certainly can stand as a key instance of the magnitude of the problem. Reflections at a general level on why the world is as it is must withstand confrontation with just such examples if they are to carry conviction in the religious mind.

The question may be asked whether it is moral evil or natural evil that represents the greatest threat to Christian belief. The religious mind seems to find human wickedness more perplexing than human-kind's vulnerability to the ravages of nature. Just because the universe is seen and experienced as a sphere of personal meaning and the work of a good and loving Creator, deliberate wickedness reaching such proportions as those of genocide strikes the religious mind as incomprehensible, a totally inexplicable surd in God's good creation. The non-religious mind seems to find natural evil a more perplexing threat to the consistency of theism. We have already seen how Mackie assimilates moral evil to natural evil by his stress on circumstance, and it is the impression of a mindless nature, careless of the individual, that was classically expressed by David Hume when he wrote that "the whole presents nothing but the idea of a blind nature, impregnated by a great vivifying principle, and pouring forth from her lap, without discernment or parental care, her maimed and abortive children".[10] This secular incredulity at the very idea of a fatherly providence, given the nature of the world in which we live, is fuelled by paradigm examples of horrific accidents and natural disasters such as the Lisbon earthquake of 1755 or the African drought today. The religious mind, therefore, assumes that there must be a good reason for the creation's present structure (taken, in any case, to be a temporary phase in the whole creative plan), whereas there seems to be no good reason for human wickedness; the nonreligious mind assumes that moral evil is explicable given the nature of the world but that the natural universe just is not what a good all-powerful God would make. In what follows I do not attempt to resolve these felt priorities. I assume that both moral *and* natural evil cry out for an explanation of their presence in God's world.

It is in some ways a curious fact that, at a time when modern science and civilisation have reduced our vulnerability to the ravages of nature, the problem of evil is felt more strongly as a threat to faith than it was in the so-called ages of faith when life was short and at the mercy of disease and plunder. This in part reflects our disappointment that progress has proved so difficult and that civilisation has itself spawned the worst wars and, not least, appalling examples of genocide. It is also partly due to modern communications and the fact that all the world's ills are daily presented to us in the newspapers and on the television screens. Our awareness of the problem of evil is virtually constant and global in its range. But the main reason why the problem is felt so acutely in the modern world is the alienating effect of scientific knowledge of the impersonal workings of nature and the consequent loss of plausibility in a personalised, providential reading of the circumstances of life. It is not surprising that this loss of plausibility has been found by sociologists of religion to constitute a leading aspect of the secularisation of the modern mind.[11] Consequently a viable theodicy will involve not only explanations of the features of the human and the natural worlds that create the problem of evil but also reformulation of the doctrines of divine providence and action in ways that do justice both to the workings of nature and their place in the divine creative plan.

III. THE "FREEWILL DEFENCE"

I shall explore first the "freewill defence", which accounts for the presence of moral evil in God's world by arguing that it is impossible—logically impossible—for God to create a world of finite free persons and at the same time to ensure that they all always act well. Their acting well must be up to them. The risk of their acting badly is therefore part and parcel of the creation of finite free persons. This means that there is a sufficient reason, morally speaking, for God to permit at least the possibility of moral evil; for without that risk the value of there being free created persons living in relation to each other and to God would not be realised. The only alternative, on this view, would be a world of *apparent* persons, of puppets or automata.

For this initially plausible argument to hold, the facts of freedom, in this strong, "libertarian" sense and its necessity to personhood must be maintained. So too must the *value* of such freedom and personality. These conditions of the validity of the freewill defence have been attacked by Mackie in his posthumously published book, *The Miracle of Theism.*[12] Mackie no longer holds the position advanced in an earlier article[13] (and refuted by Alvin Plantinga)[14] that, since a world in which everyone acted well is logically possible, an omnipotent God could have created it. For it is logically impossible even for omnipotence to *cause* a free being freely to act well. But it *is* possible, Mackie holds, for God to create finite persons *such that* they always act well of their own free will. He is able to advance this view, since he holds a compatibilist view of the relation between determinism and free will, whereby significant freedom equals absence of constraint, not the categorical freedom espoused by the libertarian. Free actions, on Mackie's view, are actions that flow from one's own nature, as one responds to all the circumstances of life. God could have made us with a nature such that in the relevant circumstances our clear perception of the facts always led us to act well. Not only, on Mackie's view, is it false to claim that libertarian freedom is inextricably bound up with being a person. We do not have that kind of freedom anyway. As already mentioned, Mackie holds that even the worst of humankind's actions, including genocide, are a product of circumstance.

What are we to make of this alleged rebuttal of the freewill defence? I do not find it very persuasive. Mackie does not do justice either to freedom or to what it is to be a moral person. Compatibilism is no way out of the deterministic impasse. The value of a moral personality, formed through free, responsible thought and action over a lifetime, cannot be achieved by advance programming. It must be up to individuals what they make of the given factors of their heredity and environment. "Libertarian" freedom, not in the sense of randomness but of one's own control over what one thinks and does and becomes, is of the essence of finite personal existence. Ascription of moral responsibility, praise and blame, presupposes such control. Neither thought nor agency would be what it is if one could not have thought or done otherwise. Both human goodness and human wickedness are what they are only because of freedom in this sense. To be a person is to have the power to act well or badly and to develop, through one's acts and acquired dispositions, a good or bad character. The point of human existence is lost if these are the only possible outcomes of prior processes (not just the "wrong sort" of prior processes).[15]

The freewill defence, then, stands. The gift of freedom is necessary to finite personal being, and if God is to create such beings, he must allow the possibility of moral evil. The positive value of having finite persons in existence to enjoy life, to develop interpersonal relationships, and to pursue the good provides a sufficient reason for God to permit moral evil, since the possibility of moral evil is *entailed* by finite personal existence, and the only alternative is no world of finite persons at all.

But what of theological objections to the freewill defence? It is not at all clear that strict predestinarianism, in a sense that denied "libertarian" free will in basic anthropology, is to be ascribed even to Calvin, let alone to Augustine. But there is a tendency in this direction, not only in Reformed theology, particularly in Zwingli, but also in that side of Thomism already mentioned in connection with Dominican anti-theodicy,[16] which stresses divine sovereignty so strongly that human free will appears an illusory phenomenon, incapable of bearing the weight of the freewill defence. The answer to all these theological attacks on the reality of human freedom can be provided only by a better theology. God's prior causality is indeed required for any creature, together with its God-given powers, to remain in being and efficacy. But if "the dignity of causality is imparted to creatures" (Aquinas) and that of freedom to men and women, it is they, not God, who are responsible for what they do, even if by the exercise of their freedom they get themselves into a state from which they can escape only with the help of God. Christianity does indeed teach that God provides that help; although it too must be freely embraced if God is to continue to treat them as persons. But the view that God's sovereignty can be defended only by ascribing to prior *determination* the human response to grace itself is not only morally incredible. It contradicts itself; for men and women, so treated, would not be persons, inhabiting a moral universe. Similarly, it may well be the case that our true freedom is God's own gift, a faithful dependence on God's enabling grace, which we could never achieve by our own efforts. But freedom in this sense still presupposes the basic fact of libertarian freedom whereby we can be held responsible for what we do and also can embrace, in penitence, the true freedom offered us by God. The free will required by the freewill defence in theodicy is not abrogated by these religious perceptions.

But there are other theological objections to reliance on the freewill defence. If we understand freedom to entail the possibility of moral evil, what of God's freedom or Christ's freedom or the freedom of the blessed in heaven? Consideration of these questions *would* lead us to qualify and restrict the thesis that personhood as such entails libertarian freedom. God's freedom entails no possibility of moral evil, since it is the freedom of one who is omnipotent, omniscient and perfectly good.[17] Such a God is indeed bound by his nature always to act well. For this reason we introduced finitude into the definition of persons liable to do evil. Christ's freedom was of course finite freedom, and so the logical possibility certainly existed of his sinning. His sinlessness consisted in the constant free choice of his Father's will. We may well wonder if his being who he was (God incarnate) did not ensure that there was no real possibility of his sinning. Whatever we may think of that christological problem, we ourselves are not God incarnate and our finite freedom does entail the possibility of wrong choice. But do we not hope to be raised to a state where in the end that possibility no longer exists? The blessed in heaven freely embrace the love and will of God without any further possibility of falling away. They exist in what Hick has called a morally frictionless environment,[18] where nothing could draw or tempt them away from the vision of God. If this is so, then it must be the freedom of souls in the making that entails the real possibility of moral evil. But the obvious rejoinder is, Why does not God place his finite free, personal creatures in a morally frictionless environment directly, if his purpose is to realise that state in the end? I postpone my answer to that question until we have considered the problem of natural evil; for at this point in the argument we come to realise that the freewill defence may not after all be self-sufficient and independent of an answer to the other question: Why does God create us in and through a natural system of interacting systems which can do us such untold harm?

IV. AN "IRENAEAN" THEODICY

Only the last-mentioned consideration brings the freewill defence into the context of specifically modern discussions of theodicy. The earlier considerations were purely logical and moral and required no reference to modern knowledge. But discussion of natural evil is bound to reflect our contemporary scientific picture of the physical universe, its elementary substance, its origin and its evolution. The popularity of "Irenaean" theodicies[19] (their anticipation in Irenaeus is interesting but fairly minimal) rests on their firm grasp of the fact that, in the light of modern scientific knowledge, we can no longer think of the world as created perfect in the beginning but must, rather, see it as a gradual process, building up the conditions and forms of life as it were from below, and letting the human world emerge gradually out of nature into spirit. The doctrine of the fall of humankind, on this view, has to be reformulated as picturing the distance from God that must be overcome before human beings can enter into the relationship with God for which they are destined.

An Irenaean theodicy in respect of natural evil proceeds in two stages, both of considerable generality, the first requiring developed scientific knowledge of the workings of nature and their relation to human life, the second requiring more theological, moral and logical reflection. The first stage involves seeing how the causes of suffering, accident and disaster are inextricably bound up with the very nature of the physical universe that makes human life possible. The second stage involves seeing how some such physical universe is the necessary condition of the creation of a world of finite persons and the values which their existence realises.

Before we examine these two stages of an Irenaean theodicy, it is necessary to deal with the summary dismissal of such approaches which we find again in Mackie's treatment of the problem of evil. For Mackie, any "instrumentalist" view of the order of nature as causally necessary to the achievement of good ends is totally irrelevant where an omnipotent Creator is concerned. "If omnipotence means anything at all, it means power over causal laws. If there is an omnipotent creator, then if there are any causal laws he must have made them, and if he is still omnipotent he must be able to override them. If there is a god, then, he does not need to use means to attain his ends. So it is idle to refer, in theodicy, to any ordinary, factual, means-end, or in general, causal relationships."[20] These remarks fail to do justice to the fact that causal relationships may turn out to be internal to the values which they make possible. This is not just a question of the obvious fact that you cannot (logically cannot) have, for example, sympathy without pain or suffering. It is a question of the much more widely ramifying considerations of the logically necessary conditions of all specifically human values, including finite personhood as such. Formed character, for instance, cannot (logically cannot) just be posited in being. It must (logically must) be acquired through repeated acts in a regular environment. (As with Mackie's earlier argument—the one refuted by Plantinga— Mackie shows himself curiously unwilling to explore arguments concerning logical possibility in detail.) We shall need to explore further such logical implications of the embeddedness of the values of creation in the actual structures of creation in our treatment of the second stage of an Irenaean theodicy below.

a. The First Stage

The first stage, however, remains at the causal level, noting the interconnectedness of the physical system of interacting systems, composed of certain basic particles, energies and forces, operating in accordance with certain basic, mathematically expressible laws, that makes organic and hence human life possible but at the same time vulnerable to accidents, clashes and malfunctions. We note how scientific knowledge renders quite implausible the suggestion that a physical universe capable of producing life might easily have been made to run more smoothly or to lack such features as viruses, tornadoes or earthquakes. A scientific understanding of the operations of nature shows how it is the very same basic substance and the very same general laws that make possible the growth and development of organic structure to the point where consciousness, sensibility and thought can appear on the scene and yet, just because they operate impersonally (without a specific intention behind each occurrence), at times frustrate personal life as subsystems within the system come into chance conflict. Indeed, the highly developed sensitivities of the human organism make it at the same time highly vulnerable to such frustration.

Our scientific knowledge also makes it quite implausible to suppose that such frustrations might easily be prevented by particular volitions of the deity. Quite apart from the consequent contradiction of the point of a world order operating in accordance with general laws, any such intervention would itself set up a new chain of causal effects requiring further interventions to frustrate new clashes, and again the regularity and reliability of the physical environment would soon be lost. Here we may agree with McCabe that it is foolish to suggest that God might have made a material world without suffering and defect. Such a suggestion is a disguised wish for no autonomous scientifically explicable world at all.

This argument goes farther than the older arguments which—quite rightly as far as they went—pointed to the function of pain in the evolution, growth and sustenance of organic life. Pain is a useful, indeed necessary, mechanism. Presumably it would not have evolved otherwise. But its destructive extremities, so the present argument goes, follow necessarily on what is good and useful for other things[21]— that is, on a regularly structured, predictable and explicable environment for the evolution and maintenance of life.

It is important to stress the level of generality at which the modern scientific view of the world enables us to answer the question, Why this pain, this accident, this disaster? Such things are explicable by reference to the general structure of the universe through which God creates and sustains us. It is not only scientifically but religiously inappropriate to look for a particular purpose or intention behind the particular pain, accident or disaster in question. But at once the religious mind rebels against the austerity of this kind of argument. It looks at first sight as if we are explaining the presence of natural evil only by resorting to a deistic picture of the universe, whereby God sets the world in motion and then leaves it to operate in accordance with the general laws of nature that he has laid down. Something will be said in the final section of this chapter about the way in which the believer finds the resources of God at work in all the circumstances of life, however disastrous, drawing good out of evil, enabling suffering to be turned to redemptive uses, evoking just such faith and experience of God in and despite suffering as have been brought to our attention by such writers as Simone Weil, D. Z. Phillips and Diogenes Allen. It needs to be stressed that it is by no means a deistic picture of the relationship between God and the human world that comes to expression in such insights into spiritual resources in a world of pain. But it may still be thought of as a somewhat deistic picture as far as causal explanation is concerned.

It is at this point that we need to explore and articulate a much more careful conception of God's providence than that which sees direct divine causality and intention behind each particular event in the natural or human worlds. A mature doctrine of providence is concerned rather to spell out, as far as humanly possible, the modes of operation of the divine Spirit *in and through* an open, yet regularly structured, world. Seeing the point of the impersonal, law-governed operations of nature, it does not seek to interpret particular events, whether good or bad, as deliberately "sent". On the contrary, it recognises that God respects the given structure of the world for good reasons. Yet it also recognises that the natural world is open and flexible enough to allow novelty and creativity and freedom. Such a structured yet open universe is seen as the field or matrix within which the divine Spirit, without breaking the God-given laws of nature, works to bring about God's purposes, further the good, and, as the process theologians say, "lure" the creation into states more closely aligned with the intended goal of the whole creative process. Such a view of divine action in and through an ordered yet open cosmos is rightly suspicious of miracle. But it does not at once resort to deism, abandoning the notion of divine action altogether. It is a great mistake to think that God could only act in the world by miracle. *Pace* Feuerbach, miracle and providence are not the same thing.

This is most clearly seen at the level of conscious response to the presence and acts of God in the human spirit. As Austin Farrer points out,[22] the paradox of grace is that I am most truly myself and most truly free when I do God's will and thereby experience God's own action in me. Equally the word of a friend, a book, a sermon, can become the vehicle of divine action in and to a human soul. In none of these cases is the vehicle purely instrumental. There is always a natural, human story to tell. The reality of human interpersonal life is respected, yet it becomes the sphere or medium of divine action. Farrer expands this insight into a theory of "double agency" whereby God's agency is recognized in or behind human agency, the latter mediating the former, without any artificial manipulation or faking of the human story. Seen most clearly in the paradox of grace, the idea of double agency is then extended and generalised to cover the whole God-world relation—the whole field of creaturely causality being thought of as open to divine action, not as the effect of one cause among others as in the notion of direct miraculous intervention, but as an ordered yet flexible matrix, brooded over by the Spirit of God, who by his presence and action draws natural stories into providential patterns and, where possible, brings good out of evil. For the potentiality for good to be brought out of evil is itself a sign of the openness of creation, despite its law-governed structures, to the activity of the Spirit. The necessary structures account for the natural evils God permits, just as God's resolve to respect human freedom accounts for the moral evil he permits. But in neither case are we driven back to a deistic picture. For neither nature nor humankind is left to its own devices. At no point do they fall out of the continuing scope of appropriate divine action. On the contrary, to speak of *appropriate* divine action is to recognise the point of *double* agency and why it is that God respects the given structures of creation. Without them, human life would be impossible. The risks and vulnerabilities of a structured physical cosmos cannot be bypassed. But God is there in the whole process, fashioning a cosmos out of chaos, leading evolution in the direction of humankind, and fashioning a world of human life out of human history and interpersonal relation. At every point the natural is respected. It is not overridden. Yet the story of humankind becomes the story of God in humanity, the story of redemption. A structured physical world and free human beings are bound to produce suffering and evil, as well as all the good of existence, life and history. But divine providence turns the evil to good, as we see most clearly in the story of Christ and his cross.

The double agency theory of divine providence avoids the reduction of God's acts to one set of causes among others in the world. It enables us to take both God and the world seriously as the very different realities that they are. In developing the Irenaean theodicy in respect of natural evil, I have tried to show how important it is to appreciate the structure and interconnectedness of the natural world—something that modern science enables us to do much more coherently and in much greater detail than was possible in earlier centuries. But equally we must learn to appreciate the Godness of God—the creative Spirit at the heart of all things, the source of all good, the personal, ethical will, making the created cosmos make itself in the direction of the final consummation.

b. The Second Stage

We must now turn directly, however, to the second stage of an Irenaean theodicy and ask why it is that the creator Spirit has to create finite persons in and through such a law-governed physical universe, and why it is that the Creator has to respect its "impersonal" structure, even when great harm is done to persons (and to sentient creatures in general) by the operations of nature. Presupposing Christian theism, the answer can only be that such an impersonal, law-governed physical cosmos (including elements of real indeterminacy)[23] is a necessary condition for the realisation of the value of finite personal (human) life. I place "human" in parentheses, since this reply can take a weaker or a stronger form. The weaker form of the reply involves regarding some such evolving physical universe as a necessary condition for the realisation of specifically human values. The stronger involves regarding it as the necessary condition for the realisation of the value of finite personal creaturehood as such.

It is important to realise that even in its weaker form this argument is not restricted to the somewhat overmoralistic view of the universe as a necessary testing ground for character and the necessary condition for the acquisition of the sterner virtues, nor to the morally dubious view that "sin plus redemption is of more value in the sight of God than an innocence that permits neither sin nor redemption".[24] It is not too difficult to see that the physical universe is necessary and thus internal to the value of human existence in all its ramifications, including artistic creativity, moral sensitivity and love. Finite personal existence posited in being some other way would not yield these values of specifically human life. But intimations of the stronger form of the argument are also found in Hick's treatment when he speaks of the necessity of setting the creature at an "epistemic distance" from the Creator and of the physical universe as acting as a kind of screen, shielding the creature from the overwhelming reality and glory of the Creator, and enabling finite personal beings to acquire their personhood, together with all its concomitant values, including that of free thought and action. Unfortunately, Hick spoils the argument by conceding to Mackie that God could have created finite personal creatures in a morally frictionless environment, such that they always acted well, and arguing only that such goodness "is intrinsically less valuable than a moral goodness which has been built up through an agent's own responsible choices through time in face of alternative possibilities".[25] But the point about epistemic distance surely requires us to suppose that building up the creature from below, in and through a regularly structured environment, is a necessary condition of finite personhood as such. Not only is the environment necessary for personhood, but so is the building up from below. The gradual acquisition of moral personality through growth into and exercise of freedom is itself necessary to being a finite person. It is not that it is more valuable if done that way. It can only be done that way. And an environment both productive of finite persons at an "epistemic distance" from God and appropriate to their gradual acquisition of free moral personality could not possibly be "morally frictionless". Some such evolving physical universe is thus the necessary condition of the existence of finite persons as such.

Once we see that an evolving "impersonal" natural world is the necessary condition for there being any kind of finite creaturely person at all, we realise that an Irenaean theodicy is both presupposed by the freewill defence and explains the susceptibility of finite persons not only to damage but to temptation. Thus the explanation of the presence of natural evil in the world is bound up with the explanation of the presence of moral evil in the world. God permits natural disasters, since without the impersonal workings of nature there could be no finite persons, and he permits human wickedness, since persons would not be persons unless they were free; but the fact that finite persons must be set in and drawn out of nature also explains their liability to err. There could not be a "morally frictionless environment" for the formation of finite persons.

I stress the word "formation", since the destiny of finite persons, thus formed, is a resurrection life which will indeed be morally frictionless. But that state cannot be posited in being directly. We now see that it is the necessary conditions of the formative process of "soul-making" that explain both moral and natural evil. Once made, once established in being through this necessary and costly process, finite persons become susceptible of transformation into the frictionless environment of heaven.

In concluding this section on natural evil, I should like to underline again how different this kind of Irenaean theodicy is from any attempt to blame natural evil (or for that matter moral evil too) on the devil. The implausibility of reference to the devil at this point (quite apart from any other moral and metaphysical implausibilities which may attach to the notion of an irredeemably evil finite pure spirit) lies in our modern understanding of the nature of matter. We cannot suppose that cosmologists and elementary particle physicists are investigating the properties and powers of corrupted and perverted material substance. A scientific approach to the study of nature can be appropriated theologically only if we take it as an enquiry into what God has made. As argued above, a scientific understanding of nature helps us to appreciate its interconnectedness and its necessary function in the evolution of life. Metaphysical and theological reflection then enable us to see the necessity of some such law-governed system of interacting systems for the emergence not only of character and virtue, not only of specifically human values, but of any free, personal creature able in the end to be raised to an eternal destiny. This means of course that we do not yet have the proper standpoint from which to judge whether the whole creative process leading to that end is worth the cost in the inevitable concomitant evil and suffering. We trust that it is, and that trust may be helped by recognition that the only alternative would be no created world of personal being and life at all.

V. THE ACHIEVEMENT OF
GOD'S PURPOSES

The theodicy outlined in the last two sections explains the presence of evil and suffering in God's world as stemming from certain very general necessary conditions of the formation of finite persons. A law-governed physical universe and freedom of the will are necessary if there are to be such persons to know and enjoy one another and their God and to pursue and embrace the highest good. From those same conditions, sadly, come all the world's ills. We are specifically urged not to look for a particular explanation for this pain, this disaster, this piece of wickedness, apart from innerworldly explanations in terms of the operations of nature and free human action. There is no hidden purpose behind such terrible things. But of course Christianity has much to say as well—and indeed primarily—about what God does, and enables his creatures to do, about the world's ills. Such considerations are part of theodicy—not in offering further explanations but in helping to render creation justifiable despite the cost. In this concluding section I shall do little more than mention these further considerations.

It is a consequence of the theodicy advanced so far that we can come to understand why God respects the impersonal operations of nature and why he respects human freedom. At the same time, we learn that divine action in the world must take a form appropriate to the nature of what God has made and is making in and through this whole creative process. As argued above, this basic fact controls a mature understanding of prayer and providence. But given these constraints, which, to repeat, are internal to the realisation of the intended values of creation, God works to bring about his purposes, to bring good out of evil, and, in the end, to raise and transform human lives, once fashioned in this necessarily arduous way, into the morally frictionless conditions of eternity.[26] One of the ways in which the world's ills may be "absorbed"[27] is precisely through that deeply religious discovery of the possibility of encountering the love of God in the depths of affliction to which Weil, Phillips, and Allen draw attention. Freed from any temptation to discern in this the *rationale* of the presence of evil in God's world, we may indeed find profound religious significance in this possibility. Kindred notions may be recognised in the possibility of redemptive suffering which already came to expression in the Servant Songs of Deutero-Isaiah and in the ways in which not only the good of self-sacrificial love but also other unexpected consequences may providentially supervene upon disastrous circumstances which in themselves we can only bewail and deplore. Most notable is the central Christian belief that the God who has ordained, for the reasons already given, this costly and painful creative process has taken its consequences in suffering, pain, dereliction and death upon himself through incarnation. The passion and cross of Christ do not explain evil and suffering, but they reveal the readiness of God, out of his great love, to subject himself, in the person of his Son, to the worst the world can do, precisely in order to win and enable the kind of experience and response in us that issues in the bringing of good out of evil and, in the end, participation in eternal life. The story of our redemption also illustrates God's way with evil and the manner of God's providential action in a world where evil and suffering are inevitable. That story does not, of course, end with the passion and cross of Christ. The resurrection anticipates an eschatological transformation which will constitute the destiny of a personal creation necessarily achieved only arduously through a world of pain. Admittedly it also shows how nothing the world can do can ultimately separate us from the love of God and his gift of eternal life. For in the end God will raise the dead. But the resurrection is no paradigm of providence. It can be thought of only as an anticipation of the end. The end itself cannot come within the present structures of creation.

The eschatological dimension to theodicy does nothing to explain the presence of evil and suffering in the world, but it helps to show the ultimate justification for creation, despite its inevitable pain. Such are the extent and extremity of evil and suffering that it would be hard to see that justification if God did not raise the dead. It is in this sense that we can say, *pace* the Dominicans, that God, if there be a God of love, is morally obliged to raise the dead. That obligation, as stressed above, is self-imposed. It is a matter of moral consistency in a God whose nature is revealed to be perfect love. Only if all the world's sufferers are raised, forgiven and transformed in order to share in the final consummation of all things has theodicy any real chance of making out its claim that the creation of finite persons, necessarily in and through an evolving material universe that can temporarily so frustrate as well as further the creative intention, is worthwhile.

NOTES

1. D. Z. Phillips, *Faith and Philosophical Enquiry* (London: Routledge & Kegan Paul, 1970), 128.

2. Stewart R. Sutherland, *God, Jesus and Belief: The Legacy of Theism* (Oxford: Basil Blackwell, 1984).

3. Herbert McCabe, "God: III—Evil", *New Blackfriars,* January 1981, 4–17.

4. Brian Davies, *An Introduction to the Philosophy of Religion* (Oxford: Oxford University Press, 1982), chap. 3.

5. Diogenes Allen, "Natural Evil and the Love of God", *Religious Studies* 16 (1980):439–56.

6. Antony Flew, "Theology and Falsification", in *New Essays in Philosophical Theology,* ed. Antony Flew and A. C. MacIntyre (London: SCM Press, 1955).

7. J. L. Mackie, "Evil and Omnipotence", *Mind,* 64 (1955).

8. John Hick, *Evil and the God of Love* (London: Macmillan & Co., 1966).

9. See the essays and discussions in S. T. Davis, ed., *Encountering Evil: Live Options in Theodicy* (Edinburgh: T. & T. Clark, 1981).

10. David Hume, *Dialogues Concerning Natural Religion,* ed. Norman Kemp Smith (New York: Oxford University Press, 1935), 260.

11. Peter Berger, *The Social Reality of Religion* (London: Faber & Faber, 1969), chap. 3.

12. J. L. Mackie, *The Miracle of Theism: Arguments for and Against the Existence of God* (Oxford: Oxford University Press, 1982).

13. See n. 7.

14. Alvin Plantinga, *God and Other Minds: A Study of the Rational Justification of Belief in God* (Ithaca, N.Y.: Cornell University Press, 1967), chap. 6.

15. Mackie, *The Miracle of Theism,* 171.

16. See Davies, *An Introduction,* 21.

17. See R. Swinburne, *The Coherence of Theism* (Oxford: Oxford University Press, 1977), chap. 11.

18. Hick, in *Encountering Evil,* ed. Davis, 44.

19. See Hick, *Evil and the Love of God,* passim; and Hick, in *Encountering Evil,* passim.

20. Mackie, *The Miracle of Theism,* 153.

21. McCabe, "God: III—Evil", 13.

22. Austin Farrer, *Faith and Speculation* (London: Adam & Charles Black, 1967), chap. 4.

23. See D. J. Bartholomew, *God of Chance* (London: SCM Press, 1984).
24. Hick, quoted from Mackie, *The Miracle of Theism,* 153.
25. Hick, in *Encountering Evil,* ed. Davis.
26. See further Brian L. Hebblethwaite, *The Christian Hope* (Basingstoke, Eng.: Marshall, Morgan & Scott, 1984).
27. To use a concept given an unduly restricted use by Mackie, *The Miracle of Theism,* 154ff.

4

HUMAN BEING

RICHARD NORRIS

I. WAYS OF BEING IN THE WORLD

Anyone who dares, in this day and age, to open the question of human "nature"—and from a theological and specifically Christian perspective at that—owes potential readers a preliminary accounting. Over what ground will the discourse move? What is the business of a theological anthropology?

There is a great deal of historical precedent to which one can appeal for an answer to these questions. Over the centuries, in connection with their handling of the themes of sin and redemption, Christian preachers and teachers have not infrequently offered analyses of the human situation. These have ordinarily taken the form of interpretative readings of the stories of creation and fall in Genesis. Their function has been to explain how the "grace and truth" manifested in Christ answers to the problems of human nature and history. At the same time, Christian divines have not infrequently set out accounts of the human constitution—accounts that seemed to them to lend support to their treatment of these more fundamental themes. From Irenaeus's *Adversus haereses* and Tertullian's treatise *On the Soul* to contemporary theological disquisitions on the meaning of "person", there is a whole series of Christian writings that can be summoned to give testimony about the standard agenda of a theological anthropology.

Inspection of such writings, however, does not suggest that there is now, or ever has been, a distinctively Christian teaching on most of the subjects they handle. Where the question of the human constitution is concerned, Christian reflection has tended on the whole to accept the commonplace wisdom of the culture in which it is set and then, in

78

handling that wisdom, to revise and reshape it critically in accordance with the requirements of the language of Christian faith and hope. Similarly, in handling the tensions of the human situation and the issues of human destiny, Christian thinking has regularly employed the linguistic codes which distill and shape its culture's perception of these problems, while at the same time it has stretched such codes by putting them to unaccustomed—and sometimes, indeed, inappropriate—uses. To be sure, there are distinctively Christian themes that inform the anthropological discourse of theologians, and one can enumerate them: the creation of Adam "after the image of God"; sin or disobedience as the root of Adam's alienation; the "new creation" in Christ as the destiny of the human animal. On the other hand, these themes have tended, it seems, to be deployed and interpreted through the use of anthropological ideas which in and of themselves are not necessarily either Christian by origin or theological in conception.

Are we to conclude from this that there is no such thing as a "Christian anthropology"? Certainly this is the case *at one level,* and it is important to say so. In spite of efforts—in every age, including the present—to read a systematic anthropology off the text of the Christian Scriptures, it is merely obvious, or should be, that those writings do not speak in ways which are directly relevant to the agenda either of a philosophical anthropology in the Greek tradition or of a "scientific" anthropology in the modern style. An explicit "doctrine of man" is no part of the Mosaic covenant, of the prophetic witness, or, for that matter, of the apostolic testimony to the Christ; and no doubt it is this fact which accounts for the eclecticism—and the variety—of Christian anthropological discourse.

To say this, however, is to assert, not that the Scriptures do not talk about human beings, but only that they do so in a fashion that is at once unsystematic, largely prereflective, and almost invariably indirect. So let it be granted that reflective anthropology—of whatever sort—is, at best, a minor item on the agenda of the scriptural books. There is nevertheless a scriptural *way of talking* about human beings, both as communities and as individuals; and it is this way of talking—embedded as it is in a cheerfully metaphorical vocabulary—which may in the end afford the most useful key to a Christian approach to the issues of anthropology.

To begin with, though, that expression "way of talking" needs some explanation. In the first instance, it does not refer to *what* the Scriptures say about human beings (though that lurks prominently in the background). Rather, it refers to the set and character of the relationships in which they characteristically locate their Adam. Human persons and communities are envisaged habitually in the setting of a relation—at once dependent and responsive—to a "Beyond" which evokes, sustains, enlivens and addresses them in and with their natural and historical world. Within this relationship, moreover, they play an active role. They are said variously to love, obey, sin, get angry, hear, see, give thanks, confess—all with reference to the God who is their sustaining "Beyond". Conversely, they are the objects or recipients in this relationship of actions or attitudes of which God is the subject: loving-kindness, judgment, guidance, forgiveness, and the like. The scriptural "way of talking" about human beings is, then, systematically *theological* in the sense that human individuals are identified and understood as such through their relationship to God. Their being, to use one of Luther's favorite phrases, is *coram Deo.* "God" is the name of the ultimate context in which and to which they are responsive.

No doubt this is an obvious enough point. What is perhaps not so obvious is the fashion in which this "way of talking" functions. Scriptural language does not set relatedness to God *alongside* other relations or sorts of relations in which human beings can stand. People are related in various ways to one another; to their forebears and their offspring; to their fields and flocks; and, for that matter, to a variety of other forces or powers in the cosmos. Such engagements, however, do not displace people's relation to God, nor are they displaced by it. Amos had to be taken from his herds and his dressing of sycamore trees to become a prophet. The set of relations that defined the one role was inconsistent with that which defined the other. In neither role, however, could he cease to be answerable to God. Distinct and concrete though it be, people's relation to God is never, in the scriptural way of talking, alternative to their other sorts of engagements, but, as it were, encompasses them. It cannot be reduced to them, but it seems, for all that, to be carried on in and through them. It is the framework, so to speak, or horizon which determines or defines the meaning of these other engagements; and in that sense it transcends them as it includes them.

How, though, is this line of thought relevant to our question about the agenda of a Christian anthropology? Every anthropology, I want to suggest, works with a model of the human person which is based, at least in substantive part, on a consideration of the *mode or style* of the relations which such a person typically sustains with the "world"—with the "other" as it impinges and is encountered in life. Through the mode or style in which the "other" is approached, treated or dealt with, there emerges, on the one hand, a tacit or explicit picture of what "world" is really like and, on the other hand, a paradigm of the person who can be so related to such a reality. If, however, our brisk and impressionistic account of the scriptural "way of talking" about human beings is broadly correct, then there is in the Scriptures just such a paradigm of the human person; and the fact that it is not conveyed directly in rigorous philosophical or "scientific" language is a matter of scant importance. In all their engagements with the world, of whatever kind, human beings as the Scriptures portray them *co-respond with* a sustaining and inclusive "Beyond" which is somehow objectified for them as a reality which can and must be answered, as "word". The implications of this way of talking are not, perhaps, perfectly clear; but they might, at least in principle, be teased out. The Scriptures do in fact contain the *matter* for a reasoned anthropology, and that matter is found in the mode or style in which their writers perceive that people are related to the "other".

It needs to be noted, however, that this account of the basis and framework of a Christian or scriptural anthropology has at least one immediate and important implication. The way in which the Bible's dominant "way of talking" about human beings envisages them and their world is not derived from a speculative impulse or a desire to settle an abstractly posed question about "human nature". It emerges out of and expresses a practical orientation to the business of human life. People who speak in this way, in other words, can only be supposed to do so because in fact they relate themselves to the world in the fashion which this particular way of talking articulates. Their "anthropology" is an implicate of their style of life, their practical way of seeing things and handling them. Hence any formal anthropological "doctrine" that is derived from the Scriptures is, in the end, simply an attempt to give a critical and reasoned account of what amounts to a cultural and religious praxis. If this is true, however, of a Christian or scriptural anthropology, then presumably it is also true of differing or alternative anthropologies. In every case, one must suppose, theoretical disquisitions on human nature are likely to be critical expressions and articulations of a mode or style of relatedness to the world that is actually *lived*.

It seems, then, that if there are a variety of ways in which human beings have understood themselves, this circumstance can be attributed—at least in part—to the fact that there is more than one dominant mode or style in which people can learn—and have learned— to address (and so to picture) their world. There is no "doctrine" about the human way of being which is not an attempt to make systematic sense of an habitual mode of engagement with the "other"; and this of course implies that people not only can *think* differently about themselves but—at least within certain limits—can *be* differently. If this is so, however, then the question of what human nature is, is not merely unsettled in theory; it is in fact and in reality an open—or better, an open-ended—question. No doubt there are satisfactorily accurate ways of telling a human person from other sorts of things in the world; and to that extent it makes perfect sense to speak of a given "human nature". That "given", however, is in some sense unfinished—underdetermined, as the phrase goes. Nature requires, as the ancients would have said, to be completed by a "second nature" which brings it to its point.

To expound a Christian—or any other—understanding of human being, therefore, can never be a matter simply of laying out an authoritative teaching which can then be affirmed or qualified or denied simply in view of "the facts". It is to project a mode of engagement with the "other", the world, that is arguably consonant both with the limitations and with the possibilities of human nature—with its givenness and with its underdetermination. At the same time—and this point requires equal stress—the very existence of such an enterprise testifies that the finishing or completion of the human animal involves its own participation, its own choice and freedom—if only in the persons of those who set out to write systematic anthropologies. The underdetermination of human nature (its "mutability", as the church fathers would have said) is the correlate of its self-determining capacity. To project a mode of engagement with the "other", then, to envisage for human persons a style of relatedness to the world, is, at base, to propose a way of understanding and handling the concurrent givenness and underdetermination of human nature, the dialectic of limitation and freedom in human existence.

This, then, must be the most basic task of anyone who is engaged in the business of expounding and assessing the elements of a Christian understanding of human nature. The material themes of a Christian anthropology—the doctrines of creation, of the image of God in Adam, of sin and fall and redemption—must be set in the formal framework of the Scriptures' "way of talking" about human existence, their articulation of a mode of engagement or relatedness to the "other"; and this framework in turn must be interpreted and assessed in the light of its handling of what I have called "the dialectic of limitation and freedom in human existence". To accomplish this constructively, however, due attention must be paid to the fashion in which this fundamental dialectic has been handled in other idioms—that is, in the framework of other understandings of the dominant mode of human relatedness to the "other". And for present purposes, it is post-Enlightenment debates about the nature and situation of human beings which are most obviously relevant, since these provide the setting in which and to which a contemporary Christian anthropological "projection" must speak.

II. SUBJECTS IN AN OBJECT WORLD

Where, though, shall we look for the characteristic note of a "modern" anthropology? The era in the history of Western culture that opens toward the end of the seventeenth century (and indeed even earlier, with Descartes and Hobbes) has arguably produced not one but many treatments of human nature and the human constitution. Even if one were to confine inquiry to the field of philosophy, how much could one find in common as between, say, the understanding of the human person in Hume and in Kant, or in Heidegger and in Ryle? The truth is, however, that it is not to the work of philosophers that one instinctively turns to see the shape of a characteristically modern anthropology. Rather, it is to that of the practitioners of the so-called "human sciences" or "social sciences". Surely it is the sociologist, the economist, the anthropologist, and the theorist of the human psyche who have been most influential in forming the modern picture of what a human being is; and here too the variety of contending views is striking—and indeed almost numbing to the brain. As between a behaviorist and a Freudian, as between a Marxist and a functionalist, there seems, again, to be little in common.

Such variety, however, may conceal a real unity—not so much of viewpoint as of *agenda*. That is to say, there may well be a unity in the modern approach to anthropological questions, a unity defined by a central issue or set of issues with reference to which different thinkers and schools of thought have taken radically differing stands. Such a unity, moreover, which is defined not by a doctrine so much as by a question or a series of questions, is likely to have its roots in a commonly accepted way of conceiving people's relation to the world, to the "other". The question then would be one, not of surveying modern accounts of human nature in all their variety, but of grasping the logic of the problem with which they deal—a problem dictated or engendered by a certain mode of engagement with the world.

Can one detect such a characteristic problem in modern ways of handling anthropological questions? A relevant clue is afforded by some remarks of Michael Polanyi:

> Man's capacity to think is his most outstanding attribute. Whoever speaks of man will therefore have to speak at some stage of human knowledge. This is a troublesome prospect. For the task seems without end: as soon as we had completed one such study, our subject-matter would have been extended by this very achievement. We should now have to study the study that we had just completed, since it, too, would be a work of man.
>
> This difficulty may appear far-fetched, but it is, in fact, profoundly characteristic both of the nature of man and of the nature of human knowledge. Man must for ever try to discover knowledge that will stand up by itself, objectively, but the moment he reflects on his own knowledge he catches himself red-handed in the act of upholding his knowledge.[1]

The human person, then, is essentially, or at any rate characteristically, "knower", Polanyi suggests; and to find out what one can say about human nature, one must give, above all and in the first instance, an account of what is involved in knowing.

This, of course, is one thinker's opinion, but it is an opinion supported by the testimony or the practice of many others. Modern philosophy, if it can indeed be thought to have its inception in Descartes's *Meditations,* is centrally concerned with the problem of doubt and therefore with the problem of knowledge. Both the debate between rationalist and empiricist and its attempted resolution in Kant's "Copernican revolution" are focused on the problem of the ground of knowledge. The character of scientific inquiry—whether into nature or into human affairs—is not merely the central concern of positivists like Neurath and of hermeneuticians in the tradition of Dilthey; it is also the issue that underlies the philosophical agenda of the thinkers whose ideas, however much they have been revised, criticized and expanded, have engendered in one way or another the principal schools of contemporary philosophy: Peirce, Husserl, and Wittgenstein.

If knowledge and science, however, are indeed the dominant themes of philosophy in the modern style, one is bound to ask why this is so. The answer cannot be sought in philosophy itself. It must, rather, be sought in the wider culture which the philosopher at once interprets, criticizes and rationalizes: that is, in the concerns, values and ideas that govern the way that people (including philosophers) see and treat with their world. And the fact is, of course, that Western culture in the modern era identifies and praises itself principally by reference to its knowledge—its ability to explain its world. Other ages have, no doubt, sought and extolled knowledge; but what they meant by that was a capacity to see and appreciate the world—to be "in" and "with" it knowingly. By contrast, the knowledge upon which modern Western culture has prided itself is a science which, because it grasps how the world works, is able to "work" the world—to predict and, at least within limits, to make and control it.

Beneath the philosophers' obsession with the problem of knowledge, then, there lies a culture's obsession with the need to explain for the purposes of control. If there is a dominant mode in which the modern individual or group envisages its relation to the world, it is that of "knower". In this relation, however, there emerges, as one would expect, a characteristic picture both of "world" and of the human person. The former is something to be explained and understood: it is "object"—which is to say that its way of being is constituted and exhausted by the fact that it answers to the interests and methods with which the knower approaches it. Conversely, the human person as knower belongs not to the world which is explored and investigated but simply to itself. Over against what it knows, it stands as autonomous "subject", the repository of effective initiative. In this capacity, moreover, the knower is preeminently the possessor of power. What is known and understood becomes "available" to the knower. It is, at least in principle, at the disposal of the human subject. It matters little whether "world" is conceived as society or as nature. In either case it becomes *in principle* malleable to the knower's purposes; perhaps not infinitely malleable, but at any rate subject, as we have said, to prediction and control.

This picture or model of the human being in relation to its world—a picture in which the status of subject is reserved to one term of the relation and that of object to the other—seems to account for many of the characteristic problems of modern anthropology. The Cartesian dualism of mind and body, frequently deplored as it is, seems to result simply from the assimilation of "mind" to subject and "body" to object; and though this interpretation of the schema may well seem naive, reasonable alternatives seem difficult to find as long as the basic schema itself is presupposed. Another problem arises from the fact that an object world must be pictured, for purposes of scientific knowing, as denuded of intrinsic value. Not only must it appear to be deprived, as Joseph Addison in effect admitted in a well-known hymn,[2] of those engaging secondary qualities which the senses delight in—sound, color, and texture; it must also be deprived of a capacity to engage the will by evoking delighted responses of respect or honor or obligation. The object of *knowledge* is value-neutral. The human person, then, is isolated as a compulsive valuer over against a valueless world; and this perception of the human situation undergirds not only certain existentialist portrayals of the individual as an undetermined quantum of pure and arbitrary freedom but also the frequent attempts on the part of philosophers and others to overcome the subject-object antithesis by portraying the object world as a distillation of universal human needs and interests or as (in part, at any rate) a mental or social creation of some sort.

Our concern here, however, is not to sketch—or even to mention—the various anthropological proposals by which this basic schema has been interpreted or qualified. Rather, it is to indicate the shape that is given to the problem of human freedom and limitation when this particular form of the "knower-known" relation is used as the dominant model for understanding what a human being is in relation to the world.

To approach this issue, it is necessary to take explicit account of two circumstances that have helped to determine the way in which this model functions in practice. The first of these has to do simply with the sort of explanation that scientific knowledge seeks. What the knowing subject grasps in a knowledge that is "scientific" is not the world as it appears. Such knowledge, in other words, is not primarily a description or classification of phenomena—not even of the patterned sequences of sense data to which Hume appealed in order to define the notion of causality. Rather, it is a detection and grasp of invariable structural factors which are taken to underlie and explain phenomena. Hence there is a systematic distinction to be made between the way things *are* and the way things *look,* and a systematic reduction to be made of phenomena to the structural factors—"laws"—which operate, more or less hiddenly, to produce them. Whether one attends to the order of the physical universe, to the experienced life of the self, or to the functioning of a social and cultural order, what really goes on and what is normally seen to go on are, almost by hypothesis, different. One might epitomize this principle by saying that scientific knowledge proceeds to explanation by way of the criticism of whatever passes for "common sense". Its capacity to control and predict, in short, depends on an operation of uncovering and unmasking, in which the factors that actually *rule* in a given sort of situation are identified.

The second circumstance to be noted—and a crucially important one—is the fact of what we can call the ambiguous location of the human person in this version of the relation between knower and known. In the scheme of Descartes, it seems, and in the early stages of the Enlightenment, it was "nature"—that is, the nonhuman world—which constituted the object of scientific inquiry. It required only time, however, for the phenomena of the human world also to become objects of such inquiry. This meant that human persons, their past and present acts, and their modes of association were assigned to the object realm. They became matter for explanation, prediction and control. In this way the human self in all of its dimensions came to suffer, as it were, from bilocation. On the one hand, it was envisaged as the autonomous self which understands and controls—which, indeed, shapes the world that is the object of its explanatory knowledge. At the same time, however, it was treated as a part of the world thus explained and controlled. It became a phenomenon to be understood by appeal to objectively operating factors—whether physical or social or psychic—which lie beneath the surface of its knowing and choosing.

This dialectic between self-as-subject and self-as-object involves much more than an intellectual puzzle. It is embodied in many of the problems of contemporary cultural and political life, for which the human individual is, on the one hand, elevated as an independent source of value and initiative, endowed with the power—and the right—to construct its own existence; and, on the other hand, treated precisely as the *object* of such a process of construction, through various techniques of propaganda and manipulation. It is not surprising, then, that this bilocation of the self has long been a theme for theoretical reflection. One thinks of the distinction between a transcendental and an empirical ego; of the division, already alluded to, of mind from body; of the psychoanalytic hypothesis of a conscious ego playing on the surface of the unconscious; of the proletariat which must seize the initiative and act because, as a matter of fact, it is in chains. In each of these themes there is an adumbration, presented no doubt in a distinctive way, of the conflict between the picture of self as the world's constructor and that of self as the world's construction.

Here, then, is the point at which one can discern the shape that is taken by the problem of human freedom and limitation under the aegis of the modern picture of humanity's relation to its world. At first glance, the human subject appears as independent—the knower and "worker" of an object world. At second glance, however, it appears as a part of the very object world which it controls and hence as absolutely bound. What is not often noted about this apparently confused picture is that the two roles in which the self occurs—that of fully autonomous subject and that of fully determined object—mutually require each other. Unless the human person is "object" in the sense required, its autonomy as "subject"—as the knowing controller of its own world—is denied. Conversely, unless the human person possesses just such an autonomy, its world does not appear as "object".

In view of this circumstance, it cannot be surprising that attempts to overcome this dualism—this bilocation, as we have called it, of the self—have on the whole been unsuccessful. The behaviorism of a B. F. Skinner may attempt, for example, to absorb the human person wholly into the object world as a system of conditioned reflexes (and thus, as it were, to absolutize the limitedness of human being); but the autonomous subject subsists, though in a hidden fashion, in the scientist who knows how best to condition human material for its own good. Again, the radical existentialist who denies that human beings have *any* objective "essence" save by their own free decision (and thus seeks to absolutize human autonomy) nevertheless envisages himself precisely as the object of such a decision. Hermeneuticians in the broad tradition of Dilthey have sought to make room for freedom within the object realm itself by insisting that the phenomena with which the "human sciences" deal are of a sort that must be "understood" rather than "explained". Yet the enterprise of "understanding" proceeds by absorbing its object into a governing context of meaning. For the relativity of phenomena to causal laws it substitutes a relativity to cultural and historical setting—that is, to "language"; and in the end this procedure seems to threaten absorption of interpreter and object alike into the surface "play of signifiers".

The fact is, then, that the modern "subject-object" schema, when it is employed to interpret the basic mode of humanity's relation to its "other", its world, runs a perpetual risk of losing track of the autonomous self which it presupposes. This fact no doubt becomes most obvious when the human person is programmatically absorbed into the realm of that which is (or is to be) explained or understood. When this occurs, the claim to freedom in the form of autonomy becomes radically inconsistent with the way in which the self is being envisaged and treated—that is, as "object". To assert the claim to freedom is to posit indeterminacy in the realm of that which must be understood as determinable: that is, to put the matter in other terms, it is to suppose that there are problems in the "world" that do not fall under rules of prediction and control. It is illicitly to insert a "ghost in the machine". The classic alternative, of course, is to relocate the ghost in a position over against the machine: to locate it, that is, as the knower and manipulator, possibly the inventor, of the machine. Even when envisaged in this fashion, however, the autonomous subject remains very much a ghost—disembodied, intangible, "transcendental". It is "spirit" as over against "nature". Furthermore, it can be related to its object realm only, it seems, by being brought once again within the latter's scope (rather as Descartes joined "mind" to the realm of "body" or "extension" by way of the pituitary gland). Freedom, it turns out, is either illicit or ineffective.

To say this, however, is not to suggest that in practice faith in human autonomy, or desire for human autonomy, is or ever has been unreal in the world of modernity. The contrary is surely the case. The subject-object schema itself is, historically speaking, an assertion of that faith and that desire. It carefully segregates limitation from the subject and envisages the "other" as determinable object precisely in order to establish the human person as controller and creator of its world. No doubt, as we have seen, the object world has increasingly tended either to absorb the autonomous subject or to exile it from effective reality. But this tendency is greeted almost universally with fear and protest. The object realm, whether it is identified as natural and physical law or as objective social and political "system", is perceived as a place of

89

exile for the human spirit, as intrinsically oppressive and dehumanizing; and such a perception simply enacts the original logic of the subject-object schema. What it expresses is no more than the basic assumption that the human self as subject is alienated when it is "relocated" as a member of an object world.

The problem, then, is not that this way of structuring the human person's relation to its world somehow "intends" to ignore or devalue the openness, initiative and freedom of the individual. It lies, rather, in the fact that it identifies freedom as strict autonomy and limitation as strict dependence, and thus constitutes them as contraries. It is, in the proper sense, a dualistic scheme. The result of this is twofold. On the one hand, as we have said, the two contraries presuppose each other because they define each other. Only in the face of an object world can autonomy be exercised; and only in relation to an autonomous subject can the world appear as object. Hence the dualism which the schema presupposes cannot be overcome apart from a reconsideration of the entire perspective which it embodies—apart, that is, from a redefinition of the very terms of the polarity of subject and object. Then, on the other hand, there is the phenomenon that we have described as the bilocation of the self. To practice self-determination, the subject must become object as well. Since, however, it remains the case that the two are conceived as contraries, the very act in which self-determination is exercised is the act in which alienation is experienced and the autonomous self is revealed as "ghost".

It may safely be said, then, that the living out of this mode of relation to the world—a mode that has its roots in the enterprise of scientific knowing—involves at least one serious anomaly which can manifest itself socially and politically as well as personally. It at once identifies freedom with ability to control and refuses dependence as inconsistent with freedom. The question then becomes, for a Christian anthropology, that of asking how this set of issues is handled if the scriptural "way of talking" about human beings and their relation to the world is adopted.

III. THE HUMAN CREATURE AMID THE CREATURES AND BEFORE GOD

I have already tried to suggest the shape of this scriptural way of talking, though only in the most general terms. The human self *co-responds* with its "other" in such wise that the "other" appears not as mere object but as something possessed of a depth and interiority—a subjectivity—of its own. It is tempting here to adopt the language of Martin Buber and say that the Scriptures set the human self, most fundamentally, in an "I-Thou" relationship with its "other"; but this would be to speak too narrowly or exclusively. The world does not invariably come at people in the role of a "Thou"; nor, for that matter, does the human self invariably respond to its world as an "I". Nevertheless the mode of relationship in question presupposes a "subject"—something with a center and integrity of its own—on both sides of the relation, even as it presupposes something that is capable of functioning as "object". The metaphor of conversation is not inept, but it must be taken in an extended sense as embracing different orders of relations between subjects as well as different orders of subjects.

A useful, if inexact, way of illuminating this understanding of humanity's relation to its world is simply to note, in historical vein, that it has its roots in a mentality that is not far removed from animism. The world and the things in it, whether they are identified as persons or not, are full of power and presence. To be in the world is to be set in relation to realities that have, so to speak, a way—even perhaps a will—of their own that cannot always be plumbed or mastered. In such a world the human person comes to itself through interaction with beings that have a dimension of mystery about them—which can be appreciated but not, in the full sense, grasped. It is no doubt true, as an earlier generation of theologians delighted in saying, that the writers of the Hebrew Scriptures "demystified" their world in the sense that they emptied it of "gods". They did not, however, reduce it to the status of a determinable object. The other remained "subject"—something less than perfectly transparent and therefore something of which the human person had not merely to give an account but to take account.

This way of perceiving or envisaging things, however, stems directly from the scriptural picture of the world, and of the human self within it, as God's creation. The doctrine of creation, of course, aims to render an account of the relation of the human person (and other creatures) to God, but it also, in the end, brings to focus an understanding of the relationship of the creatures to one another.

In the first place, the doctrine of creation pictures every finite being as not merely reflecting but embodying a divine intent. It is not Adam alone who, in the Genesis story of creation, has a place and a calling in God's purposes. Creatures animate and inanimate alike have the

Creator's will as the ground of their being. They are expressions and embodiments of that will. For just this reason, however, they are not, for Adam, mere objects of knowledge and control. To encounter another creature is always to meet something which, because of the creative intent that informs it, demands cooperation more than it invites mastery. Adam sets names to the animals, and this responsibility no doubt marks the human being out as something distinctive; but it also marks the beasts out as Adam's fellows—as creatures of whom proper account must be taken because they too mean and intend something in God's purposes.

In the second place, then, the Adam of biblical story is not set over against the world as its knower and controller, as autonomous subject. The human being's subjectivity, its awareness and initiative, have the rest of the created order as their matrix. No doubt it is Adam who brings the world into conscious focus, so to speak, as something to be assessed and treated with: so much the business of "naming" intimates. Nevertheless the story of creation locates humanity *within* the world, acting upon the "other", to be sure, but only by way of responding to it as an effective presence. Not merely in relation to other people but in relation to "nature" itself, the human person is intrinsically social: it appears as one focus of a network of engagements and connections within which it is at once dependent and active, puzzled and knowledgeable.

This picture of the human person in relation to the created world, however, simply reiterates, in another mode, the logic of the relation between Adam as creature and God as Creator. On the one hand, the doctrine of creation pictures Adam in a wholly dependent relation to God: dependent not—in this case—relatively or partially but in respect of existence itself. On the other hand, it depicts this wholly dependent creature as a being that *responds* to God in a unique way. Humanity does not have God merely as the source and horizon of its being but also brings that horizon into focus as another Subject to whom free response is required. In total dependence on God, the human being of Genesis is free in relation to God—in relation to the frame and context of its own being. Hence as Adam is both free and limited by dependence, that context is, for the human creature, at once focused and unfathomable.

In both cases, then—as over against other creatures and as over against God—the human person is limned neither as "object" nor as "subject" but as both at once. The "other" is something that Adam recognizes and answers; at the same time it is something that limits Adam precisely because it is there to ground and to demand such response. Where the other creatures are concerned, however, this responsive relationship stands very much within the wider horizon of Adam's ultimate engagement with God. If these beings are present for Adam, and Adam is answerable to them (and for them), this is a state of affairs which God has brought about. Hence in the last analysis it is God's will in them and for them to which Adam responds in treating with them. The relation of creature to Creator is the ground, and in that sense the archetype, of the creatures' relation to one another.

This being the case, however, it is in the seeming paradox of Adam's relation to the Creator that one must seek the key to a biblical understanding of humanity. And the essence of the paradox is plain: limitation and freedom are not segregated but go hand in hand. Far from being treated as contraries, they are presented in the doctrine of creation as two sides of a single coin. It is through the human creature's complete—and presumably continuing—dependence on God that it appears as a centered reality that in its own right "intends" something; and in the human being which God creates, such dependence manifests itself in an "intending" that reaches and focuses—"hears" and "sees"—God himself. This marriage of limitation and freedom, however, is paradoxical only from the point of view of a perspective that understands freedom to mean the autonomy of a subject confronted with a world of determinable objects. The paradox disappears when we recognize that it is *answerability* which is the form of freedom in biblical perspective; for answerability signifies both freedom and limitation. Freedom appears as the capacity to respond to the limiting presence of an "other" which embodies a claim upon, and hence evokes a response from, the agent. In other words, it emerges in and through dependence, as the subject is brought to awareness of self and other through a reality which both bounds and sustains it. Adam becomes free in relation to God through a divine word that confers responsibility by marking a limit. The freedom and the limit go hand in hand. The human person belongs to itself only in belonging to God.

IV. LIMITATION AND FREEDOM

The question must be, though, what, at least in general terms, this picture of Adam's relation to the "other"—immediate and ultimate, fellow creature and Creator—implies or suggests about the human individual's own way of being. What sort of anthropology grows out of this perspective on the problem of freedom and limitation? It is in this connection that the theme of the image of God and the theme of sin and the fall must be taken up; but first it is necessary to explore our metaphor of answerability a bit further.

The point of the metaphor, as should by now be clear, is to suggest that both in relation to God and in relation to other creatures, the human being is at once limited and free, a dependent subject of initiative, whose capacity for self-determination arises *through,* and not apart from, the "other". Human freedom is not an "inalienable" possession but something that emerges within a pattern of relationships.

In speaking of such engagement, however, with the dependence and limitation it involves, one hits directly upon the dimension of Adam's being which is conveyed and captured in the symbol of "body". The term "body" and its equivalents no doubt have different primary connotations for different eras and cultures. It may convey solidity and reality (as to the Dr. Johnson who neatly refuted Bishop Berkeley by kicking a stone). It may, as for much of Greek thought, suggest mere bulk: that is, distension in space, lack of coherent integrity, and hence liability to dissolution. In either case, however, to be body means to be tangible; and it is this connotation to which I want to advert here. A body is something that I can touch; but conversely it is that in virtue of which the "other" can touch me. To be body, then, is (among other things) to be touching and touched, involved in a web of relationships by which, on the one hand, the "other" attains and affects me and, on the other, I am able—and bound—to react or respond. Hence its own bodiliness, from the point of view of the human self, turns out to be a sort of office of foreign relations, a place of meeting with the "other" which at some indefinable point begins to fade into the "other". For the human being to stand, then, in a relation of answerability to its world entails its being bodily.

In this bodiliness, moreover, at least two orders of relations are embraced—orders that are normally distinguished but that in fact, where human beings are concerned, go hand in hand. As body, the human person is embedded first of all in ("physical") nature; but it is also embedded in the social world of other human beings. That is, it comes to be, finds place and identity and carries out its role, in virtue of two systems of patterned interaction to which it belongs. Both of these involve the interplay of natural energies; in the second of them, however, these natural energies constitute a world of language and symbol—a world of shared meaning embodied in gestures, artifacts, words and institutions. Adam's is an embodied life, then, insofar as it is a life beholden and dependent—touched, upheld, molded and questioned on every hand by a natural and social "other".

Every human culture has, in some characteristic way, expressed a distaste, mild or pronounced, for bodiliness and the dependencies that its "tangibility" entails. The Scriptures themselves contrast the weakness of the flesh with the power of God. The culture in which Christianity first spread saw body in its neediness and susceptibility to external influences as an occasion for the human self's alienation and consequent moral disintegration. Modern culture too, with its urge to treat body as "object" over against the self, and its analogous tendency to label cultural and social "system" as inherently oppressive and alienating, evinces its own form of this distaste. By contrast, the soul or the mind— or, in the language of more recent social and political discourse, the "individual"—has been identified as the locus of what is truly human, and this precisely because, as the focus of conscious awareness and choice, it transcends bodily embeddedness, whether in nature or in society.

It would be inaccurate to say that the Christian Scriptures are unaware of this polarity. Even the story of Adam's creation, in its more primitive form, differentiates the human being's body from the "breath of life" which informs it; and this distinction indicates that it sees human selfhood to be centered in an interior principle of growth and action that bestows a species of agency, self-determination, upon body. It would seem, then, that on the biblical view there are indeed two modes in which the human person is related to the "other". Adam is "formed . . . of dust from the ground". He is thus, as body, continuous with the rest of creation, with nature and—we might add—with human society. On the other hand, Adam is also identified with the life principle that makes body a center of self-initiated growth and action. In this mode, Adam is one for whom nature is brought into focus as—not an "object but—a given "partner" to which he responds. The polarity of body and soul is, therefore, at least incipiently present in Genesis 2. What sets the scriptural perception of human nature apart, however, is the fact that this polarity is not experienced or portrayed as an opposition. The individual's embeddedness in the world is not the contrary but a condition and presupposition of the world's becoming "partner"—a subject, in short, which Adam addresses in action and discourse.

The limitation and freedom which mark Adam's relation to the created order as body and soul also characterize his relation to God as "image". In this case, however, the two modes of the human being's existence are conveyed by the same symbol. With respect to its original, an image is secondary and dependent. This is true whether one thinks of a scaled-down model which "represents" the original or (with Calvin and others) of a mirror image. It is dependent, indeed, in two ways: on the *givenness* of the original and on the agency or set of conditions that brings it into being. In Adam's case, however, the original and the agency are identical: *God* constitutes humanity after *God's* likeness. To speak of humanity as made "after the image of God", then, is simply to reiterate—with an important twist—the point that Adam is indeed *creature.* The human being is a pure receiver of being, dependent upon God for whatever it is. It is this "moment" in Adam's relation to God that corresponds to the human person's bodiliness in relation to other creatures.

At the same time, however, as the ancients knew more clearly than their posterity, the image functions as the original. This means, of course, that it may be a delegate for its original: Adam puts names to the animals, acting, it seems, as God's *locum tenens.* But it also means that the image functions *as the original functions.* The human being is a center of creativity and initiative; and this is true, as the Genesis story suggests, not only in its dealings with other creatures but also in its encounters with God. Adam is "another" for God: does not the Lord give this creature orders? This means, however, that human willing and choosing, and hence human awareness, go beyond creatures to attain the ultimate horizon of their being. In doing so, moreover—and this is an implication of the image doctrine that nowadays is not always very clearly drawn—what they reach for is their own original and archetype. What limits and addresses Adam in the Lord's word is not an alien presence but the truth of human being. In these two sides of the doctrine of the image, then, Pascal's paradox of grandeur and misery conjoined finds its proper interpretation. The human person is the center of a web of communication. To Adam, being and life are communicated, through other creatures and ultimately from God. They are communicated "naturally", as we say; but also "socially", through the presence of the "other" in word. By so much, then, Adam is a creature marked above all by limitation, by dependence; and this circumstance is easily enough experienced as misery. On the other hand, as the center of a web of communication, the human person is enabled to respond, to answer—to bring even the infinite horizon of human selfhood into focus as something that can be obeyed or disobeyed. And here, surely, is grandeur.

The problem is, however, that on the Scripture's view of things, the one cannot be had without the other. If the horizon of human selfhood is God, that is the case because—and only because—that same human selfhood is conferred as God's gift. Human initiative and freedom open out upon a horizon that transcends the created order; but they do so because that same horizon is their ground and matrix, and because it approaches them as a claim that makes demands and thus limits them. Analogously, within the created order itself, the human being is dependent, as a bodily reality, upon the natural and social orders in which and through which it appears; and its freedom over against these orders is created as they too demand its attention to their claims. Human freedom is not autonomy but answerability; and the answerability of Adam to other creatures is a reflection and an expression of a larger and deeper responsibility to God. It is in this sense, and for this reason, that Adam lives in a world not of objects but of subjects.

Hence the "fall" of Adam consists in sin: that is, it consists in the rejection of one side of human answerability—of the dependence in which human freedom subsists. For the narrative of Genesis, sin is envisaged above all as rejection of answerability to God. Eve and her consort are happy to grasp the promise that they "will be like God"—a promise which is given in their very creation "after the image". In the end, however, they are not willing to accept the fact that this promise belongs to them not in and of themselves but in their relationship of belonging to, dependence upon, God. It is not in that dependence or the limitation which it involves that evil consists, then, but in refusal of the answerability—the openness to the "other"—which is, in the last resort, the ground of their freedom.

But answerability to God involves answerability to God's creation: which is to say that it entails both acceptance of other creatures as presences through which God's purposes are engaged and acceptance of the bodiliness through which one is dependent upon them. Only in such consent to limitation is Adam's freedom actualized. One of the curses that follows upon Adam's sin is, in effect, that he must "work" the creation, and in working it lose his openness to the "other", and in losing that "return to the ground". Rejection of answerability turns out to mean loss of self; and this, it is suggested, is the situation in which Adam is caught. Somehow the human being must learn not to be "at" things (or God) but "with" them.

The difficulty of course is that such a stance—and the understanding of the human situation that informs it—implies a life of puzzlement and risk. It suggests that in the last resort, the human person is not the knower and controller of objects but the fallible appreciator, assessor and partner of realities that impinge upon and affect its life. The "other" is present for Adam, but not wholly given in its presence. (That, indeed, is why it is and is called an "other".) Adam's knowledge focuses the world and God, but does not constrain them; and it cannot be independently and absolutely grounded, because its ground is the relationship within which it emerges—the relationship constituted by the presence of something that remains, even in its presence, "other". Thus Adam becomes, in this vision of the human situation, the partner of God and of other creatures under God, beset with all the uncertainties that partnerships entail, living in circumstances that at once demand faith and render it hard.

NOTES

1. Michael Polanyi, *The Study of Man* (Chicago: University of Chicago Press, 1959), 11.

2. See stanza 3 of "The Spacious Firmament on High": "What though in solemn silence all / Move round the dark terrestrial ball? . . . / In reason's ear they all rejoice . . ."

5

THE PERSON OF CHRIST

ALASDAIR HERON

I. "STUDIES IN THE RELIGION OF THE INCARNATION"

The general theme of the incarnation is given a great deal of space in *Lux Mundi.* Not only does the book bear the subtitle "Studies in the Religion of the Incarnation"; something like a quarter of it is taken up by three central chapters: E. S. Talbot, "The Preparation in History for Christ"; J. R. Illingworth, "The Incarnation in Relation to Development"; and R. C. Moberly, "The Incarnation as the Basis of Dogma". Yet an acute contemporary commentator, A. M. Fairbairn, remarked: "Curiously the Incarnation is the very thing the book does not, in any more than the most nominal sense, either discuss or construe."[1] On the face of it, surely a rather surprising observation!

On closer inspection, however, it is not hard to detect what Fairbairn meant. *Lux Mundi* is, by and large, far more interested in "the religion of the incarnation" than in the incarnation itself, and much more interested in the idea of the incarnation than in the person of Jesus Christ. The main focus in each of the three central chapters is not the incarnation as such but its preparation in history, its relation to "development" and its supplying the foundation for dogma. The *reality* of the incarnation as an historical event of unique particularity is largely taken for granted, occasionally referred to, but only peripherally focussed.

Lux Mundi was not in fact a symposium on Christology, nor even on dogmatic theology, though its authors largely shared a broad positive appreciation of dogma reflecting their partially Tractarian heritage. Their real concerns as evidenced in their contributions were much more apologetic, cultural and ecclesiastical—and, one might add, "anti-

Protestant" in a fashion that perhaps owed more to the posthumous influence of Hurrel Froude in the Oxford Movement than to any profound knowledge of the history and theology of the Reformation. Even their insistence on "the religion of the incarnation" seems largely determined by a certain diffused sense that "Catholic" faith is "incarnational" whereas "Protestant" belief concentrates one-sidedly on the atonement. This is made quite explicit in Illingworth's chapter, as we shall see below.

The first question with which *Lux Mundi* confronts us today is, therefore, the central one of whether its apologetic, cultural and ecclesiastical interests do not require to be deepened by more radical reflection on the person of Jesus Christ and the meaning of the incarnation than the contributors themselves attempted. Must not the rethinking and restating of central themes of theology, from the doctrine of God to the authority of Scripture, be oriented around the rethinking and restating of what the older dogmatics called the *locus de persona Christi? How* this is to be done—from what angles, in which perspectives, under what leading questions, whether "dogmatically", "existentially", "mythically" or "politically", for example, may be open to debate. *That,* however, the specifically christological task is an abiding challenge requiring to be faced, that christological issues keep resurfacing, if not always in identical form, is perhaps more obvious to us today than to the authors of *Lux Mundi* a century ago. I would therefore like to devote my contribution chiefly to a summary analysis of the approaches of these three chapters and to questions that these approaches raise for christological study and reflection today.

II. MOBERLY ON THE INCARNATION AND DOGMA

Let us begin with Moberly, as his is the chapter that might seem best able to give the lie to Fairbairn's criticism. Speaking of dogma, Moberly writes:

So far from [faith] without it being a thing more spiritual or pure, faith without it is a thing irrational. Faith in what? I cannot have faith without an object. Faith in Jesus Christ? But who is Jesus Christ? Is He a dead man? Is He, as a dead man, no longer in any existence? . . . And what then did His life mean? or His strange deliberate dying? or what connection have they of meaning or power with me? . . . The question whether He is or is not God, is one which cannot but be asked and answered. . . . Is He my living Master; my very Redeemer by the Cross; my eternal Judge? and where and how have I contact in life or soul with the benefits of His Cross, or the power of His help? . . . Faith in Him can have no meaning while these (sc. questions) are ignored.

Such passages are, however, rare in Moberly's chapter. The real focus of interest lies in classical christological dogma and in the incarnation as its *basis*. For the most part, lengthy and, to our ears, rather formal arguments about theology and science, about the status of dogma and its patristic development, predominate—and the correctness of that dogma is more rhetorically asserted than cogently demonstrated.

Moberly does indeed raise the question "how the truths of the Creed did first, in fact, introduce themselves to human consciousness", and distinguishes three stages: "first, the leading up, in the world's history and consciousness, to the life of Jesus Christ; secondly, the life and death of Jesus Christ; thirdly, the results, in history and consciousness, of the life and death of Jesus Christ". Here he puts special weight on the resurrection: if Jesus *"rose again the third day from the dead,* you have indeed already the foundation dogma of the Creed; and having that, you cannot possibly rest in it: that foundation fact will absolutely compel you to ask and to answer certain further necessary questions; and whatever intelligible answer you may choose to give them will be essentially a dogmatic definition. Who or what was this man?" It is noticeable, however, that the biblical, specifically New Testament witness alluded to here takes up barely three out of the forty-two pages of the entire chapter.

It may seem unreasonable to press these observations on Moberly's contribution, given that his subject was, after all, the christological dogma, and his concern to defend its substantial significance and importance against the notion of an undogmatic faith. Yet what surely ought to be his main theme—the person of Jesus Christ as witnessed to in the New Testament and the relation of that witness to the development of the patristic christological dogma—plays manifest second fiddle to the assertion of the "largeness and equity" of the dogma itself. "It is harmony; it is proportion; it is the protest of balanced completeness against all . . . partiality. . . . To work and think within the lines of dogmatic faith is to work and think upon the true and harmonious conception of the Person of Jesus Christ—'Quem nosse vivere, Cui servire regnare.' " I am very far indeed from wishing to dispute what is said here *so far as it goes*. But does it go far enough to draw the venerable formulations of dogma into the service of effective proclamation, to address the existential issues of faith, or even to defend the dogma itself from more corrosive sceptical challenges which cannot so easily be disarmed by the serene affirmation of its balanced fulness?

For all that Moberly insists that the question that really matters is, "Whom say ye that I am?" he seems very ready to be content with the simple answer, "Very God and very man." It is not unjust to say that his programme is set by Nicaea and Chalcedon; he sets out from them in order to return triumphantly to them. Obviously that is not, in itself, wrong. It does, however, need to be asked whether it takes us much farther along the way of discerning what the answer "Very God and very man" *means,* what it implies for the terms "God" and "man"; whether it helps as much as it should to see why the classical dogma is both true and necessary for the faith of the church.

We shall have to raise issues of this kind again towards the end of this chapter, but we should perhaps try here to make them a little more specific still. Moberly pleads for the balanced wholeness of classical dogma over against all one-sided views. This is in fact very easy to do. However popular from time to time this or that repristination of ancient heresy as modern fashion may appear, those who have seriously gone to school with the church of the fathers and the early councils are not likely to be seriously seduced by them. The real problem lies elsewhere—in the substitution of the contemplation of the dogma for the path of faith. It is one thing to be sincerely intellectually convinced of the correctness of the patristic dogmatic development, of its logical cogency given the issues and alternatives then under debate. It is something else to believe it and take its implications seriously. Moberly's argument seems more apt to the first than to the second.

Related to this is a second observation. While Moberly stresses the "very God and very man", it is the "very God" that seems to him in need of special emphasis, as "no one today disputes that He was truly man". One might be tempted to say, therefore, that Moberly's approach is "from above" rather than "from below". The notional opposition of Christology "from above" and "from below" is, however, a slippery matter and it is probably better to avoid the scheme.[2] The real trouble in either case is the effective one-sidedness which does not appreciate that the "very God" is essential to the exegesis of "very man" and vice versa. The danger is then that of sliding into some form of either Ebionism or Docetism—or, more refinedly, of allowing the emphasis on "very God" to issue in what T. F. Torrance has penetratingly diagnosed as a pervasive Apollinarianism in doctrine and worship.[3] With all sympathy for Moberly's argument, it does nevertheless appear to be somewhat exposed on this flank.

III. TALBOT ON THE HISTORICAL PREPARATION FOR CHRIST

Talbot's chapter is of similar length to Moberly's but much more tightly constructed and densely argued. If Moberly takes his bearings from the pattern of classical dogma, Talbot finds his in a philosophy of history in which the development of the classical world on the one hand and of Israel on the other each represent a genuine but flawed reaching after a new, universal religion which finally became a genuine historical possibility as a result of the incarnation. The incarnation itself is thus "a climax and a new point of departure in the historical order", as well as being "supreme, solitary, unique, transcending all analogies of experience, all limitations of nationality or generation, determined before the world was, beyond the power of any antecedents to produce". It must therefore be approached in two ways: on the one hand, "for its own unchanging truth and meaning" and, on the other, "as clothed in historical event, to be understood in its relations to what went before and followed after and stood around". It is with this second approach that Talbot is concerned, with "the relations between Christ and History" which are the necessary complement to "a right understanding of the Person of Christ".

In unfolding his argument, Talbot appeals especially to an idea that must strike us today as sounding very contemporary—that of *process*. Not that Talbot is a Whiteheadian before Whitehead, or not entirely. Process, for Talbot, is primarily a scientific and historical rather than a metaphysical concept; and while he does indeed see it as a kind of unifying concept for diverse disciplines, he is careful to recognize possible limitations when it comes to a theology of history. But we should let him speak for himself. What is it, he asks, "which specially engrosses the interest and admiration of all of us in the different branches of modern study and enquiry"?

It is the beauty of *process*. The practical men among us watch process in its mechanical form as contrived by invention. The naturalists and the men of science have to an extraordinary extent developed our perception of it in nature: they shew us its range, and its incredible delicacy, flexibility, and intricacy. . . . And the historians in their sphere do the like: it is for them, if not the beginning and end of their work, at least the most powerful of their methods, to shew the processes by which institutions, customs, opinions rise and decline.

So Talbot goes on to emphasise the "beauty of process" and the "rational element present in, or controlling our sense of beauty, which asks whence and whither, which demands unity in detail; and this finds altogether new and delightful ratification when it can see a relation, a meaning, a grouping, a symmetry, of which processes are the ministers and instruments". This "idea of beauty in process . . . we bring with us as we approach to behold the facts and method of God's Redemptive Work"; while we should not be uncritically carried away by it, we cannot wholly disown "what is so specially our own. And if our love of process is prepared to be critical, it is also prepared to be gratified: and there is opened a prospect of fresh witness to the truth of the unchanging Gospel, if it should be found that its introduction into this world is ushered in by all the beauty of process". Just such a twofold ushering in can be traced on the one hand in the preparation in the Greco-Roman world "of an environment suitable to the Gospel" and on the other in "the preparation of the organism itself" in the setting of ancient Israel.

The political, social and intellectual history of Greece and Rome brought about "the transformation of a world intensely localized and sub-divided into one as singularly united and homogeneous" and so prepared the ground for "the progress of a world-religion", indeed created the longing for it. This was "a double preparation, positive and negative: a positive preparation by evolving ideas which the Gospel could work into its own fabric . . . a negative preparation by the breakdown of human nature's own constructive and speculative efforts, and by the room thus left for a revelation which would unite the broken and useless fragments of thought and minister to unsatisfied needs". Especially significant is the failure of the two great "experiments" in this development: that of "speculative self-reliance", whose collapse became increasingly apparent after Aristotle, and that of moral self-sufficience, represented by Stoicism. Despite these failures, however, Greece and Rome developed values "which could never have been realized if all the world had been brought up in the barbarous societies of ancient Europe or under the great despotisms of Egypt and Asia''. Their contribution was "a great clearing of the stage, and a great disposing of thought and sentiment, for a religion which proclaimed a good tidings for all men without distinction of 'Jew or Greek, Barbarian or Scythian, bond or free'; for a religion of compassion; for a religion wholly spiritual and unpolitical"—a religion, however, which *"comes to* the Gentile world, and does not *grow out* of it".

Israel's history too was a process of preparation, including the dispersal of Jews throughout the Roman Empire, the strong, radical character of Jewish monotheism, the sense of national calling, of the promises given to the fathers, of the gravity of the law of God. But this history too was ambiguous, marked by a profound antithesis culminating in "the crucifixion of the Lord and all which Judaism, without and within the Church, did to extinguish the Gospel and persecute its followers in its first age". It too had known two great "experiments", the temporal monarchy and the more spiritual restoration; both also failed and "emphasize the fact that the history of Israel was in no sense working itself out towards the *production* by its own forces of the true religion which went forth from the midst of it". Yet the unique significance of Israel is that it brought what the pagan world could not: the basis for such a universal religion and the awareness that it must be based upon "not only doctrine, but fact".

The essentials of such a universal religion are summed up by Talbot in "three or four points which it is striking to find were fundamentals of the religion of Israel, and at that time of no other". He lists them as "a doctrine of God, lofty, spiritual, moral; a doctrine of man which should affirm and secure his spiritual being and his immortality; and a doctrine of the relations between God and man, which should give reality to prayer and to the belief in providence, and root man's sense of responsibility in the fact of his obligation to a righteousness outside and above himself, a doctrine in short of judgment". All this was taught in Israel's religion, but combined with an exclusivism which forbade any "attempt to make a religion by extracting the universal truths in Judaism" at the cost of abandoning the specifically Jewish history and sense of calling. "If the thing was to be done, it must be done by some power and teaching which, while extricating into clearness all that was truest in the theology and morality of Israel, was also able to show . . . that it constituted a true climax of Israel's history, a true fulfilment of the promises and prophecies". "It must be able to take Israel to witness, and therefore it must be able to convince men not only that it had a high theology and a refined morality, but that 'God had visited His people.' "

Thus far, the "two preparations", the Gentile and the Jewish, "stand apart: they go their own way. There is indeed in them a strange parallelism of common experience and human need. Both have tried their experiments, made their ventures, won their successes, gone through their disciplines of disenchantment and failure." Both in fact are at the end of their own possibilities, the one searching for wisdom and a new philosophy, the other for a sign and a saving divine intervention. "And then from out of Israel

> there comes forth a Thing in which on the one side Jews . . . find the whole spirit and meaning, even down to its detail, of the life and hope of Israel summed up and fulfilled, . . . while on the other side this same Thing was felt by "Greeks" as a "wisdom" flooding their reasons with a light of truth and wisdom *(sophia)* which met the search of philosophia *(philo-sophia)*. . . . "There came forth a Thing," or rather there came forth One, in Whom all this was done. The question rises, "Whom say we that He is?"

Talbot is clear that considerations of the kind he has developed can at best corroborate, not prove, the answer, but he suggests that "the convergence of many lines . . . to One in whom they are all combined and transcended, to One whom they can usher in but were powerless to produce, may be no slight corroboration of the answer . . . 'Thou art the Christ . . . the Son of the Living God'."

I have quoted Talbot relatively fully, because it is difficult to do justice to his argument by a summary that is any more compressed and because it raises a host of questions that are still with us today. Quite apart from his application of the idea of process in history and nature—which should not too rapidly be dismissed as a piece of optimistic nineteenth-century idealism, particularly in view of his consciously restrained theological use of it—he challenges us to reflect on whether there can be a kind of Christian philosophy of history incorporating, as his does, a special sense of a *praeparatio Evangelii* in the distinctive history of Greece and Rome, and relating the whole historical process to the incarnation as a unique event but one connected to its world-historical antecedents and consequences. He further challenges us to consider the distinctive relation of Christianity to Judaism as also the adequacy of a presentation of Christianity as the "universal religion", connecting with but transcending both Jewish and Gentile anticipations and preparations. These are all large questions, much debated in the hundred years since Talbot wrote, which can here only be signalled, not unfolded. But Talbot is surely right to remind us that questions of this sort are raised by the affirmation that the Word was made flesh in time and history in the person of Jesus of Nazareth, that "the paradox of divine mystery implied in the words, 'The Word was made flesh,' is not exhausted by a right understanding of the Person of Christ. It extends to the relations between Christ and History."

If there is a weakness in Talbot's approach, however, it would seem to lie precisely in the fact that he separates the question of "the relations between Christ and History" from that of "a right understanding of the Person of Christ", presupposing the latter in order to explore the former. Like Moberly, he approaches the person of the Incarnate Word only indirectly, from the side, as it were, through the lenses of history on the one hand and the new, universal religion on the other, what he calls the religion of the "mighty truths, speaking of what was above man, which brooded over the history of the Jews and came forth into the world with the Gospel". The inner connection between these mighty truths and the person of Jesus Christ remains vague at best in Talbot's account.

The same problem can be raised from the other side if we ask: Must not the relation of the incarnation to preceding and following history be more concretely centred on the history of Jesus Christ incarnate, crucified and risen rather than simply on "the incarnation", punctually interpreted chiefly as an event of revelation? Talbot rightly emphasises that not only doctrine but fact is of vital significance, that "God has visited and redeemed his people". In his argument, however, the necessity of the "fact" seems to lie primarily in the link between Israelite and Jewish tradition and the universal faith for which the Gentile world was hungering. Must not the "fact" itself be more fully spelt out and interpreted as itself history and the pivot of all history? That would seem to be the most central issue that Talbot's chapter lays before us.

IV. ILLINGWORTH ON THE INCARNATION AND DEVELOPMENT

Illingworth's is the shortest but also by far the most substantial of these three chapters and must be dealt with most fully. It is also in many respects still the most contemporary today; had it been lost and only now rediscovered, it could still be published as it stands as a significant contribution to themes of current debate. It anticipates some significant later trends, especially in Anglican theology in this century—for instance, the relating of Christology and cosmology by Lionel Thornton and William Temple or the sympathetic reappropriation of medieval scholastic thought by Austin Farrer and Eric Mascall.

Illingworth combines an apologetic interest—meeting the challenge of evolutionism to Christian faith—with a deliberate theological programme: the challenge is to be met by recovery of the full width and depth of the Catholic faith, specifically in its stress not only on atonement but on the incarnation and on the immanent indwelling of all created nature by the eternal Logos, the Word and Reason of God. The apparent attack made by theories of evolutionary development can thus be turned into a witness to Catholic truth; properly understand, "development" confirms Catholic conviction.

It is immediately obvious that Illingworth's concerns are still very much with us today—the question of evolution; the relation of theology, philosophy and science; the relation between God and the world; the connexion of incarnation and atonement. That apart, Illingworth displays both a wider familiarity with the history of Christian thought and a profounder grasp of apologetic argument than either Moberly or Talbot: his is by far the outstanding christological contribution to *Lux Mundi,* perhaps indeed the finest chapter in the entire volume. It falls into three sections, each very closely argued; for convenience, our exposition will follow the same pattern. We begin with the incarnation and evolution.

The "gradual acceptance by Christian thinkers of the great scientific generalization of our age, . . . the Theory of Evolution", has proved yet another "opposition of science to theology" to be "no opposition at all". Further, all great scientific discoveries are not "merely new facts to be assimilated" but involve "a new way of looking at things"; "the law of evolution . . . has rapidly extended to every department of thought and history, and altered our attitude towards all knowledge. Organisms, nations, languages, institutions, customs, creeds, have all come to be regarded in the light of their development, and we feel that to understand what a thing really is, we must examine how it came to be. . . . Our religious opinions . . . must justify their existence by an appeal to the past."

Discussion of the "various views of evolution" can also serve to show

how "popular misconceptions of . . . the Incarnation have been reme-
died; what more or less forgotten aspects . . . have been restored
. . . what new lights have been thrown upon the fulness of its meaning".
The "study of past theology" is particularly valuable as showing that
what by some are too easily dismissed "as metaphysical subtleties, or
as dangerous innovations, or as questionable accommodations of the
Gospel to the exigencies of passing controversy, are after all an integral
part of the great Catholic tradition". It can also effectively counter the
inclination of "well-meaning but ignorant apologists" to "brandish in
the eyes of men" "fragments of doctrine, torn from their context and
deprived of their due proportions" as if they were "the sum total of the
Christian faith", as a result of which all too "many mislead themselves
and others into thinking Christianity discredited, when in reality they
have all along only been criticising its caricature".

What Illingworth has in mind here is spelt out by him very clearly:

> The general tendency of thought since the Reformation has been in the
> direction of these partial presentations of Christianity. The Reformers,
> from various causes, were so occupied with what is now called Soteri-
> ology, or the scheme of salvation, that they paid but scant attention to the
> other aspects of the Gospel. And the consequence was that a whole side
> of the great Christian tradition . . . was allowed almost unconsciously to
> lapse into comparative oblivion; and the religion of the Incarnation was
> narrowed into the religion of the Atonement. Men's views of the faith
> dwindled and became subjective and self-regarding, while the gulf was
> daily widened between things sacred and things secular; among which
> latter, art and science, and the whole political and social order, gradually
> came to be classed.

This is of course a fairly sweeping judgment and one that in particular
is far from just to the Reformers, whether on the continent or in
Britain.[4] But there is certainly some truth in it, though still one-sided,
as a characterisation of certain tendencies in post-Reformation Protestantism. More significant than the historical question, however, is the
theological importance, rightly stressed by Illingworth, of seeing the
incarnation and the atonement together instead of emphasising the one
to the neglect of the other. Indeed, it is necessary to go farther still and
see that the incarnation, the cross *and* the resurrection of Jesus Christ
must all be kept in view in developing a Christian understanding of the
world of creation and history. This Illingworth goes on to do.

By contrast, "the great thinkers of the early Church . . . realized that redemption was a means to an end, and that end the reconsecration of the whole universe to God. And so the very completeness of their grasp on the Atonement led them to dwell upon the cosmical significance of the Incarnation":

> The identity of Him Who was made man and dwelt among us, with Him by Whom all things were made and by Whom all things consist; His eternal pre-existence as the reason and the word of God, the Logos; His indwelling presence in the universe as the source and condition of its life, and in man as the light of his intellectual being; His Resurrection, His Ascension,—all these thoughts were woven into one magnificent picture, wherein creation was viewed as the embodiment of the Divine ideas, and therefore the revelation of the Divine character; manifesting its Maker with increasing clearness at each successive stage in the great scale of being, till in the fulness of time He himself became man, and thereby lifted human nature, and with it the material universe to which man is so intimately linked; and triumphing over the sin and death under which creation groaned and travailed, opened by His Resurrection and then by His Ascension vistas of the glorious destiny purposed for His creatures before the world was. "Factus est quod sumus nos, uti nos perficeret esse quod est ipse."

This view of the incarnation is developed with increasing clarity from Justin to Athanasius. "It was born of no abstract love of metaphysics. . . . Its motive and its method were both intensely practical; its motive being to present Christianity to the mind as well as to the heart; and its method no more than to connect and interpret and explain the definite statements of S. Paul and S. John." In the Middle Ages, however, two "kindred errors, both concerned with an undue estimate of matter", arose: the "Arabic pantheism, and the materialism which was fostered in the medieval schools". "And how did Christian theology meet them? Not by laying stress, like the later Deists, upon God's infinite distance from the world, but upon the closeness of His intimacy with it: by reviving, that is, . . . the Patristic doctrine of the Incarnation as the climax and keystone of the whole visible creation." Illingworth concludes this section of his chapter with a chain of quotations illustrating how various medieval thinkers regarded the creation itself as a visible word of the Word, the incarnation as the consummation of creation, even on occasion as its "pre-destined climax . . . independently of human sin", and the human intellect as originating in and illumined by the eternal Logos.

V. INCARNATIONAL THEOLOGY AND
MODERN SCIENCE

In his second section, Illingworth writes, following on directly from the argument at the end of the first:

> We have now to consider whether this view of the Incarnation, which, though in the countries most influenced by the Reformation it has dropped too much out of sight, has yet never really died out of the Church at large, is in any way incompatible with the results of modern science; or whether, on the contrary, it does not provide an outline to which science is slowly but surely giving reality and content.

So Illingworth comes to his central apologetic theme, detailing five areas in which there might (wrongly) be held to be a necessary opposition between science and theology: the question of the origin of all things; the challenge of evolutionism to teleology; the origin of the human race; the objective rationality of the universe, the subjective rationality of the human mind, and the relation of both to the Logos of God; and the relation of Christianity to other philosophy and religion. In all these areas it is not, strictly speaking, the incarnation that is in view—that is reserved for the final, third section—but rather the immanence of the eternal Logos in nature and in the human intellect. Illingworth does not identify incarnation and immanence, but the inner connexion between the two is fundamental for his entire approach.

Illingworth's treatment of these issues is a model of its kind: well informed as to the state of contemporary discussion, judicious in avoiding "the rash orthodoxy, that is over eager to accept any (sc. scientific) result that tallies with its own preconceived opinions", and careful to insist upon the essential difference between what finite intellect can discover and "the vast region of possibility, which lies wholly and for ever beyond the power of science to affirm or to deny", in which region "Christian theology claims to have its roots". Doctrine can neither be demonstrated nor refuted by science; it can, however, receive a kind of deepening confirmation by analogy as science uncovers more and more of the structure of things and so permits a profounder appreciation of the "design" everywhere to be traced or of the universality of religion as testimony to the God who "left not Himself without witness". This gives Illingworth the freedom to avoid adopting on theological grounds scientific positions that may in the long run prove untenable. In view of much often bitter recent argument, his remarks on theologians and evolution are still strikingly up-to-date. So, for instance, on the question of human origins:

> Theologians first thought it necessary to contest every detail of this development . . . and some are still inclined to entrench themselves in one or two positions which they think impregnable, such as the essential difference in kind between organized and inorganic matter, or again between animal instinct and the self-conscious reason of man: while others are content to assume a sceptical attitude and point to the disagreement between the men of science themselves, as sufficient evidence of their untruth. But none of these views are theologically needed. . . . In fact the evolutionary origin of man is a far less serious question than the attack upon final causes. Its biblical aspect has grown insignificant in proportion as we have learned to regard the Hebrew cosmology in a true light. And the popular outcry which it raised was largely due to sentiment, and sentiment not altogether untinged by human pride.

Illingworth's remark about "the attack upon final causes" as being far more dangerous to Christian theology than any threat from the theory of evolution is not without significance in regard to the whole spectrum of questions he discusses as arising between theology and science. In brief, his thesis is that the Aristotelian notion of the *entelechy,* which was appropriated in scholastic theology but abandoned in post-Reformation science as it developed a more mechanical, less organismic view of reality, is nevertheless in an important sense valid. The idea of a "final cause" which teleologically shapes entities to make them more than the sum of their parts is in his view necessary both to a proper appreciation of the "design" apparent in nature and humankind, scientifically speaking, and to the theological linking of that "design" with the workings of the immanent Logos.

On this, two observations: First, it is true that no less a thinker than Francis Bacon in the early seventeenth century insisted on rooting out the notion of final causes as an essential prerequisite of scientific advance. In much the same way, thinkers of the next generation such as Robert Boyle attacked the idea of "nature", understood as if "nature" were autonomous and self-governing rather than the handiwork of God, as deleterious alike to good science and good theology. Second, however, there is a great deal of more recent accumulated evidence suggesting that while the rejection of the notion of final causes as understood in late medieval thought was indeed a necessary step, it cannot have the last word. Gestalt psychology, the philosophy of Michael Polanyi, and the physics of Ilya Prigogine, to name only three examples, all suggest that the nature of physical reality and human perception alike can be grasped only in terms of the spontaneous ordering of wholes. It is indeed in this area that the major unsolved problems of evolutionary theory still appear to lie, to say nothing of the problems which the advance of physics and cosmology and, more recently, genetic research have placed on the agenda.

To this extent, Illingworth's defence of the idea of final causes is by no means merely a piece of late Victorian nostalgia for the hallowed world of the Middle Ages, though his presentation could make it appear so. It is much the same with this as with the medieval and later deist "argument from design": the argument as such, conceived as a logical proof of the existence of God or as a piece of natural theology, is not conclusive; the undeniable existence of *order*—order of increasing, or, to use Pierre Teilhard de Chardin's term, "involutionary" complexity—in the history of the cosmos, the world and the emergence of the human race, in spite of all that the *Second Law of Thermodynamics* predicts, remains a perplexing puzzle and challenge. But I am now in danger of wandering too far from my subject and must return to Illingworth's chapter.

Illingworth closes this second section with consideration of an objection that offers him the entrée to more direct reflection on the incarnation of the Word of God in Jesus Christ:

> But when all this has been said, there is a lingering suspicion in many minds, that even if the details of the doctrine of development are not inconsistent with Christianity, its whole drift is incompatible with any system of opinion which claims to possess finality. And if Christianity were only a system of opinion, the objection might be plausible enough. But its claim to possess finality rests upon its further claim to be much more than a system of opinion. The doctrine of development or evolution, we must remember, is not a doctrine of limitless change, like the old Greek notion of perpetual flux. Species once developed are seen to be persistent, in proportion to their versatility, their power, i.e. of adapting themselves to the changes of the world around them. And because man, through his mental capacity, possesses this power to an almost unlimited extent, the human species is virtually permanent. Now in scientific language, the Incarnation may be said to have introduced a new species into the world— a Divine man transcending past humanity, as humanity transcended the

rest of the animal creation, and communicating His vital energy by a spiritual process to subsequent generations of men. And thus viewed, there is nothing unreasonable in the claim of Christianity to be at least as permanent as the race which it has raised to a higher power, and endued with a novel strength.

This touches "new ground", as we shall see below. Before we come to it, two further observations may be in order. First, Illingworth shows a remarkable confidence in the future of the human race in view of its mental capacity for adaptation. That that very same capacity could lead to the destruction of the world and the human race with it by the disproportionate development of technology to the disadvantage of geopolitics is something Illingworth could certainly not have envisaged. But we can hardly ignore the questions raised for us by the one-sided development of science, technology and living conditions in the wealthy fraction of the world over against the reality of living conditions for most other members of the human race. To say the least, there has taken place a certain shift of perspective in the last hundred years which makes us less inclined today than yesterday to put our faith in humanity's capacity for "adaptation". All the signs are that such adaptation can take place only under especially privileged conditions, conditions benefitting only a fraction of the human race: namely, that fraction which by one means or another has come to wealth and power. The great majority are doomed to go under in the struggle for life. Illingworth's concern to present a plausible *apologia* for Christianity to its enlightened despisers in the ranks of the evolutionists issues in a signal failure to consider what material, cultural, intellectual and moral conditions are required for the human development he praises, and at what cost they are to be bought.

Second, his *apologia* is developed in the horizon of a horizontal immanentism in which the outworking of the incarnation is interpreted in terms of the spread and triumph of Christianity, of the spiritual transformation of humanity and human society by the influence emanating from the divine man, representing yet a further evolutionary breakthrough, yet a further stage in the evolutionary process. That is very much a nineteenth-century perspective; its patron saint is—though not, I think, mentioned in *Lux Mundi*—Schleiermacher. Again, Illingworth could not suspect that later theological development would lead to a very serious questioning of this whole approach with its triumphalist claims for "the Christian religion".

VI. THE INCARNATE LOGOS

We quoted Illingworth above as saying that "the Incarnation may be said to have introduced a new species into the world". This thought leads into his third section:

> But in saying this we touch new ground. As long as we confine ourselves to speaking of the Eternal Word as operating in the mysterious region which lies behind phenomena, we are safe, it may be said, from refutation, because we are dealing with the unknown. But when we go on to assert that He has flashed through our atmosphere, and been seen of men, scintillating signs and wonders in His path, we are at once open to critical attack. And this brings us to the real point at issue between Christianity and its modern opponents. It is not the substantive body of our knowledge, but the critical faculty which has been sharpened in its acquisition that really comes in conflict with our creed. . . . What is called the negative criticism assumes that it cannot be true, because the miraculous element in it contradicts experience.

To this, Illingworth first offers two preliminary remarks. First, all origins are mysterious—"the origin of matter, the origin of energy, the origin of life, the origin of thought. And present experience is no criterion of any of these things. . . . If therefore the Incarnation was, as Christians believe, another instance of a new beginning, present experience will neither enable us to assert or deny, what its attendant circumstances may or may not have been". Second, "it is a mistake to suppose that as a matter of strict evidence, the Christian Church has ever rested its claims upon miracles". They have indeed served for many as a "confirmatory factor". "But to others, who in the present day are probably the larger class, it is not so easy to believe Christianity on account of miracles, as miracles on account of Christianity. For now, as ever, the real burden of the proof of Christianity is to be sought in our present experience."

What, then, is the nature of that experience? Illingworth is not slow with his answer; it may nonetheless come as something of a surprise in view of his preceding argument with its insistence on the immanent workings of the divine Logos in the cosmos and in human nature:

> There is a fact of experience as old as history, as widely spread as is the human race, and more intensely, irresistibly, importunately real than all the gathered experience of art and policy and science—the fact which philosophers call moral evil, and Christians sin. . . . We breathe it, we feel

115

it, we commit it, we see its havoc all around us. It is no dogma, but a sad, solemn, inevitable fact. . . . Man has a law of his being, a condition of his perfection, which he instinctively tends to disobey. . . . And moral evil, independently of any theory of its nature or its origin, is a plain palpable fact, and a fact of such stupendous magnitude as to constitute by far the most serious problem of our life.

But there is another fact of experience to set against this: "that there are scattered throughout Christendom, men of every age, temperament, character and antecedents, for whom this problem is practically solved: men who have a personal conviction that their own past sins are done away with, and the whole grasp of evil upon them loosened. . . . And all this they agree to attribute . . . to the personal influence upon them of Jesus Christ". "Pre-Christian antiquity contains nothing analogous to it." "It has all the appearance of being, what it historically has claimed to be, the entrance of an essentially new life into the world."

It is therefore understandable that the message of the atonement has so filled some Christian minds as to exclude all else. So they "have come to think that the other aspects of the Incarnation might be banished from the pulpit and the marketplace, to the seclusion of the schools. But this has proved to be a fatal mistake. Truth cannot be mutilated with impunity". Indeed, "this gradual substitution of a detached doctrine for a catholic creed has led directly to the charge . . . that Christianity is inadequate to life". The charge rests on a radical misconception. "The Incarnation opened heaven, for it was the revelation of the Word; but it also reconsecrated earth, for the Word was made flesh and dwelt among us." "Natural religion, and natural morality, and the natural play of intellect have their function in the Christian as they had in the pre-Christian ages; and they are still kindled by the light that lighteth every man coming into the world. And hence it is that secular thought has so often corrected and counteracted the evil of a Christianity grown professional, and false, and foul." By the same token, the religion of the incarnation is the only real answer to materialism, because it does justice to the material aspect of nature "by shewing the cause of that importance to lie in its connection, communion, union with the spirit, and consequent capacity for endless degrees of glory". So Illingworth comes to his impassioned conclusion: Christianity welcomes the discoveries of science, as ultimately due to Divine revelation, and part of the providential education of the world. It recalls to art the days when, in catacomb and cloister, she learned her noblest mission to be the service of the Word made Flesh. It appeals to democracy as the religion of the fishermen who gathered around the carpenter's Son. It points the social reformer to the pattern of a perfect man, laying down His life alike for enemy and friend. While it crowns all earthly aims with a hope full of immortality as prophetic of eternal occupations otherwhere. And however many a new meaning may yet be found in the Incarnation, however many a misconception of it fade before fuller light; we can conceive no phase of progress which has not the Incarnation for its guiding star; no age which cannot make the prayer of the fifth century its own—

"O God of unchangeable power and eternal light, look favourably on Thy whole Church, that wonderful and sacred mystery; and by the tranquil operation of Thy perpetual Providence, carry out the work of man's salvation; and let the whole world feel and see that things which were cast down are being raised up, and things which had grown old are being made new, and all things are returning to perfection through Him, from whom they took their origin, even through our Lord Jesus Christ."

VII. JESUS OF NAZARETH, CRUCIFIED AND RISEN

I have dealt so relatively fully with Illingworth's chapter because it manifestly contains a great deal that demands to be taken fully as seriously today as a century ago. The relation between theology and scientific advance, the connexion between incarnation and atonement, and the urgent need for a Christian understanding of (and dealing with) the material creation are of as pressing importance now as then, perhaps even more pressing in our changed world. At the same time, however, Fairbairn's judgment with which we began clearly applies to Illingworth's chapter too, though perhaps slightly less than to those of Moberly and Talbot. Illingworth is much less concerned with the incarnation as such than with the implications of *an incarnational understanding of creation and human life.* That is no invalid concern, and Illingworth's handling of it is masterly and instructive, but it does not appear to set up an adequate defence against the kind of position more recently advocated by Geoffrey Lampe and others, according to which "incarnation" is primarily a way of speaking about the divine immanence in creation rather than about the mystery of Jesus Christ.[5]

In making this observation today, one of course has in the back of one's mind the ways in which theology has moved in the intervening century, ways that have inevitably altered our perspectives and questions. It would be quite impossible here to offer any kind of overview of Christology since 1889, let alone a "Christology for today". But it may be worthwhile to hint at some of the stages in subsequent development that would deserve to be kept in view in any full-scale dialogue with *Lux Mundi*'s approach to the incarnation.

First, very much contemporary with *Lux Mundi* itself, continental theology, especially in Germany, was intensively concerned with newer exegetical and historical issues which set much of the agenda for the following generations. One thinks here in particular of the "quest of the historical Jesus" and its problems as well as of the rise of the "history of religions" approach to the Old and New Testaments. It is not, I think, unjust to *Lux Mundi* to say that its authors, like most British biblical scholarship of their day, were several steps behind their German contemporaries in the biblical field, both as regards the level of their information and in respect of the kind of questions they were interested in asking. At the time *Lux Mundi* appeared, so-called "lower criticism", that is, study of the text of the Bible in the light of the manuscript tradition, was coming to be accepted in British churches and universities; "higher criticism" with its concern to distinguish different sources in the biblical material and to question traditional ascriptions of authorship was still very widely suspected of illegitimate infringement of the authority and inspiration of the Bible. This was reflected in the fact that it was Gore's *Lux Mundi* chapter on the inspiration of Scripture that came in for the most bitter attack, mild and harmless though it might appear today.

In sum: *Lux Mundi,* as we have already hinted in passing, did not tackle exegetical and hermeneutical issues, nor those relating to the development of patristic theology, with the same kind of patient energy as was coming to be expected on the continent of Europe. It is significant that the contributions considered in this chapter do not, in spite of their heavy leaning on the development of dogma in the early church, appear to have engaged in depth with the work of an outstanding Oxford scholar who died in the year *Lux Mundi* appeared—Edwin Hatch. It was left to Adolf von Harnack in Berlin to take up and develop Hatch's work with brilliant originality in research and interpretation of the development of dogma in the early centuries. By contrast, *Lux Mundi* was generally content to reaffirm "the catholic faith", avoiding more detailed exegetical and historical questions.

It can of course be argued that in doing so *Lux Mundi* was performing a necessary service. At a time when there is, not without reason, widespread talk in many quarters about the "crisis of the historical-critical approach to Scripture", we can do worse than hold to the sheet-anchor of the Catholic faith as Moberly, Talbot and Illingworth all clearly did. Not for nothing have the fruits of the Tractarian movement in liturgy and hymnology long become part of the common heritage of ecumenical Christendom, both Roman Catholic and Protestant. But the aim of *Lux Mundi* was to mediate constructively between Catholic tradition and the modern world. It was, perhaps, more successful in addressing the modern world of science under the banner of evolution than in addressing the modern world of biblical scholarship and historical research of Christian origins. That is a field in which a great deal of creative synthesis is most certainly needed today if theological study is once again to recover its unity as a coherent family of disciplines. The task has certainly not become easier in the last hundred years; it is not for that reason less worth undertaking.

Second—and here we are still in the realm of what, to appropriate Talbot's words, "went before and followed after and stood around" the publication of *Lux Mundi* itself—the aversion of the authors to what they regarded as "Protestant" does seem to betray a certain narrowness of view. In the two generations before *Lux Mundi* appeared, a major group of Scottish and English theologians, some Reformed, some Anglican, had vocally and powerfully proclaimed the integral relation between incarnation and atonement as the axis on which all Christian theology turns, and paid for the fact in most cases by being relieved of their ecclesiastical charges: Edward Irving, Alexander Scott, John McLeod Campbell, Frederick Denison Maurice, Thomas Erskine, George MacDonald. The contributors to *Lux Mundi* betray little if any awareness of these men, or of their North American counterparts: John Nevin, Philip Schaff or Horace Bushnell. Nor do their strictures on "Protestantism" betray familiarity with or appreciation of the strongly incarnational theology of English Methodism. It may be added that in the years immediately following *Lux Mundi* it was the Scots Presbyterian Henry Drummond who took up the challenge to offer a theological evaluation of the process of evolution in much closer detail than Illingworth had done in his chapter. Yet *Lux Mundi* itself must surely be seen in the context of these wider movements as reflecting a common—but by no means merely Anglican—recovery of incarnational thinking, a recovery that was as much "Protestant" as "Catholic" and ought not to be played off by one side against the other.

Here, of course, the changes of the last century have altered the atmosphere very considerably. "Catholic" thinking is not the exclusive prerogative of particular churches or traditions, and "reformed" thinking has its own contribution to make to the ecumenical future. If *Lux Mundi* was inclined to set the two over against each other as opposites, we are faced with the task—itself by no means easy—of holding both together. Sometimes, indeed, it can appear to some of us in the Reformed tradition that we need to warn our more "liberal" Catholic friends against becoming "mere Protestants" in what *Lux Mundi* understood as the properly negative sense of the term!

Third—and this is the most substantial christological aspect of the matter—the twentieth century has brought with it a long series of challenges, questions and responses casting their own light and shadow on *Lux Mundi*'s programme as seen in retrospect. Karl Barth with his *Commentary on Romans* and the *Church Dogmatics,* not always popular or understood in England, yet a theological "event" of abiding significance; Rudolf Bultmann with his radically fresh contributions to New Testament research and his programme of "demythologisation"; Friedrich Gogarten with his analyses of the phenomenon of secularisation; the newer political theology articulated by the underprivileged of the first and third worlds—these are but a few of the movements challenging and reshaping theological thinking. These and others—for example, the new work done in recent decades on the relation between theology and natural science—cannot easily be reduced (or reduced at all) to a single common denominator: theological work today is marked by a diversity and variety bursting the framework presupposed and advocated by *Lux Mundi.* It may be that no common alternative to *Lux Mundi*'s approach can be discerned; but let me try to diagnose the points at which the challenge is most apparent.

These can for present purposes be reduced to two, both following from the fact that *Lux Mundi* engaged in no serious christological analysis but contented itself with the serene reaffirmation of patristic dogma. First, the contributors did not think through the implications of their incarnational concern for the doctrine of God; second, they did not focus sufficiently sharply on the New Testament's witness to the humiliation and destruction of the Incarnate Son of God. In a word, they did not even begin to develop the idea of a *trinitarian theology of the crucifixion*. Their theology of the incarnation is not in fact profoundly trinitarian, nor does it take account of the history of Jesus Christ, of the cross and the resurrection, in any but the most peripheral sense. The "strange, deliberate dying" of the Son of man seems to have been understood by them, classicists as they were, on the model of Socrates, allowing quick flight to an idealistic vision of a world suffused with divine energies and power as opposed to the world of often bitter reality. The cry of dereliction—"Eloi, Eloi, lama sabachthani?"—plays no part in their "Catholic" reflections, which it could only have intrusively disturbed.

That path may have been travellable for a privileged circle of Oxford theologians in the 1880s; it is no path for Christian theology today. Our Christian theology has to take seriously the fears, needs and despairs of the hopeless, the exploited and mistreated, in whom the image of God is daily trampled underfoot, defaced and debased. And it has to be upheld, as in so many past generations of persecution and inhumanity, by the trust that the God in whom we believe is not merely the guarantor of an incarnational world view but the Eternal that makes for righteousness.

More than ten years ago Donald MacKinnon summed up everything that I am trying to say here in an immensely powerful and moving article on the relation between the doctrines of the Trinity and the incarnation. His comments represent both the authentic continuation and the necessary deepening of what *Lux Mundi* had to say on the import of the incarnation:

What is realized in the mission of Jesus and perfected in the Father's raising Him from the dead is the very unity of God, the consistency of God with Himself in relation to His creation. We have to do with a prolonged human action that is grounded in God, that in fact provides the very rationale of creation itself. Yet it is unique because in it the very being of God is put at risk, and by the way in which it is thus put at risk, we learn, as nowhere else, what it is we *say* of God when we acclaim Him all-powerful, all-knowing, etc. It is a weakness of the western Trinitarian tradition so to conceive and so to stress the unity of God that the whole theology of the divine attributes tends to be treated independently of the treatise on the divine tri-unity, and the unity of God itself regarded as conceivable independently of the tri-unity through which it is realised:

"The hands are stretched in weakness, not in power."

So Archbishop William Dalrymple Maclagan in a Good Friday hymn, a good deal better than most. But he is wrong. It is the power of God that we must learn to define by reference to those outstretched hands. For we are not passing through the hour of a temporary *eclipse* of the divine sovereignty where we are concerned. We are witnessing its supreme assertion in the setting of a deeply estranged world, an assertion that discloses its very substance, its arcane ground.[6]

The ground of creation is not to be looked for in an immanent activity of the eternal Word *alongside* the history of the incarnation. It is most profoundly disclosed in the person of the crucified and risen Jesus of Nazareth, not only the *risen* but also the *crucified,* the crucified as the risen and the risen as the crucified. Just that plays too small a part in *Lux Mundi.* Its incarnational theology has little room or place for the harsh reality of the cross, except perhaps as a hallowed symbol—crucifixes in place of the crucifixion. The *Magnificat* can find its place there—as a splendid canticle, set to glorious music, but not as the cry of the oppressed celebrating the Lord's visitation of his captive people with all the overtones of hope, longing and expectance. For all the ignorance concerning Luther and the Reformers which they show, the contributors to *Lux Mundi* subscribed in the end to their own, perhaps distinctively Anglican conception of the "two kingdoms": on the one hand the harsh reality of the everyday world and on the other the new and true universal faith introduced by the incarnation, a religion purely "spiritual and unpolitical", riding serene over the waves and storms of time and history. Much the same view of the matter has been more recently expressed by Edward Norman in his Reith lectures. It is not wholly false but is in permanent danger of being one-sidedly interpreted as justifying an understanding of Christian faith which looks past rather than at the reality of human life and experience.

This is the decisive contrast between the approaches of Moberly, Talbot and Illingworth and that of MacKinnon. MacKinnon reminds us of Bonhoeffer's words near fifty years ago: "Only a suffering God can help." The road back to *Lux Mundi*'s vision of a world suffused by the light of the divine immanence is barred to us by an angel with a flaming sword—and the flames are not those of the transfiguration but of Auschwitz and Hiroshima, of Vietnam and Afghanistan. The harsh reality is that not only nature is "red in tooth and claw": so too are human power, human politics, human striving for a better world. For those who have ears to hear, the cry of desolation uttered by Christ on the cross is as essential a key to understanding our human predicament as the Prologue to the Fourth Gospel. It is also essential to realising who and what God himself is.

NOTES

1. B. M. G. Reardon, *Religious Thought in the Victorian Age: A Survey from Coleridge to Gore* (Harlow, Eng.: Longman Group, 1980), 433. The quotation is from Fairbairn's *The Place of Christ in Modern Theology* (1893), 451.

2. For a useful recent discussion, see Colin Gunton, *Yesterday and Today: A Study of Continuities in Christology* (Grand Rapids: Wm. B. Eerdmans, 1983).

3. T. F. Torrance, "The Mind of Christ in Worship: The Problem of Apollinarianism in the Liturgy", in his *Theology in Reconciliation: Essays Towards Evangelical and Catholic Unity in East and West* (London: Geoffrey Chapman, 1975), 139–214.

4. At least Illingworth did not go so far as Aubrey Moore in his chapter on the doctrine of God: "The only scientific theology of the Reformation period was the awful and immoral system of John Calvin, rigorously deduced from a one-sided truth." It is perhaps kinder to make no further comment on *that!*

5. G. W. H. Lampe, *God as Spirit* (Oxford: Clarendon Press, 1977).

6. D. M. MacKinnon, "The Relation of the Doctrines of the Incarnation and the Trinity", in *Creation, Christ and Culture: Studies in Honour of T. F. Torrance,* ed. R. W. A. McKinney (Edinburgh: T. & T. Clark, 1976), 92–107; the passage quoted is on p. 99.

6

THE ATONEMENT

PAUL AVIS

I. THE ATONEMENT IN THE MODERN WORLD

Definitions of the atonement convey an air of irrelevance in the modern world. They seem luxuries that we are not sure we want or can afford. Why spend time and effort asking *how* God redeemed the world when we are not sure whether there *is* a God? Why speculate about what happened long ago for the benefit of the human race when we are uncertain whether there will *be* a human race? The doctrine of the atonement will speak to us only if it can be shown that redemption *is* the existence of God in the world, that God exists for us precisely at the heart of human suffering, and that to know this is the safest assurance of the future of humanity.

The modern world places a great question mark against the doctrine of the atonement. Not only are we unsure whether there is a God to save and whether there will be a human race to be saved but our century has witnessed suffering on such a scale and of such a nature that the cross of Christ seems to take its place simply as one among the myriad crosses of humanity. If there is salvation, atonement, where was it at Auschwitz, at Hiroshima or on the Eastern Front? Such questions compel us to follow the method advocated by Karl Rahner and Johann B. Metz and make apologetics integral to the exposition of the content of Christian truth.[1] Moreover, they indicate that the question of atonement cannot be tackled apart from the question of theodicy, nor the question of theodicy apart from the question of atonement. At the root of our dilemma is the question of the nature of God. Is God a God who cannot be touched by our infirmities, but saves at arm's length by an external transaction, manipulating judicial categories to transfer us from the death camp of the condemned to the rehabilitation centre of the reprieved? Or is our God a God who pours himself unstintingly into his creation, participating in its travail and endowing it with glory, sharing in its sufferings and working through human channels for its redemption, so that the atonement—though expressed definitively and decisively in the life and destiny of Jesus Christ—comes to realisation through the loving heart and helping hand of human creatures? It was of course the question of the nature of God, of transcendence and immanence, that underlay the reconstruction of theology by the "Holy Party" in the volume *Lux Mundi*.

The problem of the atonement did not begin with the twentieth century, or even the Enlightenment. But the latter certainly determined the formulation of the problem for the *Lux Mundi* writers. The eighteenth-century renaissance of secular knowledge and enquiry challenged all received authority, including the authority of dogma. It saw itself as bringing to bear the claims of truth, justice and compassion on the dark enclaves of mystery-mongering and the suppression of open enquiry. The traditional doctrine of penal substitution could not survive its scrutiny. The objections of the Enlightenment may have rested, as Wolfhart Pannenberg suggests, on "extreme ethical individualism",[2] but their validity at this point was acknowledged by Charles Gore and his colleagues.

Of equal or perhaps greater significance than the (first) Enlightenment, is what might be called the second enlightenment—that of the human and social sciences in the late nineteenth and early twentieth centuries. With their "hermeneutic of suspicion" (Paul Ricoeur), the human sciences help us to discriminate reality from illusion. They uncover the "social construction of reality" and the economic basis of ideology. They show how we project inner conflicts and inhibitions on to the world and make supposedly objective reality in our own unconscious image. In theology we have not yet come to terms with the challenge of these human and social disciplines. We are not keen to hear the news that Christian doctrines, as well as referring to claimed revelatory events in the past, represent, in the way they are formulated and perpetuated in history, psychological needs and social dynamics. We are reluctant to acknowledge the relevance to Christian ideology of the mechanism of projection, whereby parental images, for example, become projected on to the transcendent.[3]

Though this second enlightenment, that of the human and social sciences, has important implications for the whole range of theological doctrines, not least for the doctrine of God, it has particular relevance to the atonement. The themes of guilt and punishment which figure so centrally in atonement theories are prime candidates for clarification from these disciplines. The concept of reification, whereby psychosocial structures are projected onto the screen of "external" reality and treated as objective entities, is readily applicable to atonement theories that talk of sin, guilt, the moral law, the wrath of God, satisfaction and reparation as though they were three-dimensional physical objects that could be measured, weighed, run into and moved around.

For example, Anselm's classical discussion *Cur Deus Homo?* employs the conceptual apparatus of medieval feudalism—honour, obligation, recompense—though it obviously transcends their limitations. Calvin asserts: "The guilt which made us liable to punishment was transferred to the head of the Son of God" (*Institutes* II.xvi.5). But modern writers on the atonement continue to reify matters to which the language of personal relations is more appropriate. For Gustaf Aulén, one of the merits of the "classical", *Christus Victor,* account of the atonement is that it treats sin as an "objective power".[4] For Kenneth Kirk, the problem of the atonement is how to compensate the Almighty for the "offence" offered by sinners.[5] William Temple asks, "How can forgiveness be freely given without detriment to the majesty of the moral law?"[6] Emil Brunner asserts: "Between us and God there is an actual obstacle which blocks the way like a great boulder, an obstacle so great that we cannot push it out of the way by our own efforts." Guilt is "unalterable" and "can never be undone". Even God is bound to observe "the inviolable character of the law of penalty" and cannot cease even for one second *(sic)* to maintain his purpose of law unconditionally. Divine punishment issues necessarily and inexorably from the holiness of God. Brunner speaks boldly of "the divine necessity of destruction". God's wrath is a "wall of fire". Eternal death is the penalty of unatoned sin that "God wills in his anger".[7]

All this sounds suspiciously like a God who is merely an idol steeped in our own guilt.[8] Our suspicion is confirmed when the same writers as often as not go on to assert that our penitence is not a sufficient ground to allow God to forgive. Kirk argues that "where offence has been offered, . . . a mere cessation of the offence does not restore the original relationship".[9] What he studiously does not go on to say is that penitence may do just this—for it includes sorrow and shame for what has disrupted a relationship and the desire for it to be restored. Brunner, however, will not allow that God's forgiveness can be released by our penitence. There remains the need for some "objective transaction" to make this possible. It is ethical for us to forgive one another, but not for God to forgive us. "If we say: 'God forgives if we repent', . . . this simply amounts to a denial of guilt. What has my present repentance to do with my previous guilt? . . . The sinner can never repent in proportion to his sin".[10] This sounds like sheer reluctance to accept good news (gospel), to let God be God. Who is he to say what God can and cannot do? The absurdity of representing God as wanting to forgive, but unable to forgive, is manifest. As Grotius pointed out, if God were merely a judge, bound by law, he would have no power to remit punishment of the guilty, even if it were borne by the innocent. But all punishment aims at the common good. The penal law may be relaxed. Deserved punishment need not be inflicted.[11]

It is the strength of "exemplarist" theories of the atonement that they can point to the teaching and the life style of Jesus as proclaiming in word and deed that God's salvation is at hand, that forgiveness is offered. People may repent and be restored and enter God's kingdom now. Jesus' offer of salvation in his own person was apparently not dependent on what might happen to him at the hands of men. As Edward Schillebeeckx comments: "There would have been an element of play-acting about his commitment to his message of *metanoia* and the rule of God, if he had thought and known from the start that salvation would come only in consequence of his death." His presence was "a concrete tender of salvation then and there. . . . Where he appears he brings salvation and becomes God's rule already realised. . . . Jesus proclaims the salvation to come, and at the same time by his conduct he makes it present".[12] It is Jesus and the gospel—not just Marx and Freud—who have taught us to see through the human projections of guilt, fear and anger. It is thanks to the gospel itself that men and women today are not afraid of falling into the hands of an angry God. Any parish priest can testify to the quiet confidence of the non-church-going nominal Christian who, without the comfort of the sacraments, entrusts his or her soul to a merciful creator. Compared to the major horrors that humanity has inflicted upon itself, our personal failures—though they must contribute to the cumulative weight of the world's woe—seem insufficient to provoke divine indignation against the individual to the extent evinced by past generations of preachers and divines. As J. Pohier aptly remarks: "It is not a matter of denying the existence of moral evil or the guilt of human beings, but of asking about the forces which move them to attribute to their failings consequences, the individual, collective and even cosmic magnitude of which far surpasses the degree of freedom which it is anthropologically reasonable to recognise in the human condition."[13] The battle against evil—against the oppression of the weak, against the perverted exploitation of children, against the killing of the unborn, against the systematic sadism of concentration camps—seems far more important to us, and, we believe, to God too. This is where we see "the exceeding sinfulness of sin". As Schillebeeckx puts it: "By violating humanity, the sinner is personally guilty before God."[14]

F. D. Maurice already had an answer for teaching such as Brunner's. You are not delivered, he insisted in his sermons on the doctrine of sacrifice, from a threat emanating from God, but "from your vain conversation received by tradition from your fathers" (1 Pet. 1:18); from "dark and slavish notions concerning God"; from "dread and horror of him"; from the "intolerable bondage" of thinking of God as like ourselves and as our enemy.[15] The paradox of theories of the atonement that reify guilt, sin and the supposed law of penal retribution is that while on the one hand they are crudely anthropomorphic, on the other they cut loose from the control provided by analogy: they portray God as less willing or able to forgive than we are ourselves. "Thus men in slavery of sorrow imagine ghastly creeds" (Robert Bridges).

II. THREE TYPES OF ATONEMENT THEORY?

It is often pointed out that the Christian church has not given conciliar or credal authority to any particular theory of the atonement. It only insists that it was "for us men [humans] and for our salvation" that Christ "came down from heaven". The Christian doctrine of salvation is polymorphous: theories of atonement correspond to the needs that dominate human consciousness at any particular period of history—escape from mortality and ignorance in the patristic period, from guilt and punishment in the medieval and Reformation periods, from meaninglessness and despair in the twentieth century.[16] The disturbingly relativistic conclusion of John Fenton would appear to be incontrovertible: "The content given to the title Saviour depended on what it was thought most necessary to be delivered from."[17] This certainly means that we are free to work out (the meaning of) our salvation—provided we do it with fear and trembling![18]—but in doing so, we will want to be guided by the central sacramental act of the church as it offers and receives the body and blood of Christ for the redemption of the world. This certainly places constraints on our speculations, for if we were to adopt a theory of the atonement in which the death of Christ was, so to speak, accidental and peripheral to his mission, and any meaningful sacrificial content excluded, we would be verging on the ecclesiologically untenable position that the core of the Christian message as it has been preached from St. Paul to the present day, and embodied in the liturgies of the church, had been exposed as a false ideology.[19]

For the past fifty years, discussion of the atonement has tended to follow the lines laid down in Aulén's *Christus Victor.*[20] Aulén distinguished three types of atonement theory: the "classical" type, as he called it, which proclaimed (rather than explained) Christ's victory over the hostile forces of sin, death and the devil that held humanity in bondage; the Latin or juridical model, which found paradigmatic formulation in Anselm's *Cur Deus Homo?;* and the exemplarist, "subjective" view associated with Abélard and defended by Hastings Rashdall, which sees the death of Christ as the supreme revelation of the love of God. However, the more closely we examine Aulén's classification, the less plausible the watertight separation of the theories becomes.

First of all, I would not dignify Aulén's "classical" model with the status of a theological theory. It is more a series of metaphors and images, extolling the victory of Christ and the fruits of his atonement, but failing to show how this was accomplished. The personification of sin, death and evil (the devil) reveals the poetical and mythological character of this model. As J. Macquarrie nicely points out, we should not be misled by the mythological language of triumph over the principalities and powers, as if some "objectively existing demons" had been destroyed by Christ two thousand years ago, never to trouble humanity again.[21] And as Colin Gunton has suggested, this model can be regarded as an exercise in the history of a metaphor, in which "victory" is used in a highly paradoxical sense.[22] The Christus Victor theme is first-order religious rhetoric, not second-order theological explanation.

Second, Anselmian, juridical theories now have the air of strained analogy about them. What were serviceable forensic metaphors in St. Paul become unconvincing when pressed into the straitjacket of a systematic explanation. As H. P. Owen points out:

The theories of satisfaction and penal substitution confuse moral and legal categories. In the legal sphere a debt must be paid and a penalty discharged. However, there is no such necessity in the moral sphere. On the contrary a loving father will readily waive a debt owed to him by his own son, just as he will do all he can to save his son from the self-destructive effects that his son's sins have caused. Moreover, although in the legal sphere one person can sometimes pay a debt or penalty owed by another, in the moral sphere he cannot do so. Moral responsibility is incommunicable.[23]

A further weakness of juridical theories is their isolation of the death of Christ from his person, message and life—not to mention his resurrection and the church.[24] Again, such theories—even if valid—could take us only part of the way towards a doctrine of the atonement, for the outcome of the atonement on this model is forgiveness, but forgiveness is only the beginning: it must lead to reconciliation and thence to communion with God.[25] I would endorse F. W. Dillistone's conclusion that "no strictly penal theory of atonement can be expected to carry conviction in the world of the twentieth century. . . . To appeal to a system which is either outmoded or seriously open to criticism is to bring the whole doctrine into discredit".[26]

Moreover, even basically substitutionary and penal theories, such as that of Calvin, cannot be reduced to unacceptable and discredited notions. They are not always what they seem and cannot be consigned to the rubbish dump of obsolete theological doctrines. For example, while Calvin employs the most literal propitiatory language about the death of Christ, his teaching contains elements of the classical and exemplarist theories. Certainly, Christ's work was to "procure the favour of God for us". He is "a priest employed to appease the wrath of God" and to "render the Father favourable and propitious towards us". Our sins were "transferred to him by imputation", and by the price of his blood "the justice of God was satisfied" (*Institutes* II. xv. 6; xvi. 6; xvii. 4). But Calvin asks: "How can it be said that God, who prevents us with his mercy, was our enemy until he was reconciled to us by Christ? For how could he have given us in his only begotten Son a singular pledge of his love, if he had not previously embraced us with free favour?" Calvin admits that the propitiatory language is a manner of speaking, for though our sins are abhorrent to God, he still loves us as his creatures, and it is because he already loves us that he acts to restore us to himself. Calvin quotes Augustine: "In a manner wondrous and divine, he loved even when he hated us." The tension of divine righteousness and love subsists "in a manner which cannot be expressed" (*Institutes* II. xvi. 2, 3, 4; xvii. 2). Calvin's commentary on John 3:16 is almost Abelardian: as we contemplate in faith Christ crucified, we behold "in him the heart of God poured out in love".[27] Even the implacable Brunner's doctrine is not entirely beyond redemption (!). The heart of God is poured out in sacrificial love for Brunner too. "It is indeed God who takes everything upon himself. . . . The cross of Christ is conceived as the self-offering of God. It is God who does it; it is God himself who suffers, it is God who takes the burden upon himself."[28]

James Denney's work *The Death of Christ* is sometimes cited as a late example of the juridical, objective, substitutionary model of the atonement. Rashdall frequently castigates Denney. Denney points out that to deny the substitutionary element altogether is to imply not so much that Christ died for the ungodly as that the ungodly, in Christ, died for themselves.[29] Denney formulates the problem of atonement thus: "In the very act of forgiving sin . . . God must act in consistency with his whole character. He must demonstrate himself to be what he is in relation to sin, a God with whom evil cannot dwell, a God who maintains inviolate the moral constitution of the world." Denney speaks of the "divine necessity . . . to forgive in a way which shows that God is irreconcilable to evil".[30] (The use of the words "demonstrate" and "show" is significant here.) Christ's death is atoning and substitutionary in that he offers to God, under the pressure of the world's sin and all its consequences, that perfect recognition of God's holiness which human beings should have offered. But when we accept his work in faith, he becomes our representative and we offer ourselves in union with him.[31]

Denney explicitly rejects a juridical, forensic interpretation of the atonement. "To say that the relations of God and men are forensic is to say that they are regulated by statute—that sin is a breach of statute—that the sinner is a criminal—and that God adjudicates on him by interpreting the statute in its application to his case." This would be a "travesty of the truth".[32] Denney wants to maintain that forgiveness is mediated through Christ and specifically through his death,[33] but Denney's explanation of the mechanics of this hardly differs from that of William Temple and is only a handshake away from Rashdall's view. According to Denney, God can only forgive "through a supreme reve-

lation of his love, made at infinite cost, and doing justice to the utter-
most to those inviolable relations in which alone . . . man can participate
in eternal life, the life of God himself—doing justice to them as relations in which there is an inexorable divine reaction against sin, finally
expressing itself in death." This forgiveness which leads to communion
with God is actualised as sinful human beings "open their hearts in
penitence and faith to this marvellous revelation and abandon their
sinful life unreservedly to the love of God in Christ who died for
them". Denney is arguing that if forgiveness is not just wiping a slate
clean but restoring a damaged relationship, it can be effected only by
bringing out the conditions of that relationship and somehow actualis-
ing them. The death of Christ is the demonstration and setting forth of
these conditions, which evokes penitence, faith and love from the
beholder. Thus a theory that ostensibly sets out to establish the objectivity of an atonement in which there is something accomplished and
achieved for our salvation which could not be attained in any other way
turns out to be simply a rather more profound version of the subjective
theory.

Aulén's classification of atonement theories into three types is beginning to look very shaky. This impression is confirmed when we begin
to appreciate that the threefold division involves misinterpreting and
parodying the exemplarist, subjective theory. Elizabeth Moberly points
out that Abélard's doctrine has often been viewed prejudicially—as
though a change in humanity excluded the action of God.[34] Typically,
Kirk suggests that the exemplary theory of the death of Christ—the
theory that his death reveals the heart of the Father and invites our
response—means that we could save ourselves, and, moreover, gives
no guarantee of the ultimate victory of God in the universe.[35] Even
Oliver Quick, from whom we might have hoped better things, suggests
that the exemplary theory is further removed from the New Testament
than the juridical theory. Its most significant feature, Quick suggests,
is that it abandons entirely the direct connection, so clear in the epistles
of St. Paul, between the atonement and the inauguration of a new
world by God's act in the resurrection of Christ:

Thus there is no directly *cosmic* importance at all in the death and resurrection of Christ: the order and constitution of God's universe remain exactly
the same after as before, no radically new relation of men to God has come

132

into existence, and it may well be argued that Christian theologians have no longer any interest in insisting that the body of Jesus was raised from the tomb.[36]

But surely the new creation is in the church which is his body and the meaning of the resurrection is to be found in relation to that: "If any one is in Christ, he is a new creation" (2 Cor. 5:17). These comments reveal again a hankering after some objective, external transaction, prior to and apart from human response, which is enough to eliminate any risk from God's commitment to his creation.

Brunner too parodies the exemplarist theory of the atonement, while his strictures on idealist theology are hardly applicable to Gore and the contributors to *Lux Mundi*. "The doctrine of identity—and the kindred systems of idealism and mysticism—maintain that it is not necessary that any objective transaction should actually take place, for God's attitude is eternally the same. There is no obstacle between us and God *save our erroneous idea that it exists.*"[37] The threefold typology of atonement theories, as presented by Aulén, depends on misinterpretation, stereotyping and sheer travesty of alternative theories. The true situation is much more fluid. It looks as though a constructive restatement can be eclectic with a good conscience.

III. ATONEMENT THEORIES ON THE EVE OF *LUX MUNDI*

When the Holy Party began to meet in the mid-1870s, R. W. Dale's work on *The Atonement* was just appearing.[38] It is a version of the "objective", juridical doctrine of atonement but gives it a human face. Dale's aim is to show that "the death of Christ is the objective ground on which the sins of men are remitted" (p. lxii). Dale is well aware that to explain the atonement theologians "have been driven to the most monstrous and incredible speculations" (pp. 268–69). Dale is no exponent of penal substitution: Christ "could not actually share the guilt of the human race, for guilt attaches to those and to those only who have actually sinned. Nor was there any imputation of sin—the imputation of sin is a legal fiction" (p. lxiii). But Christ did take upon himself the consequences of sin, particularly the wrath or hostility of God against sin. The cry of dereliction reveals that he was separated from the presence of God by being identified with human sin. Thus God's "hostility to our sins has received adequate expression in the death of Christ", so enabling God to forgive (pp. 342, 346). As the judge of the world and the embodiment of the eternal law of righteousness, Christ chose to endure pain rather than to inflict it (pp. 361ff., 395ff.). Dale's was an enlightened version of traditional theories, but it still ended up by making Christ bear the wrath of God in the place of sinners.

A radically liberal view that wanted to break with this tradition altogether was that of Benjamin Jowett. Jowett's essay on the atonement[39] begins with an outburst of moral revulsion against juridical, substitutionary theories of the atonement. "God is represented as angry with us for what we never did [original sin, the imputed guilt of Adam], he is ready to inflict a disproportionate punishment on us for what we are. . . . The sin of Adam is first imputed to us then the righteousness of Christ. . . . He is a victim laid upon the altar to appease the wrath of God" (p. 209). Jowett cuts through the contortions of successive acts of imputation: "We need not suppose that God ever sees us other than we really are, or attributes to us what we never did" (p. 262). He points out that interpreters of the atonement have been led astray by taking figurative biblical expressions literally (pp. 213ff.). He protests against abstracting the death of Christ from his total person and destiny: "Christ died for us in no other sense than he lived or rose again for us" (p. 260). For the Master of Balliol, the atonement was effected through our identification and communion with the living Christ.

Jowett's protests had been anticipated by F. D. Maurice in his essay on the atonement in his *Theological Essays* (1853).[40] Maurice summarised the Christian gospel as the message that God has "offered himself for the sins of the world"—a message that "brings divine love and human suffering into direct and actual union" (p. 109). Maurice refuted all theories that represented the Son as persuading the Father to be gracious. How could Christ have changed "that will which he took flesh and blood to fulfil"? In the following year (1854), Maurice gave a series of sermons at Lincoln's Inn on *The Doctrine of Sacrifice* in reply to criticism.[41] Maurice regards sacrifice as the law of the divine life and the path to our true end. In offering our souls and bodies, we find the meaning of our lives in imitation of the trinitarian life of God (p. 111). Maurice is in company with McLeod Campbell in rejecting any covenant theology that gives priority to law. God's covenant with humanity is prior to law, blessing comes before the curse. Blessing expresses the mind of God; law is rendered necessary by the false condition into which humanity has fallen through distrusting the promises (p. 139). Maurice's doctrine of the atonement is basically exemplarist—Christ's death is the sacrifice of himself in total dedication to the cause of God and humanity and reveals that there is forgiveness with God. The mercy seat of the Old Testament stands not for the propitiation of divine wrath against sin, but "he who had established the mercy-seat was the Lord God of that earth from which the foulest steam of human sacrifices was ascending to the Baals and Molochs. He was testifying there that from him came freely down the blessings which they were hoping to buy of their Gods; that he blotted out the transgressions of which the worshippers were seeking, by the cruellest oblations to escape the penalty" (p. 150). Christ's cross is, by analogy, God's "setting forth to us the one all-sufficient, all-satisfactory evidence that he *has* made peace with us . . . that the barrier between God and his creatures is removed by himself" (pp. 152–53). Luther had discovered that the righteousness of God is not the righteousness of hostility to the sinner but the righteousness that he freely bestows to make the unjust just. Maurice echoes Luther when he says: God is "the being who puts away sins *because* he is righteous, *because* he would not have the man tied and yoked to evil, *because* he would make him his free and true servant" (p. 156). The theory of penal substitution, on the other hand, is designed to enable God to forgive sins *though* he is righteous (p. 157). For Maurice the atonement was made by Christ's solidarity, sympathy and self-identity with sinners even unto death (pp. 179ff.). God's way of reconciling humanity is "to take upon him their flesh and blood, to enter into their sorrows, to feel and suffer their sins" (p. 192). Nothing that the contributors to *Lux Mundi* had to say about atonement reached Maurice's level of profundity and passion—and none of the writers I have perused in the preparation of this study approach him.

IV. THE ATONEMENT IN *LUX MUNDI*

If one failing of judicial, objective theories of the atonement is that they represent God as trying to redeem the world at arm's length, by an external transaction, the rediscovery of the doctrine of divine immanence by Gore, J. R. Illingworth and their colleagues in the Holy Party should have been conducive to a more profound and satisfying theory of the atonement. E. S. Talbot specifically states that it is "this idea of beauty in process that we bring with us as we approach to behold the facts and method of God's redemptive work". In this connection, it is interesting to take note of Aulén's claim that the idealist, monist and evolutionary thought of the nineteenth century was inherently incapable of doing justice to the realist, dualist and dramatic scheme in which the doctrine of the atonement had been classically expressed.[42] Does *Lux Mundi* bear out Aulén's contention?

The contributors to *Lux Mundi* do not disguise their distaste for crude penal substitutionary views of the atonement. They repudiate them as strongly as do Jowett and Maurice. Illingworth observes that unworthy interpretations of Christianity have drawn down the justified attacks of its critics. "Fragments of doctrine, torn from their context and deprived of their due proportions, are brandished in the eyes of men by well-meaning but ignorant apologists as containing the sum total of the Christian faith." One such caricature was the narrowing of the religion of the incarnation into the religion of the atonement in Protestantism. The fathers of the church saw the plan of salvation in a broader context. "They realised that redemption was a means to an end, and that end the re-consecration of the whole universe to God." In his essay on the atonement, Arthur Lyttelton deplores the fact that the doctrine has become so isolated and distorted as to become "almost incredible". The "unreality" of some theories "has been a disaster to the Christian faith".

It must be admitted that some contributors overcompensate for the exaggerated stress on the atonement in the narrow sense. When they speak most eloquently of the unfolding of the divine purpose, it is the incarnation as the crown of progressive revelation that fills their thoughts. For Aubrey Moore, Christianity speaks of God "leading the world by a progressive preparation for the revelation of himself as Infinite Love in the Incarnation of the Word, stimulating those desires which he alone can satisfy, the yearning of the heart for love, of the moral nature for righteousness, of the speculative reason for truth. When men had wearied themselves in the search for a remedy for that which separates men from God, the revelation is given of him who 'shall save his people from their sins'. And when reason had wandered long, seeking for that which should be real and yet one, a God who should satisfy alike the demands of religion and reason, the doctrine of the Trinity is unfolded." And Moore concludes: "It was the gradual revelation of God answering to the growing needs and capacity of man." Similarly Illingworth, in his essay on the incarnation and development, traces the manifold witness that God gave to himself from "the dim twilight of the world" until the fulness of time when the Word was made flesh. "The pre-Christian religions were the age-long prayer. The Incarnation was the answer." So far Aulén's criticism of immanental categories appears to be justified.

Some presuppositions of a doctrine of atonement are given in Illingworth's first essay, on the problem of pain, and here an unacceptably rosy view of suffering is presented. Unmerited suffering has the power to neutralise past evil and, moreover, to elevate, refine and dignify the character to an infinite degree. Unmerited suffering unites us to God, for it reflects the principle of sacrifice at the heart of the divine life. It reveals the law of vicariousness in all creation that comes to its climax and fullest expression in the cross of Christ where we see the definitive separation of sin and suffering. In a passage that cries out for critique as false ideology, Illingworth writes:

> The pleasures of each generation evaporate in air; it is their pains that increase the spiritual momentum of the world. We enter into life through the travail of another. We live upon the death of the animals beneath us. The necessities, the comforts, the luxuries of our existence are provided by the labour and sorrow of countless fellow-men. Our freedom, our laws, our literature, our spiritual sustenance have been won for us at the cost of broken hearts, and wearied brains and noble lives laid down. And this is only the human analogue of that transference of energy by which all life and movement is for ever carried on.

"And how", asks Illingworth, "should their Creator draw all men unto him, but through the instrumentality of his own great law of sacrifice?" And he speculates "whether 'in the light that no man can approach unto', where the Three are One, some higher analogue of what we call sacrifice does not for ever flame; whose radiant reflection on the universe only becomes shadow when it falls on a world of sin".

If Illingworth here at least echoes Maurice's teaching on sacrifice, Lyttelton also shows himself to be influenced by Maurice when, in his essay on the atonement, he insists that any theory must satisfy the conditions of the religious consciousness and broad human experience. But Lyttelton departs from Maurice in taking his starting point from the Old Testament law and "the tremendous fact of the wrath of God against sin". For him, the simplest and the most scriptural way of stating the doctrine of the atonement is to say that, when man could not offer an acceptable sacrifice to avert the wrath of God, Christ offered it on his behalf. But Lyttelton insists that this is no theory of penal substitution. "The sufferings and the pains of death which he endured have not been remitted to us; and that which is remitted, the eternal penalty of alienation from God, was not, could not be endured by him." Our human sufferings remain; however, they are no longer penal but remedial and penitential. "Pain has become the chastisement of the Father who loves us, and death the passage into his presence." The notion of suffering as remedial chastisement would be developed by R. C. Moberly in *Atonement and Personality.*

In Gore's own essay in *Lux Mundi,* on the Holy Spirit and biblical inspiration, he touches momentarily on the atonement. Gore sees Christ's obedience unto death as "propitiatory", in the sense of atoning, because it constitutes him the founder of a new humanity in the power of the Spirit:

> In the Spirit he offers himself without spot to God; in the power of the Spirit he is raised from the dead. All that perfect human life had been a life of obedience . . . which became propitiatory as it bore loyally, submissively, lovingly, all the heritage of pain and misery in which sin in its long history had involved our manhood, all the agony of that insult and rejection in which sin revealed itself by antagonism to him—bore it and by bearing it turned it into the material of his accepted sacrifice.

Gore returned to the subject of the atonement in *Belief in Christ* (1922), the second volume of his trilogy *The Reconstruction of Belief.* [43] The moral thrust of all Gore's thought comes through in his definition of redemption as "the actual restoration of men into the moral likeness of God" (p. 577). Gore upholds an "objective" atonement against Rashdall's recent "subjective" account. Rashdall, writes Gore, "labours in vain . . . to dislodge from its position in the Christian tradition the belief which . . . is so prominent and indisputable throughout the New Testament—that, prior to all appropriation by men, through the ministry of the Holy Spirit, of the fruits of the Incarnation, there had been on the part of Christ, as the redeemer of men and the inaugurator of the new manhood, a sacrifice offered to the Father, a sacrifice of obedience to the shedding of his blood, in virtue of which God was enabled freely to justify, or acquit, those who belong to him, and to give them a new standing ground as sons of God and members of Christ." Gore maintains that "everything in the New Testament appears to depend on this initial sacrifice of atonement, reconciliation and propitiation" (p. 590).

In Gore's assessment, critical study of the Gospels supports the view that Jesus identified with the suffering servant of Isaiah who offered himself to God as a sacrifice for the people (p. 582). Gore makes an important distinction between vicarious sacrifice and vicarious punishment and will allow no playing off of the Father against the Son: "The essential wrath of God over sin is Christ's as much as the Father's, and the pardoning mercy the Father's as much as Christ's" (p. 592). Christ bore the sins of the world (not the punishment for sins) "in exactly the same sense as all the world over the sins of men are vicariously borne by their victims" (p. 593).

V. ANGLICAN ATONEMENT THEORIES
AFTER 1900

Two major treatises on the atonement distinguish Anglican theology between the beginning of the century and the end of the First World War—the war that was to give a new momentum and urgency to the doctrine of the atonement by linking it with the question of theodicy and making the concept of a suffering God imperative. R. C. Moberly's *Atonement and Personality* (1901)[44] and Hastings Rashdall's *The Idea of Atonement in Christian Theology* (Bampton Lectures 1915; published in an expanded form in 1919)[45] retain their value and repay study. Moberly had contributed an undistinguished essay to *Lux Mundi;* he was a devout, deeply pastoral and largely intuitive thinker. His central theory of Christ the perfect penitent did not find acceptance, and his logic received rough treatment at Rashdall's hands in an article review. But as Rashdall admitted, Moberly was "one of the very few Church of England theologians to whom theology means something more than either ephemeral polemics, on the one hand, or biblical and historical learning, on the other".[46]

Moberly attempts to clarify the concept of punishment. His contention that punishment cannot cancel wrong or remove guilt undermines all penal theories of the atonement (p. 18). We might add to this that even *forgiveness* cannot cancel wrong or remove blame, but it can restore a damaged relationship. Atonement theories should resist infantile wishes to make the wrongs we have done go away and the wish to be seen as other than we are. Moberly further holds that human sufferings are corrective as long as they are accepted in a spirit of penitence, but become punitive when we harden our hearts. On this Rashdall commented: "Such an astonishing combination of opinions has never, so far as I am aware, been held before", and he astutely pointed out that this theory enabled Moberly to retain a belief in hell.[47] But on this point I would side with Macquarrie in rejecting the view that natural evil is the instrument of God's justice as incompatible with the Book of Job and the teaching of Jesus.[48]

Moberly is strong on the solidarity of Christ with humanity, but his grounds are weak. His argument is based on the vicariousness of all human life and the patristic theory of recapitulation (pp. 86ff.). Rashdall criticises this as based on an inadequate metaphysic: Moberly's doctrine of Christ's inclusive humanity is derived from "the crude, vague, shifting idea of *recapitulatio* in Irenaeus" which was elaborated by fathers and schoolmen "whose minds were steeped in the crudest form of a realism which, though derived from Plato, it would be an insult to call Platonic".[49] A more incisive criticism would be, I suggest, that Moberly is falling into the trap of attempting to establish the objectivity of the atonement apart from our human response of penitence and faith and sacramental incorporation into the church as the body of Christ. Moberly is aware of this pitfall (p. 138) and points out that the reality of the atonement can be explained only in terms of Pentecost (p. 151). But when he elaborates the notion that "from the moment when humanity triumphed in holiness perfectly divine, the Spirit of God was become, in the person of Christ, the Spirit of human holiness victorious over sin" (p. 204), he reveals that he is still ensnared in the false consciousness that wants a guaranteed ontological divine reality in this world, independent of any actual response of human beings.

McLeod Campbell had taught in *The Nature of the Atonement* that forgiveness moved by love precedes atonement which is its manifestation to humanity. In Moberly's elaboration of this theory, Christ "confessed the Father" by being in himself the manifestation of the Father to humanity and correspondingly confessed the sin of humanity by being the very manifestation of humanity in its ideal reality of penitential holiness before the Father. Where Campbell had interpreted Christ's atonement as "a perfect Amen in humanity to the judgement of God on the sins of man", Moberly stressed the penitential nature of this confession: "He voluntarily stood in the place of the utterly contrite—accepting insult, shame, anguish, death . . . nay more, in his own inner consciousness accepting the ideal consciousness of the contrite."

Acceptable—valuable—as this may be as metaphor, in hymns and prayers where we offer our imperfect penitence through Christ's perfect self-offering to the Father, it is not viable as theology. J. K. Mozley pointed out that "serious difficulties" were involved in Moberly's paradox that while true penitence is necessary for the sinner, it is possible only for the sinless.[50] H. A. Hodges dismisses Moberly's proposal as "impossible".[51] Rashdall's parting shot in his unsparing review of *Atonement and Personality* is to observe: "It is a significant fact that it should be possible for an Oxford professor of theology to write an elaborate treatise upon the doctrine of the atonement without so much as mentioning the name of Ritschl."[52] Ritschl's great work on justification and reconciliation had been published in the early 1870s, the first volume being translated into English in 1872 and the third in 1900.

Rashdall begins his own enquiry into the doctrine of the atonement, some years later, in *The Idea of Atonement in Christian Theology,* by defining the question of salvation as "the question of the way in which human souls . . . may attain to the highest ideal or true end of their being" (p. xii). Rashdall's method is to start with the teaching of Jesus in the Gospels: "What did Jesus himself teach about the forgiveness of sins? Did he teach the doctrine that sin can only be forgiven through the atoning efficacy of his death, or anything like that doctrine?" (p. 4). Randall answers his own questions thus: "The bare call to repentance as the one great pre-requisite of entrance into the kingdom, which formed the substance of the earliest teaching, implies by itself that God is willing to forgive; and it implies with almost equal distinctness that forgiveness is dependent upon no condition whatever but repentance, and the amendment which is the necessary consequence of sincere repentance" (p. 25). The teaching of the Gospels—the words and deeds of Jesus—must certainly be allowed to control the formulation of our doctrine of the atonement. And Rashdall is right to insist that conformity to certain correct beliefs and participation in certain sacramental practices cannot be supported from the Gospels as conditions of salvation. But Rashdall goes too far in eliminating the suffering Saviour, baptism and membership of the church from the Gospels' picture of salvation. In the Gospels, salvation is bound up with faith, confession of Christ, and discipleship within the eschatological community.

The sacrifice of Christ and his call to his followers to take up their own cross reinforced "the principle that love is the highest thing in human life and the highest revelation of the divine nature" (p. 46). Christ's life and death are exemplary in that they show forth the love of God and are a pattern of our response to that love. "The only [*sic*] atoning influence that can be recognised in the death of Christ, or in any other aspect of his work, is one which operates by actually helping to produce that repentance and moral regeneration upon which, and upon which alone, according to the Master's express teaching, forgiveness depends" (p. 48). Misconceptions about the necessity of Christ's death as a propitiation or expiation for sins came in with St. Paul and derived from the misappropriation of Old Testament texts (pp. 76ff.). The true interpretation was rediscovered by Abélard, who wrote: "The purpose and cause of the Incarnation was that he might illuminate the world by his wisdom and excite it to the love of himself" (p. 358). And Rashdall quotes Peter Lombard:

> So great a pledge of love having been given us, we are both moved and kindled to love God who did such great things for us; and by this we are justified, that is, being loosed from our sins we are made just. The death of Christ therefore justifies us, inasmuch as through it charity is stirred up in our hearts. (p. 438)

The cross of Christ teaches us that God sorrows over human sin and pain—Rashdall was writing during the First World War—and "a God who could contemplate such a world as ours without suffering would not be a loving God, nor would he be in the least like Christ" (pp. 452–53). A previous owner of my copy—apparently Conrad Noel—has marked the margin at this point "1941". That was indeed a dark year, but the death camps of the Nazi empire were still a ghastly secret.

Between the wars, William Temple expounded the atonement in *Christus Veritas*.[53] Rashdall had complained that theologians were so busy speculating *how* forgiveness was effected that they seldom troubled to ask what forgiveness was.[54] Temple soundly states that "to forgive is to restore an old relationship" (p. 257). He has the moral thrust of his teacher Charles Gore when he affirms: "The atonement is accomplished by the drawing of sinful souls into conformity with the divine will" (p. 259). But the problem remains as to how forgiveness can be freely given "to men so blind and callous as we are" without undermining the moral order and appearing to treat sin as trivial. It could be given, Temple replies, only "by one who was also to lay bare the heart of God and show what sin means to him, and therefore how righteous as well as deep is the love from which forgiveness flows" (p. 260). The cross, by showing what sin costs God, safeguards his righteousness while he forgives. Temple's view of the atonement is also contained in the report *Doctrine in the Church of England* of 1938 (p. 92).

At the beginning of the century Rashdall had observed that "an enormous but singularly silent revolution" had taken place in the understanding of the atonement and its place in Christian theology: "The gospel of the Incarnation has practically to a very large extent taken the place of the doctrine of the atonement." The views of Maurice and F. W. Robertson (liberal Protestants) had been imbibed by the pupils of Newman and Pusey.[55] When, on the eve of the Second World War, William Temple, then Archbishop of York, reviewed the fourteen years of the Doctrine Commission's deliberations, he detected a shift of the focus of concern in their minds and those of theologians all over the world (Temple was no insular Anglican). When the Commission had been constituted in 1922, the influence of B. F. Westcott and the *Lux Mundi* school had established a theology of the incarnation rather than of redemption (as Rashdall had noted twenty years before). And, as Temple commented, "A theology of the Incarnation tends to be a Christocentric metaphysic" (Temple had spent a lifetime developing one). A theology of redemption, on the other hand, tends "to sound the prophetic note". It is more willing to admit the irrational and unintelligible in the world. It is eschatological and looks for the coming of God's kingdom. Temple concluded: "If the security of the nineteenth century, already shattered in Europe, finally crumbles away in our country, we shall be pressed more and more towards a theology of redemption. In this we shall be coming closer to the New Testament. . . . Man needs above all to be saved from himself. This must be the work of divine grace."[56] Temple, who had always insisted that Pelagianism was the only heresy that was intrinsically damnable, would have had a contribution to make to such a theology of redemption, but his work was over in the midst of "the breaking of nations". Temple could have had no conception of the extent to which growing knowledge of the horrors of Auschwitz, Stalingrad and Hiroshima ("Their wrong is an echo defying/acoustical law, increasing not fading," R. S. Thomas) would explode not only a serene Christocentric metaphysic but make thoughtful Christians wonder whether even a theology of redemption dare open its mouth, whether atonement was not only impossible but blasphemous. No one could have predicted the ironical return of a chastened, reticent, critical theology to seeking the hope of redemption precisely in the incarnation and what it reveals of the solidarity of the Creator with suffering humanity.

VI. INTERPRETING THE ATONEMENT

The atonement is first of all a fact; it is a reality. Christians have the witness of the Spirit that they are reconciled to God through Jesus Christ. This is the strength of Schleiermacher's approach that begins from the corporate Christian consciousness. Christ *does* assume believers into vital fellowship with him and communicate "his unclouded blessedness" to them.[57] But the experience of redemption is more easily expressed in hymns, prayers and poems than formulated theologically. However, we do not need to rationalise fully our salvation. "No eye has seen, nor ear heard, nor the heart of man conceived, what God has prepared for those who love him" (1 Cor. 2:9). Schillebeeckx rightly points to the impossibility of defining salvation. "Precisely because a perspective on final salvation comes to us only in historically broken situations or experiences of meaning or meaninglessness, the awareness of final salvation is provisionally a 'negative awareness'."[58]

I am happy to continue to employ the traditional vocabulary of the vision of God as the end of salvation—a vision that, needless to say, is not merely contemplative and detached (that would be the apotheosis of false consciousness) but a vision that is conferred through purification and issues in union. Maurice and Quick[59] are surely in tune with a central theme of the Bible in teaching that humanity's true end is to offer itself to God and find its fulfilment therein. Salvation might be defined as *the union of love with the loving heart of reality.* In words that have been quoted almost too often to be usable, Dante spoke of the vision of God in which all insubordinate and carnal desires (concupiscence) were purged away and his will responded in perfect accord with the love that moves the sun and the other stars. I concluded my study of the methods of modern theology—which I subtitled "The Dream of Reason"—by alluding to these final lines of the *Paradiso* and our hope to awaken one day to the vision of a reality, before which "high imagination fails" (*Par.* 33:142), and I ended by quoting one of the biblical verses that, blended with Platonic idealism, underlies this tradition of Christian eschatology: "I shall see thy face, and be blest with a vision of thee when I awake" (Ps. 17:15 NEB).[60]

But this salvation cannot be attained without solidarity with and service to other human beings. It is not a pilgrimage of the autonomous soul, not "the flight of the alone to the Alone". Just as Barth qualified his "positivism of revelation" with the rider that the revelation of God comes to us veiled in "the garments of creaturely reality",[61] so too we must qualify the soteriological principle that salvation is from God alone, requiring no assistance from human works, with the ecclesiological—and indeed pneumatological—principle that salvation is not disembodied and detached from creaturely reality but is mediated to us through the loving heart and outstretched hand of our brothers and sisters in Christ. Christ is known through his body the church, and St. Paul speaks of the vital role that every limb and organ of the body plays in ministering to the whole. As Schillebeeckx intimates, Christology is the paradigm of God's method of salvation through the church: "In Jesus . . . the coming of God's kingdom is mediated by a human being. [Therefore] man's caring for his fellow-men is the visible form and aspect in which the coming of God's kingdom is manifested; it is the way that God's lordship takes."[62] When, at long last, at the end of his second massive volume, Schillebeeckx asks, What then is salvation for us today? he defines it as "being at the disposal of others, losing oneself to others" (as Jesus did) and working for goodness and truth in the human world.[63] I find this one-sided and insufficient, not because it is not "spiritual" or inward enough—what could be more spiritual or demand greater inner intensity than to take up one's cross and follow in the footsteps of Jesus like this?—but because it neglects the eschatological tension that draws us onwards beyond our veiled and indirect encounter with the God of salvation in this life and this world, to its fulfilment and fruition in the redemptive vision of God in heaven. But this is not another God than the one we have encountered obliquely in loving service to one another and in the face of Jesus Christ. We are never delivered from our humanity. And God has willed never to be parted from the humanity that he has created and redeemed. In the incarnation, humanity has been taken irrevocably into God. We can appreciate the following verse of William Blake as metaphor, not theology (his statement, "God only acts and is, in existing beings or men," is beyond what is permissible):

> For Mercy has a human heart,
> Pity, a human face:

> And Love, the human form divine,
> And Peace, the human dress.
> ("The Divine Image")

St. John is not far from this soteriological immanentism when he writes: "No one has ever seen God: if we love one another, God abides in us and his love is perfected in us" (1 John 4:12).

What is required, as I see it, is a holistic interpretation of the atonement in which the dichotomies that have been exploited between objective and subjective atonement and between the person and the work of Christ are healed. It is the total performance of the life and destiny of Jesus, received as the Christ within the church which is his resurrection body, and made effectual through the Holy Spirit, that constitutes the atonement:

a. Person and work.

Dietrich Bonhoeffer argued for the priority—at least in the *ordo cognoscendi*—of the knowledge of Christ's person. Who he is comes first; what he does for us, second.[64] This is a reversal of the Melanchthonian dictum: To know Christ is to enjoy his benefits—an approach endorsed by Denney when he remarks that we come to believe in Christ as the one who can do this for us.[65] I cannot see that there is any advantage to be gained either way. It smacks of false consciousness to put person before work or work before person. Paul Tillich is surely on the right lines when he suggests that Jesus' acceptance of his destiny of suffering and death made him the Christ.[66] Calvin taught that Christ's sacrifice was his whole life ("the whole course of his obedience", *Institutes* II. xvi.5). Schleiermacher, commenting on the traditional distinction between the active and the passive work of Christ, wrote: "The action of Christ without the suffering could not have been redemptive, nor the suffering without the action reconciling. . . . Redemption cannot be ascribed to the active obedience alone, nor reconciliation to the passive obedience alone, but both to both."[67] Schillebeeckx puts it suggestively when he says, "Jesus' whole life is the hermeneusis of his death."[68]

b. Objective and subjective.

We have seen clearly enough that the only theories that do justice to Christian experience are those "exemplarist" theories which interpret the cross as the outpouring of divine love to win us back to God. Even a theory such as Denney's that strives to establish an "objective" atonement conforms ultimately to the exemplarist model. Even Calvin has affinities with it. But exemplarist theories have been pilloried for being merely subjective and seeming to make salvation depend on the human response. Theologians have hankered for a guaranteed, objective atonement, prior to and apart from the penitence and faith of human beings. In that case one could propose the hypothesis: What if this supposed atonement failed to meet with faith from a single person, the cross ignored and forgotten? Would the atonement still stand? Obviously not, for no one would have been reconciled (at-oned) by it. The postulating of such an "objective" atonement, and the disparaging of exemplarist views as "merely subjective," must be rejected as the product of false consciousness. Schleiermacher is right to condemn as "magical" any doctrine of the atonement that makes "the impartation of his blessedness independent of assumption into vital fellowship with him", and to claim that "the total obedience . . . of Christ avails for our advantage only in so far as through it our assumption into vital fellowship with him is brought about".[69] Any theory of the atonement that rests all on the once and for all work of the cross to the neglect of the resurrection and the work of the Holy Spirit in the church is patently inadequate. Ritschl speaks with Luther of the justification of *the community.* Our assurance of forgiveness and our membership of the Christian community are "identical". "Only on the understanding that these are equivalents is it possible to establish the necessity of the connection asserted between the forgiveness of sins and the personal life of Christ, particularly the completion of his life in his sacrificial death."[70] As Bultmann puts it, we have "to make the cross of Christ our own". When we do, we bring to realisation the vicarious humanity of the one who identified himself with our sinful condition in order that we might become identified with the righteousness of God through our union with him by faith and sacrament (cf. 2 Cor. 5:21).

If we are doing theology within the church, we must take the eucharist, and ultimately the Last Supper, as the paradigm of atonement. At the Last Supper, celebrated by Jesus' design at the Passover season, an inextricable connection was established between the death of Jesus—an inevitable death—and the salvation of his people.[71] Bread was first offered to God and then given to men: that bread was the symbol of Jesus' body and his body the symbol of his sacrifice. In the eucharist we make Christ's offering of himself our own—a sacrifice of perfect conformity to God's will,[72] one that we cannot make for ourselves. And we receive back, under the symbols of bread and wine in our outstretched hands, the forgiveness of our sins and "all other benefits of his passion". The tokens of redeeming love are pledges of the unitive vision of God that we expect in hope.

Christ as *human* makes the perfect offering of humanity to God. His humanity is vicarious because we are incorporated in him by faith and sacrament. Christ as *God* brings into our midst the love that knows no bounds and suffers any cost. It is the knowledge of that love, as it is revealed supremely in the cross, that moves us to respond in penitence and faith by offering ourselves to be reconciled to God in union with that "full perfect and sufficient sacrifice, oblation and satisfaction, for the sins of the whole world". "In his suffering unto death," writes Schleiermacher, "there is manifested to us an absolutely self-denying love; and in this there is represented to us with perfect vividness the way in which God was in him to reconcile the world to himself."[73]

Through the Holy Spirit we are united to Christ and to one another in his body the church. In these moments of offering and receiving we discover the Spirit in our midst as the one who makes present and efficacious for our salvation the Christ who, in offering himself to the world on behalf of God, offered the world to God in himself. The Holy Spirit is the power of our participation in the person and work of Jesus Christ. By bringing the church into being through word and sacrament, the Spirit makes the atonement a reality.

NOTES

1. Cf. Paul D. L. Avis, "Fundamental Theology", in idem, ed., *Threshold of Theology* (Basingstoke, Eng.: Marshall Pickering, 1988).

2. Wolfhart Pannenberg, *Jesus—God and Man* (London: SCM Press, 1968), 264ff.

3. Cf. Paul D. L. Avis, *Theology and the Human World* (forthcoming).

4. Gustaf Aulén, *Christus Victor* (London: SPCK, 1970), 147.

5. In E. G. Selwyn, ed., *Essays Catholic and Critical* (London, 1926).

6. William Temple, *Christus Veritas* (London, 1924), 260.

7. Emil Brunner, *The Mediator* (London, 1934), 443–80.

8. Jacques Pohier, *God—In Fragments* (New York: Crossroad, 1986), 200.

9. In Selwyn, *Essays Catholic and Critical,* 263.

10. Brunner, *The Mediator,* 447.

11. Cf. Robert S. Franks, *A History of the Doctrine of the Work of Christ in Its Ecclesiastical Development* (London: Hodder & Stoughton, n.d.), 2:53ff.

12. Edward Schillebeeckx, *Jesus: An Experiment in Christology* (London: William Collins & Co., 1979), 306, 311, 152; cf. Pannenberg, *Jesus—God and Man,* 227ff.

13. Pohier, *God—In Fragments,* 237.

14. Edward Schillebeeckx, *Christ: The Christian Experience in the Modern World* (London: SCM Press, 1980), 833.

15. F. D. Maurice, *The Doctrine of Sacrifice* (London, 1879), 120ff., 148ff.

16. Paul Tillich, *Systematic Theology,* 3 vols. in 1 (Chicago: University of Chicago Press, 1967), 2:191ff.

17. J. C. Fenton, "Salvation," in Alan Richardson and John Bowden, eds., *A New Dictionary of Christian Theology* (London: SCM Press, 1983).

18. Hans Küng, *On Being a Christian* (London: William Collins & Co., 1977), 424.

19. Cf. Walter Kasper, *Jesus the Christ* (Tunbridge Wells, Eng.: Burns & Oates, 1976), 119.

20. Aulén's work dates from 1930 and was translated into English already in 1931.

21. John Macquarrie, *Principles of Christian Theology,* rev. ed. (London: SCM Press, 1977), 325.

22. Colin Gunton, *"Christus Victor* Revisited: A Study in Metaphor and the Transformation of Meaning", *Journal of Theological Studies* n.s. 36 (1985): 129–45.

23. H. P. Owen, *Christian Theism: A Study in Its Basic Principles* (Edinburgh: T. & T. Clark, 1984), 100f.

24. Küng, *On Being a Christian,* 423.

25. Cf. P. T. Forsyth, *The Work of Christ* (London, 1938), 57.

26. Frederick W. Dillistone, *The Christian Understanding of Atonement* (London: James Nisbet & Co., 1968), 214f.

27. John Calvin, *Gospel According to St John,* ed. David W. and Thomas F. Torrance; trans. T. H. L. Parker (Edinburgh: Oliver & Boyd, 1959), 1:74.

28. Brunner, *The Mediator,* 482.

29. James Denney, *The Death of Christ,* including *The Atonement and the Modern Mind* (London, 1911), 304.

30. Ibid., 294.

31. Ibid., 305f.

32. Ibid., 271f.

33. Ibid., 293.

34. Elizabeth Moberly, *Suffering: Innocent and Guilty* (London: SPCK, 1978), 23ff.

35. In Selwyn, *Essays Catholic and Critical,* 255, 258f.

36. Oliver C. Quick, *The Gospel of the New World: A Study in the Christian Doctrine of Atonement* (London: James Nisbet & Co., 1944), 89.

37. Brunner, *The Mediator,* 453 (my emphasis); cf. 523.

38. R. W. Dale, *The Atonement.* Quotations are from the 1900 edition.

39. Jowett's essay was written in 1855 and revised in 1859. Quotations are from Benjamin Jowett, *Theological Essays* (London, 1906).

40. Quotations are from the reissue, F. D. Maurice, *Theological Essays* (London: James Clarke & Co., 1957).

41. Maurice, *The Doctrine of Sacrifice.* Quotations are from the 1879 edition.

42. Aulén, *Christus Victor,* 11, and a footnote on p. 4.

43. Charles Gore, *The Reconstruction of Belief* (London, 1926).

44. R. C. Moberly, *Atonement and Personality* (London, 1901).

45. Hastings Rashdall, *The Idea of Atonement in Christian Theology* (London, 1919).

46. Hastings Rashdall, "Dr. Moberly's Theory of the Atonement", *Journal of Theological Studies* 3 (1902):178–211.

47. Ibid., 187.

48. Macquarrie, *Principles of Christian Theology,* 258.

49. Rashdall, "Dr. Moberly's Theory", 200f.

50. J. K. Mozley, *The Doctrine of the Atonement* (London, 1915), 196.

51. Herbert A. Hodges, *The Pattern of Atonement* (London: SCM Press, 1955), 57.

52. Rashdall, "Dr. Moberly's Theory", 211.

53. William Temple, *Christus Veritas* (London, 1924).

54. Rashdall, "Dr. Moberly's Theory", 193.

55. Ibid., 178.

56. *Doctrine in the Church of England* (London), 16f.

57. Friedrich Schleiermacher, *The Christian Faith,* trans. H. R. Mackintosh (Edinburgh, 1928), 361 and 431.

58. Schillebeeckx, *Christ,* 790.

59. Quick, *The Gospel of the New World,* 97, 111.

60. Cf. Paul D. L. Avis, *The Methods of Modern Theology* (Basingstoke, Eng.: Marshall, Pickering, 1986), 225.

61. Avis, *The Methods of Modern Theology,* 62ff.

62. Schillebeeckx, *Jesus,* 153.

63. Schillebeeckx, *Christ,* 838.

64. Dietrich Bonhoeffer, *Christology* (London: William Collins Sons, 1971), 40.

65. Denney, *The Death of Christ,* 230.

66. Tillich, *Systematic Theology,* 2:141.

67. Schleiermacher, *The Christian Faith,* 453.

68. Schillebeeckx, *Jesus,* 311.

69. Schleiermacher, *The Christian Faith,* 435, 456.

70. Albrecht Ritschl, *Justification and Reconciliation* (Edinburgh, 1900), 543ff., 550f.

71. Cf. Martin Hengel, *The Atonement: Origins of the Doctrine in the New Testament* (London: SCM Press, 1981), 65.

72. Cf. Schleiermacher, *The Christian Faith*, 456.

73. Schleiermacher, *The Christian Faith*, 458.

7

THE HOLY SPIRIT: SCRIPTURE, TRADITION, AND INTERPRETATION

DAVID N. POWER

I. GORE'S CONTRIBUTION

When Charles Gore wrote the essay on "The Holy Spirit and Inspiration" for *Lux Mundi,* he wished, in the climate of the advances made by liberal theology, to uphold the revelatory character of the Scriptures and to take the authority of the Catholic Church, with its episcopacy and liturgy, as the norm for the interpretation of the Scriptures. The two enemies that he had in mind were liberal theology's reduction of Christian revelation to moral sensitivity and Roman Catholic authoritarianism.

In harmony with the cultural Kantian turn to the subject, the theology of the time centered on religious experience. Its scientific interest lay in treating the Scriptures with the tools of historical criticism, taking account of the varied historical circumstances affecting the origin of the Scriptures and the work of their human authors. Gore's schema for safeguarding both the revelation of the Scriptures and the authority of the church arose from the connection that he posited between religious experience and the action of the Holy Spirit. Behind the Scriptures he saw a religious experience, which he identified with their inspiration. The culmination of human religious experience, for Gore, lay in the disciples' experience of Jesus Christ as Divine Revealer, and it was this that he found brought to expression in the New Testament. Because of their foundation in religious experience, he happily quoted the words of St. Athanasius that described the Scriptures as "a sacred school for all the world of knowledge of God and of spiritual life".[1]

With this foundation, Gore could both treat the Scriptures as historical documents, differentiating between kinds of literature and a diversity of authors, and uphold their inspired authority. There was no need to subscribe to the theory of the exact dictation of words, which he identified as the Roman Catholic position, for the criterion of inspiration could be located in the sensitivity to God and to the things of God, and to the action of God in Israelite history and in Jesus Christ, which one found in the books of the Scriptures. Furthermore, he could affirm that since the same Spirit who inspired the Scriptures abides in the church of Christ, with its episcopacy and sacrament, this assures their interpretation by the church in the same sense in which they were written. Hence, without having to retreat from the accomplishments of historical criticism, Gore could attribute both the authority of the Bible and the authority of its interpretation by the church to the Holy Spirit.

In his understanding of the church's role in interpreting the Scriptures, Gore's adherence to the important role of the episcopacy went hand in hand with a theology of baptism and a theology of creation that affirmed the primacy of the religious experience that was the work of the Holy Spirit. The authority of the episcopacy had to be exercised in tandem with the contribution that all the members of the baptized fellowship make to the interpretation of the Scriptures and with sensitivity to the action of the Holy Spirit in the entire work of creation. The episcopacy was not to be allowed to suppress the religious experience of the baptized, and the action of the Spirit in historical event was not to be allowed to let its action in the works of creation go unheeded.

The questions facing a theology of the Holy Spirit today are, in some respects, remarkably similar to those facing Gore a century ago. Some of the answers given to questions about Scripture and its interpretation by the church show a comparable concern with the proper use of historical criticism, with the location of the work of the Spirit in the church, with the church's nature as a communion or fellowship, and with humanity's communion with all the works of creation. Despite the similarity, however, the questions formulated and the appeal to experience have been rather radically transformed, as the need for a more critical appropriation of experience emerges and affects both the reading of the Bible and the estimation of its normative interpretation.

II. THE APPEAL TO EXPERIENCE

While contemporary theology continues to appeal to the experience of the Spirit in order to resolve the relationship between the authority of the Scriptures and their interpretation by the church, the meaning and the weight given to experience are not uniform. Discussing current positions on the place of the Scriptures in the life of the church, Avery Dulles has remarked: "Many tend to define revelation, as did Schleiermacher and liberal protestants, in terms of experience of the transcendent."[2] Dulles then goes on to cite what he sees as two typical examples of this appeal, the one Protestant and the other Catholic. He describes Schubert Ogden as one who holds that the ultimate sources of religious authority are the specifically Christian experience of God in Jesus Christ and the universally known human experience found in human existence as such. He then describes Edward Schillebeeckx as one who speaks of two sources of theology, the one being the traditional experience of "the great Jewish-Christian movement", the other contemporary human experience, common to both Christian and non-Christian.[3] On such a basis, the correlation between the Scriptures and an understanding of experience is the work of theology, and the way whereby to decide what teaching the Scriptures transmit to the church, and how faithful the church is to them.

Coincidental with this attention to experience in the transmission and interpretation of the Scriptures is a broader attention to experience among Western theologians in filling the void left in Western church tradition by a relative neglect of reflection on the Holy Spirit. The apparent Pentecostal renewal, with its flowering of gifts of service and ministry, has had a part to play in this, as had the accompanying attention to the need for a discernment of spirits.

At the beginning of his three-volume work on the Holy Spirit, Yves Congar describes experience of the Spirit as the perception of the reality of God coming to us, active in us and through us, drawing us into a divine communion, a friendship, an existence of one for the other.[4] Among the signs of this presence, Congar lists the fruits of the Spirit enumerated in Gal. 5:22. Throughout the three volumes, he continually writes of the action of the Spirit in the liturgy, in mystical experience, in the gifts that build up the believing community, and of their more recent manifestations in the Pentecostal movement.

Other authors have attempted a more philosophical or phenomenological analysis of this experience of the transcendent God. For example, the category of experience is so fundamental to all of Karl Rahner's theology that it is sometimes referred to as a mystagogia. Writing in particular of the Holy Spirit, he states:

Spiritual experience . . . means that God, through his self-communication ("uncreated grace"), becomes always and everywhere in grace a co-constitutive principle of the human spirit in its transcendence. . . . This transcendental experience of the radical quality of the Spirit as a result of the self-communication of God is mediated by a categorial object, because the finite spiritual nature of man only comes to awareness of itself by coming to rest in another, and it may be remarked in passing that this other is always ultimately personal.[5]

For Rahner, this radical personal presence of God to the human person in the mission of the Holy Spirit is at the root of all graced human activity, individual and collective. He was able to approach every distinct theological issue, whether it was grace, the church, the sacraments or inspiration, from the starting point of God's self-communication, brought about in the twofold mission of Word and Spirit. Human activity being an activity in the world, and in communion with the world, there are cosmic as well as personalist aspects to Rahner's theology, and these are evident in his writing on the Holy Spirit.

For other writers, however, this kind of transcendental analysis remains too abstract. Protestant and Catholic theologians alike have attempted a phenomenology of human experience which points to the ways in which it is disclosive of the divine or transcendent. Such a phenomenology of common human experience often isolates what are termed limit experiences or limit situations, the most obvious of which is confrontation with death. In these experiences, human beings are said to realize the boundaries of their own existence and the need for a ground of being to all finite existence. This analysis of common human experience can then be put in correlation with what is known through a historical and hermeneutical approach to the Scriptures and to the other sources of our knowledge of the Christian tradition.[6]

Proponents of a political theology find a lack in both Rahner's transcendental analysis and this type of analysis of limit experience.[7] Granted the advantage of the turn to the subject, both appear to remain too abstract or general in their considerations, and, at least in the case of transcendental analysis, too accepting of an unproblematic originating experience of the question about God. Political theology demands consideration of the concrete social and historical subject rather than

DAVID N. POWER

of some generic subject. Instead of working from an unproblematic originating experience, it turns to the prereligious questions and conflicts that besiege the human community in its concrete existence, asking how religious language and the affirmation of God's action in Christ and in the church relate to these.

For political theology, it is inadequate to work from conceptualizations of experience. Instead, one has to attend to the imperatives of conversion that are known through the appropriation of human consciousness and to those that echo in the proclamation of the gospel.[8] Indeed, as some see it, contemporary human experience when considered in all of its concrete reality reveals, not a humanity already before God, but a humanity torn apart by multiple alienations. These are inclusive not only of strife, struggle and oppression within human society but even of a basic and radical alienation from the rest of creation and from the earth that humanity inhabits. Such awareness calls for a profound personal, social, cultural, economic, ecological and political conversion, which can be brought about only through the practice of a profound commitment to a vision and a hope that is able to integrate all of these factors. Attentiveness to concrete human experience and to the call to conversion requires, above all, attention to the history of suffering, to the suppression of persons and voices in the enactment of human events and the pursuit of goals, and to the exploitation of the earth.

The correlation with Christian tradition then becomes the evocation of a dangerous memory, in which the memory of Christ's passion becomes inclusive of the memory of all suffering. The eschatological judgment and expectation that is expressed in Christ's Passover signals the possibility of overcoming all alienation, a possibility that has to be embodied in the practical commitment of the church to the cause of the poor and oppressed. It is from the vantage point of such a commitment that the presence and action of the Holy Spirit can be discerned and understood and that the freedom of the Spirit becomes a practical reality. For political theology, in its various forms, the rooting of a theology of the Holy Spirit in experience has taken a very concrete turn. It allies it with emancipatory praxis and finds therein the primary evidence of the gift of the Spirit. This has to have an effect on the way in which it is possible to understand the authority of the Scriptures, their normativity for the life of the church and their interpretation by it.

156

III. THE HOLY SPIRIT AND THE
SCRIPTURES

What has been reviewed thus far are various approaches to the connection between experience and the theology of the Holy Spirit. It is now necessary to ask how all of this affects the ways of understanding the origins and interpretation of the Scriptures.[9]

For one thing, current positions on the inspiration of the Scriptures are far from the psychologizing explanations that dogged earlier investigations. Already in a neo-orthodox theology, the inspiration of the Scriptures is linked with the presence of the Holy Spirit in the church. Though some would dispute the interpretation, David Kelsey has paraphrased Karl Barth's view of inspiration as "the promise of God and the Holy Spirit to be present among the faithful when these writings are used in the common life of the church".[10] All discussions of experience, in short, have to have repercussions on the understanding of the doctrinal axiom that the Spirit has spoken through the prophets and inspired the Scriptures.

There are those who take Scripture as the primary witness to the apostolic kerygma and hence as the way whereby to arrive at the historical Jesus, who is the norm of all belief. This allows inclusion of greater attention to his teaching and ministry along with remembrance of his death and resurrection. It also allows for differentiation between the several communities and traditions to whose milieu the composition of the various parts or books of the Scriptures are ascribed, and consequently between the several Christologies already apparent in New Testament times. In relation to the current life of the church, this approach has the advantage that it offers grounds in the Bible itself for a cultural diversity of religious expression within the one catholic fellowship.

There are those, however, who feel that the methods of historical criticism and historical reconstruction are inadequate. They offer much information about the formation of the Scriptures and about canonical selection, but their results are tentative and allow little for synchrony. Hence, various attempts are made to take the Scriptures as text, already distanced from its formative history and from the experiences in which its parts originated. The findings of historical critical method are kept, but they are subordinated to a reading of the Scriptures as text. In this case, their appropriation has more to do with current ethical options, and with the current historical experience, than it does with the discovery of the original experience behind the formation of the texts. It can be understood through a phenomenology of universal experience and of particular historical experience, or even through a correlation with fundamental ontological questions, but it does not depend on a retrieval of some originating experience.

In all such attempts as those here recorded, the Bible is taken as the book of the church, in whose formation and interpretation the community of faith has a vital part. This differs from positions that would see the Bible as a written word that stands distinct from the life of the church or that came into being independently of a community of faith.

One school of thought is that of canonical criticism, which turns its attention to the final canonical collection rather than to the formation of texts in themselves.[11] The determination of the canon is seen as an act whereby the community of faith set for itself the boundaries of belief and of ecclesial identity, so that it is to the canon of the Scriptures that subsequent ages give normative value in the development of tradition. Among writers pursuing a canonical interpretation, positions differ on the relation of the Bible to other early church writings. For the more traditional, the books of the Bible constitute the only inspired books, in the sense that they possess a value and an authentic expression of Christian faith that cannot be found in other writings. For others, the setting of the canon is a concrete historical judgment that locates in these works all that is necessary to the foundations of Christian faith. Other works might equally well have been included, but their inclusion was not necessary to the church. In this latter case, some expansion or some future delimiting of the canon is always a possibility. In taking the Bible as canon, one does not necessarily exclude the possibility of more convincing expressions of Christian truth, but none of these have been given canonical normativity by the church. David Tracy uses the vocabulary of *classic* to express this, calling the Scriptures "the classic judging and transforming all other classics".[12]

Taking the Scriptures as text entails giving priority to word over the reconstruction of any originating experience. It is the event come to language and formulated as text that passes into tradition in its most accessible way. This means that one looks to word for the offer of the possibilities of personal and social transformation and action, though explanations of the precise conjunction between word and action may differ. Through literary analysis and hermeneutical method, what is explored in reading the text is the relation between language and event, between language and meaning, and between language and being. The power of language, its donative character, obliges the reader or the hearer to be attentive to the being which it discloses, not treating it simply as a tool which human beings use to express their feelings, thoughts and convictions. Not only humanity's social and personal existence but even its communion with the whole of creation is expressed and formed through language and its appropriation. It is not primarily to propositional, technical or conceptual forms of speech that one listens for the revelation of being, but to poetic language. In the words of Paul Ricoeur,

> Poetic language alone restores to us that participation-in or belonging-to an order of things which precedes our capacity to oppose ourselves to things taken as objects opposed to a subject. Hence the function of poetic discourse is to bring about this emergence of a depth-structure of belonging-to amid the ruins of descriptive discourse.[13]

This is to say that poetic discourse is the language of participation, of humankind's oneness with all reality and with the ground of reality. It is not therefore the language of a spectator or of a technician. Any reflection by which a thinker stands apart from participation in being and in action has to be grounded in this kind of language and continually related back to it. Poetic discourse does indeed originate in some kind of experience of participation, but it posits distance from this through an expression of meaning that allows for the sharing of a world with others. Hence, the reading of a text and its interpretation do not depend on the ability to reconstruct an original experience, behind the text, but on being attentive to the world, or the mode of being, opened up in front of the text, and on the ability to appropriate this meaning into one's own existence. Appropriation is not automatic, since it requires an ongoing development of consciousness and freedom from the various kinds of alienation that inhibit authentic existence.

When developed as a scriptural hermeneutic, this literary attention to the text and to its world postulates convergence between the testimony given in the word and the testimony given in the hearts of believers by the Holy Spirit. It is the Spirit who frees the heart from alienation, who inspires right action, and who alerts believers to their fundamental participation in the order of things.

Ironically, the very attentiveness to language and text has led in some cases to a disillusionment with language, which only adds to the disillusionments felt with the achievements of historical reconstruction. It is said that what is meaningful in one situation is not so in another, or that the suppositions about God, the world, and humanity that are found in the Bible, for example, are inadequate to the project of unity and liberation that faces humankind in the postmodern world. Indeed, some feel that if authority is given to the Bible and to its authoritative ecclesial interpretations, the church will simply continue to absorb past ideologies and to impose these, in one way or another, upon successive generations.

One does not have to go outside the community of faith, and of those who continue to have resort to the Bible as "Word of God", to find suspicion of its ideological and potentially alienating impact. Coupled with emancipatory interest and emancipatory action, doubt about the Scriptures, their authority and their meaning, gives rise to the critique of patriarchy in feminist hermeneutics and feminist ecclesiology.[14] The whole of church tradition, beginning with the authorship of the Scriptures, is found to be distorted by use of an androcentric paradigm. Communication within the living church is equally distorted by the maintenance of androcentric structures that function in the exercise of church authority and ritual. Liberation requires a reconstruction of church structure, and a historical reconstruction of the originating Jesus movement. This is not so much revealed as veiled in the canonical Scriptures, so that feminists are interested in the compilation of a canon of writings, distinct from the Bible, in which the emancipatory interest of women-church is given expression.

Feminist hermeneutics, in its various forms, appears to maintain an interest both in historical reconstruction and in the power of language as such. Feminist interpretation uses the methods of historical reconstruction to discover an experience of God and of Christ behind the text of the Scriptures, but it is not so much the experience to which they directly give expression that is sought as that which the patriarchy that engulfs the Scriptures succeeds in hiding and distorting. At the same time, the interest in paradigmatic expression indicates a belief in the power of language, as well as the trust that there are forms of speech or discourse that communicate an authentic emancipation or freedom. In any case, the criterion for judging the veracity of interpretation or the emancipatory power of language does not lie in the success of interpretative methods as such but in the promotion of the emancipatory interest and commitment of women-church. For this reason, the Bible does not serve as an archetype for Christian experience or as a classic that judges all classics. It is, rather, a prototype in which one finds the signs of conflict between the emancipatory message of Jesus or of Old Testament events, on the one hand, and the oppressive measures of patriarchal culture, on the other. Whether the interpreter looks for the authentic originating experience or for the power of a language that frees, it is clear that the criterion of truth lies not in the text as text but in the emancipatory praxis of the community. Since language, however, must always function in the service of this freedom, memories are revived and stories are retold and images of speech are reborn. An important factor in this rebirth of discourse, coupled with emancipatory praxis, is the new naming of Spirit that reveals her activity in emancipatory praxis. Fundamentally, a theology of the Holy Spirit is grounded in the experience of the conflict between freedom and oppression, as these are known in the various ways in which they come to expression. This location of the Spirit in emancipatory praxis is more fundamental and authentic than an attribution of the Scriptures to the inspiration of the Spirit.

Though there are considerable differences between the positions on revelation and on the use of the Scriptures in theology that have been here described, it is possible to point to a quite common trend. This is the trend to locate the power and action of the Spirit at the juncture between experience and the interpretation of the biblical tradition. With an increasing interest in emancipatory praxis, this has to play a part in the unfolding of that relation. Moreover, the contours of language and discourse are more carefully examined, in lieu of a more abstract quest for ideas, concepts or messages, and these are seen to have a profound impact on meaning. By and large, one could say that the process of interpretation is itself a pneuma-praxis, based on the persuasion of the role of the Spirit in the originating events, in their initial communication, in the action of the interpreting community, and in the interpretation itself. This can be quite compatible with the persuasion that alienating distortions occur both in the original expression and in the ongoing interpretation, so that criteria of discernment are necessary. It is from pneuma-praxis that a reflective pneumatology would need to be developed. A pneuma-conscious hermeneutics, however, cannot be developed without a pneuma-conscious ecclesiology.

IV. SPIRIT AND CHURCH

As theories of inspiration and hermeneutical methods appeal to experience, and as the Scriptures are spoken of as the canon of the church, the more important it becomes to see how this relates to a theology of church. Rather than confine the role of the church to the formulation of propositional statements, it is necessary to see the transmission and interpretation of the Christian faith within the total context of church life. For that reason, writers look to the role and effects of mystical experience, of liturgical assembly, of missionary action, of practical commitments, and of Pentecostal phenomena. They associate all of these with the power of the Holy Spirit operative in the community of faith, giving rise to a Spirit-conscious church as context for hermeneutics and praxis.

The church is a community and discipleship that gives witness in the world to the coming of God's rule, through the power of the Spirit of the risen Christ. The gifts of the Spirit that abound in the community do not need to be explained through their psychological effects, but they can be discerned through attending to the consciousness and intentionality of persons who have been converted through the belief that in the resurrection of Christ a new horizon opens up to human history. The church looks back in memory to the ministry and Passover of Jesus Christ, and from this derives the hope of the eschaton and of full human freedom in the love of God. It is called to be a prophetic body, and more and more it is becoming clear that communities of faith have to be praxis-oriented, having a critical role in society in favor of greater human mutuality and of a freedom in love in which the fundamental equality of persons is recognized.

From the call to exercise a critical role in society, there follows the demand on the church to be self-critical, to revise its own horizons and positions and its public stance on human issues. From the general awareness that the church is always both holy and sinful, there follows the need for a continual conversion that can integrate into the love of God all that is called for in the human enterprise, inclusive of economic, political, social and ecological factors. All of this constitutes the Spirit-filled context and action within which the Christian tradition is interpreted and oriented to practice.

The liturgical assembly has long been recognized as a privileged locus in which the Scriptures are proclaimed, transmitted and interpreted.

Present considerations require a sensitive reconsideration of how this comes about, since the church's worship is so highly affected by ritual and institutional structure and office. The authority given to the bishops to officiate at liturgy goes hand in hand with the authority given to them to interpret. While the role of ordained ministry in the church is affirmed, it would be a mishandling of the doctrine of the Spirit simply to conclude to a *de iure divino* justification of given forms of church office, without relating them to other manifestations of the Spirit in the church. This would be a violation of the consciousness that the Spirit's activity is present in all and that it has an eschatological character.[15] It is in the power of the Spirit that God's word is heard anew, that the resurrection of Christ is newly perceived as the promise of humanity's release in Christ's death from the ultimate alienation of death. It is in this power that Christian faith is handed on and newly interpreted, integrated into historical and cultural, and even into political, settings through symbolic mediation and practice. It is within the horizon of hope and memory that charisms flourish and provide the grounds on which church office is established and renewed. Because the perceptions, interpretations and symbolic mediations of meaning cannot be mapped or planned on a straight line, charisms cannot be discerned or judged on the pure assumption of the juridical continuity of office or official forms of ministry. On the contrary, the renewal of office, both in action and in form, has to be submitted to the criterion of the presence of charism. In allowing for future developments in church office, the past is remembered not only for the model of its juridical forms but, even more important, for the manifestation of its charismatic action.

Naturally, those who are most critical of the ideologies inherent in church statement and church structure, such as feminist writers, are the most critical of given official models and the most open to alternative forms of ministry. The way in which the church reshapes its structures is part of its living interpretation of the Christian fact. It is an enterprise in which the renaming of the Spirit and the reformation of church structure go together, the trend today being toward greater mutuality within the body than is allowed for by rigidly male and hierarchical structures.

V. SPIRIT, LITURGY, INTERPRETATION

Because of the place assigned to liturgy in the transmission and interpretation of the Christian faith, a special word needs to be said on

163

this score. Despite the simple-sounding tag, *Lex orandi, lex credendi,* the examination of liturgical texts and ritual is quite complex. To develop criteria necessary for the evaluation of any particular liturgical tradition, one has to attend both to the nature of liturgical language and to its distortions.

In the first place, consideration needs to be given to the relation between liturgy and culture. While faith is given expression in liturgy, it also has to be borne in mind that liturgical expression mediates between the community of faith and the surrounding culture. Not only does it take up images, rituals and stories of the faith tradition but it also assimilates experiences and symbols of the surrounding culture.

In the second place, one needs to recognize that in this very process there can be a distortion of language and its meaning, especially in the ways in which liturgy is affected by cosmic imagery and the images of power which it adopts from culture and cultural institutions.

Three criteria can be used in evaluating liturgical expression and its role in transmitting and interpreting the faith tradition. The first of these criteria pertains to the fullness of language. How well, it can be asked, does a rite keep alive the different forms of discourse that originate in the biblical works and that properly belong in worship? Narrative, parable, wisdom and prophetic forms, thanksgiving, lamentation and intercession are outstanding forms of liturgical expression, which cannot afford to be stifled in celebration without detriment to faith and interaction. The second criterion has to do with adequacy to experience as formed by culture. How do liturgical formulation and celebration relate to the dominant culture, not necessarily to affirm its values but certainly in a way that commands attention? Are Christians enabled through liturgy to see their identity as Christians in relation to their cultural identity, or does the liturgy represent a world that has little to do with all else that pertains to the common experience? The third criterion for the evaluation of a liturgical tradition is that of celebration's relation to the orthopraxis of gospel freedom and the solidarity of the community with the suffering. Worship is not so self-contained that it can guarantee its own truth, if by truth we understand that which leads through conversion to communion with God. What it represents is the living memory of Jesus Christ and his presence in community and world through the action of the Holy Spirit. The ethical values which it fosters are a necessary part of this representation. If therefore the ethical implications are dimmed by celebration and appear to be unassimilated by community members, one has to query the liturgy's effectiveness in expressing and transmitting the faith of the scriptural tradition.

For any hermeneutic that is adopted in the interest of retrieving Christian mutuality in place of hierarchical inequality, and especially for women-church in the struggle against patriarchy, the development of alternative structures and of alternative liturgies is part of the hermeneutical enterprise. These may actually be generated by a collective and creative memory that is expansive in its recall of the Christian past. Going outside the biblical canon or outside the formal liturgical canon for common memories is a factor in this creativity. How God is named, how the Spirit is named, how Christ is imaged, of whom memories are kept, what interaction is fostered between the members—are all affected by the sources in which memory is sought. While such initiatives must certainly in turn be subjected to critical discernment, they keep the church in mind of the fact that God's grace may be hindered by institutional factors and by ideologies absorbed into the life of the church. They also point to fresh possibilities of being church. As such, they are to be seen as an important effect of the action of the Spirit in the transmission and interpretation of the Christian tradition and in the shaping of believing communities.

VI. THE POWER OF THE WORD

In the midst of the questions raised by emancipatory interest about the authority of the Scriptures and their ecclesial interpretation, theology must still ask how the Christ-event is brought to expression in such a way that it mediates its grace to humankind. Questions about the authority of the Bible have to be met, even while affirming the power of God's Word. Perhaps the difficulties are met by a twofold move. First, one can go from suspicion about the use of language and the cultural institutionalizations of a living tradition to an attentiveness to that in language which, even in the midst of distortions, continues to question present existence and its presuppositions. There are features in language use that unmask the value conflicts that appear in the writing of texts. To the extent that these value conflicts are made apparent, the text can still show the power that an event brought to speech has to reshape reality. When the event in question is that of a divine action in human history, those features of speech or discourse which unmask conflicts show how the action questions and challenges humanity and manifests the hope of that which lies beyond humanity's own power to achieve. Just what those features of discourse are requires continued and refined sensitivity to the force of metaphor and to all the forms of discourse that in literary texts intersect and interact among themselves, so as to raise fundamental issues about belief in God and the desire for salvation from evil.

Because we are dealing with language's power to address human persons in such a way as to raise fundamental faith questions, hermeneutical method also has to make the move to a better understanding of the human subject, personal and collective. Thus it can show how language and its message are appropriated, how it is allied to emancipatory praxis, and what it unveils of the transformative dynamic that is inherent to the human and that needs to be set free by divine grace. Sensitivity to the power of discourse to challenge perspectives and raise fundamental questions, correlated with a refined knowledge of the human subject, offers a heuristic pattern of language, as it opens up to the community of faith the possibilities of grace that are given to humanity through the mediation of the originating event and experience of God's mercy in Jesus Christ. At the same time, because of the alliance between language expression and emancipatory praxis we are able to locate the action of the Spirit in the church as it testifies both to the event of Christ and to the presence of grace in human hearts.

The relation of biblical hermeneutics to general hermeneutics has to be recognized in this operation. The specificity of biblical discourse is that it points to events and, in the Christian tradition, to the one outstanding event of Jesus Christ, in which God's love and mysterious reality are revealed. With all human discourse, it shares the power to raise fundamental questions about human life and about humankind's being in the world, but it relates these questions to what has been manifested in Jesus Christ about humanity and about God.

Hubris would have us seek fulfillment through our own effort, or at least lay claim to the control of meaningful experience. It is on this account that distortions creep into language and cause it to sanction a variety of alienations in the human order or to distort the relation between humanity and the cosmic order. The manipulation of persons and of earth's resources goes hand in hand with a manipulation of language in the service of self-interest. The illusion that the human person can posit the origin and power of its own future can, in effect, be broken only by breaking the illusion that it is the point of origin of its own language and that it has complete control of its use. In the midst of the various distortions to which language is in its use subjected, one has to be able to hear the word that is not so much spoken by the human as spoken to it. Re-creative word does not so much break forth from the speaker as break forth in the speaker. It is rooted in a sense of the giftedness of the speaker's own being and of the giftedness of the existence which the speaker shares in communion with all being. In societies that are largely ordered by an interest in productive and technological capacities, or in those where priority is given to the rule of order, this kind of word is quite still. Yet there remain persons and places in whom or in which it continues to erupt, as it can also at times break through in the language of public order.

Since it carries within itself the conviction of a God-given regeneration and redemption, the Christian community distances itself from the forces of Enlightenment that place the hope of the future in humanity's own achievements. It is, however, prone to those inclinations which mask the power of the word about redemption by a desire for ordered knowledge or ordered existence. Hence the church itself is constantly challenged by the word of faith that is spoken by those who share the experience of oppression and suffering, and in that very suffering discover the hope of Christ's Passover. In attending to what is proclaimed from the Bible, or to what is celebrated in liturgy, or to what is passed on in tradition, the church needs to listen keenly for a word that speaks from a deeper experience of redemption than do the paradigmatic patterns of speech adopted from patriarchal, hierarchical or technological cultures.

Another way of putting this proposal is to say that the fundamental power of language, as it comes to speech in the Spirit, is united with emancipatory desire and praxis, each informing the other and testing the other. What is appropriated in faith from the discourse of Scripture, worship and tradition is the effort to be free, the promise of being gifted with freedom through God's grace, and the awareness of that communion which unites all persons and all creation in the wonder of this gift. In other words, what is appropriated is not so much propositional content as the use of those forms of language which free by disorienting and questioning and thus allow the imagination and hope of a fuller, even of a utopian, existence. Whatever power the patterns or paradigms of speech adopted from dominative cultures have to silence or misrepresent what is experienced in God's Spirit, this same Spirit gives

167

the power and the freedom to hear an alternative word. In the reading of or the listening to the Scriptures, and in the celebrating of the liturgy, a word can still emerge that unites with Christ and that arises from a consciousness of the gift of redemption, and that can be heard by those who are united through the Spirit in compassion and hope, even in the midst of suffering. Basing ourselves on this wager, a more technical analysis of the forms of speech that occur in Scripture and worship can be put to the service of hearing and understanding God's voice, speaking though it does in often flawed human speech. The emancipatory power of language itself, as it arises in, rather than from, those who share a deeper communion with Christ, or as it appears in the interplay of words, metaphors and forms, can alert us to the issues that lie beneath the value conflicts that are evident in biblical texts, in traditional ecclesiastical formulations, and in acts of common worship. It is by calling on human consciousness, and by appealing to the testimony of the Spirit in the human heart, that the word of Scripture and worship echoes the Word of God. That is why what is said or what is heard has to be tested over against the strength of a person's or a community's commitment to emancipatory praxis. For a better understanding of this, something more needs to be said about the emancipatory power of discourse, and then about the dynamic of the human subject to which word makes appeal.

VII. FORMS OF DISCOURSE

It is widely asserted, in hermeneutical theory and in theology, that the meaning and possibilities of human existence have to be brought to expression in narrative.[16] The inner coherence of human life, the meanings of existence which can be shared by many, the relation between past, present and future, emerge in story. In the Scriptures, of both the Hebrew and the Christian Bible, narrative is the fundamental form of discourse and shows the primacy of events in the redemptive action of God. It is the primary form in which event is brought to speech, so that its meaning and power can be transmitted. Since, however, it is clearly possible for narrative to be put to the service of ideological domination, one looks for the liberating force of biblical narrative in that twist of metaphorical usage which suggests a subversion of humankind's more common expectations of God and of divine order. That this is not immediately apparent is all too evident from the readings of the Scriptures that appear to confirm instinctual desires for clear propositions of truth and authoritative forms of government. These readings can come from the fact that we look to the Scriptures for knowledge and order, and so fail to attend to the niceties of language in which those value conflicts appear that appeal to the human heart and to that which is at the root of human existence. The Spirit within us calls upon us to listen with keener ears to the twist in the stories that subverts more surface interests and expectations, thus revealing unrealized but deeper possibilities of freedom and being. Such twists occur, for example, in the locating of victory over death in the death of the innocent, in the convergence of God's judgment on humankind with the judgment of the courts on Jesus, in the sending of a woman as apostle to those who, by reason of intimacy with Jesus and by reason of cultural supposition, thought of themselves as apostles, or in the way in which Jesus' judgments of people differ so evidently from the judgments made in virtue of the law.

Whatever the twist within the story, there is something about narrative that favors the common order, the established form of things, expectations of continuity, and authoritative interpretation. At any rate, it can easily be put to the service of these interests. It cannot therefore stand by itself, and hence attention has to be given in biblical hermeneutics to parables and eschatological sayings and to songs of lamentation as well as of blessing. These are forms of discourse that call on us to be attentive to the realities of human experience that cannot be captured in public order, or that are neglected by it, as they call on us to be aware of the disruptive and disorienting manner of God's presence in human history.

In looking back to redemptive events, the work of historical criticism certainly enhances the reading of the text. Nowadays, this is complemented by sociocritical methods that indicate society's or church's plausibility structures, so that the value conflicts that emerge when covenant or gospel is proclaimed become more evident to the reader. However, rather than depending on historical-critical methods to put us in touch with an originating event or experience, it would seem that the Christian community must recognize that it is attention to speech and to word that makes it harken to God's Word, since the power of an event is communicated necessarily through discourse. It is not necessary to be naive about the meaning of the expression "God's Word", as though it were necessary to identify a written or proclaimed text with divine speech in the same way in which one identifies a human word.

The term is analogous, indicating that God's redemptive power works in human lives and in human history through the convergence of the Spirit at work in the heart with that which in the flawed forms of human speech appeals to the heart and points to, or testifies to, the redemptive power of God at work in certain events that have been recorded for us.

Following out this explanation, one could adopt the distinction made between the Bible as archetype and the Bible as prototype.[17] It would be taken as archetype were one to glean from it a definite model of God, Christ or church that continued to serve unchanged in all subsequent developments of faith and practice. As prototype, it introduces us to the conflicts that emerge with the occurrence of revelatory events and with the proclamation of the gospel, and thus alerts us to the play of language within which value conflicts and meanings come to expression. The testimony of the Spirit, through the desire for God and for the freedom of God's gift that it inspires, complements the written and the spoken word and thus guides the church in the continuing process of interpretation that is allied with emancipatory praxis.

VIII. THE HUMAN SUBJECT

Placing the action of the Holy Spirit at the juncture between the interpretation of the Scriptures and emancipatory praxis involves some working understanding of the human subject. The following ten points are intended to summarize the direction that such an understanding takes.

1. Being stands forth in language, and it is only through language that the human person comes to conscious appropriation of human freedom and of participation in being. There is no access to the knowledge of things, just as there is no access to self-knowledge, except through language. While language serves discursive and practical purposes, its primary form is symbolic and representational. The language of poetry and the language of philosophy, or of philosophical theology, are complementary to each other and need to remain in dialectic.

2. Human existence is fundamentally intersubjective and participatory. It is related not only to contemporaries but also to forebears and descendants, not only to humans but also to the world of nature.

3. Human history is not experienced as an ordered sequence, in which causal relations between epochs and events are apparent. It is sensed to be simultaneously "discontinuous" and "connected". Narra-

tive and the institutions of civilizations attempt to express its meaning, beyond discontinuity and disruption, thus forging an awareness of being-in-time within some transcendental unity.

4. The concerns of participation and the quest for unity are expressed in the language of the Beginning and of the Beyond, and it is with this that the sense of the divine in relation to the human is connected. This is eloquently expressed by Eric Voegelin, from whom the following quotation is taken:

> Though the divine reality is one, its presence is experienced in the two modes of the Beyond and the Beginning. The Beyond is present in the immediate experience of the movements in the psyche; while the presence of the divine Beginning is mediated through the experience of the existence and intelligible structure of things in the cosmos. The two models require two different types of language for their adequate expression. The immediate presence in the movements of the soul requires the revelatory language of consciousness. This is the language of seeking, searching, and questioning, of ignorance and knowledge concerning the divine ground, of futility, absurdity, anxiety, and alienation of existence, of being moved to seek and question, of being drawn toward the ground, of turning around, of return, illumination and rebirth. The presence mediated by the existence and order of things in the cosmos requires the mythical language of a creator-God or Demiurge, of a divine force that creates, sustains, and preserves the order of things.[18]

These two kinds of language in fact run together, and are fused in the symbolism that expresses the divine presence, because it is in the events and experiences of history that take place within the cosmos that pneumatic consciousness develops as a participation in both Beyond and Beginning. Thus the sense of a personal divine presence and that of a cosmic presence intersect, necessarily go together and complete each other, even while running the risk of splitting off from each other or alternately being gobbled up, one by the other.

5. Participation in being, together with others and with cosmic forces, is fundamentally expressed and constituted through the kind of language that is called poetic and by that praxis which is fostered by the imagination that explores the possibilities of participation. Poetic language reveals the mythopoetic core of being, projects and breaks open the world in which humans belong and in which they find their own-most possibilities of being and action. Because of the double concern with Beyond and with Beginning, within poetic language the use of

171

metaphor is crucial, since it has the power to unite the two. In its appeal to the mythic image, metaphor can redescribe and reshape reality through a predication that unites the mythic quest with ordinary human experience and with the consciousness of a divine presence in the movements of the soul.

6. In appropriating the meaning and reference of poetic discourse, there is no appropriation without interpretation, no interpretation of text without self-interpretation, no self-understanding without dialogue, no grasp of the parts without a sense of the whole, and none of these without the verification of praxis.

7. The sense of being-toward-death that haunts the individual, and the puzzle of historical discontinuity that plagues generations, are positively retrieved and even reversed within the life of a community and within traditions that cross generations. The foundation of tradition is the narrative of historical events that distances the meaning of the event from its original historical circumstances and participants, and thus makes it accessible to future peoples, as it also frees the text itself from the original writer's intentions. This makes text and event available to an ongoing interpretation. As this is never disassociated from self-understanding, individual and common, interpretation is always open to an ongoing revision.

8. Interpretation and appropriation occur within the limits of human finitude, and are subject to the distortions of those who falsely seek to transcend these limits, with exorbitant claims to power and knowledge. Modesty is possible only to those who keep alive a sense of the need to receive from an Other, an awareness of dependence in all existence and doing, and a preunderstanding of the coincidence of the fullness of being with the infinitude of desire.

9. The tendency to close off further interpretation, together with the wish to build secure social and psychological structures for living, emerges in the solidification of myths and the fabrication of ideologies. Interpretation therefore has to have its underside of demythologization and demystification.

10. Cultural, military, economic, political and even ecclesiastical imperialisms build on the ideologization of structures of power. In breaking open the meaning of being and the possibilities of participating in ultimate reality, poetic language subverts imperialisms of every sort. By this same token it expresses the cry of victims and of those who continue

to yearn for true freedom and a communion founded on freedom. No human society that is attentive to this cry can totally suppress the emergence of a praxis that changes persons and structures in favor of a fuller realization of the potential for being. The locus for the fullest expression of God-given freedom and of humanity's communion with all of reality, in mutual enhancement, is the struggle against oppression, in the solidarity of desire and hope.

IX. THE SPIRIT AND THE ECONOMY
OF SALVATION

In Gore's essay in *Lux Mundi*, he could make a relatively simple connection between the experience of the Spirit, scriptural inspiration and scriptural interpretation. This correlation has become more complex because of critical approaches to language, to church structure, and to the biases of ecclesial interpretation. Since this involves a more critical understanding of human experience, it means greater difficulty in identifying God's Spirit within this experience. A good grasp of the hermeneutical process is in fact the avenue to a theology of the Spirit's role in the development of the Scriptures and their interpretation, and simultaneously in the work of salvation. It has been said in this essay that the power of the Spirit is made manifest at the point of conflict between oppressive and alienating forces on the one hand and the desire for freedom and wholeness on the other, and that this affects not only relations within the human community but also humanity's solidarity with the entire creation. Consciousness of the desire for freedom and wholeness, knowledge of the ways in which language brings this to expression, even within an otherwise prejudiced speech, and practical commitments that favor the oppressed and solidarity with creation are the critical elements in the interpretation of the Christian tradition. They are likewise the ways in which the power of God's Spirit is at work.

In effect, this approach makes possible a retrieval of the images and symbols of the Spirit that are found in Scripture and tradition, especially liturgical tradition. This point could be elaborated upon at length, but a few words will have to suffice, given the limits of the essay.

I would like to note three points from an essay on the Holy Spirit in Scripture.[19] First of all, the author notes that in both the Old and the New Testament the term "Spirit of God" has a rich and multiple significance:

Directly intending the imagery of wind or breath, it naturally carries such connotations as power, life, vitality, inspiration, etc. In the context of the religious experience of the Judeo-Christian tradition where the divine was experienced as highly transcendent (YHWH, God-Father), the multifaceted wind-breath imagery was quite suited to evoke the sense of divine power experienced within creation.[20]

Second, this author notes that rather than being portrayed as one with whom humanity enters into communion, the divine Pneuma is represented as that which internally constitutes the encounter with God and the communion of salvific realities. In a footnote, for example, he indicates:

> Divine *Pneuma* is experienced as so radically immanent that the New Testament does not tend to refer to *Pneuma* with the language of personal encounter (I-Thou) but it is rather through the Spirit that we address the transcendent God as Father and Jesus as Lord.[21]

Third, according to the same author, it is not possible to take account of the work of the Holy Spirit by limiting consideration to the human community:

> Human spirit with its self-realization in community is not the only locus of the immanent divine power which is Spirit. We have spoken of "mankind's shared depths". We have further intimated that mankind shares its "depths" with the universe. . . . In the context of a dynamic, evolutionary, processive world-view, it might be expected that the cosmic dimension of the Spirit symbol—only seminal in the scriptures—become a rich source of theological reflection.[22]

To these three points one would want to add two others, namely, the way in which the Scriptures connect freedom with the Spirit and the way in which they designate the Spirit as eschatological gift. The two points coincide, for example, in Paul's Letter to the Romans, where the writer joins the experience of the Spirit with being freed from the bondage of flesh and fear. Of this, James Dunn writes:

> In Rom. 5.2ff. . . . the key point is the eschatological dimension of the believer's sufferings. Suffering and hope go together. Suffering does not deny or contradict hope. On the contrary, hope arises together with suffering (vv. 2f.); indeed hope arises out of suffering (vv. 3ff.). . . . The creative role of suffering and the creative role of the Spirit (v. 5) are two sides of the one process.[23]

In exploring the immanent, cosmic, eschatological and liberating imagery which expresses the power and action of God's Spirit, one would have to investigate the place that it has in the different kinds of language through which liberating and integrating experience is brought to speech and connected with historical events and expectations. Not only narratives and prophetic discourse, but even more eschatological sayings and hymns of anamnetic praise and lament would need to be examined. Here, however, this can only be mentioned in passing, indicating the possibility of retrieving such discourse in the midst of emancipatory praxis.

X. THE SPIRIT IN GOD

Ultimately, the liberating power of the Spirit brings creation into a communion of love with God, and this communion can be adequately expressed only in doxology. Addressing the theology of the Spirit in a paper entitled *Spirit of God, Spirit of Christ,* [24] the Faith and Order Commission of the World Council of Churches notes the doxological foundation of trinitarian theology, suggesting that the way to a theology of the immanent Trinity would need to take its point of departure in doxology. [25] Since, however, even the church's expression of praise can be distorted by ideological patterns of speech and ritual, it may be more correct to say that the perfecting of our communion with God is the perfecting of our praise and that this cannot be done without overcoming division, oppression and alienation. The Spirit who liberates at the same time perfects creation in a doxological communion with the Godhead, in the memory of God's Word made flesh and in reverence of God the Origin. How the Spirit unites humanity and creation in this relation of praise and commemorative hope to God as Origin and Word has to form the basis for any possible understanding of the place of the Spirit within the Godhead. As the above-mentioned document states:

> Conceptual distinctions between the "economic" and "immanent" Trinity, or between "temporal mission" and "eternal procession" should not be taken as separating off from each other two quite different realities which must then be somehow re-connected. Rather, they serve to witness to the triune God as the living God. In calling upon God, we turn and open ourselves to the God who is none other than he has revealed himself in his Word. This calling upon his name is the essential expression of

doxology, that is, of trust, praise and thanks that the living God from eternity to eternity, was, is and will be none other ("immanent Trinity") than he has shown himself to be in history ("economic Trinity").[26]

In his chapter in *Lux Mundi,* Charles Gore was able to complete his discussion of the Spirit's role in Scripture, interpretation and human experience of the divine with a theology of the inner Spirit of God, relating it to the experience of the Spirit in the church. If a comparable program were to be pursued here, it would be a matter of asking whether an understanding of the Spirit's communion with Utterer and Uttered could emerge from our understanding of the liberating power of the Spirit which brings a healed humankind and all of creation together in a communion of praise with the God who is revealed in Jesus Christ. One would also have to ask how this affects the *filioque* controversy which has divided Christianity's historical churches. However, the treatment of the relation between Spirit, Scripture and hermeneutics has been so protracted that this latter task cannot be taken up here. Suffice to say that if the healing and liberating power of the Spirit is not appropriated by the church, then indeed the praise and the knowledge of God are stunted.

It has been the primary purpose of this chapter to discuss how the development of hermeneutics, especially in the light of its critical turn, affects understanding of the action of the Spirit in Scripture and tradition. Gore in *Lux Mundi* had already incorporated an understanding of experience into this relation, but this needed to be pursued further. In particular, it has been deemed important to show how awareness of the distortions of language, ritual and structure affect the interpretation of Scripture and the work of tradition. The importance given to praxis, its commitment to liberation, and the multiple conversion which it postulates suggested that the action of the Spirit be located at the point of conflict between the forces of alienation and liberating action. This then becomes a criterion for the ongoing interpretation of the Scriptures and a key to the deep meaning of its language. It is out of the suffering and hope born of this conflict that the Spirit of God leads the church forward to communion with God and allows it to appropriate Scripture and tradition as God's word, in which the events of divine action in history and cosmos are given expression, so that their grace and their meaning can be discerned even in the midst of flawed human discourse.[27]

NOTES

1. Charles Gore, "The Holy Spirit and Inspiration", in *Lux Mundi,* 285, quoting Athanasius, *De incarnatione* 12.

2. Avery Dulles, "Scripture: Recent Protestant and Catholic Views", in *The Authoritative Word: Essays on the Nature of Scripture,* ed. Donald K. McKim (Grand Rapids: Wm. B. Eerdmans, 1983), 251.

3. Ibid.

4. Yves Congar, *Je crois en l'Esprit saint* (Paris: Les Editions du Cerf, 1979), 1:15–16.

5. Karl Rahner, "Experience of the Spirit and Existential Decision", in *Experience of the Spirit,* vol. 99 of Concilium, ed. Peter Huizing and William Bassett (New York: Seabury Press, 1974/76), 41.

6. For a survey of this approach in contemporary literature, see David Tracy, *Blessed Rage for Order: The New Pluralism in Theology* (New York: Seabury Press, 1975), 91–118.

7. Cf. Johannes B. Metz, *Faith in History and Society* trans. David Smith (New York: Crossroad, 1980); and Matthew Lamb, *Solidarity with Victims: Toward a Theology of Social Transformation* (New York: Crossroad, 1982), 117–21.

8. Lamb, *Solidarity,* 116–52.

9. For two helpful surveys, see Dulles, "Scripture", 239–61; and Pheme Perkins, "Biblical Scholarship and the Church: The New Testament—The Church's Book", in *CTSA Proceedings* 40 (1985):36–53.

10. David H. Kelsey, *The Uses of Scripture in Recent Theology* (Philadelphia: Fortress Press, 1975), 212.

11. A recent presentation of canonical exegesis is Brevard S. Childs, *The New Testament as Canon: An Introduction* (Philadelphia: Fortress Press, 1984).

12. David Tracy, "The Particularity and Universality of Christian Revelation", in *Revelation and Experience,* ed. Edward Schillebeeckx and Bas van Iersel, vol. 113 of Concilium (New York: Seabury Press, 1979), 113.

13. Paul Ricoeur, "Toward a Hermeneutic of the Idea of Revelation", in *Essays on Biblical Interpretation,* ed. Lewis Mudge (Philadelphia: Fortress Press, 1980), 93.

14. Rosemary Radford Ruether, *Sexism and God-Talk: Toward a Feminist Theology* (Boston: Beacon Press, 1983), 12–46, 93–115; and Elisabeth Schüssler Fiorenza, *In Memory of Her: A Feminist Theological Reconstruction of Christian Origins* (New York: Crossroad, 1984), 1–95.

15. See the articles by B. Mondin, H. Häring and H. Meyer in *Conflicts About the Holy Spirit,* ed. Hans Küng and Jürgen Moltmann, vol. 128 of Concilium

(New York: Seabury Press, 1979) for different approaches to office and the Holy Spirit.

16. For the source of this interest in biblical studies, authors often point to Gerhard von Rad, *Old Testament Theology,* vol. 1, trans. D. M. G. Stalker (New York: Harper & Row, 1962).

17. Fiorenza, *In Memory,* 33–34.

18. Eric Voegelin, *The Ecumenic Age,* vol. 4 of *Order and History* (Baton Rouge: Louisiana State University Press, 1974), 17–18.

19. Edmund Dobbin, "Towards a Theology of the Holy Spirit", *The Heythrop Journal* 17 (1976):5–19, 129–49.

20. Ibid., 19.

21. Ibid.

22. Ibid., 148.

23. James D. G. Dunn, *Jesus and the Spirit: A Study of the Religious and Charismatic Experience of Jesus and the First Christians as Reflected in the New Testament* (Philadelphia: Westminster Press, 1975), 328.

24. *Spirit of God, Spirit of Christ: Ecumenical Reflections on the Filioque Controversy,* Faith and Order Paper 103 (London: SPCK; Geneva: World Council of Churches, 1981).

25. Ibid., 7.

26. Ibid., 10.

27. This article has of necessity been limited to the link between the theology of the Holy Spirit and the theology of biblical inspiration. Hence, in closing, it is fitting to note a few of the works available in English in which the theology of the Holy Spirit has been more fully developed in recent years: Yves Congar, *I Believe in the Holy Spirit,* 3 vols. (New York: Crossroad, 1983); James D. G. Dunn, *Jesus and the Spirit: A Study of the Religious and Charismatic Experience of Jesus and the First Christians as Reflected in the New Testament* (Philadelphia: Westminster Press, 1975); Alasdair Heron, *The Holy Spirit* (Philadelphia: Westminster Press, 1983); William Hill, *The Three-Personed God: The Trinity as Mystery of Salvation* (Washington, D.C.: Catholic University of America Press, 1982); John V. Taylor, *The Go-Between God: The Holy Spirit and the Christian Mission* (Philadelphia: Fortress Press, 1973). Note also the two volumes of Concilium: Huizing and Bassett, *Experience of the Spirit,* vol. 99; and Küng and Moltmann, *Conflicts About the Holy Spirit,* vol. 128.

8

THE CHURCH

GEORGE LINDBECK

I. THE STATE OF THE QUESTION

The aim of this chapter is to do for our day what Walter Lock did for his in his *Lux Mundi* essay on the church. He sought to formulate the theological case for Catholic doctrines in a way that fit the situation, and we shall try to do the same. The situation has changed, however, and so also must the means. A different ecclesiological vision is needed to sustain Catholic claims, and the claims themselves need to be reformulated ecumenically. The vision of the church which we shall explore is that of the messianic pilgrim people of God typologically shaped by Israel's story. Our chief concern is with the contemporary applicability and possible consequences of this ecclesiological outlook. But before turning to these aspects of our theme in the last three sections, we must deal in the first three with its present status, biblical grounding, and long eclipse during most of the two thousand years of Christian history.

Ecclesiology is a dogmatically undeveloped area. As historians remind us, there have been until recently no comprehensive pronouncements on the nature of the church in any major Christian tradition. Much has been said about it, but not what it is. There are, for example, the four *notae ecclesiae,* spoken of in the ancient creeds: one, holy, catholic, and apostolic. The Reformation confessions add to the list. The church is said to be, among other things, *creatura verbi,* the creation of the word (cf. Confessio Augustana VII), but it is also in its visible form a *corpus mixtum* of the elect and the reprobate (Westminster Confession, 25.5). These, however, are attributes that can also be predicated of other subjects. Authentic preaching and sacraments together with Scripture and pure doctrine can also be described as creations of the word which are one, holy, catholic, and apostolic. The same properties have often been attached to what has been conceived as a pure and invisible communion of faith, hope and love. Furthermore, is not Israel also composed of the faithful and the unfaithful, the saved and the unsaved? The traditional attributes neither uniquely identify nor comprehensively describe the church.

Not only church doctrine but also theological reflection has been lacking in this area. Until a hundred years before *Lux Mundi,* a chapter of the kind that Walter Lock wrote would have been a novelty. Specific topics such as ecclesiastical structures and discipline were addressed at length (as, e.g., by John Calvin in Book IV of the *Institutes* or Richard Hooker in his *Laws*), but separate treatises on the church as a whole are modern phenomena. Among all the major theological loci, ecclesiology has been the last to develop.

Furthermore, even after ecclesiological treatises began to proliferate, it was long before "people of God" became a central motif. H. F. Hamilton published a two-volume work on the subject in 1912,[1] but little else appeared for the next two decades. After that, however, there was a spate of studies of the theme even though they have never preempted the field. Identifications of the church as primarily "sacrament", "body of Christ", or "worshiping community", for example, have remained important.[2]

Yet by the time of the Second Vatican Council, the weight of biblical research in particular was such that "messianic pilgrim people of God" received equal status together with "sacrament of unity" and (perhaps) "institution of salvation" as an ecclesiologically fundamental concept.[3] No one of these three characterizations is given precedence, however, and their interrelationships are not defined. The result, in effect, is to accord dogmatic approval to three different ecclesiological options (and perhaps more, for there is no suggestion that the list is exhaustive). People-of-God ecclesiologies are neither more nor less admissible than the other kinds.

From an ecumenical perspective, however, they have a definite advantage. Unlike the two major alternatives in *Lumen gentium,* they are as congenial to evangelical concerns (by which, in this chapter, I mean those of the Reformation) as to Catholic ones,[4] and they are at least as influential in non-Catholic as in Roman Catholic circles. For a discussion, such as the present one, which aims to be ecumenically catholic, they constitute the doctrinally warranted starting point for thinking about the church.

Yet doctrines, as Karl Rahner in particular has emphasized,[5] are beginnings as well as ends. They lead beyond themselves. Over and over again in church history, magisterially approved formulations have been overshadowed by others which came to seem more adequate. This could happen in the present case. Perhaps some other way of thinking about the church is preferable in our or in any situation. It is up to the reader to be the judge of that. Yet whatever the ending, there are both doctrinal and ecumenical reasons for beginning with the messianic pilgrim people. This is the way of viewing of the church which currently has the greatest prima facie claim to ecumenical catholicity.

II. BIBLICAL EVIDENCE

In order to sustain such a claim, however, a view of the church must be biblically warranted. It must, above all, be consistent with the total witness of Scripture as this centers on Jesus Christ. Without this, it can be neither catholic nor ecumenical. In addition, correspondence with scriptural patterns of thought is normally regarded as enhancing biblical backing. There are, to be sure, occasions when a scriptural outlook on a particular topic must be abandoned out of faithfulness to the central message or out of concern for intelligibility and practical effectiveness. The New Testament tolerance for slavery can be cited as an example. Its replication in our postbiblical circumstances would be, for all contemporary churches, directly opposed to Christ Jesus, not to mention unintelligible and practically counterproductive. Conceivably something similar might hold for biblical ways of thinking about the church. Perhaps they never were fully adequate to the gospel, or perhaps they have become inadequate in the course of time. Yet despite this possibility, it has been the general conviction throughout Christian history that, other things being equal, correspondence to what Scripture says is desirable. Departure from its patterns may be admissible, but only when there are good reasons for it.

This has been recognized even in trinitarian and christological doctrine. The nonbiblical formulations of Nicaea and Chalcedon have over and over again been treated by their advocates as unfortunate necessities forced upon the church by the needs of a new situation (such as, according to Athanasius and his fellows, the heretical misuse of scriptural language). We shall assume that the same rule holds in ecclesiology. Biblical conceptualities may be supplemented or displaced, as at Nicaea and Chalcedon, but only if this is necessary for the sake of greater faithfulness, intelligibility or efficaciousness. The burden of proof is on those whose fundamental categories for thinking about the church are nonbiblical.

In the light of these considerations, it is impossible to avoid the exegetical question of what were the biblical ways of understanding the church. The answer to this may be decisive and is in any case important for ecclesiology.[6]

Fortunately we need only ask what Scripture meant by the church when it is conceived primarily as the people of God. On this, something close to a scholarly consensus seems to exist. Problems arise and the consensus dissolves chiefly when one turns to a prior question: Is the church of which the Bible tells us primarily the people of God, or is some other designation more fundamental? Does one get closer to its essence if one calls it, for example, the body of Christ, or the community of the Spirit, or the worshiping assembly, or an event, an institution, or a liberation movement? The scriptural references can be looked at from any one of these or many other angles, and which approach does most justice to the data is exegetically undecidable. We are here inclosed in what has come to be known as a hermeneutical circle, for our preunderstandings help determine what we take to be relevant data.[7] Squaring this circle is out of the question, and we shall therefore proceed on the doctrinally and ecumenically mandated hypothesis that the church was primarily the people of God in the biblical writings, and ask what that meant.

The historical and exegetical support for this ecumenically catholic hypothesis is strong (whether stronger than for other hypotheses is what we shall not discuss). The early Christians were a Jewish sect. They believed in a crucified and resurrected Messiah who authorized them, some of them believed, to welcome the uncircumcised into their fellowship, but this did not diminish their desire to maintain their legitimacy as Jews. All the categories they possessed for their communal self-understanding were derived from the Hebrew Scriptures (usually, to be sure, in the Greek Septuagint version). These were their only inspired text, and they interpreted it as Jews. It was natural that they should understand their communities as *ekklēsia,* as *qahal,* the assembly of Israel in the new age. (For once philology and etymology cohere with broader historical considerations.)[8] Thus the story of Israel was their story. They were that part of the people of God who lived in the time between the times after the messianic era had begun but before the final coming of the kingdom. Whatever is true of Israel is true of the church except where the differences are explicit.

Four heuristic guidelines for reading the New Testament references to the church are suggested by this historical background. First, as befits those who thought of themselves as a people, early Christian communal self-understanding was narrative-shaped.[9] The church, in other words, was fundamentally identified and characterized by its story. Images such as "body of Christ" or the traditional marks of "unity, holiness, catholicity and apostolicity" cannot be first defined and then used to specify what was and what was not "church". The story was logically prior. It determined the meaning of images, concepts, doctrines and theories of the church rather than being determined by them. Just as the story of the Quakers is more fundamental than descriptions such as "church of the poor" or "church of the wealthy" (for they have been both), and the story of the French is more fundamental than "monarchy" or "republic" (for France has been both), so also in the case of the church.

A corollary of this priority of story was that "church" ordinarily referred to concrete groups of people, not to something transempirical. An invisible church is as biblically odd as an invisible Israel. Stories of the biblical realistic-narrative type can only be told of agents and communities of agents acting and being acted upon in a space-time world of contingent happenings. Thus to say that it was empirical churches in all their actual or potential messiness of which exalted concepts and images such as "holy" and "bride of Christ" were predicated is an analytic implicate of the primacy of narrative.

For the early Christians, in the second place, Israel's history was their only history. They did not yet have the New Testament or later church history as sources. Israel's history, to be sure, was seen through the prism of Christ, and this made a profound difference; but yet, to repeat, the Hebrew Scriptures were the sole ecclesiological textbook. The only inspired stories available to the church for its self-understanding were the stories of Israel.

A third rule is an extension of this second one. Not only was Israel's story the early Christians' only communal story but it was the whole of that story which they appropriated. It was not only the favorable parts, such as the Old Testament accounts of faithful remnants, which they applied to themselves. All the wickedness of the Israelites in the wilderness could be theirs. They might rebel, as did Korah, or perish for fornication, as did three and twenty thousand in the desert (1 Cor. 10:5–10). These happenings, Paul tells his readers, are types *(tupoi)* written for our admonition (v. 11). As of old, judgment continues to begin in the house of the Lord (1 Pet. 4:17), and the unfaithful church can be severed from the root no less than the unbelieving synagogue (Rom. 11:21). It can, like Eve, yield to the wiles of the serpent and lose its virginal purity (2 Cor. 11:1–4). One can imagine early Christians going on in more extreme situations, such as later developed, to say of the bride of Christ what Ezekiel said of the betrothed of Jahweh (Ezekiel 16; 23): she can be a whore worse than the heathen. As was earlier noted, when the New Testament is silent we need to turn to the Hebrew Scriptures, the ecclesiological text par excellence, to discover how the early Christians thought about the church.

In opposition to most later exegesis, therefore, the relation of Israel's history to that of the church in the New Testament was not that of shadow to reality, or promise to fulfillment, or type to antitype.[10] Jesus Christ alone is the antitype or fulfillment. He is depicted as the embodiment of Israel (e.g., "Out of Egypt have I called my son", Matt. 2:15), and the church is the body of Christ. Thus Israel's story, transposed into a new key through Christ, becomes prototypical for the history of the church which is its continuation rather than its fulfillment.

From this it follows, in the fourth place, that Israel and the church were one people for the early Christians. There was no breach in continuity. A new age had begun, but the story continued and therefore also the people which it identified. The French remain French after the revolution, the Quakers remain Quakers after becoming wealthy, and Israel remains Israel even when transformed by the arrival of the eschaton in Christ. The church is simply Israel in the time between the times. The continuity of the story and the identity of the people are unbroken.

Discontinuity and nonidentity are problems in the New Testament, not for the church per se, but for unbelieving Jews on the one hand and gentile Christians on the other. The apostle Paul says of the first group in Romans 11 that they have been cut off, but that this can happen does not differentiate them from Christians. Churches also, as we have already noted, can be severed from the root. They can, in the even more vigorous language of Revelation, be spewed forth, expectorated (Rev. 3:16). Yet when this occurs, it does not alter the identity of the people of the promise. "The gifts and the call of God are irrevocable" (Rom. 11:29). Unbelieving Jewry will ultimately be restored. Furthermore, postbiblical Judaism which has not heard the gospel (and how can it hear in view of Christian persecution?) lives theologically before Christ and cannot be equated with the unbelieving Jewry of which Paul speaks. Nothing in his account prevents us from saying that the synagogue, like remnants in ancient Israel, is at times more faithful to God's will and purposes than are unfaithful churches. In any case, in the one New Testament writing in which the problem is directly addressed, Judaism after Christ is as inalienably embraced as the church in the continuous overarching story of the single people, consisting of faithful remnants and unfaithful masses, which stretches from the patriarchal period to the last days.

So strong was this sense of uninterrupted peoplehood that the only available way to think of gentile Christians was, in Krister Stendahl's phrase, as "honorary Jews".[11] The uncircumcised, "alienated from the commonwealth of Israel", have become "fellow citizens . . . of the household of God", "fellow heirs, [fellow] members of the same body, and [fellow] partakers of the promise" (Eph. 2:12, 19; 3:6). This inclusion of the Gentiles is represented in Ephesians as the most wondrous aspect of the work of Christ. Where there were two, there is now one, the new man in Christ (Eph. 2:11—3:11), the beginnings of the new humanity, the third race of which the early fathers spoke. Thus has begun the gathering of all humankind into God's people, the promised ascent of the nations to worship in Zion, the crowding of the Gentiles into the heavenly Jerusalem. But Zion does not change identity: the twelve apostles are commemorated on the foundations of the walls of the New Jerusalem, but its gates are marked with the names of the twelve tribes (Rev. 21:12). The inclusion of the uncircumcised in the covenant with Abraham by means of the new covenant in Christ did not, for the earliest Christians, constitute the formation of a different people but rather the enlargement of the old.

From this perspective, not only the enlargement of the people but also its other special features are functions of life in the new age, not changes in identity. Who and what the people is becomes more fully

GEORGE LINDBECK

manifest now that the Messiah has come. The bride of Yahweh is the bride and body of Christ. The Spirit is now offered and may be poured out on all flesh as it was not before (Acts 2:17ff.). Thus the *ab initio* trinitarian calling, constituting, and empowering of God's people stands revealed. It is a new epoch of unheard-of possibilities and actualities, not a New Israel, which begins at Pentecost.

The early Christian appropriation of the story of Israel, needless to say, differed greatly from situation to situation. Sometimes the differences look like contradictions even in the same author. It is, for example, hard to reconcile what Paul says of unbelieving Jews when encouraging the persecuted Christians of Thessolonica (cf. 1 Thess. 2:14–15) with his later discussion in Romans 9—11. The church is scarcely ever spoken of as the people of God in the Johannine literature, and in Hebrews, it is sometimes said, it is platonized. Yet there is nothing surprising in this. The use of ancient tales to shape the identity of the nascent church required many twists and turns. If one follows the story line, these intertwine into a single narrative (not systematic) whole; but if not, they fragment into distinct and perhaps incompatible ecclesiologies. It is perhaps only in a people-of-God approach that one can speak responsibly of a basically unified New Testament understanding of the church.[12]

III. POST-BIBLICAL ECCLESIOLOGY

This understanding, however, did not persist. It became increasingly unintelligible and inapplicable as circumstances changed. Modifications developed in part to maintain faithfulness to the christological center, but these led at times to unfaithfulness. We cannot assess the present situation in ecclesiology without first noting some of these changes in Christian communal self-understanding.

Modifications of biblical patterns of thought started in the very first generations. The hardening of the opposition between synagogue and church led even Jewish Christians, as such documents as the Letter of Barnabas illustrate, to reject the notion that unbelieving Jews remained part of God's people. Faithfulness became the mark of election, and election, conversely, became conditional on faithfulness. The doctrines of predestination and of salvation *sola gratia,* insofar as they persisted, tended to be applied only to individuals and not to communities. Heretical groups were more and more regarded as not really the church at all. They were not seen after the fashion of the ancient prophets as the adulterous spouse whom the Lord may cast out for a time but without divorcing.

A second development was that the church quickly became wholly gentile: it ceased to be sociologically a Jewish sect. It became intellectually and practically impossible for gentile Christians to think of themselves as naturalized citizens in the continuous, uninterrupted commonwealth of Israel. Thus not only was the synagogue excluded but the one people of God was broken into two peoples, the old and the new. This created the problem of how to relate them, and the solution was to read the Scriptures as if Israel were the type, no longer simply of the coming kingdom and of its instantiation in the person of Christ, but also of the church, which thus became the antitype, the fulfillment. The more unsavory aspects of the history of Israel were no longer genuinely portions of the history of the church but were projected exclusively on the synagogue.

These modifications, it will be observed, are quite explicitly changes in the scriptural people-of-God pattern rather than simply new applications. Yet despite the monstrous offspring they ultimately engendered, they cannot be flatly condemned as simply unfaithful. They were the historically (i.e., contingently) necessary conditions for the church's appropriation of Israel's story. Without that appropriation, so we may plausibly speculate, Gnosticism would have wholly triumphed, the Marcionite rejection of Israel's Scriptures and Israel's God would have become universal among Christians, and the Nazi heresy that Jesus was not a Jew would have become orthodoxy from the second century on. Because the modifications were the only available alternative to utter subversion of the christological center, they can be regarded, despite their magnitude and consequences, as scripturally faithful interpretations of the story of the church.

Such excuses become increasingly unworkable, however, after the Empire was converted and persecuted Christians became the persecutors. Anti-Semitism was the paradigmatic problem, but it needs to be seen as an acute manifestation of a more general disease. The dissonance between antitypical claims to fulfillment and empirical reality was the central difficulty. The church was now a *corpus mixtum* composed overwhelmingly of visible sinners rather than visible saints. The pressure was great to refer its high claims, not to the overall pattern of communal life, but to segregated aspects: to pure (ultimately infallible) doctrines, to individualistically (and, in vulgar understanding, magically) efficacious sacraments, and to divinely established institutions. Even these developments, to be sure, were not in every respect anti-scriptural. They might be compared, perhaps, to the Israelite monarchy which God consented to *contre coeur* (1 Samuel 8), and yet also mightily used to preserve his people and prepare for the Messiah (Jesus sprang from the Davidic line). In somewhat similar fashion, so one could argue, the imperial church preserved the faith amid barbarian chaos, converted Europe, and was the cradle of the first civilization to become worldwide (whether there is anything messianic about Western-spawned modernity is another question). Be that as it may, however, the antitypical pretensions of Western ecclesiastical establishments (from which Reformation state churches were by no means wholly exempt) could not but evoke sectarian reactions (which, incidentally, have not been so strong in the East where Caesaropapism, whatever its faults, muted churchly arrogance).

The sectarian solutions to the church's dilemma have on the whole been less biblical but not uniformly less faithful to Scripture than the earlier Catholic ones. They have been less biblical because for the most part they have no longer understood God's people in terms of Israel's story but rather have been modeled after New Testament depictions of fervent first-generation communities especially as found in Acts. Yet however unbiblical one may think the ecclesiology of, for example, the Quakers, it is hard to deny that such groups have at times been faithful remnants amid the faithless masses. Insofar as they were protest move-ments against Constantinian churches, the sects were in general scrip-turally justified, but they are also deeply problematic. The intense effort to make the empirical reality of Christian communities conform visibly to images of antitypical fulfillment can have consequences in some ways worse than institutional triumphalism. The arrogant self-righteousness of the company of the visibly holy compares ill with the concern for publicans and sinners sometimes found in churches that conceive of themselves as arks of salvation, as hospitals for sick souls.

The difficulties in traditional ecclesiologies, whether Catholic, Refor-mation, or sectarian, have led in recent centuries to new ways of think-ing about the church which depart even farther from biblical patterns but which, once again, can have scriptural authenticity. Not only is Israel's story abandoned but also the referential primacy of empirical communities. Something other than these communities is really the church, is really the subject of the claims to antitypical fulfillment, with the result that ecclesial arrogance of either the Catholic or the sectarian types is no longer theologically legitimate.

For example, the church is characterized denotatively (not simply connotatively, or predicatively, or in some promissory or other illocutionary mode) as event, or mission, or liberating action, or the new being in Christ, or the fellowship of the Spirit, or the communion of Christ's justifying grace which works in anonymous as well as explicitly Christian ways. For the most part, any suggestion that the church is invisible is stoutly resisted. Rather, it necessarily takes visible form, and in some interpretations referential primacy is accorded to what is empirically or experientially identifiable (e.g., event, mission, or liberating action). Nevertheless, however observable or experienceable the main referent may be, it is not first of all a people. It is not empirical churches in all their crass concreteness. These latter are rather imperfect manifestations, realizations, participations or thematizations of the church's true, eschatological reality.

Thus if our exegetical approach is right, what for the Bible are predicates are in these modern outlooks turned into subject terms. The reference of these terms is not a concrete people of the kind whose identity is rendered by realistic narratives, and it must therefore be described in some other way. Systematic ecclesiology replaces the story of the people of God. This is what happened in recent centuries in almost all major theological outlooks whether Catholic or Protestant.[13]

Yet, we must now recall, there are good reasons for these developments, and unbiblical ways of thinking about the church are not necessarily unfaithful. They have in some cases eliminated occasions for anti-Semitism and ecclesial arrogance by making the antitypical church something other than the empirical churches. In this and other respects they may be more genuinely Christian than their predecessors. It would be artificial but not impossible to write a history of ecclesiology in which increasing departures from the Bible were correlated with increasing closeness to Christ.

The question arises, however, whether the progression we have reviewed has reached its end. Perhaps the incipient return to a people-of-God ecclesiology noted at the beginning of this essay can now be carried farther. In dealing with this question, we shall first comment briefly on the applicability of this ecclesiology in the present situation and then deal in two concluding sections with some possible applications.

IV. APPLICABILITY

There are a number of familiar ways in which the present period is becoming more like the Christian beginnings than the intervening ages. Christendom is passing and Christians are becoming a diaspora. The antagonism of the church to the synagogue has been unmasked (we hope definitively) for the horror it always was. Ecclesial pretensions to fulfillment have become obnoxious to multitudes of Catholics and Protestants alike. Some of the reasons for distorting and then rejecting the scriptural people-of-God ecclesiology are disappearing, and perhaps its original version is again applicable.

Certainly there are reasons for wanting to apply it. For it, there is no church except the empirical churches,[14] and this emphasis is badly needed. The empirical churches are losing the loyalty and devotion of their members. Special-interest enclaves are replacing comprehensive communities as the locus of whatever shreds of communal identity the isolated individuals of our society retain. The conviction that the churches even in their crass concreteness have a crucial place in God's plans has weakened. All these considerations call for a return to Israel's story as a template which helps shape Christian communities. These communities need to be understood as witnesses that God has chosen no less irrevocably than he chose Israel to testify to his glory in both their faithfulness and unfaithfulness, in both his mercy and his judgment. Their election needs to be recognized as abiding even though they too may be severed by disobedience from the root (Rom. 11:21). Portions of the chosen people may lose their identity, they may be destroyed as was the Northern Kingdom, but that does not alter the unconditionality of the election of those which remain recognizably Jewish or Christian even when they apostatize. God chastises them when they err—indeed, he does this with special severity—but as his chosen ones, beloved above all nations.

Such convictions have made of Jews the great exception to the sociological and historical generalizations that apply to other nations and have enabled them, despite their dispersion and small numbers, to be a major force in history (not least, it should be recalled, when they were wholly in the diaspora). History shows that Israel's story has unique ability to confer communally significant meaning on whatever happens:

190

it has, one might say, unrivaled power to encode successfully the vicissitudes and contradictions of history. Christianity, it can be argued, has urgent need to make greater use of that same biblical tale if it is to be comparably tenacious and flexible in maintaining its identity as a people irresistibly called (and ineluctably failing) to witness by selfless service of all humankind to the universal yet thoroughly particular God of Abraham, Isaac, Jacob, and Jesus.

It must be added, however, that there are as yet few signs that this is happening. On the right, apocalyptic conservatism is on the rise, but this, despite its often ardent support for the Israeli state, not only thinks of Christianity as the replacement of Judaism but restricts the church to the company of the datably converted. On the political left, liberationists selectively appropriate episodes from Israel's history, especially the exodus, but use these as legitimating precedents for their own campaigns, not as applicable to comprehensive gatherings of sinners and saints, oppressors and oppressed, tyrants and liberators. More generally, despite such dubious phenomena as Jews for Jesus, Christianity continues for the most part to be as gentile in its self-understanding as ever, and few Christians are in the least inclined to think of themselves as even remotely analogous to a Jewish sect or honorary Jews. As long as this is the situation, a biblically Israel-like understanding of the church will not be intelligible or efficacious, and in a sense not even scripturally appropriate: many Christians would react by becoming even more Marcionite than they already are.

Yet uncertainty about applicability does not preclude discussion of applications. Some of these must be outlined in order to illustrate how the code of Israel's history may be used in our day as, in the first century, to understand who and what the church is. Attention will focus on the identity of the church in relation to, first, its mission and unity and, second, its unifying structures. The result is a very partial treatment of the church. It fails to start, as a full-scale ecclesiology would, with the people of God as worshiping community created by the Father through the Son in the power of the Holy Spirit, constituted by the proclamation of the gospel in word and sacrament, and bearing joyous fruit in works of suffering love. These basal dimensions are discussed, however, elsewhere in this volume, even if not from a specifically ecclesiological perspective, while questions of the institutionalization of church order are at present the ecumenically most intractable ones. It is, then, the identity and the mission of the messianic pilgrim people in relation to its ordering structures which are the topics of these concluding remarks.

V. IDENTITY AND MISSION

The church's story, understood as continuous with Israel's, tells of God doing in this time between the times what he has done before: choosing and guiding a people to be a sign and witness in all that it is and does, whether obediently or disobediently, to who and what he is. Both God's mercy and God's judgment are manifest in the life of this people as nowhere else.

This is what the narrative is about. By remembering that this is the subject matter, we can identify the church in the twentieth no less than in the first century. It is true that the church looks very different in these two periods, but then so did Israel in the wilderness, under judges and kings, and in exile. The encoded historical data vary, and so do the descriptive results, but the identifying code is the same and therefore also the identified people.

The referential force of this narrative code can be analyzed into distinct aspects. First, the identity and being of the church rests on God's election, not on its faithfulness. Second, as an implicate of this, the elect communities are stamped by objective marks which are both blessing and curse depending on how they are received. Eating and drinking, Paul reminds us, can be unto judgment (1 Cor. 11:29) and not only life, and the same applies to circumcision and baptism, the *shema* and the *apostolicum*. Even when the sacraments are spiritualized, as by Quakers, the profession that the Christ spoken of in Scripture is the Lord can be a publicly unmistakable brandmark of the group's election. Third, election is communal. Individuals are elect by virtue of visible membership in God's people. Last, the primary mission of this chosen people is to witness to the God who judges and who saves, not to save those who would otherwise be damned (for God has not confined his saving work exclusively to the church's ministrations). It testifies to this God whether or not it wills to do so, whether it is faithful or unfaithful. The final consummation which has begun in Christ is proleptically present in this people as nowhere else, but so also is the eschatological judgment (1 Pet. 4:17; cf. Amos 3:2 and Jer. 25:29).[15]

The church thus identified sounds Catholic in its comprehensiveness, Calvinist in the unconditionality of its chosenness, and Lutheran in its possibilities of unfaithfulness while remaining genuinely the church;

but the total effect, not surprisingly, is more Jewish than anything else. This is true, first, in reference to who are designated individually and communally as part of the church. The church consists of those, whether atheists or believers, reprobate or regenerate, who are stamped with the marks of membership in elect communities.[16] Baptism may be easier to ignore than circumcision (though secular Israelis are adept at doing so), but God remembers. Nor does communal degeneracy erase election. The Amhara and the Falasha in Ethiopia may resemble the animist tribes which surround them, but if one admits they are Christian and Jewish respectively, one is obligated to accept them as fully parts, even if defective parts, of the elect people. Similarly, the apartheid churches of South Africa are no less churches than the black ones they oppress, just as sixteenth-century Catholics and Protestants were part of the same elect people as the Anabaptists whom they jointly slaughtered, and just as the Gush Emmunim and Peace Now advocates, not to mention the warring sects of whom Josephus tells, are and were fully Jewish. To put this point in the terminology of the social sciences, the people of God consists of cultural-linguistic groupings that can be meaningfully identified by ordinary sociological and historical criteria as Christian or Jewish (even though their chosenness, needless to say, is known only to faith). This is what is meant biblically and, in the present perspective, theologically by a people.[17]

Also Jewish sounding is the church's mission. It is above all by the character of its communal life that it witnesses, that it proclaims the gospel and serves the world. This revolutionizes one traditional understanding of proclamation, of evangelization. While it is crucial that all kinds of human beings—Greek, barbarian, female and slave as well as Jew, male and free—be fully part of the community, sheer numbers are, at most, of tertiary importance. Christians have as much reason as Jews to eschew heedless invitations to outsiders (whether rootless or adherents of other religions) to bear the burdens of election. The possibilities of damnation as well as of salvation are increased within the people of God (think of the story of Ananias and Sapphira in Acts 5 or, as far as that goes, of Judas). The Bible gives us no warrants for saying that all those who do not become Christians are, in any case, excluded from the coming kingdom, although it cannot be said of them as of Christians that salvation, the kingdom, is already present among or in them (Luke 17:21). The purpose of that presence of salvation, furthermore, is witness, and it is up to God to add whom he will to the company (Acts

2:47). Churches should not imitate the Pharisees, whom Jesus condemned for compassing land and sea to make proselytes (Matt. 23:15), but should rather follow the practice that prevailed in the first centuries of prolonged catechesis. The primary Christian mission, in short, is not to save souls but to be a faithfully witnessing people.[18]

It would be a mistake, however, to conclude from this in the currently popular fashion that the church's mission is therefore primarily *diakonia* in the sense of serving the needs of humanity at large. Christians are responsible first of all for their own communities, not for the wider society. It is by the quality of their communal life that God wills them to be a light to the Gentiles. This does not mean that the chosen people is more important than the world. On the contrary, its role is instrumental: it exists in order to witness to the nations. It does this, however, not primarily by striving to save souls or to improve the social order, but by being the body of Christ, the communal sign of the promised redemption, in the time between the times. When serving the world results in the neglect of the household of faith, the church becomes not a sign but a countersign, a contributor to that human confusion which is the opposite of God's design. It comes to resemble the philanthropist who loves humankind at a distance but not his neighbors or family in need. Its primary task should be to build up sisters and brothers in the faith, not to liberate the oppressed everywhere; and it is only through performing this task that it becomes a liberating force in world history.[19]

This makes mutual responsibility of all for all crucial to the church's mission and witness. The need, the shame, the glory, and the health or sickness of any one part belong to all. One must aid the distressed communities and seek (by protest from within rather than from without) to correct the wayward ones. This part of the biblical outlook, present in both the Hebrew Scriptures and the apostolic writings, has been better preserved among Jews than Christians. The black Falashas, for example, once they are acknowledged as Jewish, are the special responsibility of Jews everywhere. Contemporary ecumenism moves part of the way in this direction but generally stops short with mutual respect between the churches and invitations to dialogue. Even the ecumenically minded do not generally recognize as their special business the superstition (and now the suffering) of the Ethiopian Copts, the shame of Maronite massacres of Shiites (we are much more concerned about the indirect Israeli responsibility), the apartheid oppressiveness of the Dutch Reformed churches in South Africa, or the electronic vulgarity of television evangelists. Contemporary Christians are concerned about these problems, but no more so (and perhaps less) than about superstition and suffering among non-Christian tribes, massacres in India or Iran, or violence and pornography on the screen. Once the traditional understanding of mission as the saving of souls is abandoned, the task of witnessing tends to become indistinguishable from that socially responsible righteousness, that commitment to peace, justice and freedom, to which all human beings are called. The problem is not only practical but theological: it is difficult in most ecclesiological perspectives to legitimate greater concern for Christians than for non-Christians. Perhaps the only way out is a people-of-God perspective in which the mutual concern of all the churches for each other's worship, faith, fellowship and action becomes of paramount importance precisely for the sake of missionary witness to the world.

VI. MINISTRIES OF UNITY

It is in the context of this mutual responsibility of all for all that we now turn to the question of structures of churchwide unity. These are not fundamental. Mutual care can be exercised in some circumstances without institutionalized ministries of unity (as, e.g., by the collection for the poor of the church in Jerusalem which Paul so energetically promoted). Furthermore, the local ministries of word and sacrament are, by common consent, basic. Disputes over these, however, have not led to schism to the same degree as have those over the wider structures, over the historic episcopacy and the papacy. It is therefore with these that we shall deal.[20]

The use of Israel's story leads to results that are ecumenically catholic, but the way of getting there has resemblances both to Protestant functionalism and traditional Catholic institutionalism. On the functionalist side, it is clear that the leadership structures of the chosen people changed to fit new circumstances. Moses was followed by judges and kings, and the rabbinate developed in the exile and the diaspora. (Prophets, needless to say, were also important, but authentic prophecy is not easily institutionalized, if at all, and is not our present concern.) Further, when the kingdom was divided between north and south, both monarchies were for the most part treated in the canonically edited text (even though the final redaction was southern) as legitimate, and worship at Shiloh as well as at Jerusalem was acknowledged. The functionally sensible rule of international law that effective control in the long run establishes legitimacy has scriptural precedents. If Christians have anything to learn in this respect from Israel's Scriptures (which are also its own), then disputes between the Greek, Roman and Reformation churches over which has the more valid ministerial orders and/or sacraments are misplaced.

The same scriptural story also has, however, Catholic implications. These implications, to be sure, are not necessarily antifunctional, but they do oppose the widespread Protestant pragmatism which makes of structures a simple adiaphoron, a matter of theological indifference or even dislike. Israel's history, like that of any other sizable and enduring people, makes clear that continuity and tradition are functionally important. Long-surviving institutions, like long-surviving species, can incorporate in their genetic code a wealth of evolutionary wisdom unmatchable by conscious calculation. Or, to make a somewhat similar point less metaphorically, the symbolic weight acquired by durable structures can be incomparably more powerful (for good as well as ill) than anything devised *de novo* to fit contemporary needs. Not only episcopacy and papacy can be cited but also such non-ecclesiastical structures as universities, the American Constitution, and the British monarchy. So also it was in Israel. As in all traditional societies, the old was to be preferred unless divinely or historically countermanded (and, given God's rulership of the universe, the two are not unrelated). This is not surprising. Whatever else the elect people may be, it is genuinely a people which, by God's will, is not exempt from, even if it is not captive to, the same constraints that influence other human collectivities. In short, a historically embedded functionalism has a Catholic thrust.

Further, however, the structurally Catholic aspects of Israel's narrative are more than functional. It is God who guides his people and orders their common life. The monarchy was established by God even though, as the text explicitly points out, he acted reluctantly in response to what his people thought was historical necessity (1 Samuel 8). Except for the period of the divided kingdom, he always supplied leaders or a single center for the whole people (even if, as during the long diaspora, this was no more than the holy land as an object of longing rather than as an actual possession). Leadership has been recognized as providentially authorized. When one form disappeared to be replaced by

196

another, it was rarely because of internal revolt. The prophets merci-
lessly denounced the abuses and corruptions of the leaders, but they did
not doubt that they had been divinely appointed. Even Paul, according
to Acts 23:2–3, did not deny that this was true of the high priest of his
day whom he called a "whited wall". When it came to the Jerusalem
leadership of the infant church, his own account of his attitude is
poignant. He did not want to go to Jerusalem to consult with James,
Peter, John and the others of repute (though "what they were makes
no difference", he adds) about the gospel he had been preaching to the
Gentiles, for that could not be challenged. It took, he tells us, a "revelation" to compel him to go (Gal. 2:2–6). It is almost as if he feared a
conflict (which in fact did not take place) between an irresistible force
and an immovable object, both divinely authorized. In summary, then,
leadership structures are treated in the biblical texts as *de iure divino,* as
Catholics would say, and yet also as changeable human law, *ius huma-
num,* to bring in the Protestant note.[21]

While this narrative way of thinking about church structures may be
as nearly Protestant as Catholic, its consequences are Catholic, though
without repeating the claims that have been most objectionable to the
Reformation churches. The starting point is the conviction that God's
providential guidance of his continuously existing people did not stop
with biblical times. Only if one believes that the Spirit has guided the
church in the past can one trust God to guide it also in the present and
in the future. Tradition counts. Structures that God has used and is
using have his authorization and are not to be lightly discarded. Ruptures in continuity are to be avoided except when absolutely necessary,
and even then the search for precedents is important.[22]

In the second place, then, the preference is for the reform of past
structures, not their replacement. The burden of proof is on those who,
for example, reject the historic three-fold ministry as this ministry is
recommended in the Lima text, *Baptism, Eucharist and Ministry.* The
case for it need not be that it is demonstrably superior to other ministerial orderings, but simply that it can be congruent with the christological center of the faith (which anyone who believes God did not desert
his church from the time of the first centuries is bound to admit), and
that it is not irrational or impractical (which in view of its present use
by some three-fourths of all Christians seems incontestable). If so, the
respect for tradition which trust in God's guidance of the church in-

volves requires churches that do not have it to adopt (and adapt) the historic polity for the sake of unity whenever this is practically feasible (which in periods of transition such as the present it often is).

This case, however, does not meet the Protestant and Reformation objection that Catholics have in fact claimed far more for their structures than is warranted by their providential origins and use. They have held that the historic episcopate in particular was founded directly by Christ and the apostles, has existed continuously ever since, guarantees the apostolicity of the church's faith, and is irreversibly indispensable to the *bene esse,* or *plene esse,* or even the *esse* of the church. Under the pressure of historical evidence, providentially guided development has now generally replaced dominical or apostolic institution, the possibility that apostolic faith may sometimes be more fully present in nonepiscopal churches is admitted, and there is no effort to say that bishops are necessary to the being of the church (if so, how could one account for the nonepiscopal churches of the first century?), but the claims to irreversibility and to the necessity for the well-being or the fullness of being of the church continue to be generally maintained. These are the sticking points for many Protestants who otherwise have no objection to the apostolic succession. Even when their *amour propre* is not wounded by the doubts raised regarding their own orders and sacraments, they view the claim that a specific ordering of the church is permanently optimal as infringing on God's freedom, confusing law and gospel, and endangering the principle that human beings, including church communities, are justified by faith, not by works. It is *status confessionis* under these circumstances to be nonepiscopal.[23]

Even Catholics who are sensitive to the force of this objection, however, are inclined to think that it underestimates the degree to which episcopacy is intertwined with the foundational features of the church's origins in the immediate post-biblical period. The episcopate emerged early and was, in its original form, much the most successful institutional expression and support in Christian history of that mutual responsibility which we have seen to be at the heart of the church's mission. Letters to the churches and collections for needy saints in distant places may have sufficed to maintain churchwide mutuality in the New Testament period, but not when the group of apostolic leaders who were personally acquainted with each other passed from the scene. Then the device of requiring each new bishop to be approved and consecrated by neighboring bishops was hit upon, and this developed into an interlocking network covering the Mediterranean world which was both flexible and tenacious enough to contain in a single communion orientations as antithetical as those of Tertullian's Carthage and Origen's Alexandria. (It is misleading to call this a monarchical or monoepiscopal system, for without the requirement of validation from neighboring churches, one bishop in one place does not unify.) Profane historians are as likely as Catholics to conclude that it was chiefly this institutionalization of mutual accountability which explains the astonishing success of the originally Catholic minority (for most Christian groups were at first nonepiscopal) in becoming the overwhelming—and therefore catholic—majority. It is to this episcopally unified church, furthermore, that all the major Christian traditions owe their creeds, their liturgies and, above all, their scriptural canon. If these latter are inexpungible, why not also the episcopate? No wonder many Catholics think of it as ineradicable, and they may be right. Yet, on the other hand, the reader of Israel's story cannot but observe that the leadership structure in the comparably decisive period of Jewish history did not survive.[24] The question of irreversibility cannot be settled by appeals to Israel's story. The story provides a framework for reflection, not a formula for automatically settling disputes.

The same holds true for the basically similar problem of papal primacy[25] which divides Orthodox and Anglican Catholics from Rome. Many of these, as well as a not inconsiderable number of Protestants, see no difficulty in admitting the providential origins (and, in that sense, divine institution) of the papacy, and they agree that it has greater potentialities for ministering to the unity of the church universal than any other existing institution, and yet they resist the contention that Rome must be at the center, and that this is irreversibly true.[26] Although they believe it important for the sake of unity to have at the very least a *primus inter pares* among the bishops, and take it as self-evident that both the weight of tradition and contemporary standing point to the Bishop of Rome, yet it seems to them worse than pretentious to affirm as a matter of faith that God will always will it so. After a time when both were approved, the center in ancient Israel shifted from Shiloh to Jerusalem, and then Jerusalem was destroyed and leadership in various forms was located elsewhere (though Jerusalem in transformed ways has always retained a unifying role). Why may not similar developments occur within the church? Was not God free to choose Constantinople, or Moscow, or Canterbury, and might not his choice in the unforeseeable future fall on some as yet unimaginable institutional structure in Africa or the islands of the sea?[27]

Yet this unsolved question of the irreversibility of papal and/or episcopal structures is by itself too marginal, some would say, to justify the division of the churches.[28] The very fact of union, when or if it comes, would make the continuing disagreement practically nugatory. All the churches would, in effect, be acknowledging the historic ministries of unity as God's gifts to be renewed and used in his service, and expressing their thankfulness that these did not disappear at the time of the ruptures in the eleventh and sixteenth centuries. They would at the very least hope that God would not again permit such ruptures or, even worse, the cataclysm of the complete loss of these ministries. The Roman Catholics among them would also believe as a matter of faith that this cataclysm would not occur, but it is hard to see what the operational differences between trustful hope and formal belief would be under these circumstances. This marginality of the issue of irreversibility could be maintained in the context of any historically informed ecclesiology, but it is reinforced by thinking of the church in terms of its unfolding story as the pilgrim people of God.

Of greater consequence than the difference between hoping and believing is the question of why the Catholic structures are important, and here the answer is clear. The historic episcopacy (with or without the papacy, for the latter is impossible without the former but not vice versa) is the only ministry that exists to promote the unity and mutual responsibility of the worldwide church. Those churches which lack it have no substitute. To the degree that they are concerned about unity and mutual responsibility, it is to this ministerial ordering of the church they need to turn.

This, however, is not likely to become clear except to the degree that there is a renewal of the episcopal pattern of the early church. The unifying power of that pattern, it will be recalled, lay in the reciprocal dependence of otherwise independent local churches. None could have leaders except those approved and consecrated by their neighbors. A vertical continuity through time in the laying on of hands was involved in this, but that was not what unified (think of the *episcopi vagantes*). It was, rather, the horizontal mutual responsibility for leadership which was the genius of the arrangement, the chief element in its apostolicity. Only traces of this pattern still remain. Even in the nonpapal episcopal churches the emphasis tends to fall on diachronic succession in office rather than the synchronic mutuality of neighboring communities. If something approximating this early Catholic episcopate were restored, the resultant worldwide network of tenaciously interconnected yet organizationally self-reliant churches might well have competitive advantages similar to those of the early Catholics.

The best case for the papacy, perhaps, is that without it there could be no return to this earlier pattern in the Roman half of Christendom, or perhaps anywhere. Other churches also need its help. To the degree that Rome became the nurturer of a worldwide communion of mutually accountable yet largely autonomous churches, it would prove itself even to some of its sternest critics the God-chosen center of the whole.[29] The heirs of the first phase of the Reformation would welcome this development. They could then become what they claimed to be in the Augsburg Confession, a reform movement within the Roman Catholic communion rather than outside.[30]

Other ways of envisioning the church's Catholic unity are also compatible with this story-shaped understanding of the church. The Faith and Order organic model as outlined in *In Each Place: Towards a Fellowship of Local Churches Truly United* (Geneva: World Council of Churches, 1977) owes much to Eastern Orthodox insights and could easily be adapted and adopted. One could do the same, though perhaps not so easily, with the model of a communion of communions which underlies the Anglican/Roman Catholic dialogue, and which, in a form that embraces all the major Christian traditions, received eloquent exposition in the last of Karl Rahner's books.[31] There are yet other possible descriptions of the unity for which to strive. The church's story is incomplete, and how God will lead cannot be known beforehand.

Yet however the goal is described, it must take into account both Catholic and evangelical concerns. The messianic pilgrim people which is the body of Christ in history needs unifying institutional structures. These structures are to be assessed and reformed functionally by the evangelical touchstone of whether they help the churches witness faithfully by all they are, say, and do to Christ, in the power of the Spirit, and to the glory of God the Father. These structures, however, as Catholics stress, are also gifts of God to be gratefully received and obediently used to his glory. Episcopacy can be one such gift to the whole church, and perhaps papacy also. God will lead.

NOTES

1. H. F. Hamilton, *People of God: An Inquiry Into Christian Origins* (London: Oxford University Press, 1912).

2. For the pre-Vatican II literature, see the incomparably thorough survey by Ulrich Valeske, *Votum Ecclesiae* (Munich: Claudius Verlag, 1962).

3. These three descriptions of the church are simply juxtaposed in the first three chapters of *Lumen gentium,* the Dogmatic Constitution on the Church. For further discussion and references to the literature, see George Lindbeck, *Future of Roman Catholic Theology* (Philadelphia: Fortress Press, 1970), 32–33; and H. Rikhof, *The Concept of the Church* (London: Sheed & Ward, 1981). For many of those in English-speaking countries who began their theological careers in the 1950s, including myself, Bishop J. E. L. Newbigin's *Household of God* (London: SCM Press, 1953) has been influential. Under the rubric "Congregation of the Faithful", it integrates the "people of God" motif with "Body of Christ", and "Community of the Holy Spirit" into a trinitarian pattern which could provide a wider framework for the present sketch.

4. This does not mean that a sacramental understanding of the church is necessarily unevangelical, but rather that it is often regarded as such. See, e.g., a comment such as that of F. W. Katzenbach: "Im Gegensatz zu Lindbeck . . . halte ich die ekklesiologische Verwendung des Begriffs 'Ursakrament' für gefährlich." In *Oecumenica: Jahrbuch für ökumenische Forschung 1967,* ed. F. W. Kantzenbach and V. Vajta (Gütersloh: Gerd Mohn, 1967), 222, fn. 40.

5. See, e.g., Karl Rahner, "Current Problems in Christology", in *Theological Investigations* (Baltimore: Helicon Press, 1961), 1:150 and passim.

6. A somewhat fuller version of much of the material in the next two sections is to be found in George Lindbeck, "The Story-Shaped Church: Critical Exegesis and Theological Interpretation", in *Scriptural Authority and Narrative Interpretation,* ed. G. Green (Philadelphia: Fortress Press, 1987), 161–78.

7. My understanding of this circle as it affects theology is heavily dependent on David Kelsey, *The Uses of Scripture in Recent Theology* (Philadelphia: Fortress Press, 1975).

8. Krister Stendahl's summary of the philological and etymological evidence in *Die Religion in Geschichte und Gegenwart* 3d ed., 3:1297–1304, is both precise and concise.

9. I am chiefly indebted to Hans Frei for my understanding of narrative and its place in Scripture. See Hans Frei, *Eclipse of Biblical Narrative* (New Haven: Yale University Press, 1974); and, most recently, idem, "The 'Literal Reading' of Biblical Narrative in Christian Tradition: Does It Stretch or Will It Break?" in *The Bible and the Narrative Tradition,* ed. Frank McConnell (New York and Oxford: Oxford University Press, 1986), 33–77. For further details on my indebtedness to Frei, see George Lindbeck, *The Nature of Doctrine* (Philadelphia: Westminster Press, 1984), 113–24.

10. It is noteworthy that the Second Vatican Council is ambiguous on

THE CHURCH

whether the church as well as Christ is the antitype "mystically prefigured" by
Israel (in the Declaration on Non-Christian Religions, no. 4). It is therefore
wrong to attribute to it an unequivocal continuation of the older view as seems
to be done by B. Klappert, *Israel und die Kirche* (Munich: Christian Kaiser
Verlag, 1980), 19, with whom in most other respects I am in agreement.

11. Krister Stendahl, *Paul Among Jews and Gentiles* (Philadelphia: Fortress
Press, 1976), 37.

12. I have dealt somewhat more fully with the topics of the last two paragraphs in the essay cited in n. 6 above.

13. Karl Barth, despite his popularization of the nature of the church as
event, is in large part an exception to this generalization. The story-shaped
people of God embracing both Christians and Jews is usually referentially
primary in the later volumes of the *Church Dogmatics.* It is well to observe in
this connection, however, that the popularity of the designation "people of
God" in recent ecclesiology (manifesting itself not least in the second chapter
of the Vatican II's Constitution on the Church) does not necessarily indicate
a return either to narrative or denotative concreteness. Often "people of God"
is treated as an attributive rather than a denotative term. Thus, for example,
Paul Minear discusses it as an "image" of the church logically comparable to
others such as "body" or "bride" (*Images of the Church in the New Testament*
[Philadelphia: Westminster Press, 1960], 66–104). In such an approach, "people of God" becomes competitive with other attributions, and warnings against
overemphasis may seem appropriate (as in fact happens in Raymond Brown,
The Churches the Apostles Left Behind [New York: Paulist/Newman Press,
1984], 60 and 83). One author who in practice recognizes that "people of
God" in the Bible, like "America" in ordinary usage, is usually a denotative
term, and that, when employed this way, it makes no more sense to inveigh
against overuse than in the case of "America" or "church" when those are the
referents of discourse, is Nils A. Dahl, *Das Volk Gottes,* 2d ed. (Darmstadt:
Wissenschaftliche Buchgesellschaft, 1962).

14. All the bodies that profess the Lordship of the Christ Jesus witnessed to
by the canonical Scriptures in ways that purport to be consistent with membership in, e.g., the World Council of Churches would qualify as "empirical
churches" for the purpose of this essay. As we shall see, some bodies that are
not in fact acceptable for World Council membership, such as those which
approve apartheid, are neverthless "empirical churches" on this reckoning
because of what they as communities "profess" or "purport" to affirm. Greater
precision than this, while important in some contexts, does not seem to be
necessary for the following discussion.

15. Salvation and damnation in the ultimate sense depend on decision for or
against the Messiah, for or against the kingdom, and as this is for the most part
possible only for those who hear the message within the context of communities
that look for or know the Messiah, it is there that both salvation and damnation
are chiefly present. Because Christian anti-Semitism has made the message

203

inaudible within the synagogue, this double presence, as was earlier suggested, now applies chiefly to the church. For a further discussion of this thesis, see Lindbeck, *The Nature of Doctrine,* 55–63.

16. This outlook can be used to support rather than undermine the increasing contemporary concern in all churches about "indiscriminate" baptism. When the psychosocial dimension is lacking in an initiatory rite, it turns in effect into play-acting and therefore lacks the traditional condition for validity that a right intention, "the intention to do what the church does", be present, not only in the celebrant but also the other principals. It was because of this condition that pagans, because they presumptively did not intend to rear their children as Christians, could not have them baptized. It is no doubt right to trust God to supply for deficiencies of intention and therefore not "rebaptize" in doubtful cases, but this does not excuse that acquiescence to the profaning of sacred things which has become increasingly rampant as dechristianization has emptied baptism of psychosocial content. That content remained powerful under Christendom: baptism was not play-acting. It made one a Christian, and being Christian, however distorted in understanding and practice, was fundamental to personal and communal identity, i.e., to peoplehood.

17. In modern pluralistic societies it is admittedly difficult to draw the boundaries between "cultural-linguistic groupings". Many individuals are socially alienated or unlocated in such a way that they do not belong to any "people" *(ethne, laos,* or *genos)* in the classical and biblical senses of these terms. Even in the case of highly assimilated Jews, not to mention secularized Christians, it is often difficult to say whether or not they belong to the Jewish people in the biblical and classical "cultural-linguistic" sense. Perhaps "no people" (1 Pet. 2:10) is a way to classify deracinated modern masses of whatever provenance. For a discussion of religions as cultural-linguistic systems (and therefore, by implication, of their adherents as constituting "peoples"), see Lindbeck, *The Nature of Doctrine,* 30–45.

18. These remarks apply chiefly to diaspora situations such as those of the first centuries and, increasingly, the present. Where the socioreligious identity of those "evangelized" is already Christian, an emphasis on bringing as many people as possible into the churches can be construed as a call to the unfaithful to become faithful. From this perspective, the basic purpose of much Protestant revivalism since the days of Edwards and Wesley is unimpeachable, however questionable some of the techniques. Yet another set of problems is posed by mass conversions such as those which occurred after Constantine, among the northern barbarians, and on some modern mission fields (the Khazar would be a medieval Jewish parallel). When, as in such cases, one socioreligious identity collapses and multitudes seek for a new one, the church cannot deny entry. It should no doubt seek to insist on a prolonged and exacting catechumenate as did Ambrose, Chrysostom, and Cyril of Jerusalem in the face of the masses seeking baptism after the Empire became officially Christian. Yet such devices have repeatedly failed, and whole societies have become nominally Christian,

with the result that membership becomes easy, almost automatic, and totally comprehensive. The justification has been that there is no salvation outside the church (which does not necessarily mean that it is easy within it) or, more evangelically expressed, saving faith comes only through the gospel message, and this message is unlikely to be heard outside communities of faith. Whatever the merits of such reasoning when Christendom is intact, it invites disaster when Christendom fades. The churches now increasingly consist of people who have been culturally and linguistically dechristianized and yet retain a residual attachment to the ancestral faith. Return to stricter standards of membership seems imperative if distinctively Christian identity is to be maintained, but this means abandoning the notion that it is the church's business to entice as many as possible by catering to whatever is currently popular whether on the conservative right or the progressive left.

19. One necessary though not sufficient condition for the liberating developments within Western history has been the persistent effort of the church to be the church: to break the power of tribal traditionalism so that Christian serfs could marry freely and choose church vocations; to preserve the freedom of the church over against secular authority; to order church life democratically (as in the case of the Reformed tradition); to abolish slaveholding among adherents (as in the case of those Quakers and Moravians with whom, in effect, abolition started). The stubborn deviancy of Judaism has exerted a structurally similar liberating influence. Like all worldly liberations, those stemming (in part) from the communities of biblical faith have not been unambiguously good. This becomes particularly evident when one thinks of modern science, of laissez-faire capitalism, and of secularized messianism, not least in its Marxist form. (Freudianism should perhaps be added to the list given the crucial role of Freud's Jewishness in his theory-building according to some recent studies.) None of these liberating dynamisms would have been possible, so historians plausibly surmise, in a culture uninfluenced by biblical faith. Yet these have contributed to many of the horrors as well as glories of our contemporary world. The chosen people and its messiah have indeed brought release to the captives (Isa. 61:1; Luke 4:18), but this release has also been not peace but a sword (Matt. 10:34). Such world-transforming consequences can be seen in the biblical perspective as the use God makes in both mercy and judgment of the witness of his people; but it is the witness, not the transformation of the world, which is their mission. It is this which they are consciously to pursue. The consequences are unknown and unknowable byproducts which must be left in the hands of God.

20. The Reformers shared the early Catholic consensus that the ministry of word and sacrament is divinely instituted, and they also understood ordination as sacramental, i.e., as a rite whereby God in response to the prayers and actions of the community empowers for service. Their objections to calling ordination a sacrament were directed against late medieval views that it conferred a special personal sanctity and made priests members of a privileged caste rather than

servants of the gospel. (See George Lindbeck, "Karl Rahner and a Protestant View of the Sacramentality of the Ministry", in *Proceedings of the Catholic Theological Society of America* 21 [1967]: 267–88). In any case, the medieval distortions and the later Protestant disregard of the early Catholic consensus are now being overcome among both Roman Catholics (Vatican II) and non-Catholics. In church-oriented ecumenical circles, even if not on popular and ecclesiastical levels, the understanding of the ordained ministry articulated in the Faith and Order Lima document, *Baptism, Eucharist and Ministry,* is now widespread. Further, it has been generally agreed both in the sixteenth century and in the contemporary ecumenical movement that the wider unity of the church should be given synodal and conciliar expression. It is the question of whether it should also be papally and/or episcopally structured which has been the divisive issue.

21. This point that one and the same institutional structure may be both of divine and of human right played an important role in the Lutheran and Roman Catholic discussions of the papacy, and seems to be widely accepted. For contributions to those discussions, see George Lindbeck, "Papacy and 'ius divinum' ", in *Papal Primacy and the Universal Church,* ed. P. C. Empie and others (Minneapolis: Augsburg Publishing House, 1974), 193–207, and C. Peter, "Dimensions of *jus divinum* in Roman Catholic Theology", in *Theological Studies* 34 (1973), 227–50.

22. This is not simply a "natural law" argument to the effect that health in ecclesiastical as in legal systems depends on respect for precedent. As the Gospels make clear, and as increased historical knowledge of his milieu confirms, Jesus was much more traditionally Jewish than Christians have generally supposed. It was what he did and what was done to him, especially the crucifixion and the resurrection, not his teachings per se, which were the novelty. The new is enduringly significant to the extent that it renews and transforms the past rather than destroys it; but the avoidance of destructive loss in the face of apocalyptic newness requires profound respect for tradition (which, needless to say, must be sharply differentiated from unwillingness to change). This is one reason Paul the traditionalist has in the long run been much more powerfully innovative than the gnostic antitraditionalists.

23. This pattern of argument had its origins in the Lutheran Reformation of the sixteenth century, but, with the disappearance of belief that there is a single biblical pattern of church organization, it is now widespread also among other Protestants. It can be used against dogmatic anti-episcopalianism as well as against dogmatic pro-episcopalianism (as happens, e.g., in the Lutheran churches of Sweden and Finland, where the retention of the historic succession in the face of free-church absolutism becomes, in effect, *status confessionis*).

24. I take this comparably decisive period to be, not that of Jamnia, but that of the formation of Ezra's pentateuchal Torah during the exile (as James A. Sanders in effect argues in his *Torah and Canon* [Philadelphia: Fortress Press, 1972]).

25. I abstract from the question of infallibility which concerns the nature of doctrine more than it does that of organizational structures, and needs to be considered in reference to the Bible and the church as a whole as well as councils and popes. See Lindbeck, *The Nature of Doctrine,* 98–104.

26. This is essentially the position taken by the Lutheran participants in the official American dialogue with Roman Catholics reported in Empie, *Papal Primacy and the Universal Church.* Papal primacy is acceptable but not the claim to irreversibility.

27. The question of irreversibility, it should be noted, is that of continuity, not of permanence of structural forms. Location in Rome is not essential (there was, after all, the Avignon interlude); and, as Karl Rahner speculatively suggested (in an interview which has not been published in the *Theological Investigations*), the papal function could be exercised by, e.g., a committee of three whose jurisdictional powers might be no greater than that of the secretary of a Quaker meeting or the Stated Clerk of a Presbyterian General Assembly (the examples are my own). What is essential, however, is that such transformations take place by papal self-limitation, not by imposition from, e.g., a council, or by revolution. It is the continuity of the institution which is said to be guaranteed, and therefore also the irreversibility (= infallibility) of the corresponding dogmatic development. Even if the pope never again spoke ex cathedra or exercised "immediate and universal" jurisdiction in the sense of Vatican I, the possibility of doing so under appropriate circumstances (if or when these should ever recur) would remain.

28. See George Lindbeck, "The Reformation and the Infallibility Debate", *Teaching Authority and Infallibility in the Church,* ed. P. C. Empie and others (Minneapolis: Augsburg, Publishing House, 1978), 101–19, 312–16, esp. Thesis 5, 315–16, for a fuller discussion of the potentially marginal character of disagreements over the irreversible (i.e., "irreformable" or "infallible") character of at least some dogmatic decisions and, by extension, of the structural developments to which they refer.

29. Decentralization of the type envisioned here would make possible great variations in Jewish-Christian relations (which, as Karl Barth among others has noted, may well be crucial to the future of the church), in ecumenical developments, and in canon law between different localities and regions. Christians in one area might be in a position to move much faster on some matters than those in other areas, and this would, of course, be reflected in the candidates they proposed to lead them (for initiation of episcopal candidacies would be a local matter as in the early church). If the proposed candidates in a given region were consistently in favor of, e.g., communion with the local Anglicans and/or the ordination of women, and these candidates were acceptable to neighboring churches, Rome would have difficulty in persistently refusing its consent. If it were to do so, to mention one difficulty, some sees might be left vacant indefinitely. The papal role in such a situation could be to mediate between regions of the church that disagreed on these issues so that different local practices

could develop without schism. Nothing similar to this, needless to say, is likely to occur in the next generation or two apart from world-historical or ecclesiastical events of the magnitude of World War II or Vatican II. But, on the other hand, there is no reason to suppose that the possibilities of upheaval and change in the next half century will be any less than in the last fifty years.

30. While the Augustana has come to be regarded as Lutheran property, it was in its origins more nearly a pan-Reformation manifesto than were any of the other sixteenth-century confessions. See Brian Gerrish, "Strasbourg Revisited: The Augsburg Confession in Reformed Perspective", *The Augsburg Confession in Ecumenical Perspective*, ed. H. Meyer (Geneva: Lutheran World Federation, 1981), 129–61.

31. This was written together with Heinrich Fries, *Unity of the Churches: An Actual Possibility* (Philadelphia and New York: Fortress Press and Paulist/Newman, 1983). The most recent report from the international Lutheran and Roman Catholic dialogue, *Facing Unity* (Geneva: Lutheran World Federation, 1984), proposes a model of the unity Christians seek which corresponds more closely to the one outlined here.

9

THE SACRAMENTS

THEODORE RUNYON

I. MATTER AND SPIRIT

Francis Paget, later bishop of Oxford, views the sacraments not only as central to worship but as the "unsurpassed expression" of that doctrine which the authors of *Lux Mundi* term central to Christian faith itself—the incarnation.[1] Just as in the historical figure of Jesus the divine has made itself available in human flesh, visible to the eye and understandable to the ear, so in the sacraments the incarnation continues to be the model of divine-human communication. The Savior makes himself available through water, bread and wine: physical and material— visible, tangible, tastable—yet transmitting a reality which includes and transcends the physical as such.

What undergirded the *Lux Mundi* enterprise—and made it so appealing to many of its readers—was the conviction that a religion grounded in the doctrine of the incarnation could successfully confront the main intellectual challenges of the time. "Materialism" was the challenge to which the sacraments could speak most directly. The *Lux Mundi* authors sought to view materialism not as a dire threat to genuine Christianity but as a stimulus that forced into awareness resources of the faith hitherto unapparent. Paget regarded a "false spiritualism", which rejects the body and the material world, as the chief misunderstanding of Christianity in the popular mind of his time.[2] And materialism, he claims, has "done a valuable service in correcting the exaggeration of a one-sided spiritualism". From the incarnation flows the "sacramental principle", which sees the physical universe not as disjoined from or antithetical to the spiritual but rather views the two as interpenetrating: the physical and material are infused with the transcendent and

209

spiritual, and the spiritual communicates itself through the this-worldly and material. "Sensible objects, agents and acts [become] the means or instruments of Divine energies." The saving and sanctifying transcendent power is "conveyed by means . . . taken from this world, and addressed to human senses".

According to Paget, the fact that Judaism served as the seedbed of Christianity reinforced this affirmation of the material world, for Judaism was a nation and a people with a history "replete with forecasts of the consecration of material things, . . . encouraged to look for the blessings of Divine goodness through sensible means". There was no need to "dislodge the sacramental principle out of the minds of those among whom our Lord came". The purpose was not to destroy but to fulfill this Jewish heritage through the

> embodiment of grace in ordinances: the designation of visible agents, acts, and substances, to be the instruments of Divine virtue—this principle is so intimately and essentially woven into the texture of Christianity that it cannot be got out without destroying the whole fabric.

If materialism posed a major challenge to the ingenuity and resources of the Christian faith at the end of the nineteenth century, what is a comparable challenge today? To be sure, materialism has by no means disappeared as a threat in our time. Yet reductionist materialism, which seemed so potent in the last century, has been largely discredited by philosophical materialists themselves, many of whom in the meantime have come to recognize the inexhaustible nature of values traditionally called "spiritual" and the limitations of reductionism. Moreover, for Paget the issue was posed in the framework of the perennial mind/matter problem or spirit/body dichotomy. And a solution was sought on the intellectual level in terms of satisfactory metaphysical relations. In our time the issue is more practical, for the form that the threat of materialism takes (as much or more in the West as in the Eastern bloc with its official materialism) is the acute problem of the *ecological crisis,* which is a problem not just for the intellect and consciousness but for the environment, for health, for economics and the whole material base. This is a crisis brought about by systems—East and West—that have made the production and distribution of material goods and the increase of material wealth their chief aim but in the process are destroying and exhausting the material resources upon which all life and future generations depend. Can the doctrine of the sacraments say something to "materialism" in this form? Obviously there are many other issues in the life of society and of the church to which the sacraments can speak, but for purposes of illustration we will address ourselves primarily to this one in the conviction that, if it can be shown how the sacraments illumine an issue that is among the most pressing of modern life, we will have demonstrated today what *Lux Mundi* sought to do for its time. Its purpose was "to present positively the central ideas and principles of religion, in the light of contemporary thought and current problems", and thus to engage in "the real development of theology". It defined theology as

> the process in which the Church, standing firm in her old truths, enters into the apprehension of the new social and intellectual movements of each age: and because "the truth makes her free" is able to assimilate all new material, to welcome and give its place to all new knowledge, [and] to throw herself into the sanctification of each new social order.

This "sanctification of the social order" requires the transformation and modification of the individuals and institutions that comprise it.

One positive contribution that dialectical materialism in its contemporary form of "critical theory" has made to theological reflection is to call attention to the responsibility of thought to modify behavior. To paraphrase Marx, as long as theology simply *"interprets* the world", its effects on systems and structures will be minimal. "The point is to *change* it." Religion reduced to the private sphere and predilections of the individual cannot serve as the agent of change which *Lux Mundi* seeks when it calls upon the church to "throw herself into the sanctification of each new social order". Ideas that do not lead to change in structures and behavior have the effect of reinforcing the status quo. Sacramental worship at its best, however, is always a praxis, a way of being and thinking about God, self, community and world, that is acted out and reflected upon in a process that leads to an ever new and more profound understanding of reality as well as intervention in it. This is what the "sanctification" of both the individual and society today involves. Thus, in what follows, the praxis element will never be far from our considerations.

II. KINGDOM AND SACRAMENT

If there has been a characteristic paradigm shift in theology from the end of the nineteenth century to the present, it is the shift from incarnation to *kingdom* as the organizing motif. This is by no means a denial of the central role that Christology plays in all Christian thought. It is, rather, the attempt to do justice to what scholars agree was at the center of Jesus' own ministry. His healings, his exorcisms, his commandments, his parables—even his supper with his disciples—anticipate the kingdom. They are signs and first fruits that appear wherever Jesus' words, as agent of the kingdom, are truly heard, judgment and forgiveness are received, and God's intended order of justice and love is reestablished. The repentance *(metanoia)* for which Jesus calls is a turning away from the world as it is now constituted and toward the future as constituted by the One who is addressed in the "kingdom prayer" with the petition, "Thy kingdom come, thy will be done on earth as it is in heaven." This is the context in which Jesus' words to Pilate in the Johannine account must be understood, "My kingdom is not of this world." The "world" to which he refers is the present age, presided over by the likes of Pilate, Herod and Caiaphas, which will be superseded by the age to come presided over by God's own agent of justice, the Son of man. Although the new age will be a radical transformation of the present, in neither the Old nor the New Testament is it envisioned as a volatilization of this present material world into a realm of pure spirit. It is precisely *this* world that is the object of God's redeeming activity, for it is this world that is God's creation which he will not abandon! Under the sign of the rainbow it is to be transformed and restored, not annihilated. Therefore, the sacraments are to be understood as *signs of the kingdom* within this cosmic drama and overarching purpose.[3] Indeed, material evidences and actions—food, drink, clothing, housing, visitation—become the clearest indication of participation (or nonparticipation) in the power of the kingdom (Matt. 25:31–46).

In a section entitled "The Eucharist as Meal of the Kingdom", the ecumenical document *Baptism, Eucharist and Ministry* claims that "the eucharist opens up the vision of the divine rule which has been promised as the final renewal of creation, and is a foretaste of it".[4] According to Yves Congar, sacrament cannot be understood apart from this notion of the renewal of creation. But he joins this with the doctrine of the incarnation by saying that, with the incarnation of the Son into the life of this world, "God had irrevocably decided" for renewal:

> Seen in this light, the notion of sacrament assumes dynamic value; it is related to the world and its history. It becomes the concrete historical

expression of God's design for salvation in this world, the sign and instrument through which God works out his decision to intervene with his grace in mankind and in creation in order to make them achieve the end for which he had destined them from the beginning.[5]

Moreover, in this renewal no sharp line is drawn between the human and natural worlds, for their futures intertwine,[6] as the prophet envisions the future:

> With righteousness [God] shall judge the poor,
>   and decide with equity for the meek of the earth. . . .
> The wolf shall dwell with the lamb,
>   and the leopard shall lie down with the kid,
> and the calf and the lion and the fatling together,
>   and a little child shall lead them. . . .
> They shall not hurt or destroy
>   in all my holy mountain;
> for the earth shall be full of the knowledge of the Lord
>   as the waters cover the sea. (Isa. 11:4, 6, 9)

Indeed, as St. Paul later describes it, the creation itself will benefit from the redemption of humanity through Christ (just as the world of nature now suffers under the burden of human corruption):

> For the creation waits with eager longing for the revealing of the sons of God; . . . because the creation itself will be set free from its bondage to decay and obtain the glorious liberty of the children of God. (Rom. 8:19, 21)

As Jesus assembles his followers for a final meal, he enacts a parable which in summary fashion dramatizes his own life as a servant of the kingdom, a kingdom whose first signs according to his preaching are the forgiveness of sins and God's love poured out for the reconciliation of all who are open to the good news of divine mercy. As they begin the meal, he says to them, "I have earnestly desired to eat this passover with you before I suffer; for I tell you I shall not eat it until it is fulfilled in the kingdom of God" (Luke 22:15–16). As he passes the cup he says, "From now on I shall not drink of the fruit of the vine until the kingdom of God comes" (v. 18). With these words and actions he transforms the paschal meal, a meal of remembrance that celebrates the faithfulness of God in the past, into an eschatological feast, the foretaste of the age to come.[7]

What is this kingdom for which Jesus risks everything? And how can bread and wine serve as indications of its coming and at the same time be identified with Jesus' own life and mission?

In the hands of Jesus, the bread and the wine, symbols of the old order and the previous covenant, become signs of the new covenant of grace that is the hallmark of Jesus' interpretation of the kingdom. To receive them is to receive the very substance of his life given for the kingdom as he understood it. To participate in that life is to receive eschatological food and drink, the new creation in its promissory form, the earnest *(arrabōn)* of that which is to come. "The eucharist is the meal at which the messiah feeds His people as a sign of the feasting in the coming kingdom."[8] To receive bread and wine from Christ is therefore to receive the power of the kingdom, which was the driving force in his existence as he embodied and lived out the intention of God. This is why, according to Paul, one cannot "eat the bread" (i.e., partake in who Christ was in his body, his very being) and "drink the cup" (i.e., partake in that for which he poured out his life's blood) and not eat and drink the kingdom of God. To participate in the sacramental power of the new age and yet to operate habitually in terms of the selfishness, injustice and insensitivity of the old order is to partake "unworthily" and to invite judgment and dire consequences (1 Cor. 11:20–32).

III. FROM KINGDOM TO CREATION:
THE ECOLOGICAL SETTING

Once we have grasped the eschatological quality of the sacrament as revealed in Christ, we are in a position to look back from the *eschaton* to the *proton,* from kingdom to creation, and to look at the creation with new eyes. Turning to the first chapters of Genesis, we discover that the ancient Hebrew stories of origins open up the character of our relationship to the world afresh. Indeed, it could be said that in the hands of the Creator, the world itself serves as the *first sacrament,* the first and most basic use of the material to communicate and facilitate the divine-human relationship. Christ's own giving of freedom through bread and wine to humankind is prefigured in the Creator's bestowal of freedom to the creatures as God entrusts to male and female the care and protection of the world and calls upon them to use it in ways consistent with the divine intentions (Gen. 1:28ff.). The very term "image of God" may have been used by the priestly authors of Genesis 1 (which was written during the exile in Babylon) in conscious analogy to the

214

custom of the Babylonian emperor who, when he had conquered a new territory, set up an image of himself in the capital city of the province and appointed a governor, a viceregent, who ruled by virtue of the authority vested in the image.[9] If this combination of image and governor was indeed in the minds of those who in the first chapter of Genesis set forth the Hebrew perception of human life, it stood in stark (and perhaps even polemical) contrast to the official view contained in the Babylonian epic of creation, *Enuma elish.* In that saga, humankind was created as slaves to do the work of the gods so the gods might be at rest. The Hebrew historical consciousness had originated, however, precisely in the revolt against slavery. Their God had called them not into slavery but into a suzerainty covenant, into co-responsibility for the world.[10]

> And God blessed them, and God said to them, "Be fruitful and multiply, and fill the earth and subdue it; and have dominion over the fish of the sea and over the birds of the air and over every living thing that moves upon the earth." And God said, "Behold, I have given you every plant yielding seed which is upon the face of all the earth, and every tree with seed in its fruit; you shall have them for food. And to . . . everything that has the breath of life, I have given every green plant for food." And it was so. And God saw everything that he had made, and behold, it was very good. (Gen. 1:28–31)

The gift to humanity of the world entrusted to our care is therefore the most fundamental sacramental act. In and through it are mediated those interrelationships which are basic to human existence: our relationships to the world, to God, and to ourselves. First, as an inheritance granted to us, the world provides us with the material base for the independence of mature daughters and sons. Second, as a stewardship, the world links us in a special way to the Creator, for in giving us this gift, God gives not just some*thing.* In, with, and through the sacramental gift we receive God's own self as "our Father". To *parent* is to create a life related to oneself yet free, an independent center of will and action. In giving us the world, God both undergirds us with a Parent's love and affirms us in our maturity and responsibility to care for that which has been entrusted to us. Third, in these sacramentally mediated connections to God and creation, we receive our relationship to ourselves and each other, our identity and calling as co-responsible and mutually answerable creatures.

The implications of this sacramental relationship to God and the world for a theology of ecology and an ethic of responsibility are evident. But just as evident is the fact that humankind is far gone from the original divine intention. We have separated the gift from the Giver, the inheritance from the Testator, and acted as if it were our own with no answerability—either to the Creator, or to our fellow inhabitants of the planet, or to future generations. The ironic result of this willful absconding with our inheritance has been not increased freedom but fateful bondage. The world is becoming an ever more intolerable burden, an ominous fate and threat, our own white whale from which, like Captain Ahab, we cannot disentangle ourselves, though it carry us with it to our destruction. This apocalyptic turn of events impresses itself upon the imagination of the present generation and makes it very difficult to see the world in its basic sacramental reality. How can we envision it as the continuing "gift of the Father's unfailing grace"?

It would be easy to accuse the church of failing humankind at this point. Too often the church has been unaware of the larger meaning and cosmic implications of the sacrament, and has fostered a timid, truncated, narrowly ecclesiastical understanding, content to settle for religious practices in a sacred corner of the world where it controls the sacramental keys to heaven—yet has lost the keys of the kingdom and its world-transforming power. But such accusations would serve no useful purpose. As the authors of *Lux Mundi* recognized, often a new situation and new challenges are necessary for the church to discover its own treasures. They were writing at the very beginning of a recovery of the eschatological, world-historical dimension of Christianity. The nineteenth century had begun to suspect that the original Jewishness of the Christian message had been obscured by layers of Hellenistic and Neoplatonic interpretation which had transformed Jesus' message of the kingdom into an otherworldly metaphysic. Paget was aware of the importance of the recovery of Jewishness for sacramental theology. Nevertheless, his interpretation of the kingdom was still conceived in terms of an idealist "realm of souls", those nurtured by the sacraments to look beyond this world for salvation. The natural world and its preservation did not enter the picture, because there was not yet an awareness of impending crisis.

How can the redemptive mission of Christ extend not just to humanity but to the rest of creation as well? How can God's "purpose which he set forth in Christ as a plan for the fulness of time, [serve] to unite all things in him, things in heaven and things on earth" (Eph. 1:9–10)?

The corruption which has entered history through human irresponsibility now affects the whole planet. Can God's grace in Christ have an effect equally profound? The starting point for this fundamental transformation is to be found in the sacramental event itself.

If the world as we now experience it is unrecognizable as the gift of a loving God; if it has become more threat than promise, more a tragic destiny in which we are embroiled than a sacred trust over which we have been granted control; if it is the domain of "principalities and powers" rather than the creature of God: how then can the sacrament, deeply embedded as it is in the materiality of our world, represent both the fallen world and Christ? Are they not antithetical? It is precisely at this point, however, that the redemptive work of Christ becomes most evident.

In the hands of Christ, the sacrament is presented to us as *the world in its original and eschatological form.* He takes the bread and the wine, which are products of our ordinary world—and therefore related to the complexities of international grain cartels, embargoes, starvation, alcoholism, and all the other ways in which God's good gifts have gone awry—and turns them into signs of his kingdom of justice and love. He does this by identifying them with himself and his mission—his body, his life's blood—just as he did with the paschal bread and wine at the Last Supper. Having joined them with his life for the kingdom, thus raising them to their eschatological destiny, he hands the bread and the wine back to us to make us participants in that kingdom by sharing its first fruits *(aparchē)* which nourish us along the way.

Because this bread and wine are signs of the *resurrected* Christ, they bring with them the unquenchable assurance that he cannot finally be defeated. Therefore, as overwhelming as the task of stewardship of the world may seem, it is not meaningless or without ultimate purpose because it joins us to Christ's own redemptive work of bringing order out of chaos. In the end he will prevail! Because this bread and wine are also signs of the *crucified* Christ, we are reminded that responsibility always involves suffering and sacrifice. There are no guarantees of progress, no promises of easy victories. Yet the signs communicate to us that profound and persistent love that sustains us even when faced with defeat, assuring us that "neither death, nor life, . . . nor principalities, . . . nor powers, nor height, nor depth, nor anything else in all creation, will be able to separate us from the love of God in Christ Jesus our Lord" (Rom. 8:38-39).

217

IV. BAPTISM

If the eucharist is the sacrament that nourishes us along the way by making us participants in Christ's redeeming and renewing work in the world, baptism is the rite that inaugurates this identification with Christ and his body, the church. Baptism "unites the one baptized with Christ and with his people".[11] It places the person in a new context by incorporating him or her into the ongoing history of Christ's kingdom mission.

Baptism, like eucharist, is thus best understood within its original biblical, eschatological setting. It identifies the one baptized with the new age which Christ is bringing. As Geoffrey Wainwright observes:

> For the Christian community, meaning is in the making: life is oriented towards God's ultimate purpose, and history-making is the way to the attainment of that purpose both for individuals and humanity as a whole; the most characteristic Christian rituals [eucharist and baptism] are therefore predominantly transformative in character.[12]

Although in baptism today attention is directed primarily to the individual being baptized, it is probably accurate to say that in biblical times, in the awareness of both the congregation and the baptizand, the larger context was more prominent. They viewed the event, first of all, as occurring at a crucial moment in *world history* as part of God's intervention and saving acts; and second, as an event in the life of the *church,* to which God is adding daily in order that it might be the body of Christ at work in the world; third, the *individual* is consequently understood as identifying with, and being incorporated into, this larger picture—washed, cleansed, and made part of God's new history in Christ Jesus and sealed for the age to come by the Spirit (Eph. 1:3–14). Let us look more closely at these three aspects of baptism.

First, according to Mark's account, Jesus' original and fundamental message was, "The time is fulfilled, and the kingdom of God is at hand; repent, and believe in the gospel" (Mark 1:15). Jesus understood his own ministry within *the cosmic framework of events* that would reestablish God's order and reign over the world. This reign would not be arbitrarily imposed, however, for God seeks those who serve not out of compulsion "but in the new life of the Spirit" (Rom. 7:6), who obey not out of fear or self-interest but in the genuine partnership of inner conviction, gratitude and love, which God's grace alone makes possible. Thus the kingdom is heralded both by Jesus and the early church with the freeing announcement of God's radical mercy and love, even toward the "ungodly" (Rom. 5:6). Thus the events that accompany the dawning of the new age are acts of forgiveness which usher in the age of reconciliation (2 Cor. 5:17ff.) and cut through the vicious circles of sin, guilt, judgment and recrimination that have only added to the world's misery. Baptism occurs in the setting of these new possibilities that God has opened up, accompanied by the urgent call to respond: "Behold, now is the acceptable time; behold, now is the day of salvation" (2 Cor. 6:2).

Second, there is a keen awareness that God has taken the initiative in Christ Jesus to create a community, the *church,* instrumental to the kingdom in word and deed. This community is called variously the people of a new covenant (Hebrews 8), the renewed Israel (Galatians 6), the body of Christ (Romans 12; 1 Corinthians 12; Ephesians 4), and the fellowship of the Holy Spirit (1 Corinthians 12; Ephesians 4) (the Spirit was universally recognized as the inaugurator of the age to come [Acts 2:17ff.]). The church is therefore God's creation, understood as preceding the individual and providing the environment in which the power of the kingdom is extended. God saves by creating a people of the covenant. "You are a chosen race, a royal priesthood, a holy nation, God's own people" (1 Pet. 2:9). Here as in the whole Hebrew tradition, salvation is unthinkable apart from community. This people is where God's rule is first recognized and where, through worship, proclamation, nurture and service, the new reality begins to penetrate the old eon. This priority of the communal is the continuing truth to which the practice of infant baptism legitimately bears witness. Just as God's activity in history precedes the individual ("While we were still weak, at the right time . . .", Rom. 5:6), so the saving community precedes the individual believer and the individual finds his or her identity within the calling of the church. Understood in this way, all baptism is (qualitatively) *infant* baptism, regardless of the maturity of the person, for all enter into the community as "babes in Christ", needing the training, nurture and sustenance of the community if they are to grow in the awareness, understanding and performance of their role as members of the body of Christ.

The third emphasis is complementary: the identity and vocation granted the *individual.* In baptism the individual person is commissioned, made a disciple, and given a mission. The "people of God" is

219

created for a purpose: in order to "declare the wonderful deeds of him who called you out of darkness into his marvelous light. Once you were no people but now you are God's people; once you had not received mercy but now you have received mercy" (1 Pet. 2:9–10). The awareness of mercy and the consciousness of reconciling love are events that take place in the hearts and lives of persons—or they do not occur. As important as groups and movements, structures and institutions are for the realization of societal goals, discipleship requires committed individuals. Therefore *all* baptism is (qualitatively) *"adult"* baptism, regardless of the age at which it takes place, because it has as its aim *responsible discipleship* in the world. It creates active agents of the kingdom, those who have themselves tasted the grace and mercy of God and whose lives are dedicated to extending that power. This aim is clearly stated in the practice of baptizing those who have come to the "age of responsibility", but it is also recognized in the practice of confirmation, especially where this is understood as the confirming by the individual and the community of the vocation given with baptism. This vocation is closely tied to loyalty to Christ. "In that the name of Jesus Christ is named over the neophyte, he is committed to Jesus as Lord, belongs to him, and owes him obedience."[13] The World Council of Churches' *Baptism, Eucharist and Ministry,* and its accompanying Commentary, recognizes the complementarity of the baptismal practices traditionally termed "adult" (or "believers") baptism and "infant" baptism. "Both forms of baptism require a similar and responsible attitude towards Christian nurture,"[14] and both view baptism as laying the foundation in divine grace for lifelong commitment and service. This mutual recognition, that different baptismal practices are in fact complementary and serve to preserve the larger meaning of baptism as cosmic, communal and personal, is one of the real accomplishments of the ecumenical movement and represents a genuine advance over the situation at the time *Lux Mundi* was written.

In the context of the ecological crisis, however, it is also important to see baptism and its confirmation as renewing of the *image of God,* taking up anew the responsibility to care for the world entrusted to humanity. Every child entering the world is burdened with the accumulated sins of previous generations. Each could claim, "I am not responsible for what generations before me have done to poison the atmosphere of the planet, both physically and morally." The waters of baptism, by enacting God's grace and new beginnings, cleanse us from the necessity to make excuses and to justify and defend ourselves in the face of the situation of ecological deterioration in which we find ourselves. The point is not to assign blame but to open up the possibility for freely accepted responsibility in the present for the future. Baptism accomplishes this by renewing in us the vocation of the image of God. This is the history-making function of baptism and the way in which the praxis of the church can serve to transform the praxis of the world.

Such an understanding of baptism contrasts of course with the popular view—especially in old Christendom where baptism became virtually automatic—that allowed baptism to serve in a merely sociocultural way as consecration of the status quo. Such a distortion appears as a travesty in the light of the eschatological and transformative intention of the rite. It tames and trivializes baptism and robs it of its ability to mediate God's renewing power. Part of the church's responsibility today, therefore, is to shock traditional Christian societies into an awareness of the revolutionary import of celebrations that have become all too conformist and harmless. In third world and non-Christian cultures the intended role of baptism and the eucharist can often be seen more clearly, where a lively church functions as the leaven of hope in society.

V. UNITY

It is ironic that the sacraments, which are the sign of the unity of the church in Christ, have been the occasion for some of the most bitter divisions. At the time of the writing of the *Lux Mundi,* for example, the sacraments had contributed to factionalism among Anglicans. In one sense, this is a testimony to the sacraments' historic importance and meaningfulness; for individuals, churches and nations do not quarrel over what to them is unimportant. Nevertheless, these conflicts have proved a scandal to the non-Christian world, and the ecumenical movement has rightly set about to try not only to repair the damage but to build a new positive consensus, based on solid biblical and historical grounds, which can enable the sacraments to serve as the basis for unity and common mission rather than the occasion for strife.

An encouraging example of this new trend is the document, already referred to, *Baptism, Eucharist and Ministry,* a product of the World Council of Churches' Faith and Order Commission. Often termed the "Lima Document" after the city in which it was finalized, it spells out substantial areas of agreement among Protestants, Orthodox, and

Roman Catholics. This process of convergence has already resulted in mutual recognition of baptism among many bodies, and in table and pulpit fellowship among some, and it may eventually flower into fuller communion across lines that continue to divide the body of Christ. Moreover, the conviction is becoming increasingly widespread that sacramental fellowship *(communicatio in sacris)* practiced *before* full doctrinal agreement can be achieved could be a strong impetus toward genuine unity. The sacraments would then be allowed to exercise the healing power that all parties agree they possess.

The tension which continues regarding intercommunion is but an example of the creative tension that is the mark of the eschatological nature of the church and of the salvation it brings to the world. In one sense, the new has already arrived. We recognize the power of Christ and his Spirit where the church is alive and faithful. As individual Christians we live partly in the old order, partly in the new, tasting just enough of the first fruits to yearn for more. But this is our destiny and our calling, to be heralds of the new creation in the midst of the old, nurtured and strengthened with identity and purpose by the sacraments.

NOTES

1. The sacraments in fact mesh into the entire "body of doctrine".

2. Cf. Robert W. Jenson's observation that most non-Christian religions, at their more sophisticated levels, tend toward nonembodied representations of the divine: *Visible Words* (Philadelphia: Fortress Press, 1978), 29–30.

3. Cf. an earlier version of the argument here presented, "The World as Original Sacrament", *Worship* 54, no. 6 (November 1980):495–511. Note also Alexander Schmemann, *For the Life of the World,* rev. ed. (Crestwood, N.Y.: St. Vladimir's Seminary Press, 1973), and idem, *The Eucharist: Sacrament of the Kingdom* (Crestwood, N.Y.: St. Vladimir's Seminary Press, 1988).

4. *Baptism, Eucharist and Ministry* (Geneva: World Council of Churches, 1982), 14.

5. Yves Congar, "The Notion of 'Major' or 'Principal' Sacraments", in *The Sacraments in General,* ed. Edward Schillebeeckx and Boniface Willems, vol. 31 of Concilium (New York: Paulist Press, 1968), 28.

6. Cf. *Lumen Gentium,* chap. 7, par. 48, in *Vatican Council II,* ed. Austin Flannery (Collegeville, Minn.: Liturgical Press, 1975), 407.

7. Cf. Alasdair I. C. Heron, *Table and Tradition* (Philadelphia: Westminster Press, 1984), 54, 152ff.

8. Geoffrey Wainwright, *Eucharist and Eschatology* (New York: Oxford University Press, 1981), 94.

9. Gerhard von Rad, *Genesis* (Philadelphia: Westminster Press, 1961), 58.

10. Cf. Walther Eichrodt, *Theology of the Old Testament* (Philadelphia: Westminster Press, 1967), 2:127ff.

11. *Baptism, Eucharist and Ministry,* 2.

12. Geoffrey Wainwright, *Doxology* (New York: Oxford University Press, 1980), 121.

13. Eduard Lohse, as quoted by Jenson, *Visible Words,* 130.

14. *Baptism, Eucharist and Ministry,* 5.

10

CHRISTIAN ETHICS

KEITH WARD

I. OLD-STYLE NATURAL LAW

Does the Christian faith have anything important and distinctive to say about ethics? The question poses a dilemma. If it has nothing distinctive to say, then there is really no such thing as "Christian ethics". But if it is distinctive, that seems to imply that there can be no common ground between Christians and non-Christians, that Christians are doomed to remain cut off from the rest of the human race in their own moral ghetto. Neither alternative seems very palatable. Fortunately these are not the only alternatives. Indeed, the route that Christian moralists have taken for most of the time has been to claim a large extent of common ground between all people of good will and sound knowledge, but to add that there is a distinctive Christian content which completes and to some extent transfigures this common ground. This is the route of natural law, not in itself an especially Christian idea at all.

The idea of a natural moral law arguably begins with Aristotle, but certainly is to be found in quite a developed form in the Stoic philosophers. For them, it was the idea that, in addition to the positive laws of particular states, there is a law for humankind as such, discernible by human reason, laying down the fundamental principles of justice. This law is related both to nature and to reason. For the Stoics, nature is a rational organism, with its own inherent laws of growth and decay. The rational discernment of these laws, these patterns of change in a rationally ordered universe, reveals the principles in accordance with which the wise will order their lives. This double reference to reason and the natural order, and the perception of the well-ordered human life as a microcosmic repetition of universal principles of order in the universe, expresses a particular view of the nature of morality, as a conformity to cosmic order, rationally perceived.

The Christian church took over this complex of ideas; and in the work of Thomas Aquinas they were integrated into a more explicitly theistic perspective. Now God was conceived as the transcendent creator, pure and perfect Spirit, the ocean of unlimited existence *(pelagus substantiae infinitum),* who creates the world out of overflowing goodness. The eternal law for creatures is rooted in God's design for the finite world; and the natural law is the rational perception by creatures of that eternal law—the pattern in the divine mind of how things are intended to be. In accordance with Aquinas's general mode of argument from the world to God as its cause, human reason apprehends God's design by examining the structures of nature. There is no direct intuition of the divine being. Knowing that nature is created purposively, reason can discern the purposes of nature by examining the phenomena themselves. For Aquinas, there is certainly a revealed law of God, enshrined in the Bible and especially in the records of the life and teachings of Christ. The natural law, however, is knowable by all people, using reason alone. What it discloses is the natural inclinations of human beings, the proper fulfilments of things in the created order. Its basic axiom is that good is to be sought and evil avoided. And we know what is good by knowing what is rationally desirable by beings of the nature humans have. There is a complicated set of implicit references here to divine purposes, to the inherent purposes of nature, and to the rationally desirable goals of human life. All these factors are believed to cohere in a providentially ordered universe. Thus it comes to be thought that anything which frustrates a natural purpose of nature is morally wrong and that what advances such purposes is morally desirable.

With the collapse of Aristotelian physics and the rise of the physical and biological sciences since the seventeenth century, it is no longer obvious that these factors do cohere. Do the inherent purposes of nature express the divine purposes for the world? Indeed, are there any purposes inherent in nature at all? Are human desires consonant with any natural purposes there may be? And is human reason not set in opposition to desires, so that the best we can do is to suppress them, and there is little hope of ordering them into any harmonious hierarchy? One of the main motivating factors behind natural law thinking is to find a common basis for moral beliefs, which all people, of any faith or none, can accept. But if we remove God, and a particular view of God as ensuring the sort of coherence between these diverse factors that Aquinas requires, can anything remain upon which to base agreement?

Even before the rise of the sciences, the Reformation had produced some scepticism, especially in the Lutheran tradition, about natural law. For if one sees nature as a fallen realm, it may no longer reflect God's purposes; and human reason may be so disordered that it is no longer capable of discerning them by its own inherent power. One is then thrown back on a much more direct appeal to revelation, as the source of Christian moral insights. Far from natural law providing the common ground for all moral thinking, it turns out to express just one of many contestable and fragmented perceptions of the basis of morals, and indeed to be one chief cause of moral dispute and disagreement.

In Aquinas himself, the prescriptions of natural law were few and rather vague—survival, some form of sexual ordering of society, and some striving for knowledge and happiness are the rather general goods that one is bound to pursue. The subsequent development of the tradition within the Roman Catholic Church has become much more specific and detailed. This is at its most evident in matters of sexuality, where it is taken to be the purpose of nature in sexual activity to procreate children. Then any act that frustrates that purpose, whether in masturbation, contraception or resort to artificial means of procreation, is ruled out as illicit, on grounds of natural law. Far from securing the agreement of all rational people, this proves to set the Catholic Church in almost solitary opposition to the generality of human beings, on these issues. It is, to say the least, ironic that a methodology meant to secure the agreement of all people of good will is now the greatest stumbling block for a great many people to acceptance of the moral teaching of the Catholic Church.

The attempt to find a rational basis for morality has not been wholly abandoned by those who stand outside that Catholic tradition, however. It is clear that any such attempt cannot presuppose the existence of God, since that is highly disputable. Nor can it use the terminology of "purposes of nature", since no Darwinian, even in the most general sense, can accept that nature has purposes. One can quite consistently say that God has a purpose in creating the universe, and that God has specific purposes for particular parts of nature, without being committed to the essentially Aristotelian belief that the structures of nature are of themselves purposive. For most biologists, human beings are products of largely random mutations, and any moral appeal to a shared common ground must take that into account. In short, one must abandon any reference to purposes of nature as such—though, of course, that should not be taken to imply that the structures of nature can be ignored. One must, however, remember the words of T. H. Huxley, in his famous lecture, "Ethics and Evolution", that nature as we observe it is so bloody and callous that the only morally respectable attitude is to oppose it in the name of compassion and humanity.

It still remains a plausible contention that all moral rules must ultimately be justified by reference to the existence of goods—of worthwhile states of affairs. The idea that some rules are just binding in and of themselves, for no further reason except some allegedly self-evident intuition, seems arbitrary and irrational. As the Hebrew Bible puts it, "The Lord commanded us to do all these statutes, to fear the Lord our God, for our good always" (Deut. 6:24). Even the revealed laws of the Torah are not simply to be obeyed blindly, simply out of obedience to an omnipotent creator. They are to be obeyed, certainly. But God gives the rules for a reason, not by some arbitrary whim. And that reason ultimately lies in the realisation of human good and well-being.

Admittedly it can be hard to see how some of the rules of Torah are for human good—the rule that one should not eat meat with blood in it has no very direct link with human well-being. However, such rules must be seen in the context of the setting apart of the people of Israel for the service of God. Doubtless developed from tribal food taboos, they come to have the function of reminding the Israelites that, in every act of eating in order to survive, they are to remember their election by God to a special vocation and destiny. Such rules make each meal a sacrament of the divine calling; and it is in that way that they relate to human well-being, and indeed to the deepest level of well-being, human relationship to the creator.

II. UNIVERSAL GOODS

If moral rules must be justified by reference to human goods, one can go on to ask whether there are any goods that might be universally accepted by anyone who reflected upon his or her own life and desires. Are there any universal human goods which all agents would have a good reason to choose for their own sake? The immediate response is to say that there are an infinite number of such goods, from listening to symphonies to digging the garden; eating a good meal to writing poetry. These are certainly things that people find worth choosing for their own sakes; yet they are not universal—not everyone likes writing poetry, though perhaps everyone can see how it may be intelligibly chosen.

If we are to speak of universal goods, we have to move to a more general level and ask whether there is anything that human agents, as such, would have good reason to choose. I think that one can make out an argument for the existence of such a class of goods, and that they can form the basis of a universal natural morality, upon which Christian ethics can proceed to build. The argument consists in asking whether there are certain necessary conditions of being a rational choosing agent in the first place. Clearly, there are; for such an agent must have knowledge of what the choices are between. It must have the freedom and power to make a choice. And it must have some capacity to appreciate and enjoy specific states, so that it can have a reason for choosing states that give pleasure or happiness over states that bring pain or suffering.

Sometimes, as in hedonistic utilitarian theories, pleasure has been taken to be the only intrinsic good. But that turns out not to be such a simple criterion of choice after all, since pleasures are very various, often incommensurable, and impossible to calculate in advance. What does seem to be true, however, is that if pleasure of some sort was not present, there would be little reason to choose some states in preference to others. Pleasure or happiness is a necessary condition of rational choice, but not a sufficient one. And it should not be thought that there is just one sort of thing called "pleasure", which could perhaps be measured on a Benthamite calculus. Pleasures are infinitely various, and it is probably better to say that one chooses activities or states that bring pleasure than to say that one chooses pleasure in itself.

Any rational agent has a good reason to choose states or activities that bring pleasure over states that do not, other things being equal. Happiness may not be the only good, but it is a universal good, since the concept of happiness is necessarily involved in the concept of being a rational agent. As I have suggested, knowledge is also necessarily involved in this concept, as is the power of choice and reasoning ability. In addition, one needs to add that rational agents are not isolated atoms, living alone. They are almost always, and perhaps necessarily, members of a society of similar agents, upon whom they depend for learning language, gaining knowledge, having a range of choices made available, and participating in social practices that extend their capacities for many different sorts of action. One can therefore add that another universal good is the good of membership of a society, the members of which can be of help to one another.

Thus from examination of the concept of what is involved in rational agency, of what is *meant* by the term "good", one can obtain a list of universal and necessary goods. These will be, put most succinctly, the goods of happiness, knowledge, rationality, power, freedom, and friendship or social cooperation. Every rational agent has a good reason to choose these things and to avoid their contraries—pain, ignorance, foolishness, weakness, slavery, and enmity or misanthropy. To say they have a good reason to choose such things is not to say that they all want to. Human desires may be disordered in many ways. Part of moral argument is to show how such desires are irrational and in the end self-defeating.

If this account, or something like it, is acceptable, then morality is not just a matter of motion or purely personal choice, in which people may differ radically. There are objective values—the goods we all have reason to choose—and rational moral principles will be those which help to maximise those values and to eliminate their contrary disvalues. Where this account differs from traditional natural law accounts of the rational basis for morality is that it seems to have dropped all reference to the structures of nature. In one sense, it does refer to human nature, conceived as rational agency; and that is a traditional Christian idea. It discovers its basic values by reflecting on what it is to be a human rational agent, and on basic human desires; so it does root its values in certain natural facts about human beings, their desires, aims and goals. There is a certain continuity with the moral tradition of natural law. What is neglected is the idea that the physical structures of nature are themselves morally determining.

III. PHYSICAL STRUCTURES

The reason why Christians have often wanted to take physical or biological structures as morally determinative is founded upon the belief that God has created these structures, so that they must express the divine will. So if sexual organs have the biological function of procreation, that is how God intends them to be used, and any other use is wrong. Sexual organs clearly have the biological function of procreation. They can only be explained as means by which human beings and mammals in general procreate. Even if this particular method of reproduction has evolved by random mutation, it is presumably what God intends, at least in the general sense that God set up the universe so that it would develop in this way. Even at this stage, however, one cannot say that God intends every natural process—the growth of cancer cells, earthquakes and volcanic eruptions, early death by leukaemia. One might say that God intends there to be a physical universe in which such things will happen. But it would be grossly immoral to infer that it is wrong for us to try to prevent cancer, earthquakes or leukaemia. God might intend the universe to have this sort of general structure. But God surely also intends that we should eliminate suffering wherever we can, without causing other great ill effects.

Accordingly, we have to use another independent criterion in assessing whether or not natural processes can be interfered with. If some natural process causes great suffering, then it is our responsibility to frustrate or modify it. It is certainly not a sufficient moral argument that the process is natural, and so cannot be interfered with, however much suffering it causes. If the "natural" results in suffering and destruction, we must frustrate it if we can. Moreover, we will not thereby be frustrating God's purposes; for God's purpose is that we should eliminate suffering if we can, not that we should let nature take its course, whatever harm befall.

At this point, there is usually an attempt to redefine "natural" so that it covers only cases with generally good outcomes. So cancer is not natural, but pathological; it is a disease or defect, not a natural process at all. This seems to me the same sort of desperate expedient as Boethius used when he said that since God can do anything, but cannot create evil, therefore evil cannot exist. A "natural" process must now be defined as one that results in a healthy state of the human organism. Yet that will not do; for human beings all naturally die. Thus the word "natural" tends to slide between its Aristotelian sense of "in accordance with its inherent tendency to realise fully its proper nature" and a sense in which it means, "what is normal for the species or type of thing in question". If we cannot decide what is natural by just looking at the facts and counting cases, we are almost certainly having to import an independent moral criterion into our definition. When I say that what is natural is what is conducive to health, I am assuming that health is a good state. Health is itself an evaluative term, referring to what is desirable and rationally choosable. What is happening is that I am interpreting the natural in terms of some universal good. I then call any physical process that frustrates this good "un-natural". But now, if it turned out that sexual intercourse resulted in great illness, it would become un-natural. And the point is made—it is not enough to look at the physical structure; one must also ask about the goods that structure realises or frustrates.

This question assumes great importance in the case of human parents who carry defective genes. Suppose it could be predicted with virtual certainty—as it sometimes can—that any child born to two specific parents will be so deformed that it will die at or very soon after birth. In such a case, the act of sexual intercourse will result only in pain or defect. It is, of course, possible to say that the couple should not have intercourse. But the fact remains that a natural process would here result in a morally disastrous end. Even though the process in general creates great goods, in this clear and specific case it does not. Is it a very plain moral axiom that we should not frustrate a process that *in general* tends to good, when in a specific case it leads to harm? This sounds suspiciously like saying that we should not stop automobiles which in general convey people safely, even in a specific case when we can predict that the wheels will fall off.

So the question remains, Why is it wrong to frustrate a natural process, as such? God may indeed will the process to issue in procreation in general, but not necessarily in every case—not, for example, where it leads to harm. The most plausible inference from this situation seems to me to be that procreation should continue to take place by means of intercourse and that it is right and proper for it to do so. But where intercourse leads to undesirable ends—to grossly handicapped children, for example—it is not mandatory that the possibility of conception should be left open in every case.

The moral question that must be put to the "natural process" view is this: Does God intend every act of intercourse to leave open the possibility of procreation? The Roman encyclical *Humanae Vitae* asserts that God does and that this can be known by human reason. I am not sure that such very particular details of the divine will are open to human reason. But insofar as I can judge of the matter, it seems that God intends human beings to procreate, and normally to do so by means of intercourse, that being the only possibility open to the vast

231

majority of human beings at present. This by no means entails that each act of intercourse must leave open the possibility of procreation. Nor does it rule out the possibility of procreation by artificial means, where there are good reasons for that. Nor does it entail that the only legitimate use of the sexual organs is to attempt procreation (or at least not preclude it). Though intercourse is undoubtedly a means of procreation, I see no reason why that should be its only function, or even a necessary function on every occasion. Indeed, when infertile couples have intercourse, they can be quite certain that procreation is not a possible goal for that activity. Yet the activity is quite a proper and desirable one, since it maintains and expresses a relationship of love. Once again, it is quite unclear to me that human reason can tell that God would not wish couples to use intercourse to express love, while artificially frustrating the procreative aspect of genital activity, as undesirable in a particular case. One might feel that it would be wrong to frustrate the procreative aspect in principle and completely within a marriage. But even then there might be special cases, when great genetic disorders would be passed on to any resultant child. My general point, then, is that reason is not able to descend from the general perception that intercourse and procreation are biologically connected to very detailed knowledge of what God intends in specific difficult cases. It is not that one would ignore the structures of nature altogether—that would be foolish. It is only that there is no reason to feel morally bound by those structures, where they clearly result in harm. And there is no reason for permitting the causing of harm in specific cases, just because a physical process in general leads to the realisation of great goods.

The physical and biological structures of the natural world must always be subordinated, in morality, to the realisation of those universal goods which all free agents have good reason to want. Such a view has, I think, quite a good claim to the status of a universal common ground obtainable by all people of good will and reflective disposition. The Roman Catholic moral tradition would not dissent from this. It would wish to add to it the proviso that human beings must also respect and not frustrate the inherent order and purposes of nature, as ordained by God. Since I do not add that proviso, might it not be said that I have paid too high a price for my universal morality? I have omitted God and the doctrine of creation from it entirely; and that can hardly be satisfactory for a Christian.

IV. THE SUPREME GOOD REVEALED
IN CHRIST

I began by saying that one should seek a basic common ground for morality, if possible, and that the Christian faith would complete and transfigure it. But how does this come about? The most general answer is that it does so by a doctrine of the supreme goal of human life, its truest fulfilment and release from all those conditions which frustrate and restrict it. Traditionally put, the goal of human life is the beatific vision, the vision of God in glory. The biblical idea of God is one that sees the supreme being as the subject of the highest possible degree of precisely those universal goods which were elicited by reflection on the conditions of being a free rational agent. That is not surprising, since the biblical God is, above all, a dynamic, active God who freely creates all things and brings people into fulfilling relationship. God is the primal subject, and human personhood can be properly understood only as a faint image of God's unlimited personal being.

As these universal goods are found in the divine being, they are transformed so as to be found in a form far transcending our comprehension. Nevertheless, in the person of Christ, one sees a visible "image of the invisible God" (Col. 1:15); and we can say that the divine perfections can be perceived in Christ, in a way suited to our capacities, even if divinity in itself remains beyond our grasp. If we would see how universal human goods are transfigured in God, we must look to the person of Christ. That will correct and direct our perceptions, enabling us to see the temporal goods truly as reflections of eternity.

First, then, God is happy. But that word hardly begins to convey the quality of beatitude. Perhaps a better word, though rather archaic, is "blessed". Or we could think of the joy that Christ gives and no one can take away. The psalmist says, "In thy presence there is fulness of joy" (Ps. 16:11); and that quality of joy is one of the fruits of the Spirit, which must have been manifested very fully in the life of Jesus, the man above all others filled with the Spirit. This is not a joy which ignores the sadness and suffering of creatures. It is, rather, the joy of the resurrection, which always bears the marks of the cross, and has become what it is only because of the cross. The Christian hope is that our mourning shall be turned into joy—not simply replaced by joy, but itself taken up and transformed by a healing, reconciling touch that wipes away all tears, but does not simply forget them. Sorrow comes to an end, but joy is limitless; and the joy expressed in Christ is a joy that has seen and endured death and risen triumphant.

It must not be thought that joy compensates for sorrow, as though equal quantities of each could balance out. It is, rather, that the sorrow which we endure is itself used by God to bring into being forms of value that otherwise could not have been. The sorrow is not a mere means to the joy, as though God creates it in order to bring about joy. In some way unknown to us, sorrow is a necessary consequence of the nature of this creation and of the choices that free creatures within it have made. While not directly willing that suffering to be, and while commanding that it should be eliminated wherever possible, God can yet ensure that it is used positively, that it will not be in vain, so that it contributes to a special sort of joy. It follows that many of us cannot yet share fully in that joy, but we may glimpse it in part, as we become sharers in the gifts of the Holy Spirit.

Second, God is all-knowing. God knows the secrets of every heart and is present everywhere. But this knowledge is not a mere registering of facts. When the Bible speaks of knowing, it has in mind a depth of personal acquaintance, of delight in appreciating another, and of full understanding. When it is said that God knows us, as when it is said that a man knows a woman, this knowing is a unitive and appreciative activity. Such knowledge opens up endless possibilities of new under-standing and vision; and it sets before us an idea of heaven as an unlimited growth in new forms of acquaintance, which will be perpetu-ally fresh and invigorating. The sort of knowledge that is good in itself is a knowledge that loses itself in contemplation of a rich and complex beauty. In this sense, God is the supremely beautiful, and knowledge of God brings to fulfilment all our capacities for reverent contempla-tion.

Third, God is wise. It is not only that God can always produce valid arguments but that the connections of things are seen, the meanings that God has in fact brought to be. God never acts in vain, or impul-sively or without discrimination. Wisdom is the understanding of how to bring things to their true fulfilment; and the wisdom of God is seen in the divine relation to each human soul, as God seeks to draw from it a unique and personal response to the ideals set before it.

Fourth, God is powerful. There is nothing that is beyond God's power. Yet again, this power is not primarily exercised, as we see it in Christ, in acts of terror and destruction. God is the creator, and divine power is the free creativity which spontaneously brings new things to be; which does not constrain them but draws from them their own potentialities. It might be better, then, to speak of creativity than of power, and to think of God not as a completed, changeless perfection in every respect, but as an unlimited source of new values in infinite variety.

Fifth, God is supremely free. God is not constrained by any other thing and does not suffer from the things that restrict our freedom—disease, old age and death. If, in Christ, God may be said to suffer for our sakes, it is essential to Christian doctrine that Christ rises from death and is victorious over it. God may take the form of a servant, but this is by free choice and election. Even in the form of human weakness, God never ceases to be the ruler of the universe in all its immensity. The supreme paradox of divine freedom is that it is able to subject itself to the forms of weakness, in the flesh of Christ. But this is not a loss of freedom. On the contrary, it extends freedom immeasurably, since only God is free to do what we could never do, in a giving of self to the utmost for the sake of creatures. From the manifestations of God's being in Jesus we learn a new and larger definition of freedom—that it consists not in doing whatever one wants but in giving up one's being for others. The person who is truly free from all attachments is not, on the Christian view, merely apathetic—though indeed *apatheia* is one of the traditional virtues of the Christian fathers. Divine freedom, however, is not just freedom from attachment. It is the freedom to give oneself to others out of love.

So, sixth and above all, God is love. God does not exist in solitary perfection. God is the creator who brings others to share in the divine life, who makes human creatures brothers and sisters of the creator by assuming a nature like theirs. And, mysteriously yet evocatively, the doctrine of the Trinity suggests that even in the interior being of God, if we may speak of such a thing, there is a reality more akin to loving relationship than to some monadic singularity. Christian tradition is united in seeing in God more than a plain undifferentiated unity. While Christianity is uncompromisingly monotheistic—there is only one God—yet God is in some manner a diversity-in-unity. The lover, the beloved and the relationship of love itself in some way subsist in God;

or we might say at least that this is a more adequate image of divinity than one that sees only unity, "the One", without contact or complexity of any sort.

If one asks how these things are known of God, one must turn to the biblical tradition of revelation, to the gradual deepening of insight into the nature of the One who speaks through the prophets in judgment and salvation. For the Christian, the person of Jesus must be seen as the culmination of that prophetic tradition. The nature of the joy that God gives is fully seen only in the ecstatic surprise of the resurrection. In that event, the shadowlands of Sheol become the portals of Paradise, and one has a foretaste of the kingdom in which all tears are wiped away and a true and lasting peace reigns. The nature of divine knowledge is seen in the person who was acquainted with grief, who knows our sorrows. It is a sharing, a unity of being; and in the beauty of the risen Christ, God offers us a Lord to whom absolute devotion can be given and yet who also comes to live within our hearts. Divine knowledge is not bare lists of facts; it is a reverent treasuring of good, and it is Christ who opens up the riches of this goodness to us. Divine wisdom is seen in the immediate grasp which Jesus had of the needs of those he met. Though Jesus has been seen as the Logos, the Wisdom of God through whom the world was created, this wisdom is not limited to the intellect; it is manifested in the ability of Jesus to grasp the particular and the unique and call from it what is good and fruitful. Divine power is seen in Christ as accepting suffering, not simply obliterating it, yet bringing from it a unique sort of good. And divine freedom is seen in the washing of the disciples' feet, for it is a freedom which is not restricted by pride or disdain.

V. TRANSFORMATION

The whole may be summed up by saying, quite simply, that in Jesus God is disclosed as a God of love, a God who shares and redeems. If in the life of this person there is indeed that insight into the being of God which the apostles claimed to see, then all those universal human goods which Christians may share with all people are transformed into a new, paradoxical dimension. It is a paradoxical dimension because it is in some ways the reverse of what might have been expected. One might expect to find in God the maximisation of bliss, knowledge and power. Then one could form the concept of a being who, like Aristotle's "best of all beings", had no acquaintance with the sorrows of the world, and whose omnipotence, more actively displayed than by Aristotle's God, could dispose of all things effortlessly and without risk or disadvantage. There is a place within Christian reflection for the notions of divine impassibility and omnipotence. Surely it is true that the creator and Lord of all cannot be moved to inordinate passion and cannot be forced to do things against its almighty will. Yet the perception of God that has arisen through the life of Jesus of Nazareth compels us to confess that this God has truly become flesh, has assumed the materiality of the world, with all its contingency and obduracy, into the divine being. That makes a difference to our view of God, and, one may say, even to God. God has eternal beatitude, but God suffers in the person of Jesus. God has supreme power, but undergoes the suffering of the cross that all people may be drawn to the divine through a freely given response of love. God has complete freedom, but takes the form of a servant so that we may pattern our lives completely on that paradigm.

If the supreme goal of the Christian life is to attain the beatific vision, this requires that we pattern our lives on the nature of God. For we shall see clearly the object of our love only when we become like it in some degree—or perhaps ultimately only when it has itself suffused our lives by its own love, which is itself. In the Sermon on the Mount, Jesus exhorts us to be perfect, as our Father in heaven is perfect. That does not mean rampaging in power and terror, like some cosmic despot. It does not mean being supremely apathetic, like a God who feels nothing. It means following the pattern of Christ, in love, service and compassion. The cross is rightly seen as being central to the Christian vision of morality, for it shows the form that the power of God takes in a world crucified by its own violence.

It can be seen that the Christian vision does not countermand the account of natural morality in terms of universal and necessary human goods. Those remain proper goods, founded in the will of the creator who has shaped human nature in its essential characteristics. But it does not merely add another dimension to those goods, as though Christian ethics was an optional second tier to the moral life. It radically transforms the way they themselves are seen. I shall sketch out eight ways in which it does so. In this way I shall try to show how Christ may properly be seen as the light of the world, as its supreme moral exemplar, even though he did not explicitly teach many precise or radically new specific moral rules. And I shall suggest how Christian ethics may be taken to be authoritative, on the grounds of its revelation in Christ, without this undermining true human autonomy and freedom of choice.

a. Positive Formulation

In the first place, the universal goods are in themselves fairly minimal. All that is said is that all rational agents have good reason to avoid pain, ignorance, weakness and enmity. That is important enough, in a world where torture and oppression are commonplace and where it needs to be continually reaffirmed that such things cannot be morally justified. But they hardly place before people any sort of compelling vision which might arouse them to action and enthusiasm. In a Christian perspective, these goods become much more definite and positive. One is to seek for a positive joy, an interior delight which is truly possible only when the object of joy is such that it can never be destroyed or removed; that is, when its object is God. One is to seek for appreciation of beauty and a sensitivity to the feelings and experiences of others; for the wisdom to discern carefully and judge appropriately; for personal, unique forms of creative action; and for forms of social cooperation that can enable sharing and fellowship to flourish. These positive interpretations of human goods flow ultimately from a perception of the nature of God as it is seen expressed in Jesus. Yet they carry definite implications for social policy and conduct. The details of such policies naturally need to be worked out with care in particular situations. But there can be little doubt that a Christian social ethic will seek to build a form of society, wherever possible, which maximises the opportunities for all to appreciate beauty, to engage in creative pursuits, and to cooperate freely in activities that serve the needs of others. Any society that curtails in an avoidable way the opportunities of any person or class of persons for such creative work, cooperative service and care for the environment must stand condemned by Christian moral standards. There is a definite vision here of a society of free, cooperating, creative and caring persons. Though one cannot legislate for human hearts, one can devise forms of society that make such values easier to attain. It is a Christian obligation to do so, for these are the things which delineate the kingdom of God, so far as it lies within human power to realise.

b. Binding Character

Second, as well as giving a positive interpretation to intrinsic human goods, the Christian faith adds an important element that makes them binding upon human beings. It is quite possible for a humanist to formulate these values without reference to God. It is also possible for the humanist to regard it as a matter of obligation to pursue them, both personally and socially. Yet the notion of obligation is more securely founded for a Christian; it is for the Christian essential and inescapable, in a way that it is not for a nontheist. For Christians will regard it as a matter of the will and command of God that they should pursue human goods. It is not some sort of option or personal decision. It is not a free commitment to a set of principles that one thinks, hypothetically, to be worthy of embrace by all rational agents. It will never be irrational to see that all rational agents will not in fact live by such principles; and so to adapt one's own conduct, to compromise with the times, and to say that the hypothetically normative is not practicable in fact. Christians, however, will believe that they are commanded by God to obey the divine will; for them, there can be no rational putting aside of duty in the name of expediency. When God speaks, the human will must obey. This notion of divine command has been made the subject of some criticism by philosophers who find it somehow degrading or infantile for human beings to be commanded. It is more fitting to human dignity, they think, that we should decide our moral principles for ourselves, and decide whether or not to pursue them. But Christians should not capitulate to the notion that divine commands are somehow irrational or arbitrary, to be obeyed without question simply on the authority of some unexamined text or blindly followed authority. That is a travesty of the situation—though there are plenty of Christians only too ready to present travesties of their faith, unfortunately. God's commands are for human good. God, as supremely knowing and wise, knows what is for our good. Yet God does not issue commands in simple form, to be simply followed without question. The New Testament, the central Christian scripture, contains very few simple and direct commands that are addressed to the generality of humankind. Almost always, there are prescriptions of a rather cryptic nature made in very particular situations, which need to be spelled out with much care if one is to perceive their wider implications. In the New Testament there is a picture of the life of Jesus which presents recommendations to poverty, self-giving love, forgiveness, even of enemies, honesty and fidelity. Those recommendations, to be found summarised effectively in Matthew 5—7, are so cryptic that there are many diverse interpretations of them in the history of moral theology. They are hardly precise or simple. What they do, we may say, is to set out a series of signposts to human good, in the light of the reality of a loving creator. They help to effect that transformation of intrinsic human goods which Christian faith requires. What God commands is that we should forswear anger, lust, infidelity, revenge and hatred; that we should seek "love, joy, peace, patience, kindness, goodness, faithfulness, humility and self-control" (Gal. 5:22–23). Although these are not simple, in that their implications need to be carefully worked out in complicated personal situations, in another sense they are very clear— only too clear to most of us. They act as a continual judgment upon our lives and put forward to us an ideal that we never attain. For Christians, it is not infantile to pursue such ideals or to let ourselves be judged by them. Nor are they freely chosen, as though we would not pursue them unless we had thought them up entirely by ourselves. They are placed before us by the life and teaching of Jesus, and made binding upon us by God, whose judgment there is no evading. So one element essential to Christian morality is the element of objective obligation, whether we choose it or not. That adds a force to morality which is often lacking in accounts which in the end leave it up to us which principles, if any, we choose to live by.

c. Eschatological Goal

A third element that Christian faith adds to natural morality is the placing of moral action within a context of human life, seen as intended by God to end in union with God, through grace. For Christians, morality has a purpose. It is not simply a set of rules or even intrinsic values, to be pursued solely for their own sake. Humanists often make much, at their best, of the necessity to pursue value for its own sake alone, and not for the sake of any external rewards or punishments. And it is certainly right to pursue the good because it is good, and not primarily for some other reason—because it will make us happy, for instance. Yet, as Immanuel Kant uncomfortably saw, there are problems in this world about the effective realisation of good. I may commit myself to bringing about good for its own sake. But what if I come to judge that it cannot be brought about? That all my best efforts are doomed to end in failure? That every dream of utopia ends in the imposition of tyranny or a collapse into anarchy? What then? The humanist has no defence against a final scepticism about the possibility of realising goodness in the world; for if it is not realised on earth by human effort, it will never be realised. The good should still be realised. But will it not come to seem absurd, in a morally neutral or even hostile world?

What Christian faith does not proclaim is that the good should be sought because we will thereby attain heaven or escape hell. Indeed, the "Catch 22" of Christianity is that if you do good in order to get to heaven, you are still acting out of self-interest. If you are self-interested, you cannot get to heaven. So nobody who strenuously tries to get to heaven will ever make it; and presumably the only people there have been taken to some extent by surprise. This is only the doctrine of salvation by grace (put in an admittedly exaggerated form, which should not be taken too seriously). The truth in it is that Christianity teaches that God should be sought for the sake of God alone, and not for the sake of the happiness this will bring. Nevertheless, the gospel proclaims that God can be found; the search for God, if it is a response made in repentance and faith, will not be in vain. God can be attained; and in that good, supreme happiness can indeed be found, as long as it is not the subjective state of happiness which is itself the real object of the search.

Christian hope is for the establishing of the kingdom of God; and this is a moral goal which God will realise, whether in this physical universe or, as the Bible often seems to suggest, in a renewed and remade "heaven and earth". There is a difference between the Stoical attitude which remains true to good even when good seems inevitably to be defeated, and the Christian commitment to the hope of a final realisation of goodness in creation. Christianity is distinctive, not in its commitment to goodness, but in combining it with a hope for fulfilment, while accepting that all our efforts may fail so far as we can see, this side of the resurrection. I do not hope for immortality, as Kant taught, because I need to believe that *my* happiness will be proportioned to *my* virtue, but because God promises that the demands made of us will, if rightly responded to, issue in the realisation of the kingdom. Good will not finally be defeated, though the resurrection may seem puzzling and mysterious to our obscured vision. The good we pursue for its own sake will be established—that is a belief which gives an added intelligibility to the pursuit of morality, and so markedly increases the rationality of moral commitment.

d. Divine Calling

Fourth, God not only has a general purpose for creation which will be achieved at "the end of the age". God has particular purposes which are worked out in the lives of individuals as they are called to specific tasks and activities. The notion of a "calling" or vocation is centrally rooted in the biblical tradition of the calling of Abram out of Ur, of Israel out of Egypt, and of Mary to be the mother of Jesus. It means that some moral issues will be quite particular to individuals, and not generalisable to everyone of the same sort. The call to heroic sanctity or to some special task—whether it be ordination or social work—can be seen by the disciple as a matter of moral obligation; yet it may not be seen as binding upon all people in similar circumstances. What this means is that morality will not be seen primarily as a matter of general rules or principles. There are, I have argued, universal moral values, but they do not exhaust the realm of morality. They need to be specified in particular situations, and so, even such things as the course of life that one adopts may be seen as moral matters. Morality is thus seen as a general matter for the sorts of claims God makes upon one in the whole of one's life. It is not some sort of minimally acceptable set of general rules but a matter of personal response to particular claims and requirements. For a Christian, I suggest, ethics has an irreducibly individual dimension. That means that no area of life can be excluded from ethical consideration, from the prayerful reflection on what God requires. That is one reason why Christian ethics is not spelled out, like the Torah, in a set of rules. It is set forth in a life, whose pattern must be brought to each person's own situation, so that in the light of it, personal decisions can be made about what one is going to do and what actions one is going to undertake. The whole of life, we might say, becomes a moral matter for Christians. Yet one does not wish to say that every moment is a matter of painful duty. It is rather that, once morality is connected to the idea of the will of God, and it is seen that God has particular purposes for specific individuals, then it is always a proper question to ask what God's will for me is, now. I cannot decide that just by asking what I could will anyone else in a similar situation to do, however helpful that procedure may be in ruling out certain courses of action I am tempted to take. It may be that we are called to be "a city set on a hill" or a lamp that "gives light to all in the house" (Matt. 5:14–15); and in that sense, I may feel called to act in a way I

242

would not require of anyone else. If morality is a response to the perceived will of God, and if Christians are called to be disciples of the Lord in a special way, that is just what we might expect. They will be called, not to dominate the world, but to be the servants of all, to reconcile and forgive, to be the hands and feet of Christ.

e. Habits of the Heart

Fifth, as the teachings of Jesus make clear, Christian morality is concerned not only with outward conformity but with the attitudes of the heart. It is concerned not only with what we do but with the sorts of persons we are. Christians are enjoined to have the mind of Christ, and that means a renewing of our inward attitudes. As opposed to any view that sees morality primarily as a matter of social rules governing relationships between people, Christian morality is primarily a matter of what one is in oneself. Social rules are there, but the first question must be: Are the fruits of the Spirit manifest in me? Is the life of Christ at all perceptible in me? It is not enough, for Christian morality, that one should keep the Ten Commandments by refraining from harming others in various ways. The Christian is to pursue an interior quest for personal perfection; and while outward behaviour may be impeccable, yet if there is impurity of heart, then the Christian ethic has not been followed. I am not, of course, suggesting that outer behaviour and inner attitude can be wholly separated. A morality that consisted solely in the cultivation of inner feelings would be pietistic in a bad sense of being inward-looking and ineffectual in renewing the world. An incarnational faith must be concerned with the material and bodily as well as the spiritual and inward, with the public and social as well as with the individual and private. Nonetheless, Christian ethics does insist that the values it pursues are to be realised in oneself. It insists that there are duties to oneself as well as to others.

f. Self-Transcendence

Christian morality can thus be seen as a morality of self-realisation. It aims at the realisation in oneself of creativity, sensitivity and wisdom. Yet once again the Christian perspective gives a paradoxical interpretation to this idea of self-realisation. So, sixth, the Christian is bound by the words of Jesus, "Whoever seeks to gain his life will lose it, but whoever loses his life will preserve it" (Luke 17:33). What is to be pursued is not my own fulfilment, insofar as I am the subject of such fulfilment. The emphasis must rather be on the object in which fulfilment is to be found. Ideally, the disciples of Jesus are to abandon themselves wholly to the divine will, to be so filled by the Spirit of God that their work is the work of the Holy Spirit in them. Such abandonment requires a renunciation of everything that holds one back from God, and so of all attachments and desires that encourage pride and partiality to oneself. Self-realisation is not to be thought of as the pursuit of happiness as and when one wishes. What is required is, rather, a rigorous disciplining of the self, so as to render it wholly amenable to the will of God. God gives fulfilment to the pliant self, as it finds its essential being in its free surrender to the very root and basis of existence. It may be better to speak of self-transcendence, whereby the self moves delicately between renunciation and fulfilment, finding its freedom in allowing the divine Self to come to birth within it. Such a morality of self-transcendence is only fully intelligible in a theistic framework. It gives a special interpretation to talk of realising values in oneself, ensuring that the values themselves, and not the self, are the objects of desire.

g. *Responsive Love*

But, for a Christian, talk of "values" is too abstract and impersonal. It is hard to think of values as existing objectively or of oneself as being related to them in a vital and living way. The Christian thinks, not of abstract values, but of a personal and living God, as the object of reverence and love. So a seventh element of a Christian view of morality becomes clear—that the Christian moral life is a response to a personal being, not some abstract notion of duty of value. I have spoken of Christianity as imposing a sense of obligation, in the form of divine commands. Yet those commands issue from a being whose essence, as revealed in Christ, is love. They are, properly speaking, not so much commands as refractions of divine perfection in a broken world. If we were fully alive to God, we should not obey God by a sort of compulsion. We should be irresistibly drawn by love and do what God desires simply out of the glad desire to do so. A constant metaphor used in the Bible for the relationship of God and creatures is the analogy of marriage, of love between man and woman. In a good marriage, each partner does things because he or she wishes to please the other out of love. Duties exist only to remind them of things that love, were it still fully alive, would gladly and spontaneously do. So the ideal of Christian morality is to obey God spontaneously out of love. Human duty is the remembrance of a partially destroyed or ineffective love. This consideration adds a very powerful element to natural morality. Christians should not only seek intrinsic human goods because they believe it is right to do so. They should seek to realise them out of a love for God which impels them spontaneously to do so.

b. Works of Grace

A final, eighth, element in the Christian view of morality is the astonishing claim that it is not we who are to realise love out of our own resources. It is God who is to pour the divine love into our hearts, so that, as Augustine puts it, the love with which we love God is God's own love, given to us by the Holy Spirit. It is the love of God which constrains us. And that is not our love for God as object, but God's love placed within our hearts and working within us: "It is no longer I who live," as Paul puts it, "but Christ who lives in me" (Gal. 2:20). This is the final meaning of living by grace, so that the theological virtues are the results of the divine working in us. Technically they are "infused" and not self-made. They are the works of grace. They are the expressions of the Holy Spirit in the lives of her children. So, as a final paradox, Christian morality consists not in trying hard to be good but in allowing ourselves to be loved; not in giving but in receiving the love which God freely offers us in Christ.

VI. NEW-STYLE IMITATION OF CHRIST

I have tried to show how faith in the God of our Lord Jesus Christ does not undermine natural morality, yet does not leave it untouched. It is not merely that faith sets morality in a wider context of beliefs about human nature and destiny, though it does that. Nor is it that faith adds some additional duties, such as those of worshipping God, though it does that too. As Calvin so insistently stressed, Christ is the Lord of all life, and at his touch everything is transfigured. As God raised human nature by assuming it into the Godhead, so human morality is raised to a new level when illuminated by Christ. Putting it rather schematically, we might say that Christian morality is *revelatory,* in setting before us the goal of human life in the vision of God, and making moral values positive, binding and realisable. It is *exemplary,* in setting before us a particular pattern in the life of Jesus, to be appropriated in our own unique way, inwardly and by a self-transcending response of love. And it is *charismatic,* in being finally reliant wholly on the grace of God for the new and eternal life which it seeks to bring to birth.

Christian morality is thus utterly distinctive, as Christ himself is utterly distinctive. Yet it does not stand just as an arbitrary and odd option in human history. It may intelligibly be seen as a transforming fulfilment of natural morality, as it seeks to make the world fully personal, and thereby realise the image always implicit in it and, Christians believe, made clear in Jesus, of finite selves made transparent to the Self of all, whose essence is love.

But if I began by seeming to leave too much of Christ out of morality, I may have ended by seeming to base too much on a Christ of whom, historically speaking, we know so little. Have I not made an enormous amount depend upon the revelation of God in Christ, just at a time when biblical scholars are unsure about what the historical Jesus did or said? I have expounded a view of morality as an *imitatio Christi*; but how can one imitate one of whom one is virtually ignorant?

I think the point is a fair one. Moral theologians, like doctrinal theologians, have to take full account of critical studies of the biblical documents; and we cannot base doctrines on a careless scattering of texts as we might once have done. But are things really quite so bad? I have not, after all, based huge doctrines on a few scattered texts. Nor have I made anything rely on certainty about the details of the smallest events recorded in the life of Jesus. I would doubt whether biblical scholars have established beyond reasonable doubt that we know little or nothing of the historical Jesus. It seems to me that we can be fairly sure of the main characteristics of his life. What I have appealed to is the general record of a life of humility, forgiveness, poverty, honesty and love; a teaching of the coming of the kingdom which was preached primarily to the poor, the sinners and the outcasts of society; and a life that ended in crucifixion and resurrection. Without some sort of belief in resurrection, Christian faith makes no sense. And in the light of that primary belief, one can be fairly clear about the character of Jesus' life and teaching, as a healer and proclaimer of God's free forgiveness to all who repent. So it is not the tiny details of Jesus' teaching that we need in order to found a doctrine of the *imitatio Christi.* It is a pattern of a life that is taken to show the nature of God in a new way, a life of service, death and resurrection. That pattern is, it seems to me, left clear by the most critical biblical scholarship.

It is important to say, however, that the exemplary model of the life of Christ does not depend solely on study of the Gospel texts, even though they provide a test against which any account of the life of Jesus must be measured. In fact, the model is found very clearly in the New Testament letters, which refer only very briefly and generally to the biographical details. What is primarily important is the experience of new life in the community of the church, as the Spirit brought to birth in those early disciples what they took to be the risen presence of the Lord. I do not wish to erect a great division between the historical Jesus and the Christ of faith. But it is true that our exemplary model of Christ is one that was developed out of the experience and reflection of the earliest disciples; it is what Christ was seen to be, in the experience of committed faith in his risen presence. The Gospels themselves were pieced together within such communities of faith; and the records of his remembered life are reconstructed with reverence and care in the light of belief in his raising to life by God. We are not thereby believing just in the theories of some early Christians. But we are following the pattern of their perception of God, as it had been renewed by the preaching of those who had walked with Jesus during his ministry. The historical Jesus is the irretrievable matrix upon which the gospel records have been formed. We thus receive them as perceptions of faith which pattern our own response to God. On such a view, there is no strain between full acceptance of critical study of the biblical documents and a commitment to the recorded life of Jesus as the exemplary model of our own response to God and the charismatic channel of the divine love to us.

VII. THE LETTER AND THE SPIRIT

Christian morality is founded upon authority, for such a model of the divine nature is not just dreamed up as some sort of imaginative enterprise. It is based on the life of one who was believed to proclaim the character and demands of God with a force and clarity which seemed quite unique. Yet this appeal to authority is not of the sort that simply produces biblical texts as uncriticisable answers to moral problems. On the contrary, the testimony of the epistles is that the letter of the law (i.e., the biblical rules for personal and social morality) had been brought to an end by the new life of the Spirit. Christian attitudes to authority should be determined by the biblical documents themselves; and the teaching of the New Testament gives some sharp guidelines on precisely this matter.

In Matthew's introduction to the Sermon on the Mount, he maintains that Jesus taught that the whole of Torah, even down to its dots and commas, must be kept (Matt. 5:17–19). The apostles who had known Jesus personally all apparently continued to keep the Torah themselves, and they argued vehemently over whether new gentile converts should keep it. The compromise of the Council of Jerusalem (Acts 15) suggested that circumcision could be given up but the food laws should be retained. Before long, however, all the food regulations of Torah were abandoned, and few Christians today would even think of keeping them. We need to remember that this was a bone of contention in the early church. The strongest evidence that Jesus did not teach the abandoning of Torah lies in the fact that those who had known him were reluctant to give it up and were only persuaded by Paul (who had never known Jesus personally) and a new vision to Peter. The surprising situation is that, within a few decades, the early church seems to have completely reversed the remembered and recorded teaching of Jesus, at least if Matthew is to be believed. What this suggests is that Christian attitudes to morality are not to be based on the authority of a written code, like the Torah.

The written codes are not just to be discarded as useless. One needs to reflect upon them and ask what underlying principles are contained in them. But they are not in themselves binding. Rather, they need to be assessed in the light of the life of Christ, the reality whose personal life and presence is the new law set in the hearts of his disciples. One might hold, then, that following the testimony of the New Testament itself, moral authority is not to be found in written codes but in prayerful reflection within the community which patterns its life upon Christ and wishes to be filled with the mind of Christ.

It would be sadly ironic indeed if one then took the written codes of the Gospels or of Paul as finally binding in ethics. And it would be misguided if the community itself became some sort of oppressive authority, stifling individual reflection by the weight of group pressure. These are dangers to which Christians are always prone. But the remedy for such dangers is not to abandon authority. It is to stress those elements of creativeness and rationality which God calls us to utilise to the utmost, but to stress that, in a Christian context, they are always to be utilised as responses to the self-disclosure of God in the person of Jesus Christ, and so to be disciplined and directed by the patient guiding power of the Holy Spirit.

As I conclude, I am painfully aware of the vast issues I have left untouched—nothing on liberation theology; nothing on nuclear deterrence, justice and peace; nothing on genetic experimentation and medical ethics. I plead that there is much good material to be found elsewhere on those vital issues but very little on the one issue I have chosen—the distinctiveness of the Christian contribution to ethics. If Christ is the light of the world, then our conduct must be shaped by our response to him. What, then, does he show that will illuminate the natural morality of all well-intentioned human beings? That is what I have tried to clarify a little. I have argued that he gives to morality a depth, an importance, an inwardness and an attractiveness which is capable of transforming our whole attitude to it. This fact is itself a strong argument for the rational acceptability of the Christian faith. It also means that Christians have a duty and a claim to tackle moral issues as an integral part of their commitment of faith. They have no privileged access to simple answers. But the Christian tradition contains the resources to stimulate and lead serious ethical reflection and to challenge any comfortable acceptance of the moral status quo. Finally, it is Jesus' lived proclamation of the kingdom that gives moral vision and hope to the world. And that is the distinctive element which gives Christian ethics a vitally important place in the moral debates of the modern world.

11

CHRISTIANITY AND POLITICS

DUNCAN B. FORRESTER

I. CHRISTENDOM AND ITS END

Since W. J. H. Campion wrote his chapter on "Christianity and Politics" in *Lux Mundi,* the context and the content of the discussion have changed so dramatically that it is hard to trace lines of continuity, although they certainly exist. The tone of Campion's essay is one of confidence in the recognized complementarity of church and state within the *corpus Christianum,* in the unchanging validity of "Christian principles" derived from an assured system of doctrine and addressed by the church to the state, and in the responsibility of the church to act as the guardian of morality and of values within a social and political structure which was on the whole regarded as "given". This confidence has in the last century been deeply eroded, if not quite destroyed, by forces of change that have instigated fundamental challenges to tradi- tional theological ways of thinking about politics. But the changes in the social and ideological context of the church and of theology have not simply resulted in a failure of nerve; they have also opened up new possibilities and encouraged fresh forms of theological exploration, freed from the constraints of old schemas. There is today an abundance of thinking and writing about Christianity and politics, and vigorous controversy. The scene is confusing, and full of the clash of arms at night; yet perhaps these turmoils may be the labour pains of a new political theology which is striving to be born.

It is no more than a truism to suggest that we live in the post- Christendom era. Christendom, in the sense of a society that attempted to order itself in the light of the Christian faith, and in which Christian- ity was the dominant or even monopolistic religion and world view, is believed to have started with the reign of Constantine and to have lasted in Europe and in North and South America until more or less modern times. Christianity became the official cult and the civil religion of the state; prelates and leading churchmen became the chaplains to the powerful; and Christianity performed the standard functions of a civil religion in legitimating the established order, inculcating in the populace obedience and the other civic virtues, and acting as a powerful social cement. The theory was that the truths of Christianity were to shape the social, economic and political order; in actuality a powerful argument can be mounted to the effect that this "establishment" of the Christian faith was simultaneously its subversion.[1] Christianity took over the role of the old pagan civil religion of Rome, and in the process came increasingly to mirror significant features and fulfil major functions of the old paganism. But one may also argue that Christianity never resolved itself totally into the received pattern of a civil religion for, as Machiavelli realized far later, it had a character that made it impossible for it to be more than a rather indifferent and halfhearted form of civil religion. But the unavoidable change was this: from the time of Constantine, Christianity has had to engage with a whole new agenda of political issues and devote itself to the development of (in Max Weber's phrase) an "ethic of responsibility" as well as an "ethic of absolute ends".

The first four centuries of the Christian era saw the development of a range of political theologies which suggest the spectrum of perennial possibilities for the development of Christian political theology. We may define this spectrum by reference to three ideal types which we may loosely associate with Eusebius at one extreme and Tertullian at the other, with Augustine somewhere about the midpoint.

Eusebius is the apologist for imperial rule and the propagator of a Christian civil religion; he sees the earthly role of the emperor as a reflection of, and a kind of participation in, the kingly omnipotence of God himself. The emperor is God's vicegerent and representative on earth. Occasionally Eusebius will even speak of the emperor as a Logos and an intermediary between the cosmic and the temporal orders. The coming of Christ and the flowering of the Roman Empire are complementary and almost simultaneous manifestations of divine providence, which may be celebrated together. Eusebius tends towards an Arian theology; unitary monotheism lends itself more easily to a justification of the universal rule of the one emperor than could a more thoroughly trinitarian position. Because the emperor is so closely linked to God, opposition to the emperor becomes opposition to the God he represents; a challenge to the political order is understood as a threat to the cosmic order and an invitation to chaos. Sedition and heresy are almost identified with each other, as are piety and patriotism. The state is declared to be sacred. This is political theology in the classical tradition, continuous in style, function, and to some extent content, with the political theologies of the old pagan emperors. It goes far beyond the early Christians' belief that they sustained the empire through their prayers.

By contrast, at the other end of the spectrum, Tertullian saw the church as a kind of counterculture to be sharply distinguished from the secular society which was doomed to destruction. Because Christians are citizens of the Jerusalem that is above, they are aliens in this world and should have nothing to do with politics or with secular power. Within the church, believers live by their own standards and await the passing of the temporal order. As a parallel community, living by radically other standards, the church is a challenge to political society and suggests an alternative way of ordering life. A fellowship of love without compromises with power might not seem obviously capable of generating a political theology. But it revitalized classical political thought by presenting a viable alternative understanding of community and resisted all efforts to sacralize politics or politicize the gospel.

With Augustine we find a radically different mood. He has a *political* theology, it is true, sparking between the two poles of the *civitas terenna* and the *civitas Dei,* but he holds back resolutely from divinizing any temporal order or earthly ruler as he strives to discern the signs of the times, the clues to God's working in the history of his age. Indeed, he boldly relativizes the pretensions of earthly power. He allows only a heavily qualified endorsement to any political order whatever. In sharp contrast to Eusebius, he taught that the Roman Empire was, and always had been, corrupt. The earthly city is fragmented and partial and at best is capable only of sustaining a tenuous peace and justice based on the balancing of opposing interests. This is indeed good, but not the highest good. Human beings should seek a greater good, and owe total and unqualified allegiance only to God and his city. This city of God is indeed relevant to the affairs of the *civitas terenna,* but is not to be identified with the church as a visible institution. Augustine is not with Tertullian in seeing the church as more or less identifiable with the City

252

of God; the institution is not to be absolutized any more than is the state.

These three contrasting modes of political theology are to be found appearing again and again in the history of ideas, along with various mixed forms. The Eusebian mode motivates believers to establish or restore, and then sustain, a Christian society. Theology after the style of Tertullian sees the church as the perduring manifestation of the divine society, proclaiming the gospel and witnessing to the relevance of an absolute ethic, a challenge and an alternative to all existing political orders. Augustinian thought refuses to assimilate the two cities to each other and disconcertingly affirms that even a "Christian" civil government is no more than a temporary and relative expedient. Secular politics in Augustine was taken seriously, but relentlessly excluded from the sphere of the sacred, so that this kind of political theology moved in a quite different atmosphere from the Eusebian sacralizing of the political order or the tendency in Tertullian to see the church as a pure manifestation of the divine society.

It has become conventional to assert that we now live in a post-Christendom situation, and to look back patronizingly to the attempts to revive a rather romanticized version of medieval society on the part of Maurice Reckitt, V. A. Demant and the Christendom Group, or even T. S. Eliot in his *The Idea of a Christian Society,* with its ringing pronouncement that

> the Christian can be satisfied with nothing less than a Christian organization of society—which is not the same thing as a society consisting exclusively of devout Christians. It would be a society in which the natural end of man—virtue and well-being in community—is acknowledged for all, and the supernatural end—beatitude—for those who have an eye to see it.[2]

But if that kind of political theology has had its day with the recognition that Christendom has passed away beyond recall, there remains an urgent need for a post-Christendom political theology, more akin presumably to Augustine or Tertullian than to Eusebius, not wistful but forward-looking and missionary, taking the political realm with profound seriousness, but never absolutizing it. For a political theology must stay resolutely in the public realm and engage with the ideologies, structures and practices that are to be found there. In a post-Christendom situation the temptation is to evacuate the public realm and retreat into the private sphere. This temptation may be resisted only by a theology that realizes that Christian faith, precisely because it is concerned with seeking the kingdom of God and his righteousness, precisely because it is confession of a particular and universal Lord, cannot avoid relating to the omnipresent civil religions and political processes that shape men and women so profoundly, for good or ill. Christianity cannot separate itself from the political realm, but it must not allow itself to be absorbed into that realm, assimilating its values and proclaiming them to be the values of the kingdom—what Lesslie Newbigin speaks of as the "Constantinian trap".[3]

Romantic and wistful political theology in the Eusebian mode lingers on and has its attractions for large and influential churches in particular. But, interestingly, in regions like Latin America with high levels of religious practice, there is nonetheless a recognition that Christendom is past and beyond recovery. The need of today is a political theology more related to the present and the future than tied to the past, a political theology that is capable of interpreting the specifics of what is happening and encouraging a faithful responsive praxis. The widespread confusion in the churches about how to respond to the breakup of Christendom or, rather, to the belated recognition that Christendom collapsed long ago—produces political theologies that are often tentative, exploratory and modest, making few claims to universality or finality because they are, very properly, rooted in specific and varied contexts, and because they relate to a church that is gradually and tentatively moving from understanding itself as a dominant social institution to seeing itself as a pilgrim people seeking the City that has foundations.

II. THE INADEQUACY OF A SECULAR THEOLOGY

The process of secularization provides a significant part of the explanation of the collapse of Christendom. We are not concerned here with the debate among sociologists about the nature, impact and significance of secularization. It is enough to register that the process is one of the decline of the influence of institutional religion and of religious observance, a development that appears to be closely linked with modernity. The Christendom model fitted a more simple, face-to-face society; urban, industrial, mass society provides a less congenial setting for the traditional forms of organized religion. The generalization is, of course, too simple. Mary Douglas argues that the secular person is "an age-old cosmological type, which need have nothing to do with urban life or modern science".[4] But, having firmly and properly knocked on the head the romantic notion that "primitive man is by nature deeply religious", she then proceeds to acknowledge that in modern society with its emphasis on individual freedom, its vast and formless social conglomerations, and its impersonal types of communication, traditional churchly expressions of religion have a hard time of it. It is not, of course, that religion *as such* has been erased by secularization. Sects, operating on the margins of things, frequently flourish exceedingly; the practices known by sociologists as "implicit religion" are amazingly widespread; astrology and the occult attract at least as much attention as ever; media evangelists conduct operations that in scale and turnover rival some significant corporations. This last is a reminder that in some situations which are obviously "modern", urban and industrial, organized religion flourishes, but in a form that is itself thoroughly secularized and reflects and reinforces the values and procedures of secular society. The electronic church, for instance, presents the strange paradox of those who claim to be evangelicals suggesting insistently that salvation can be bought. But even when all allowances have been made and every appropriate qualification entered, it is in general true that in modern societies institutional religion plays a less significant role than it usually did in the past. There is less religious influence over "the way things go", religious institutions are weaker, and fewer people participate in the life of the church.

Many theological assessments and interpretations of secularization have been surprisingly positive. Friedrich Gogarten, for instance, argued that the world has been secularized by God in Jesus Christ. This means that we should not approach the world with religious veneration. It is set free to *be* the world. Human beings are free and responsible adults, heirs of all things. They are set free to relate to God in faith and to love the world and the neighbour for their own sakes, not as a path to salvation. Dietrich Bonhoeffer appears at first glance to hold a strikingly similar position. He affirms secularization and argues that believers must accept a world that has "come of age". He rules out of court any nostalgia for Christendom and even for religion, convinced that the Christian "must live a 'worldly' life and so participate in the suffering of God".[5] But whereas Gogarten at one stage flirted with the "German Christians" and seemed to find their views similar to his, Bonhoeffer's worldly life style led him into complicity in the plot to assassinate Hitler. As he wrote of the political involvement that led directly to his arrest:

> It is an experience of incomparable value to have learned to see the great events of the history of the world from beneath; from the viewpoint of the useless, the suspect, the abused, the powerless, the oppressed, the despised—in a word, from the viewpoint of those who suffer.[6]

This emphasis lay largely unexplored by those who saw themselves as the heirs of Bonhoeffer. Instead, they pressed forward with a theology that affirmed and indeed celebrated the secular and the modern. Harvey Cox's paean of praise for the *Secular City* (1965) regarded it as the fruit of a God-given process of secularization which presented new opportunities of freedom, maturity and responsibility. Arendt Th. van Leeuwen saw the worldwide spread of secularism and Western technology as a continuation and culmination of the Christian world mission.[7] Denys Munby in his *The Idea of a Secular Society* (1963) called on Christians to embrace the values of a secular society. This style of political theology in retrospect seems too easy an accommodation to the spirit of the age, singularly lacking in prophetic questioning and critical edge. The panegyrics for secularization for the most part forgot, what Bonhoeffer could never overlook, that a secular society may be diabolic, idolatrous and exploitative and that people who had come of age did not cease thereby to be sinners. Nor did many notice that secularization in society might well involve the desecularization of the church, that in a modern society where the alliance with folk religion and civil religion was loosened it might be possible for the church to recover a greater Christian authenticity.

The secular theologies of the 1960s did not withdraw from the public realm or cease to ask questions about what God was doing in history. Nor did they deny the spiritual significance of the social and political order. They attempted a theological interpretation of their times, yet ended for the most part with a Eusebian sanctification of secularism and a celebration of the secular city which amounted to little more than reflection and endorsement of the superficial optimism of the day. Such theologies were quite incapable of taking the measure of the secular human being who exploits the neighbour and destroys the environment. Secular theologies flourished simultaneously with the optimistic theologies of development; the world economy was seen not as competition nor as exploitation but as a structure of cooperation among nations all engaged in moving towards universal prosperity. When that bubble burst, secular theology went with it, to be replaced by theologies of liberation or of revolution. Secularization may be experienced as emancipation by some; but others find it means oppression for them. The lesson to be learned is that while secularization continues to be a major dimension of the context to which any serious political theology must relate, neither accommodation to secularism nor the sanctification of the secular is the way forward.

III. THEOLOGIES IN A PLURALIST SOCIETY

There are modern secular societies that are not pluralist, in the sense that they have one dominant ideology or political theology (even if in some cases an atheist one!), usually supported by a pattern of ritual to which a large proportion of the population owes some kind of allegiance. On the one hand, the Soviet Union, with its elaborate development of Marxist-Leninist ritual to complement the "establishment" of Marxism-Leninism as the official "political theology" of the state is a case in point.[8] On the other hand, in Latin America where upwards of ninety percent of the population see themselves as Roman Catholics, the only form of political theology that could be viable must be a Catholic one, and the real conflicts are about who speaks for the church, which side the church endorses, and what kind of practice is congruent with the gospel. In most other contexts, secularism and pluralism have developed together. But secularism and pluralism are not the same thing, and a political theology that responds to secularism may be very different from a theology that takes pluralism seriously. We may accept John Habgood's argument that in a pluralistic nation, although there is no one dominant or universally accepted ideology or world view, there still must be enough agreement on values, goals and underlying assumptions to hold the nation together and give some basic sense of national identity. A radically pluralistic society with a state that is entirely neutral is inconceivable; there has to be some minimal consensus to provide the necessary degree of coherence. Habgood is right in suggesting that certain times of crisis bring to the surface the consensual basis which exists even in an avowedly plural society. In time of war, for instance, the churches, otherwise regarded as increasingly marginal, find themselves moved towards the centre of the stage.[9] But there are problems for the development of a political theology in a pluralistic society, whether religion is in the wings or in the limelight. In particular there is little possibility of a Eusebian political theology proving viable or attractive, either in the shape of a general endorsement of pluralism (although Figgis[10] and Munby[11] tried such a project) or as a call to return to "the idea of a Christian society".

A political theology for a pluralistic society which recognizes, as it should, the proper autonomy of the political, and knows it cannot count upon a general acceptance of the truth of Christianity, has to commend itself by the cogency of its argumentation and the illumination which it offers. Two rather different examples of what I have in mind are Reinhold Niebuhr and R. H. Tawney. Niebuhr started from the conviction, confirmed by his experience, that Christianity provided a more authentic account of human nature and destiny than any of the alternatives on offer, a thesis he argued in detail in his Gifford Lectures, *The Nature and Destiny of Man* (London, 1944). On this basis he developed his brand of Christian realism, which produced such illuminating analyses of current events and critiques of policy options that it was profoundly influential on political scientists and international relations experts, including many who had no Christian commitment. It was not as much the fact that Niebuhr moved with confidence between fundamental Christian beliefs and the analysis of political events as that he produced insights that were not easily available elsewhere, and thereby commended the Christian faith as the most profound and accurate portrayal of the human condition, with its limitations and possibilities. Niebuhr's thought shaped the still influential school of "realists" in international relations theory, led by such persons as Hans Morgenthau and George Kennan, who found it possible to detach Niebuhr's political conclusions from his dogmatic premises, and thus made Niebuhrian realism available far more widely in a pluralistic society.

An alternative approach to the doing of theology in a pluralistic and secular society may be represented by R. H. Tawney. Tawney was a committed Christian believer with a somewhat uneasy relationship to the institutional church. But he was in no sense a professional theologian. He was a close associate of Archbishop William Temple as well as one of the most influential figures in the Labour Movement and the Workers' Educational Association. The key to understanding Tawney's thought, and the place where he makes the most explicit connections between his theological views and his political, social and economic positions, is his *Commonplace Book*. There he made clear his belief that politics must be founded on morality, and morality must spring from belief in God:

> The essence of all morality is this: to believe that every human being is of infinite importance, and therefore that no considerations of expediency can justify the oppression of one by the other. But to believe this it is necessary to believe in God.[12]

And in more specific matters as well, he sought to ground his belief that social criticism presupposes some kind of religious belief. "The social order," he wrote, "is judged and condemned by a power transcending it."[13] His political goals, his ideal for society, and his understanding of human beings were all rooted in Christian soil:

> In order to believe in human equality it is necessary to believe in God. It is only when one contemplates the infinitely great that human differences appear so small as to be negligeable [*sic*]. To put it (an)other way, the striking thing about man is that he is only a *little* lower than the angels themselves. When one realizes this, it is absurd to emphasise the fact that one man is, even so, lower than another. . . . What is wrong with the modern world is that having ceased to believe in the greatness of God, and therefore the infinite smallness (or greatness—the same thing!) of *man,* it has had to invent distinctions among *men.* It does not say, 'I have said, "Ye are Gods!" ' Nor does it say, 'All flesh is grass'. It can neither rise to the heights nor descend to the depths. . . . What it does say is that *some* men are gods, and that some flesh is grass, and that the former shall live off the latter (combined with pâté de foie gras and champagne) and this is false.[14]

In his early published works such as *The Acquisitive Society* (1921) and *Religion and the Rise of Capitalism* (1926), Tawney argued that theology since the Reformation and the beginnings of modern capitalism had progressively abandoned any attempt to shape or influence economic and political activity. Possessive individualism and mammon worship have increasingly taken over from Christianity—and few people have noticed what has been happening. The issue is therefore at heart a religious one. "Compromise is as impossible", he wrote, "between the Church of Christ and the idolatry of wealth, which is the practical religion of capitalist societies, as it was between the Church and the State idolatry of the Roman Empire."[15] Therefore in these early writings he calls upon the churches to combat the capitalist idolatry of mammon worship and give a lead in working for a juster, freer and more equal social order.

Tawney's later writings, from *Equality* (1931) onwards, are far less *explicitly* Christian. It is not that his values or his vision have changed significantly. It is true that he began to despair that the churches could or would give the sort of vigorous and effective lead that he considered proper for them, but he continued to be a Christian, consciously rooting his political and social views in his religious beliefs. He now saw the need to address a more plural society and commend his views to those who did not share his faith. Accordingly *Equality,* like most of his later writings, has little in it that is explicitly Christian or theological. But it is a profoundly Christian and theological work nonetheless, of a sort that may provide a kind of model for a political theology that is appropriate in a secular and pluralistic society. In the end it contributed powerfully to the emergence of an egalitarian-welfare consensus in postwar Britain, something that would have been quite unlikely had it been a more explicit and exclusive Christian statement; and it also invited people to consider the grounding of their values, and thus in an authentic sense it was a commending of Christianity, an apologetic or evangelistic work.

It is no part of my task to compare Niebuhr and Tawney in detail. Niebuhr was undoubtedly the greater theologian, Tawney the more impressive social scientist. Niebuhr was at his best in dealing with conflicts of interest, Tawney at advocating a fraternal sense of community. But Niebuhr had a vision of fellowship beyond conflict, and Tawney knew much about conflict, power and entrenched interests. They shared an unusual capacity for holding simultaneously in view the Christian vision and the ambiguities and complexities of the political process in which the vision may be in part realized. Their projects and their impact show that it is possible to have a viable "Augustinian" political theology in a plural and post-Christian society. Neither thinker reduces Christianity to a mere political ideology or proposes a restoration of Christendom; each takes the gospel on the one hand and the complexities of political life on the other with profound seriousness. They pass the test laid down by André Dumas:

> A good political theology does not consist either in watering down the Gospel or in idealising politics. Each needs to help the other to incarnate the Gospel, rather than reducing it to an impotent idealism, and to demystify politics, rather than making it into a false gospel.[16]

Our problem is not that in secular, plural societies political theology is impossible. It is, rather, that doing theology in this context is particularly hard, and we have few people of the insight and ability of Niebuhr and Tawney engaged with the question of how to develop and communicate relevant political theology. And since a secular and plural society is one where there is much uncertainty about fundamental values and little agreement on ways of looking at the world and understanding human beings and human fellowship, a theological contribution is in some ways more urgently required than ever.

IV. THE SCOPE OF THE STATE

Contemporary political theology has to relate to changes in the role and understanding of the state. Traditionally, theology has seen the state as, first, a restraint upon the antisocial and sinful impulses in human nature, a "dyke against sin", and, second, as having a positive, if limited, role in sustaining relative justice and peace, in providing for the poor and the weak, and in supporting the church in its separate spiritual function. Particularly in the Catholic and Calvinist traditions, the positive role of the state was stressed, along with an insistence that it should not overstep its boundaries and infringe the responsibilities of the church or of other fundamental social orders such as the family. In modern times there have been advocates of pluralism who have seen the state as little more than a neutral referee, ensuring that the competition between rival interest groups and ideologies does not get out of hand. This allocates to the state a much more limited role than that of guardian of the common good and implies that we can have a state that is totally neutral and committed to no particular values. A useful antidote to such unreal notions may be found in the Marxist claim that even a state that claims to stand above the clash of competing interests is in fact either the tool of the dominant class or itself parasitic on all the classes. Few, if any, modern states have been convincing exemplars of the minimalist, neutral referee model. Far more characteristic of the twentieth century has been the totalitarian state, the state that recognizes no boundaries to its claims and inevitably becomes idolatrous. A classic and courageous Christian response to such a state was the Theological Declaration of Barmen of 1934:

> We reject the false doctrine, as though the State, over and beyond its special commission, should and could become the single and totalitarian

order of human life, thus fulfilling the church's vocation as well. We reject the false doctrine, as though the Church, over and beyond its special commission, should and could appropriate the characteristics, the task, and the dignity of the state, thus itself becoming an organ of the State.[17]

Liberal democratic societies may not have experienced totalitarian dictatorship, but they also have seen a major extension of the activities of the state, and of people's expectations of what the state is capable of providing. The advent of the welfare state was widely welcomed by Christians when it was established in most liberal democracies in the 1940s and 1950s, and it brought with it a more positive theology of the state as essentially benign and capable of effecting relatively painlessly a thoroughgoing reform of the social order. More recent right-wing critics, such as Irving Kristol, regard it as "the paternalist state addressing itself to every variety of 'problem' and committed to 'solving' them all—committed, that is, to making human life unproblematic."[18] Political scientists of eminence hold that the sphere of the state has so expanded that major nations are teetering on the brink of ungovernability. "Governments have tried to play God. They have failed. But they go on trying. How can they be made to stop?" asks Professor Anthony King.[19] Theologians may justly be uneasy about states that "play God" or pretend "to make human life unproblematic". But this should not force them back to a minimalist, "night-watchman" understanding of the state or lead them to cooperating with neo-conservatives in "rolling back the frontiers of the state" and denying it a positive role, representing the common good and defending the weak and the poor in areas such as welfare. There is much need for a theology of the contemporary state which is positive yet realistic and which takes fully into account that the state of today is not the state of New Testament times, and substantially different in its responsibilities and limitations from the state of the nineteenth century. Yet political theology is more than a theology of the state; it is theology done in relation to the political dimension of life.

V. THEOLOGY NEITHER PRIVATIZED NOR POLITICIZED

Any political theology adequate for today has to steer between Scylla and Charybdis, the twin seductive perils of a privatized and a politicized

Christianity. Johann Baptist Metz, the German Roman Catholic theologian, has traced the withdrawal of religion from the public realm since the Enlightenment.[20] Religion has, he argues, increasingly become concerned with subjectivity, with the individual in isolation from the social context, with domestic and family life, and with private morals. Privatized Christianity makes few claims to being true in a public, examinable way and abandons any attempt to "intervene" in public affairs. It is a domesticated faith. Western Christianity has become, in Metz's words,

> an extremely privatised religion that has been, as it were, specially prepared for the domestic use of the propertied middle-class citizen. It is above all a religion of inner feeling. It does not protest against or oppose in any way the definitions of reality, meaning or truth . . . that are accepted by the middle class society of exchange and success.[21]

It is thus entirely compatible with the loose and highly secularized forms of civil religion characteristic of modern Western societies. It can coexist without tension with even the most pagan and arrogant of them.

It is this privatized version of Christianity which is advocated and praised by many contemporary conservatives such as E. R. Norman and Enoch Powell. "Man the individual is in a permanent and irresolvable tension with man the social animal," writes Powell; "he is born as an individual, he dies as an individual, and if there is forgiveness and redemption, he is forgiven and redeemed as an individual. It is to man the individual that the Gospel speaks."[22] There is no such thing, Powell argues, as a Christian social and political doctrine, and there is an impassable gulf set between Christian belief and the world of politics.[23] E. R. Norman sees Christianity as concerned with "the ethereal qualities of immortality" rather than engaging with the political order. A privatized Christianity is for him the only, and the preferred, alternative to a politicization in which the content of the faith is distilled into a heady idealism which reflects precisely the contours of contemporary secular liberal ideology. Norman's warnings about the dangers of politicization, although presented in very exaggerated form, deserve to be heeded. The problem is that both privatized and politicized Christianity give unqualified endorsement to one ideological tendency. A politicized theology runs into all the problems of the Eusebian approach; a privatized theology in some ways seems related to Tertullian's position, but it is impoverished by the lack of an ecclesiology that takes seriously the church as a sign of the kingdom. Each in its own fashion is no more than an unbalanced and partial version of the Christian faith.

Despite Norman's strictures on liberation theology as a prime instance of politicization, it is necessary for any viable political theology today to have a critical openness to the insights of liberation theology. We may learn from the liberation theologians, while keeping in mind their repeated assertions that their theology cannot be detached from its context and transplanted as it stands to another environment. Certain emphases of liberation theology are, however, of general relevance to the development of political theology. In the first place, liberation theology is not afraid to engage with contemporary political ideologies and philosophies. The West's difficulty in producing a viable political theology is probably connected with its reluctance or inability to enter into serious dialogue with contemporary social and political thought and reality. It is not surprising that theologies which attempt to address contemporary public issues without serious social analysis using the best tools available are so often vacuous and unhelpful. This also involves taking praxis seriously; faith is not just an intellectual choice but a commitment to a way of life. "It is in praxis", writes A. Fierro, "that political theology finds its matrix and nutritive soil, for it is a theology that is faith's reflection on political praxis in our day–on the praxis of Christians in particular."[24] And where Christians are not engaged and committed, where little is happening in the church, we can hardly expect a lively political theology to emerge. Accordingly, in the second place, liberation theology is unashamedly rooted in the life of the church. It takes the church seriously as a sign of the kingdom and an agent of God's purposes, itself a political organization, and one that operates unavoidably in the political realm. And the church is part of the social order, interacting in a range of ways with the class ordering of society and necessarily implicated in class struggles. Political theology is not free-floating theory, or "academic" in the narrow sense, but a critical service to be rendered first to the church and then to the life of the world. Third, liberation theology takes sides with the poor and oppressed. There is perhaps a sense in which theology has always had a kind of preferential option for the poor, however formal and however spiritualized. Often this has been the cover for an option for the rich and powerful. Liberation theology seeks to unmask the real role of theology and asserts that the best place to do theology is not among the powerful, where the "chaplain-theologian" understands and sympathizes with the tensions and dilemmas faced by decision-makers, supports them and informs their consciences, but among the poor and powerless, the recipients of policy rather than the makers of decisions. Finally, liberation theology stresses the political relevance of the Bible and of Christian doctrine in a way that is fresh and challenging. The Bible is sometimes interpreted in a simplistic way, it is true, and doctrine occasionally seems to function as little more than an ideological weapon. But this stress is an important corrective to those who believe that Christianity is devoid of political content or that its political implications have to be so distilled and filtered before they may be applied to current situations that they lose all Christian distinctiveness in the process.

VI. MARKS OF AN ADEQUATE
POLITICAL THEOLOGY

An adequate contemporary political theology will be contextual—that is, closely related to the specifics of the social, economic and political situation in the region in which it is developed—and also classical, interpreting and relating the biblical and theological tradition to the context. It is likely to show certain general characteristics, the most significant of which, it appears, are that it will be a *confessional,* a *trinitarian,* a *visionary,* a *demystifying,* and a *prophetic* theology. The stress may fall in different places in specific situations, but the characteristics themselves are complementary and necessary.

a. A Confessional Theology

A *confessional* theology is clearly *theology,* operating within the Christian theological tradition. It will not be a pious sugarcoating to a secular ideology or a Christian afterthought to an essentially untheological argument. It will grapple seriously with the complex issues involved in relating Christian belief and political praxis, aware that this is a dialectical operation, not simply the application of independently arrived at theory to political reality. It will often be tentative and fragmentary and modest, aware that the Christian faith does not provide us with a ready-made blueprint of the good society and that in political matters, as in others, Christians usually "see through a glass darkly". Confessing the faith has inescapable political implications, but it is only occasionally, and usually in times of crisis, that the political implications of the

265

faith may be confessed with great assurance. And then it is more commonly a No than a Yes that is expressed. The reason for this is explained by Bonhoeffer, himself a notable "confessor", as follows:

> The Church cannot indeed proclaim a concrete earthly order which follows as a necessary consequence from faith in Jesus Christ, but she can and must oppose every concrete order which constitutes an offence to faith in Jesus Christ, and in doing this she defines, at least negatively, the limits for an order within which faith in Jesus Christ and obedience are possible.[25]

It was just this kind of No that was expressed in the Barmen Declaration of 1934. Since Hitler made claims that were radically opposed to the claims of Jesus Christ, Nazism was incompatible with Christian faith. Here was a new paganism which put the nation, the race and the Führer in the place that should be occupied by Christ alone. With hindsight one may suggest that Barmen, for all the immense courage that went into its making and for all the patient, suffering witness of the Confessing Church, put too much stress on protecting the integrity of the church and too little on standing with the Jews and the other victims. But Barmen demonstrated a determination to act confessionally and to allow faith to shape practice. More recent declarations by major ecumenical bodies that the practice of apartheid is sinful and its theological justification heretical are in many ways similar, in that the church recognizes and declares that to confess the Christian faith excludes some courses of behaviour and is incompatible with certain ways of thinking. And a confessional stand is normally something that is "a cry from the heart" and "something we are obliged to do for the sake of the gospel in view of the times in which we stand", as the Dutch Reformed Mission Church declared in explaining its Confession of 1982, which proclaimed:

> We reject any doctrine which, in such a situation, sanctions in the name of the gospel or of the will of God the forced separation of people on the grounds of race and colour and thereby in advance obstructs and weakens the ministry and experience of reconciliation in Christ.[26]

To act in such a way is not to reduce the confession to a political manifesto but merely to take seriously that Christian faith has political implications, that it is impossible to witness to the truth of the gospel without denouncing false gospels, and that no compromise is permissible with idolatry.

But confessing the Christian faith in relation to politics is in most circumstances a complex, contentious and ambiguous matter. If theology remains at a high level of generality laying down "Christian principles" of a rather vague variety, it will be regarded as almost totally irrelevant to the hard decisions which have to be taken in politics. If, on the other hand, the mediation between faith and political choices is such that the distinctively Christian elements are filtered out and we are left with purely prudential conclusions, or conclusions that are clearly determined by some secular ideology, it may justifiably be felt that Christian faith has little or nothing to offer, and a Christian political theology is impossible. Despite the fact that in a crisis the political implications of the gospel may appear simple and unambiguous, it would be romantic and naive to believe that working on the interplay between Christianity and the world of politics is other than a complex, if necessary, task.

b. A Trinitarian Theology

The faith that is confessed is *trinitarian*. The most politically relevant and distinctive element in Christian faith is its trinitarian nature. It is this which gives Christian political theology its specific shape and role. Pagan political theologies, and most markedly the political metaphysics of monotheism which undergirded the late Roman Empire, provided a legitimation of strong centralized authority. They did this by providing simple or sophisticated analogies between the cosmic and the political orders which in practice sacralized the political status quo and identified piety with unquestioning loyalty to earthly authority.

This kind of political theology continued to influence Christian thought from early times right up to today. We have already mentioned how Eusebius developed a theology that celebrated and affirmed the special status before God, and in relation to God, of a Christian emperor and a Christian empire. It is surely significant that this system, which had so many echoes of pagan political theology, was rooted in a stance that was Arian rather than trinitarian. Only so could comparisons be drawn between Jesus Christ and the emperor Constantine, and the heavenly rule of one God and the earthly rule of one emperor. Even theologians of the standing of Thomas Aquinas did not carry a trinitarian understanding of God consistently through to their political thinking—for him too the authority of pope or emperor is justified by analogies with the rule of the one God in heaven. The argument is based entirely on monotheistic grounds, not on the mystery of the triune God. In similar vein it has been argued that nineteenth-century liberal theology's unease with, or disregard of, trinitarian theology opened the possibility of its capitulation to culture, and its tendency to sacralize the nation and its purposes.

In a notable short monograph, *Monotheismus als politisches Problem* (Leipzig, 1935), Erik Peterson argued (clearly in the face of Nazism's endeavours to construct, on a Christian or a pagan basis, a justifying ideology) that a Christian political theology is impossible, for three reasons. First, the Trinity points to the mystery of fellowship within God but does not provide a model for structures of authority or domination—indeed, quite the opposite, for it is inherently subversive. Second, the figure of Jesus suffering at the hands of the political and religious powers, coupled with the recognition that "God was in Christ", places a fundamental question mark against political power as it is exercised, and against all political structures, particularly the more totalitarian ones which make extravagant claims for themselves. And, third, the eschatological hope of *shalom* can never be identified with earthly peace. Neither the Pax Romana nor the best of earthly political orders is in fact the Pax Christi.

History, however, shows countless attempts to produce Christian political theologies. But Peterson is surely right in suggesting that political theologies that are no more than legitimations or sanctifications of an existing order sit uneasily with an orthodox trinitarian faith. A trinitarian political theology must surely be a questioning theology, constantly referring to "the disturbing memory of Jesus". It does not reject authority and espouse anarchism in utopian or millenarian fashion. It respects authority but seeks its transformation into the servant authority which Jesus commended to his disciples in contrast to the lordship of the kings of the Gentiles, and exemplified fully himself as the one "who came not to be served but to serve and to give his life as a ransom for many". And, finally, a trinitarian political theology is concerned with proclaiming, seeking, awaiting, anticipating and celebrating the forms of loving fellowship which are promised, of which we have a foretaste in the worship of the church, and which are a present reality in the heart of the mystery of the Trinity.

c. A Visionary Theology

A viable political theology will have a *visionary* element. In other words, it will be concerned with hope, with goals, with long-term objectives, with the fundamental values which religion implants in a culture over many centuries, with ideals and ends which need constant refreshment and renewal. A political theology has a responsibility to sustain a Christian social and political vision so that technical discussions and the pursuit of short-term objectives may be viewed *sub specie aeternitatis.* This is a vision which motivates and orientates; but it is not itself policy, and only becomes a programme at the cost of its integrity. The vision is concerned with ultimates and therefore relativizes many more immediate concerns. The Christian vision is eschatological and is expressed either in poetic and symbolic language or as a kind of negative eschatology—the kingdom is not this, not that.

If the sustaining of vision is a continuing responsibility for theology, and the Christian vision is recognized as having inescapably political content, there still remain dangers. The vision may be treated as a pipe dream, a way of escaping from engagement rather than an incentive to commitment to specific political options. It may be allowed to become private, vacuous and irrelevant; or the attempt may be made to declare the vision of immediate applicability as a political programme. Accordingly, the proper stewardship of the Christian vision is no simple task, but a responsibility laid squarely upon the shoulders of theologians and a particularly important component of any political theology.

d. A Demystifying Theology

In the fourth place, a contemporary political theology will exercise a *demystifying* role. The theologian here operates like the little child in Hans Christian Andersen's story of the emperor's new clothes: shaking himself free from ideological blinkers and social conditioning, he says what he sees. The child is not an "expert"—the "tailors", and in a more prudent and responsible way the courtiers, are the experts. Nor is he a decision-maker; that is the role of the emperor. King, courtiers and adults in the crowd are all caught up and bewildered by the contrived mystique of power manipulated for their own advantage by the "tailors". The child stands with the weak in *sancta simplicitas;* he tells the simple truth because he is not yet constrained by social pressure to deny it. His word destroys the mystique of power, revealing the emperor to be but a vain and fallible human being like the rest of us. The idolatry of power cannot survive the truth-telling of the child.

It is perhaps good for theologians, and political theologians above all, to be reminded from time to time of the saying about only those who become as little children entering the kingdom of heaven. For theologians have been accused, with no little justice, of mystifying politics, of declaring the established order to be God-given and sacred, of using mystification as an agency of social control. A major responsibility of the theologian is to ask questions, questions that sometimes appear at first to be naive, like the questions that Jesus asked. But the questions are deceptively simple; they show up ignorance masquerading as wisdom. The child in the story expresses the absurdity of the situation. The laughter he provokes cuts the emperor, and the tailors, and their collusive pretensions down to size. And the child does more than ask questions; he says quite simply what seems to be true to those who stand outside the circle of power, who are not experts, who are ignorant of the technical arguments but capable of seeing through the pretensions and the mystifications of power.

There are similarities here to Paulo Freire's conscientization. The little boy frees himself and others by shouting out the truth that the emperor has no clothes. But conscientization is more than a naive, childish—or childlike—apprehension of reality; it involves a critical and active grappling with reality in the light of social analysis. It leads directly to the call for the overthrow of all oppressive structures. The point here is that there is no such thing as a view of reality which is totally free from ideology, no access to reality which does not employ some form of social analysis.[27] Thus any political theology that takes seriously its demystifying responsibilities still has to work out its relation to current forms of political thought and political responsibility, learning how to discriminate between them and use them as searchlights to illumine social reality rather than as blinkers or blindfolds, and above all not acceding to the inordinate claims which are as characteristic of political ideologies as they are of those who exercise political power. Just as there can be no pure theology which does not interact with secular philosophy, so there can be no political theology which simply recounts the "brute facts" of social and political life without any interpretation or analysis save that which derives exclusively from the content of the Christian revelation. Political theology must relate to, but dare not become the captive of, the political ideologies of the day, if it is to understand the situation in which it operates and secure the ability to transform and evangelize that situation.

e. A Prophetic Theology

A contemporary political theology will, finally, be *prophetic*. The prophetic role relates in a more specific way to policy. It is impossible for a responsible political theology to remain indefinitely at the level of principle, generality or vision. We do not really understand a principle or a vision until we know how it might be implemented. But questions of policy are more contentious and divisive than statements of principle, and it is not uncommon for theologians on this account to duck discussion of policy. Prophecy is concerned with the actualities of power. When George Bell, Bishop of Chichester, denounced the area bombing of German cities during the Second World War on moral and theological grounds, he was dismissed as unrealistic and utopian and was accused of advocating a course of action that was quite contrary to the dictates of prudence and sound strategy. But years later, distinguished military commentators argued that Bell and the tiny handful who publicly endorsed his views at the time had in fact been advocating the more prudent and realistic, as well as the more moral, line. Prophecy is capable of reaching beyond what appear to be the immediate counsels of prudential ethics.

But there is also the danger that prophecy that is not rooted in careful social analysis may not take proper account of the complexities of the situation and the ambiguities that are faced by the decision-makers. John Habgood has argued that "to be close to those in power is to have firsthand knowledge of the complexity of the actual choices facing them. This has a devastating effect on prophetic certainties. And actually to share responsibility is even more devastating."[28] The point is well taken but must not be pressed too far. Decision-makers and the powerful are not the only ones who need sympathy and understanding. Those whose lives are affected by decisions, especially small and voiceless groups, have an even more pressing claim to be heard by the theologian.

Political theology as prophecy points steadily towards individual responsibility. Political, economic, scientific and strategic decisions are made and implemented by men and women, and affect men and women. Neither the market with its "invisible hand" nor the state should be reverenced as powers following their own principles and beyond human control. The prophet constantly reminds people that they bear responsibility not just before an electorate but before God for their actions and their decisions. And since in a sinful, broken world not infrequently the choice is not between good and evil but between courses of action which are all acknowledged to be imperfect and problematic, theology must seek to sustain with the promise of forgiveness and grace those who strive to act with integrity and do not evade responsibility.

The Christian faith cannot avoid a responsibility for the public realm. Because it is committed to seeking first the kingdom of God and his righteousness it must stand for justice and for peace, it must speak for the poor and the oppressed, and it must support, challenge and disturb the powerful. As the sign and foretaste of the kingdom the church cannot but be a critical force in society, sustaining vision, denouncing oppression, and announcing the hope of the gospel. And theology from its insights into the heights and depths of the human condition, the possibilities of fellowship and the constraints of sin has a distinctive and indispensable contribution to make, confronting fatalism, challenging narrow prejudices, and nourishing all that makes possible a social and political order fit for human beings, who are the children of God.

NOTES

1. See, e.g., Alastair Kee, *Constantine Versus Christ: The Triumph of Ideology* (London: SCM Press, 1982).

2. T. S. Eliot, *The Idea of a Christian Society* (London: Faber & Faber, 1939), 34.

3. Lesslie Newbigin, *The Other Side of 1984* (London: British Council of Churches, 1983), 37.

4. Mary Douglas, *Natural Symbols* (Harmondsworth, Eng.: Penguin Books, 1970), 36.

5. Dietrich Bonhoeffer, *Letters and Papers from Prison* (London: SCM Press, 1956), 166.

6. Bonhoeffer, cited in Gustavo Gutiérrez, *The Power of the Poor in History* (London: SCM Press, 1983), 231.

7. Arendt Th. van Leeuwen, *Christianity in World History* (London: Edinburgh House Press, 1964).

8. See especially Christel Lane, *The Rites of Rulers: Ritual in Industrial Society—The Soviet Case* (Cambridge: Cambridge University Press, 1981).

9. John Habgood, *Church and Nation in a Secular Age* (London: Darton, Longman & Todd, 1983), 28ff.

10. N. Figgis, *Churches and the Modern State* (London, 1913).

11. D. Munby, *The Idea of a Secular Society* (London: Oxford University Press, 1963).

12. J. M. Winter and D. M. Joslin, eds., *R. H. Tawney's Commonplace Book* (Cambridge: Cambridge University Press, 1972), 67.

13. Ibid., 68.

14. Ibid., 53–54.

15. R. H. Tawney, *Religion and the Rise of Capitalism* (London: John Murray, 1929), 286.

16. A. Dumas, *Political Theology and the Life of the Church* (London: SCM Press, 1978), 20.

17. *The Theological Declaration of Barmen,* 1934, par. 5.

18. In R. Mishra, *The Welfare State in Crisis* (Brighton, Eng.: Harvester Press, 1984), 29. On this theme, see further Duncan B. Forrester, *Christianity and the Future of Welfare* (London: Epworth Press, 1985).

19. Anthony King, "Overload: Problems of Governing in the 1970s", *Political Studies* 23 (1975): 296.

20. Johannes B. Metz, *Faith in History and Society* (Tunbridge Wells, Eng.: Burns & Oates, 1980), esp. chap. 3.

21. Ibid., 45.

22. Enoch Powell, review in *Theology* (1983): 475.

23. See also Enoch Powell, *Wrestling with the Angel* (London: Sheldon Press, 1977).

24. A. Fierro, *The Militant Gospel* (London: SCM Press, 1973), 182.

25. Dietrich Bonhoeffer, *Ethics* (London: SCM Press, 1955), 324.

26. G. D. Cloete and D. J. Smit, eds., *A Moment of Truth: The Confession of the Dutch Reformed Mission Church 1982* (Grand Rapids: Wm. B. Eerdmans, 1984), 3–4.

27. For a critical account of conscientization and its role in liberation theology, see Dennis P. McCann, *Christian Realism and Liberation Theology* (Maryknoll: Orbis Books, 1981).

28. Habgood, *Church and Nation in a Secular Age,* 105.

12

RATIONALITY, THE SCIENCES AND THEOLOGY

DANIEL HARDY

I. THE INTERFACE OF CHRISTIAN FAITH AND THE SCIENCES

There is a prima facie reason for the concern of Christian faith with knowledge and rationality, and therefore with the sciences and the pursuit of rationality. For, at the least, Christian faith is concerned with humankind's attempt to understand the position of the human being in the world, and Christian theology with attempts to do so in a fully disciplined manner, wherever and however this is done. Because of the importance which they have assumed for the understanding of human life in the world, and because of the importance of their method in doing so, the sciences must be considered by Christian faith and theology. This is no longer an optional "extra" to faith and theology, if it ever was such. The sciences and theology meet in the understanding of humankind in the universe, and in the discipline of that.

It should not be a case of unilateral interest on the part of Christian faith. Insofar as faith and its theology actively manifest their concern, the sciences in turn are bound to be concerned with theology. It is a sad feature of our day that this reciprocity is most frequently seen only where there is conflict—for example, in those episodes, remembered or present, where theology is seen to be restricting the freedom of science and scientists are defending science.[1] There are much more sophisticated accounts of the intersection of the concerns of the two, in which theology and the sciences are seen to be of assistance to each other; but these are largely ignored by those (from either side) who see unwelcome interference as the only possible relation between the two.

There are two places at which theology and the sciences necessarily intersect, *the very fact of human existence in the world* and the *understanding and development of its basic conditions.*

1. The existence of humankind in the universe is the given location, not only for humankind and the universe but for Christian faith. Whatever this existence is, it is the condition for both humankind and its faith and theology. Therefore, insofar as *either* the results of the sciences and technology *or* those of faith affect the situation of the human being in the universe, they will affect each other. And each, the sciences and technology, on the one hand, and Christian faith, on the other, must take account of the effects of the other.

It is surprising to look back to the time when *Lux Mundi* was written and find that the effects of the sciences and technology upon humankind could largely be ignored in restating Christian faith. Likewise, the consequences of faith upon humankind in the world could be seen to be of such a kind as not to impinge upon scientific understanding of humankind. But that can surely no longer be the case for either; the situation of humankind in the universe is deeply affected, even mediated, by the sciences and technology on the one hand and by religious faith on the other. Globally, but particularly in the prosperous places of the world, human understanding and life are infused by the sciences to a remarkable degree. Most of the benefits and necessities of life as we know it are provided with the assistance of the sciences, and the advances with which people are most concerned—as well as the problems that accompany them—are those in which the sciences play a very large part. Furthermore, it is evident that the sciences are important for all levels of society and for all of their activities, even those which at first sight seem most remote from the world of the sciences. And few would wish it otherwise. On the other side, the importance of religious faith for the situation of humankind is now no longer ignored either; the effects of religious world views—or the lack of them, as in what is (somewhat dubiously) called secularization—is seen as increasingly important.[2]

2. It should also be evident, however, that in important respects the position and the content of the sciences and of theology occupy a mediating role for each other in their understanding and development of the basic conditions of humankind in the world. As T. F. Torrance has suggested, "Our understanding of the ongoing universe itself cannot but enter into the coefficients of our theological statements."[3] The sciences and technology have had a deep effect on the disciplined

search for (and development of) the basic conditions of humankind. The means by which the understanding and development of these conditions are pursued are now mediated through the practices of the sciences and technology, frequently with the assistance of those (e.g., philosophers) who assume the role of reflecting on these practices in order to purify them. On the other hand, the position and the content of faith and theology are of no small importance in the understanding and development of the basic conditions of humankind in the world.[4] The mediation by both the sciences and theology of the basic conditions of humankind in the world deserves recognition by both.

That is not to say that their mediation is invariable. On the contrary, in recent years notions of the position and the content of each have varied considerably, with consequent variations in the view of their relations. (1) When science was seen in positivist and antitheoretical terms, Christian faith was seen to depend on direct experience, whether in Christ-formed knowledge of God (Karl Barth) or in the experience of salvation rooted in the justifying act of God (Rudolf Bultmann)— each a positivist and antitheoretical account. The claim about their interaction was therefore that faith and the sciences were positive and antitheoretical but offered sharply different possibilities, each useless in the view of the other, of knowing the human being in the world before God. (2) When science was seen to allow a larger place for theory, as falsifiable conjecture, theology assumed the position of falsifiable conjecture which required justification by appeal to experience, usually cumulative rather than instantaneous.[5] Correspondingly, the view was taken that the relation between the sciences and theology had to be settled by "empirical" means, by "looking at developments in the sciences . . . and then thinking about any possible implications they might have for Christian theology".[6] (3) When the sciences came to be seen as interpretations making use of world views or paradigms, faith was also seen as interpretation of the world through models and paradigms. And the effects of the sciences upon faith were seen as those of one form of interpretation of the world on another, because the means of reflecting upon them were mediated by a view of the sciences as theory-dependent interpretations.[7] In all these cases, reflection on the nature of science and religion and their mutual interaction is conditioned by the possibilities which it is thought the sciences and theology afford for understanding: positivist, empiricist, and idealist (a modern form).

Given the importance of science and technology, on the one hand, and of faith and theology on the other, for the conditions of humankind in the universe, it is easy to lose sight of their limitations. In regard both to their effect upon the condition of humankind in the world and also to the requirements of their theories, the claims and demands of each sometimes prove excessive.

In practice, both can be seen as incurring expenses that are disproportionate to their benefits. This is most obvious, perhaps, in the case of the sciences. The expense of scientific research has frequently risen to levels that are unbearable within limited resources. As scientific research advances, its requirements—in terms of equipment, energy and talent—increase geometrically as the results available at one level of inquiry are exhausted and the researchers proceed to the next level. The infinite possibilities of research are necessarily limited by what is economically possible in one locality.[8] The technological counterpart of this problem is in the transference of the benefits of scientific research to large numbers of people, which requires an exponential increase in the use of resources. To achieve this transference is frequently impossible within the limited resources available in one locality. The exploitation of natural resources there or elsewhere is often required, an exploitation that is unacceptable for the future of humankind as a whole or for the future of the natural environment. But much the same is true in the case of religion, where the advance of religious institutions places heavier burdens on those who bear them, often without being able to call upon wider resources.

In theory also, their demands frequently prove excessive. Within both the sciences and religion, there has been a strong tendency to idealize the means and goal of inquiry and to impose these idealizations as normative. In the sciences, "knowledge" has been taken to be that which is supported by—or at least not falsified by—good evidence from observation and experiment. Of course, the byproduct of this set of notions is the establishment of an elite of those who are most practiced and effective in observation and experiment; they are thought to be the guardians and practitioners of knowledge. With that goes the credit for historical achievements: it is thought that the knowledge produced by the sciences and their practitioners was responsible for most major human achievements through the past few centuries. Since the Renaissance, as human beings have concentrated on the task of improving their situation, it is seen that the sciences developed the most efficacious means of pursuing this task—sometimes through ongoing corrections in the direction of their work, sometimes through more sustained considerations of the nature and derivation of the skills by which they worked—for example, sensibility, understanding and judgment. In Christianity, "faith" was idealized in similar fashion, as that which exercised a total claim on the believer, while also providing the grace by which it should be exercised. Hence, much as knowledge was supported by observation for the sciences, faith was supported by the presence and power of its "object".

Each has produced what could be called a "confinement in factuality". For with such knowledge (in the case of the sciences), or such faith (for theology), the result takes on the character of a self-evident state of affairs—a "fact" or a "belief"—which is to be assumed and which requires no further examination. That is very like the view of scientific statements that was accepted by the scientific positivists of the Vienna Circle: "In science there are no 'depths'; there is surface everywhere. . . . Everything is accessible to man."[9] Whether in the sciences or in theology, such "facts" could then be used as an unexamined axiom, from which conclusions could simply be drawn. In theology, such an axiom might be: "It is the case that God (who is of such and such a sort) is . . . , that he created the world (simply originated it) and all that is in it (with their established characteristics) . . . , that he redeemed humankind (transforming it into the likeness of himself)." Resting in such notions, whether scientific or theological, as if they were "facts" involves treating the particular meaning ascribed to them as equivalent to that to which they refer, as if the referents themselves were as accessible as the meanings ascribed to them. In effect, this confines the referents to the limitations of the referring expressions.

The attractions of the old notion of a unified and unchanging basis for epistemology and ontology for science as well as for religious people continue very strong, for obvious reasons. The medieval description of God, which so closely approximated to that notion, continues—largely unmodified—among Christians; and they are strongly inclined to the supposition that God himself is the one, unchanging basis for all knowledge and reality. But while they may be able to sustain it in its own terms, they hold this view without being able to sustain it by reference to present-day notions of epistemology and ontology. And many questions have arisen within theology, producing a tension between "foundationalism" and "constructivism". Like one form of objectivism in science, a foundationalist position in theology finds in revelation (for example) a content-rich source from which statements can be derived, while constructivism, like relativism in science, suggests that all concepts are culture-derived though perhaps employing "thick descriptions" to maintain their content-rich material.[10]

The high cost of such attractive and usable idealizations in the sciences and theology should be recognized nonetheless. There are two difficulties with treating them as normative. One has to do with their adequacy as indications of what occurs in the sciences and theology; in so simplifying that which is achieved in knowledge and faith, they may be untrue to the complexity of the process by which they are achieved and maintained. Indeed, they may prevent an adequate account of the relation of the sciences and theology: their simplicities may blind them to the commonality between the two and thereby keep them apart. The other difficulty has to do with making them normative: if their derivation is too narrow, they cannot be used as universally normative. If, for example, the "facts" of the sciences are derived from the sensible and repeatable, observation and experiment, they cannot be treated as normative in other matters. Or, if the "facts" of Christian belief are derived from faith through grace from God, in such a way as to exclude matters of scientific "fact", they cannot be treated as normative in wider areas. While—insofar as they are adequate to the practice of science or faith—they can be treated respectively as normative for the sciences or faith, their use must be limited to that domain. Of course, this will not be the case if their derivation is not so restricted, as when one considers both the world *and* God. This is what lies behind the refusal of many scientists today to employ an axiomatic-deductive method and that of theologians to begin from a priori suppositions about God's presence to the world.[11]

It could also be claimed that the use of such restrictive approaches has other and wider consequences. On the one hand, it so limits the interaction of the human being with that which is to be known as to promote a nearly mechanistic interrelation of the two, excluding from science and faith those who seek a relation with the conditions of humankind in the world which is more free. This search is the source of the mysticism, pluralism, and aestheticism, and even the anarchic tendencies, found within and beyond the community of practising scientists today.[12] "If it feels good, do it!" and "Believe what you will" are the sorts of slogan that have a very wide appeal; and they form the basis of life and understanding for very many people, subject only to the constraints within which those persons live. Such views undercut the contribution of the sciences and theology, leaving it unclear how the stability and the developments that they have afforded to human-kind can have come about.

On the other hand, the application of such restrictive methods in the sciences and theology is frequently enervating. Using such methods in the sciences will sap the energy of reason from other areas of sense-related life and understanding, expropriating achievements in these connections and requiring them to admit that their work is esoteric and unscientific. Likewise, in theology, using a restrictive notion of faith will sap the energy from other aspects of life and understanding, de-taching the "real God" from the "real world". Recent scientific discov-eries of order emerging from spontaneity, and theological emphases on "nonorder", testify to the search for more dynamic methods.[13]

Of course, the recognition of the limits of the methods of the sciences and of theology opens a space for those attempts to speak of knowledge and faith beyond the narrower norms. But it does not in itself restore the credibility of knowledge, faith and their relatedness. It is to that task that we must address ourselves in this essay.

How does one reappropriate the possibility of knowledge and faith in their proper relationship? One important way is to begin from their commonality in humankind. This suggests that both are intrinsic fea-tures of fully human life and understanding in the universe. In other words, the concentration or integrity of life as lived, and the most concentrated act of the human mind, are intrinsically human activities. And as such they can be the subject of endless human activity, whether in the sciences or in the humanities. But it can also be said that they are intrinsic features of humankind's life before God, and as such directed to their source. "Knowledge of God is the basic act of the human mind and . . . faith in its intellectual aspect is the adaptation of the reason in its response to the compelling claims of God as he makes himself known to us in his Word."[14] If these things are so, then natural life and the sciences, while having their own norms which disallow specific reference beyond the domain of the natural world, are also manifestations of the direction of human life and understanding to its source and end. The sciences and theology are separate but inter-dependent. But it does not suffice simply to point to this intersection or to claim it. That only states schematically what needs to be reappropriated.

Why should this be so? Why will it not suffice to repeat the intrinsic connection of that which is fully human to that which is of God? It is primarily because both the sciences and theology, in the forms in which we know them, are increasingly dislocated and disempowered by a new context, a new basis for understanding, which is overtaking both of them. As we will see later, it is hardly appropriate to refer to a dislocation of such magnitude by such neutral words as "context" and "basis", for they will require a vastly different understanding of the sciences and theology and their relation.

Our reappropriation of the relation between the human and God must allow for this, and the conclusion of this essay will suggest how it may do so. But before we attempt to do so, we must face questions about the nature of knowledge and rationality and how they are made possible by God, and how such knowledge and rationality are mediated through materiality and history. In other words, we must attempt to reappropriate the intrinsic connection of knowledge and rationality, as mediated in materiality and history, to the nature and presence of God. That is a task which requires a wide discussion of the issue, as that has appeared through the centuries. Within this discussion, we will need to face the kinds of distortion that afflict the understanding of God, knowledge and rationality, materiality and history, and that have severed the proper connections between them. Doing so is unavoidable, and really requires much more space than we have available. We shall therefore have to be quite selective, focusing particularly on features that are often overlooked.

II. KNOWLEDGE, RATIONALITY AND THEIR POSITIVE CONTENT

Knowledge, what is that? Rationality, what is that? Perhaps, above all, they are refinements of what human beings have acquired through wisdom, their own or received from some source, problematic as the notion of wisdom may be. As such, it would seem that, though they may be refinements of the achievement of wisdom—and may seem very different—they are ultimately inseparable from it. They are also implicated in whatever may be the character of wisdom. One consequence of this might be that, because wisdom is concerned with more than rationality and knowledge, they are not to be dissociated from whatever else is involved in wisdom. If wisdom is also concerned with certain goals for rationality and knowledge which lie beyond what they are, preeminently with the achievement of goodness and beauty, or with their achievement in human life in the world, then rationality and knowledge are not to be dissociated from these goals or "values". Whatever it is in which the respective refinements of rationality and knowledge consist, these refinements should not omit the consideration of their use in bringing about goodness and beauty. If rationality and knowledge are connected with wisdom, they are indissolubly connected with goodness and beauty, through their derivation from wisdom if not directly.

Through the centuries, most views of rationality and knowledge have followed the basic features of this picture. They have done so selectively, to be sure, but they have in the main done so. Look, for example, at the strategies that are commended for the development of knowledge. At first glance, it seems a particularly modern strategy to suppose that knowledge and its movement are to be assimilated to the "positive content" of knowledge, that to which knowledge refers in order to be knowledge, or the "object" by relation to which knowledge is considered to be knowledge. If this supposition is made, knowledge is that which incorporates this positive content, and knowing—the movement to knowledge—is then seen to be the pathway to the incorporation of this positive content, whereby knowledge is derived from this content. But further thought shows that this is essentially the strategy followed by all theories of knowledge through the ages. We will look at examples of this in a moment, but not before considering several other issues.

On the one hand, the positive content of wisdom to which knowledge is to be assimilated in order to be knowledge seems simple; on the other hand, it seems exceedingly dense. As the goal of all knowledge it seems to have the possibility of being maximally informative for knowledge, while also being appropriately conducive to other aspects of the well-being of humankind in the world. These qualities lead to the supposition of its simplicity.[15] On the other hand, as manifested in knowledge it seems to be so mysteriously deep as to require it to be seen as a complexity in which various aspects or levels are present. This depth leads to the supposition of an inner complexity which is incapable of being known without comparable complexities in the structure of knowledge (such as those seen in the use of basic categories or in the attempt to establish an inner proportioning or dynamic for knowledge), and in the relation between knowledge and other aspects of the well-being of humankind, such as goodness and beauty.

Another issue has to do with the question of rationality. We have spoken so far of the assimilation of knowledge to the positive content of wisdom. Seen in such a way, knowledge has its source in, and is authenticated by, the positive content of wisdom; and rationality does not as such appear, except perhaps adjectivally to show when knowledge has become "rational" knowledge by virtue of its "proportioning" to the positive content of wisdom. But insofar as the content of wisdom is seen otherwise, as an agency or in terms of a consciousness, the way is open for knowledge to be considered also in terms of agency or consciousness, a knowing. Seen in such a way, the activity of knowing becomes important. In other words, attention can shift from knowledge as such to the instrument of knowledge, from the state of knowledge to the activity of the agent who knows—his or her rationality. And if this is to be assimilated to its proper content, it is an assimilation of knowing-activity or rationality to the agency of wisdom or rationality. This assimilation may be marked by the simplicity and the complexity of the agency of wisdom; the assimilation is not necessarily a simple correspondence but may also be seen as the inner proportioning of the agency of knowledge.[16]

A further issue arises over the position of the material (sensual) and the historical. If knowledge is to be assimilated to timeless and immaterial wisdom, or rationality to a perfect (because changeless) agency of wisdom, the consequences of materiality and change must—so far as possible—be avoided. But if, as later became the case, materiality and change are seen to be the medium of wisdom and rationality, it is an important task to employ the material, sensory observation and historical understanding in assimilating knowledge and rationality to wisdom and its agency. Here again, the issue is often that of identifying the simplicity and complexity of wisdom in the simplicity and complexity of the material and the historical.

III. VARIETIES OF ASSIMILATION TO WISDOM

Such considerations permit us to identify in a few major examples a fundamental pattern of knowledge, and of rationality, through the ages. We see that Platonism assimilates knowledge to the "positive content" of an absolute whose inner complexity is the eternal forms.

In such a case, there is a clear direction of knowledge to a transcendent content, even though that content is rather abstract. But much later, attention is directed more explicitly to the positive content of the rational human mind, with the transcendent assuming the position of a guarantor or informant. With attention switched to rationality, for example, Cartesianism assimilates rationality to the rational content of the mind, as guaranteed by the perfection of God. Locke's view gives much more importance to materiality and history, and finds rationality in the right judgment of sensory and historical content. With consciousness of the world taken as the mediation of wisdom, Kant (like Descartes) assimilates rationality to the rational mind as it is exercised upon the material and historical world. With a still more active view of consciousness of the world as the mediation of wisdom, Hegelian idealism assimilates knowledge to the movement of Spirit as it moves from abstractness through concreteness to the self-possession of wisdom. But in all these cases, "positive content" for knowledge or rationality is found in the mind, either by itself or in its relation to the world, and only guaranteed (or attracted to itself) by an unconditioned or absolute. The absolute, already abstract in Plato, is seen only in its operation on the mind.

In each case, actual knowledge or rationality—knowledge on the way to being knowledge, so to speak—is considered the mediation of this positive content; insofar as it is knowledge, it has become so through assimilation to that positive content; and the dynamic of knowledge or rationality is seen as a growth to a mediation more adequate to that content. For Platonism, it is the dialectical ascent to the eternal forms, so far as that is accessible to human beings, which combines an exemplary searching for truth with the happiness which is the concomitant of such a search;[17] for Cartesianism, it is a rational ascesis by which human knowing is purified in accordance with the perfection of God; for Locke, it is education in analysis and judgment; for Kant, it is the rational redevelopment (through the agency of transcendental reason) of the activity of human understanding; for Hegelian idealism, it is the self-transcending rationality of Spirit culminating in Spirit's self-appropriation in its object; and so on. All alike presuppose that knowledge or rationality (as the case may be) occurs when its "positive content" is achieved and that knowing is rightly ordered in accordance with this content.[18]

This is, perhaps, the notion that underlies the claim that "we have, in the West, no ways of knowing, rational or irrational, that we can describe without Greek models of description."[19] For, underlying every one of these views of knowledge is the supposition that the basic pattern characteristic of Platonism—assimilation to "positive content"—should be followed, even if the kind of content that is supposed is altered very radically (from a transcendent content to one found in the human mind or spirit).

Associated with this strategy has been another, that of dualism. It has been typical of the pattern we have described, and also of its variants, that the "positive content" to which knowledge has been assimilated has been, shall we say, protected from interference or contamination by what is seen to be inconsistent with its character. At the most fundamental level, this has meant that knowledge or rationality itself is distanced from the very positive content to which it should be assimilated. That is to say, in the knowledge of this content, there is also an unknowledge, because, in some basic sense, human understanding as such interferes with—or in extreme cases contaminates—the positive content of knowledge.

What it is that is problematic for knowledge is differently conceived. Often, as in the more intellectualist views of knowledge, the senses are held responsible, as though every ascent of knowledge to wisdom were weighted down by the impulses of the body. Hence, in the Platonist-Augustinian view, the purity of "truth" cannot be expected to arise from the senses,[20] any more than, in the Cartesian view, rational certainty can arise from the senses. At the very least, there is a dichotomizing of truth and bodiliness.[21] But sometimes it is the movement of the world which is blamed: "What constantly changes cannot be grasped."[22] If so, knowledge cannot arise from the contingent except by grasping the (timeless) truth of contingent events, whether for a Plato or an Augustine or a Descartes.

New views of the senses and of history slowly arise with the Renaissance, however, and thereafter it is not the senses or the changeable as such which are regarded as contaminating knowledge but their improper use. Knowledge requires to be derived from the senses and history, and—as in the empiricist view—rational judgment cannot arise from innate ideas given in the mind or from the accepted truths of the past; they are the contaminants and must be set aside in favor of a fresh derivation of knowledge from the senses and history contextually understood.[23]

A further stage occurs with Kant and Hegel. There too, the assimilation of knowledge to its positive content requires stringent safeguards: it must arise from the senses and history; yet it must be of such a kind as to guarantee itself as knowledge. Kant provides these safeguards by excluding potential contaminants: *(a)* Knowledge is sharply distinguished from what has not been touched by the rationality of the forms and categories that are operative in all knowing, from the sensual/historical as it is merely "in itself"—the phenomenal from the noumenal; *(b)* knowledge is sharply distinguished from that which is less than rational—knowledge from deficient knowledge (which includes that of the self, the world and God); and *(c)* knowledge is sharply distinguished from those activities which are not knowledge in that basic sense at all, those which have to do with goodness and beauty. In Hegel's idealism, the assimilation of knowledge to its positive content requires consideration of the achievement of this positive content through historical change: knowledge is achieved through its passage into the sensory and the historical, and the repossession of knowledge from this passage. The sensory and the historical are necessary to the movement of rational Spirit itself, but they are contaminants insofar as they are not raised to the true (i.e., the rational) quality of the Spirit. Hence, Hegel's view of the achievement of the positive content wherein knowledge consists requires not simply those contingent dualisms (of infinite and finite, e.g.) which Spirit "creates" and transcends but also the subordination of those movements which are less than absolutely rational, whether they be aesthetic, religious or even historical. In all cases, the very attempt to proceed to knowledge involves the elimination of what is considered to be incompatible with the positive content which is the heart of knowledge.

It is a significant aspect of these dualistic strategies that they procure full knowledge and rationality by concentrating on "purity" of knowledge itself, what we have termed its "positive content", and excluding the impure. The exclusion of the impure serves the pursuit of purity. The consequences, of course, are very serious, for everything that is inconsistent with this "positive content" must be eliminated, whether arising from the senses and materiality, from the less-than-rational self or from a rich transcendence. Viewed from the standpoint of the Judeo-Christian tradition, they are barren rationalisms.

Such strategies lie at the heart of traditional views of knowledge and knowing rationally, and form the core of traditional views of the sciences and epistemology. The differences introduced by different suppositions about what is the "positive content" of knowledge (or rationality), and about what are its appropriate mediations, make the strategies seem more different than they are; their basic pattern is very much the same, directing knowledge or rationality to their positive content or "wisdom", correcting them accordingly, and eliminating "contaminants" through exclusion by dualisms.

This fundamental pattern has provided a vehicle of astonishing power for Western thought, even where the pattern is adapted very extensively. What remains of it and what now to do are the chief questions facing us in this essay. But that it does remain can hardly be questioned, even in those who today claim fundamental shifts in "paradigms" of thought.[24]

IV. THE COMMONNESS OF PATTERN IN KNOWLEDGE AND CHRISTIAN FAITH

The pattern that we have been tracing suggests that knowledge and rationality, in their fullest senses, occur when they are assimilated to their positive content. Knowledge and rationality are, in a sense, mediations of their own positive content. Whether this positive content is strictly within the possibilities of human knowledge and rationality or requires reference to a higher "wisdom" is a matter of disagreement. And the kind of "higher wisdom" that is present is also a matter of disagreement, whether it is an absolute or something richer in content and whether the presence is attracting or informing. These issues are often resolved by sleight-of-hand, where a particular thinker simply adopts a consistent position without argument.

Nonetheless, the pattern has been a constant accompaniment to Christian thought in the West, and there are striking affinities between the two at many points. Indeed, there are thinkers who advance the much stronger claim that there is a necessary connection between the two and that modern science not only *did not* but *could not* have arisen apart from Christianity. For example, it is said that

> the scientific quest found fertile soil only when this faith in a personal, rational Creator had truly permeated a whole culture, beginning with the centuries of the High Middle Ages. It was that faith which provided, in

sufficient measure, confidence in the rationality of the universe, trust in progress, and appreciation of the quantitative method, all indispensable ingredients of the scientific quest.[25]

The contribution that Christianity made is impressive, even if only because the richness of its understanding of God, of materiality, of particularity and of history provided a constant attraction to the sciences, bringing them out of the barrenness of Platonism to search for richer understanding of the mind and its operation in materiality, particularity and history.

But how much of the pattern that we have traced was attributable specifically to Christian faith? The possibility of knowledge through assimilation to the positive content of wisdom? No. The supposition of simplicity and depth in this wisdom? No. The possibility of rational agency through assimilation to the agency of wisdom? No. The mediation of wisdom in the natural order of matter and history? No. All of these have other sources as well. But the possibility remains that Christianity, concentrating these emphases in its own powerful presentations, coauthored the pattern, emphasizing certain features, and thereby added immensely to the power of this pattern in the West. That is not, however, to say that the connection of Christianity and modern science was, or is, necessary—only that there is a massively important contingent connection between the two, whereby each is significantly affected by the other. It is another question, which we must face later, whether the connection of Christian faith is necessary for the well-being and acceptability of the sciences—and perhaps of both Christianity and the sciences—today.

The issue of the relation between Christianity and this pattern for knowledge is not so easily settled. The argument that we have just put is based on what is discernible through the history of culture, on the fact that "things have happened this way". From that point of view, there is an intimate link between Christianity and the pattern of knowledge which is in general use in the West, but the link is a contingent one because the two have happened to develop together. The argument traces the pattern of knowledge used in the West and its affinities with Christianity; the form of the argument is a posteriori. But to Christian faith, many of the characteristics of the pattern of knowledge appear as contingent in a different sense: knowledge has happened according to this pattern because it is of the nature of knowledge that it be assimilated to the positive content of wisdom and be so through history. To put it slightly differently, Christian faith sees it to be of the nature of wisdom that it generates knowledge in and through history. And it sees that this generation of knowledge has occurred broadly within human life, as well as specifically in Judeo-Christian experience, the one as a broader correspondent of the other more specific one. So the affinity between the broader generation of knowledge and the more specific one arises because of their common source in the generative power of wisdom, because they are both contingent upon the generative power of wisdom.

Nor is this view limited to Christian faith. Insofar as one who knows recognizes that this knowledge is generated by the positive content of wisdom, and acknowledges that the same generativity also occurs in the more specific ways of the Judeo-Christian tradition, he may recognize the affinity between the two, not simply as an accident of history but as contingent upon the nature of wisdom.

It is particularly interesting to recognize that by this account, the affinity between the two—knowledge and Christian knowledge, both deriving from the nature of wisdom—may be recognized in both static and dynamic forms. Hence knowledge occurs, and occurs in and through history, and in both cases occurs through its assimilation to the positive content of wisdom. This may be recognized both by anyone who knows and by the Christian who knows, who should therefore be able to see the affinity between them occurring both in the static occurrence of knowledge and in the dynamic achievement of knowledge in and through history.

The argument can be put more readily without such circumlocutions. The wisdom to whose positive content knowledge is assimilated through history, and which is thus known a posteriori, is found, in Christian faith, to have as its positive content the God who presents himself for human beings to know in history, known also a posteriori. The affinity between the two, which may be seen as an accident of cultural history, is shown in Christian faith as arising from the nature of wisdom itself. Nor is this confined to Christian faith: insofar as, for one who employs this pattern of knowledge, wisdom is recognized as that which gives itself to be known in history, such a one has some degree of affinity with the Christian. And that recognition is widespread among those who employ the pattern. But the claim that the one who employs the pattern of knowledge is therefore dependent upon theological ideas must be treated with some caution.[26]

V. ASSIMILATION TO WISDOM IN THE JUDAIC TRADITION

From the beginning, there is an intermingling of the pattern of knowledge that we have discussed with the subject matter of theology. We must now look much more carefully at the positive content that is provided for the pattern of knowledge in the Judeo-Christian tradition.

The supposition of the presence of wisdom in the natural world in such a way that its positive content might be the determinant of knowledge is to be found in Greek attempts to identify the "powers" of nature through mythology, and in Judaic summaries of wisdom manifest in the practice of wisdom. But despite such similarities, there are many qualitative differences between the Judaic and the Greek presentations. There is, for example, far greater passion about the importance of wisdom and its implications for the practice of life among the Jews, whereas among the Greeks there is far more patience with the development of exact statements of the conditions through which knowledge can be gained and society can be rightly ordered. There is a difference, therefore, in the form of their concerns, even in their similar concern for assimilation to wisdom.

Not disconnected from this is the more vivid awareness of time and movement which is to be found in Hebrew understanding, and the determination which is exercised upon knowledge by one who will be there (in the future) as he himself desires and wills to be there:

> (And he said:)
> Thus shall you say to the sons of Israel,
> I AM THERE sends me to you.
> (And God said further to Mosheh:)
> HE,
> the God of your fathers,
> the God of Abraham, the God of Yitzhak, the God of Yaacob,
> sends me to you.
> This is my name in world-time,
> my remembrance for generation after generation.[27]

In both cases, the Greek and the Hebrew, wisdom is seen to be itself and yet present in knowledge and practice as their determinant despite the inadequacy of human beings to receive it. As we saw before, its positive content is "maximally informative" and therefore simple, but also exceedingly dense; its presence in knowledge requires extensive elucidation in law and practice—as witness the extensive presentation of laws and practical wisdom to be found in the Old Testament. There is a great deal of hesitancy about elucidating the implications of this density for wisdom itself; and where this is done, it is never done in such a way as to confine the positive content of wisdom to a law-like pattern.

There is a greater willingness among the Jews to speak of the agency of wisdom, however. The selfsameness of wisdom (in its simplicity and density) arises not from its regularity but from its self-determination—which may at times seem changeable. Correspondingly, the agency of wisdom is seen to be the positive content of responsible action on the part of "Wisdom's" people. So there are the foundations of a notion of human rationality which is proportioned to the positive content of the agency of wisdom, in addition to the notion of human knowledge assimilated to the positive content of wisdom.

A further distinction arises over the issue of the importance of materiality and sensuality. For Platonic understanding, anything—even beauty—that is associated with materiality and sensuality is too far distanced from the ideal, the positive content of wisdom, to act as a medium of wisdom; the dialectical ascent to wisdom must begin outside materiality. And even Aristotle does not altogether overcome the distancing of materiality from wisdom.[28] But materiality is not so distanced from wisdom in Hebrew understanding. It is not simply the "place" through which there is an epiphany of the wisdom, but itself the mediation of wisdom. Hence, human territory and behavior are themselves mediations of wisdom and its agency. Why else should one worry about being in a strange land?

Likewise, history is of greater importance for the Hebrew than the Greek. Here one should note the character of the Old Testament text, which—apart from law and wisdom—is predominantly concerned with the interweaving of historical narratives through which the identity of God and his people is established. They are not therefore to be treated as time-neutral transparent screens through which the timeless purposes of God are to be discerned but as historical mediations of the wisdom and purposes of God. To be sure, this poses a most difficult question for the "nature" of wisdom. Is it "substance-like", so that "all events,

291

ideas and movements in history have at bottom something in common, which manifests itself in them all and makes it possible to understand them" in terms of that "common" thing?[29] It is only with difficulty that wisdom is seen otherwise than as a "common thing" with a singular positive content which is the point of reference for all knowledge. But this other view is undoubtedly the implication of the Hebrew understanding of history. By that standard, a "substance-like" notion of wisdom appears a simplistic abstraction.[30] To understand wisdom in its mediation in history, and to assimilate knowledge or rationality to the positive content of wisdom or its agency, therefore, demands a *hermeneutic* of wisdom.

There is another dynamic present in the Old Testament than the historical one, though the one is not readily extricated from the other. This is the dynamic of praise, whose elements are readily discernible, particularly in the psalms. There is reference to an addressee, the Lord, whose identity and position are established, not only by who he is but by what he has done and will do. Those who address themselves to the addressee are identified, self-involvingly and imperatively; and when and where the address of praise is and should be offered (that is now and always, here and everywhere) are established. And the movements and modes of activity by which praise is offered are designated; economic activity (offerings), political and social activity, personal activity and symbolic means of praise are the most usual.[31] Hence praise is seen as a comprehensive activity representing all that humanity is and does, always and everywhere; nothing stands outside of it, "framing" it as it were. And, even more important, it is drawn out of humankind by the positive content of God (his position and his activity, for example), and it is directed to "raising" God through celebrating his presence throughout the world—or, alternatively, mourning his "absence" from where he "is".[32]

This movement of praise is significant for knowledge and rationality. It establishes the relation between the positive content of wisdom (or its agency) and knowledge (or the knower) or the mediums of wisdom (materiality and history) differently, thereby avoiding the supposition that wisdom is fixed and substance-like or that there is—or should be—a fixed correspondence between them. Instead, wisdom (or its agency) and knowledge (or the knower) and the mediums of wisdom are drawn to their proper excellence in God and his truth. Hence in praise—openness to that excellence—the very notion of God and what is truth are opened through a simple yet dense affirmation. Simultaneously, the direction and mode of assimilation to that truth are expanded according to the truth of what is attended to. Still again, the movements and modes of human activity are reproportioned through their assimilation to this truth. The effect of this is to avoid hypostatizations or "substance-like" thinking at every point. Truth, wisdom, rationality, cognition, practice, economics, politics, society, persons and symbols are all "desubstantialized" in this movement of praise. Only insofar as they are "raised" by their assimilation to God do they become what they are.[33] This has important implications for the expansion of wisdom, knowledge and history, as we shall see later.

The movement which is to be seen in praise significantly affects knowledge and rationality in another way. It is a noticeable feature of Greek understanding that it prescinds from the particular, moving immediately beyond this to the universal; every particular is seen as an instance of its universal form or of universal categories—the universal imposed on the particular, one is tempted to say. And the consequences of this are found eventually in Descartes and Kant, for example, who develop theories of universal rationality through which particulars are to be seen if they are to be known (or acted upon) rationally. Hebrew understanding, by contrast, always finds the universal in the particular. To be more accurate, it begins from the particular in its spatiotemporal location, those factors which "place" it and manifest its particularity, preeminently its economy or selfness in its history, and—where human beings are concerned—society, polity, persons and communication. And this "location" or particularity is then expanded in praise to be "everywhere", without displacing other particularities. The universal is therefore a world of particulars, each contingent upon its place yet joined by an expanding truth found in the praise of God.[34] The consequences of this way of thinking are found much later in medieval nominalism, the Reformers, the inductive thinking of Francis Bacon and modern observational science.

With these considerations in mind, we can also see that the Western notion of progress is attributed to the Jewish understanding of history only by a considerable oversimplification. It is true that, for the Hebrews, history is important as the medium of wisdom in the world, but "progress" is an example of a "substance-like notion" which is a simplistic abstraction of wisdom as present in world history. Whatever is the presence of wisdom in world history, it does not permit the "Every day in every way I grow better and better" philosophy of progress. There is, therefore, no clear line or "key" to the development of knowledge or rationality, of the kinds suggested by Descartes or Locke or Kant. It is unlikely that there is even a dialectical line of development of the sort found by Hegel; even the line of abstraction, concreteness and self-possession appears too simple and "substance-like" a notion of the presence of wisdom in the mediation of history. The course of history itself needs to be "raised" to become a fit vehicle of the positive content of wisdom.

VI. ASSIMILATION TO WISDOM IN JESUS CHRIST

It is precisely this set of emphases which are taken up and given a fresh concentration in Christian understanding; and it is through the recognition of these emphases that the arrival of Christianity is to be seen—they form the preunderstanding with which one must approach the task of understanding Christianity. Thereafter, through the centuries of the Christian era in the West, it is primarily through the fresh concentration of these emphases in Christian understanding that the influence of these factors upon subsequent views of knowledge and rationality is exercised.

It is in no small part due to a preparedness for the particular that one man, Jesus Christ, could be seen as the concentration of wisdom in its presence in the world. This man, furthermore, is seen as imparting, not a theory of wisdom which has a general form, but the presence of wisdom in the practice of life for those who are assimilated to it in practice.[35] The imparting is seen, furthermore, to carry the "maximal information" in which the simplicity of wisdom or God consists, while also being so mysteriously deep as to require extensive elucidation:

There were many other things that Jesus did; if all were written down, the world itself, I suppose, would not hold all the books that would have to be written. (John 21:25, Jerusalem Bible)

Such assertions recognize the intrinsic similarity of Jesus to the wisdom which he presents.

The same characteristically Jewish willingness to speak of the agency of wisdom—as the positive content of responsible action—is also found in relation to Jesus. It is seen in Jesus' preparedness to accept his position as one who by his agency imparts wisdom, which is recognized by those who hear him doing so: "He taught them as one who had authority" (Matt. 7:29). There are two things noticeable in this. On the one hand, the activity of Jesus in knowing seems to be assimilated to the agency of wisdom (God), though in a fashion appropriate to his humanity: he constitutes goodness himself but also retorts, "Why do you ask me about what is good? One there is who is good" (Matt. 19:17). On the other hand, there is—in Jesus' agency or activity in knowing—the mysterious simplicity and depth associated with the agency of wisdom in God. In both respects, we find within his imparting of wisdom an active agency which appears to be the imparting of the agency of God in the imparting of wisdom. Hence, there is in Jesus a, if not the, concentration of the agency of wisdom, of rationality.

It is obviously expected by Jesus that those who respond to his agency will be assimilated to his (and hence God's) agency of wisdom—having in them "the mind of Christ" (1 Cor. 2:16)—as they deal with the world around them. In other words, they are to perpetuate his agency in wisdom, though obviously within their limitations. It is for that reason that the attempts of Jesus' followers to grasp the truth of him, his life and death and his teachings, are not, so long as responsibly done, at odds with his own agency, even if the forms in which they do so—typically interpretations and teachings—are not the same as that of his life and teachings. Interpretation is exactly what Jesus' followers should do, and rational interpretation, in the form of statements of teaching and practice, is a perpetuation of the agency of Jesus in the impartation of wisdom. These are not, therefore, to be dismissed as the result of the interference of human beings or of a "rationalizing" of his life and teachings.[36]

This issue appears again in later, particularly postmedieval, Christian theology, where the issue of consciousness looms large. In late medieval nominalism, as well as in John Calvin and in Francis Bacon, human awareness assumes a pivotal position. In such discussions, the issue is how human awareness makes a freely rational response to the pattern of God's agency in wisdom as found (in concentrated form) in the "book of nature" and the "book of God's Word", according to the pattern of God's agency as found in Jesus Christ. But, helped by the didacticism left from certain kinds of medieval and Ramist scholasticism, this was met by various kinds of attempts to confine the agency of human consciousness in predesignated patterns. At that point, the right attempt to assimilate the agency of rational consciousness to

Christ's agency of (the agency of God's) wisdom was deflected into an abstractive view of logic which was quite at odds with it, evidently drawn from an abstractive view of the Logos as found in Greek philosophy. As a result, the freely rational response to the pattern of God's agency in wisdom was overwhelmed by rationalism. That was a radical distortion, a caricature, but it was readily enough mistaken for Christianity. And subsequent attempts to provide for free scientific inquiry were set up in conscious opposition to this caricature of Christianity.

But the story of the concentration of wisdom in Jesus Christ is not fully told by considering his agency of wisdom. There is also the question of materiality to be faced. We recall the Jewish preparedness to find materiality as the mediation of wisdom. This was not some abstract "quiddity" with which they were concerned, but the materiality of being bodily, living and dying in a place with others, related to them through the mediums of exchange (economics), social organization (polity), interpersonal relationships and communication. And so it is necessary also to see the wisdom presented in Jesus Christ in these terms, not as preeminently a person independent of these factors and occasionally addressing them, but as one whose being and behavior is the presence of wisdom in those mediums. Nor is his reality to be seen "shining through" these mediums, epiphany-like. He is to be seen as the coincidence of wisdom with them, and not accidentally so.

Separate though they are often made to seem in modern discussions, such dimensions (even the word makes them seem separate!) as bodiliness and life, community, exchange, social organization, interpersonal relationships and communication always meet in the reality of life in the world. While the Jews fully realized their practical importance, and the importance of wisdom for them, what we find in Jesus was one in whom wisdom reconstituted such dimensions of materiality. To consider how he did so would require a wide-ranging discussion of his reconstitution of the ways in which things and people in the world are "placed" in space and time (through their being, life and death), their sociality, economy, polity, interpersonhood and communication—far more than can be attempted here. But throughout, we find him changing them from *within what they are* and thus assimilating them to wisdom. For him, like the Jews, what they are is highly particularized as *this* place, sociality, economy, and so forth. But within these, he manifests freedom from the close restrictions of the particularities to which the Jews had tended to confine them, and correspondingly a finding of wisdom in and for other particularities, a fact that can readily be seen in his comings and goings between Jerusalem and alien territories like Galilee or in his freedom from accepted practices of sociality, economy, and so forth.

There is good evidence that Jesus' representation of wisdom in these factors of materiality was passed to those who responded to them—insofar as they were assimilated to the wisdom manifest in him in their materiality. This can be seen in Paul's freedom to find (and also enhance) the reconstitutive presence of Jesus everywhere. Paul is free to travel and to be with others in compassion, as in the case of those with whom one was not normally free to relate, the aliens and outcasts, the Gentiles. Places remain important, but the astonishing missionary journeys of Paul seem to be motivated, not simply by a personal call, or sustained by the companionship of Christ. They had more to do with his discovery of the presence of Christ, and hence the transformative wisdom of God, in the materiality of the world itself. He found that the world itself was not empty but filled with the presence of Christ, and in him the wisdom of God. The materiality of the world was Christlike, and in that was present the wisdom of God, so much so that traveling the world was for him a constant finding of Christ and the purposes of God. With that came a transformation of the "ordinary" materiality of the world, its societies, its economics, and so forth. For example, he found that the peoples of the world were—at least partly—the bearers of Christ's presence; speaking to them was a constant rediscovering of Christ. If wisdom was found in the particularities of places, societies, economics, and so on, for Paul the determining element of particularities was found to be Christ: they were Christomorphic. This is the basis for Paul's conviction that Christ is the head of all creation and salvation, without confinement to place.

But how was the materiality of the world filled with the transformative wisdom of God in Christ? To put it briefly, it was reproportioned in accordance with the wisdom of God as present in Christ. And this reproportioning called forth an acknowledgment of praise in which materiality recognized its own positive content as arising from the action of God. The reconstitution of materiality by Jesus, as well as the sharing of others in that reconstitution, was therefore intimately linked to the return of materiality to its source in the wisdom of God.

As we saw earlier, the dynamic of praise in the Old Testament consists in the direction to God of movements and modes of activity (bodily, living, economic, social, political, etc.) which are themselves based in the factors of materiality which we have since discussed. But with the presence of the wisdom of God in materiality in and through Jesus, these movements and modes of activity in materiality are reproportioned. In order for this reproportioning to have its full effect, however, it must be acknowledged—the appropriate form for which is praise. When they acknowledge this reproportioning, they acknowledge the one through whom they are reproportioned.

It was evident to the early Christians that there is a richness in the movement by which the wisdom of God was present in Jesus and that this richness reconstituted things. This was in striking contrast to other wisdom:

> Where is the wise man? Where is the scholar? Where is the philosopher of this age? Has not God made foolish the wisdom of the world? For since in the wisdom of God the world through its wisdom did not know him, God was pleased through the foolishness of what was preached to save those who believe. (1 Cor. 1:20–21, New International Version)

In effect, God in Christ reconstituted not simply wisdom but the material factors in which wisdom was present, and this was known insofar as those material factors acknowledged it. Participating in this dynamic is what is important. It cannot be "possessed" by worldly wisdom, only received and returned in praise. So those who do not "take possession" of wisdom may be drawn in praise to the excellence of God's wisdom through its presence in Christ, if they allow the mode by which they apprehend to be expanded or developed in accordance with that to which they attend.

This has vast implications for the activity and results of knowledge. The actual source of wisdom—the wisdom of God—cannot be hypostatized by human beings as "their" wisdom. Instead, the excellence of it draws human wisdom beyond itself, expanding and developing it according to the wisdom of God insofar as it will allow its mode of apprehension to be expanded in such a way as to be suitable to the excellence of the wisdom of God. But this wisdom of God is also present in materiality, in Jesus and those who are formed by the presence of Jesus. As such, it reproportions all materiality, to such a degree that nothing can be hypostatized or substantialized; all the factors of materiality are reproportioned to the excellence of the wisdom of God which through Christ is present in them. So there is no longer the constancy of order—everything in its place, knowing its place—which was the case with the older views of wisdom, whether Jewish or Greek, but order itself is reproportioned by this "new" wisdom of God in the material world through Christ. Praise is the human being's participation in this reproportioning.

But it must also be seen that this reconstitution is not complete. It might be more accurate to say that it is varyingly completed, in some ways more so than in others, and for some not so at all. To put it somewhat differently, there is an "unhealed wound" in praise, which is healed in varying degrees, both in the human participation in movement toward the wisdom and in the reproportioning of all things in their relations.

Most basically, there is the partly unhealed wound of life itself. For life itself, which is the basis for praise, is lived only by healing over the threat of death. "I will sing to the Lord as long as I live; I will sing praise to my God while I have being" (Ps. 104:33). This is the wound which is again and again opened by the threat of death, whether for nations (as for the Jews in the Holocaust) or for individuals, and which appears to end the possibility of praise (Ps. 119:19). Apart from that, there are situations in which all relationships, including that with God, whether for societies or individuals, are blocked, as a result partly of damage inflicted and partly of the integrity with which those thus damaged maintain themselves; and self-defensiveness (to preserve the self) is often combined with self-negation (self-destruction). More frequently, capacity for relationships of all kinds oscillates. And beyond the question of capacity for relationships, there is the still more difficult issue of the proportioning of relationships in a manner suitable to the partners. "Pay all of them their dues. . . . Owe no one anything, except to love one another" (Rom. 13:7–8).

The problem is whether such wounds can be healed, and if so how. Is praise possible any longer, or is it only singing on the tomb of God? Is even lamentation, praise in the darkness, possible? "What does your greatness mean, Lord of the universe, in the face of this weakness, this decomposition, and this decay?"[37] What does praise mean in such a threat to the life of a whole people, in which all proportionalities are lost, or indeed for any person for whom relationships and proportions are lost? It may appear simply a goad: "Why do You still trouble their sick minds, their crippled bodies?"[38]

The intractably strange answer given by Christianity is that the wisdom of God which is present in Christ and which—through our praise—reproportions all things is in those alienations of life and its material circumstances which Christ suffered, and there begins its reconstitutive work—only to be continued by those who share in this alienation and find the proportions of new life in praise.[39] Only in such a fashion does participation in the wisdom of God through Jesus Christ heal, restore and reproportion.

To what view of history does this lead? It was clear enough that the Jewish understanding of history was based on no supposition of a "common thing" with a singular positive content which is the point of reference for all understanding in and of history, and that what was necessary is a thoroughly historical interpretation of the appearance of wisdom in history, a hermeneutic of wisdom. That view remains in Christianity, but it is allied with a new positive content. Wisdom is now found in materiality and history through the presence of Jesus as the concentration of wisdom. And this concentration of wisdom is present in the extreme alienations of life and its material circumstances, there to reconstitute and reproportion them. Wisdom in history is therefore known as alienation and reconstitution, and by those who share the life of the one in whom it is alienated and reconstituted.

History itself is also seen as wounded and reconstituted. There is no constant presence of a triumphant wisdom of history, nor is there the possibility of possessing the healing power of wisdom, its source or its effects. Instead, God's own excellence appears through the rediscovery, not only of the meaning of history but of its manifestation in materiality, in what is called the kingdom of God. Therein is the reproportioning of humankind and the world.

All this is the positive content of wisdom so far as Christianity is concerned. And it is assimilation to this positive content—in praise particularly—which for Christian faith constitutes (and heals) knowledge and rationality. It is, of course, possible to summarize the content in either of two forms, as knowledge or as the direction of rationality. But for either, it can be said that the positive content is only knowable (or rational) through assimilation to it in the factors of materiality and history; and this requires assimilation from the position of one estranged from it.[40] As knowledge, the content can be summarized in the doctrine of the Trinity; as the direction of rationality, the content can be summarized as personal faith seen as an active and involved knowing achieved through what is sometimes called "in-dwelling" which is at the same time "outer-directed" to the agency of wisdom in God.[41] While neither ontology nor revelation is irrelevant to these summaries, the positive content to which knowledge and rationality are to be assimilated calls into question the use of traditional notions of ontology and revelation.

VII. THE RATIONALIZATION OF CHRISTIAN TRADITION

In various ways, the wisdom of God thus represented by and through Jesus in the factors of materiality was reinterpreted by means of philosophical ontology, just as the representation of the agency of wisdom was reinterpreted in terms of philosophical epistemology. So, likewise, the dynamic of praise, in which things reproportioned acknowledge the source of their reproportioning, was reinterpreted by such philosophical hierarchies as "the great chain of being".

It began very early. Sometimes, as in the Book of Revelation or in Augustine's *City of God,* concern for the purity of wisdom itself led to the kind of dualistic view in which the purest form of this materiality was to be found in an otherworldly place supervening upon this world, but more often the concern for this wisdom in material existence took its shape more from Greek sources. And this translated the concern for wisdom present in the factors of materiality into quite a different form, in which they were largely divorced from materiality itself in a search for supramaterial "quiddities" like "substantiality" (instead of spatio-temporal and historical place), "metaphysical personal essences" (instead of living beings), and so on. And the ubiquitous transformative presence of Christlike wisdom in materiality was restated in such abstract notions, through the use of which it was actually detached from the very materiality in which it had been present.

The same retranslation appeared much later in a different way. Concern for the same factors of materiality is found in the division of the sciences found in Bacon's *Advancement of Learning;* there it was placed in the dynamics of history and mediated in the dynamics of consciousness, in which was to be traced the activity of wisdom imparted by God. After Bacon, however, the freedom of consciousness to discover wisdom from God in the book of nature and the book of God's word was swallowed up in the disciplines and conclusions of the separate sciences. As each of the sciences developed, the freedom of consciousness was confined by the norms of the separate sciences. These separate sciences were themselves rationalized forms of the ancient Christian concern with the factors of materiality. (The ancient concern with place became the sphere of physics, with animate beings that of biology, all the while searching for the "economy" or "politics" of nature in natural law. The ancient concern for societies became the sphere of sociology, for economy that of economics, for social organization that of politics, with the media of human contact that of semiotics.) In effect, consciousness and the world which it studied lost contact with the presence of wisdom in consciousness and materiality. Reference to the wisdom of God present in materiality was forgotten. It was replaced by reference to the human being's own consciousness of the world, rationalized either through particular pursuits (in the separate sciences) or by a general theory of rational consciousness (as in Descartes, Locke, Kant and Hegel).

Why did the sciences turn in this direction? One possible explanation is a fundamental error about the "positive content" of knowledge and rationality, which led to a certain kind of search for simplicity and depth within knowledge of the world (particularly within each of the factors of materiality) or within the rationality of the knower, with the result that this positive content was itself emasculated.

The search for knowledge of the world was developed through the separation of the sciences, there being a science for each one of the factors of materiality. Indeed, there was an analytical severance of their connections with each other, in effect relocating the positive content of knowledge within each one—a fact which explains the monopolistic tendencies discernible in the sciences. Furthermore, the preferred method within each field was to proceed to this positive content in its simplicity through the use of an analytic method reaching level by level back to what was the heretofore hidden inner "reality". If in physics, for example, the deepest "substantiality" of things or laws of nature was sought, the search proceeded by the discernment—usually through measurement—of more and more exact quantities and regularities. As thus used, the analytic method itself was a particular avenue to simplicity, to that which was deemed to be the maximally informative—regarding matter and motion in these cases—in the mysteriously complex depths of a particular factor of materiality.

And, having begun within a separate "science", the search for this maximally informative content went on, attracted by a kind of absolute positive content. Yet such a narrowly conceived positive content proved shadowlike and vacuous. In other words, an abstractive method produced an abstractive result. That which was found to be maximally informative was also abstract from normal material existence and from the source from which material existence derived. As we found to be the case in Greek philosophy, there was a loss "at both ends"—in the richness of materiality and in the richness of wisdom. Thereafter, one could reconstruct the relations of such abstractions only by means of artificial connections.[42] Though neither the development of the separate sciences nor the search for maximal informative content was in itself problematic, they became so when they were used to produce an abstraction from materiality in place of the simple materiality which they sought, and when they lost the richness of the positive content of wisdom.

Much the same happens where there is a search for simplicity and depth within the knower. If an ideal of pure rationality is set up, in effect this establishes a pure positive content to which the practices of rational thought are to be conformed. The way by which thought can be assimilated to this pure positive content is to search for the simplicity of rationality (pure reason in its use) amid its complexity (forms and categories), and then to employ these in thought. But this actually divorces thought from the richness of that which is thought (the "world" in Kant's terminology), from the richness of the thinker (the "soul"), and from the richness of the wisdom of God present in and for both. Again, there is a loss "at the ends" which is only matched by a loss in the dynamics of knowledge.

It is worth adding at this point that the subject matter of Christian faith itself may suffer the same loss if, like a science or a notion of pure rationality, it wrongly conceives its positive content and searches for "pure faith". This is avoided only when there is a full reproportioning of faith to the wisdom of God in Christ.

VIII. ARE KNOWLEDGE AND RATIONALITY NOW TO DISAPPEAR?

Perhaps it can now be seen that notions of knowledge and rationality as they operate in the sciences and in Christian faith are related at important points. Both operate with a common pattern, concerning themselves with the assimilation of knowledge to its positive content. But their use of the pattern is so different that they are frequently at cross purposes in the area with which we are primarily concerned, that is the possibility of knowledge and rationality.

There are many ways in which they draw deeply on each other, their differences notwithstanding. From Christian tradition comes the emphasis of wisdom (or agency of wisdom) present in knowledge (or its agency), a wisdom that is rich and nonabstract, simple and deep, where for the sciences the emphasis is on abstractive positive content (whether in knowledge or rationality). From Christian tradition comes the emphasis of wisdom present in particularities (or the particularity of awareness) for those fully assimilated to its effect on particularities, while from the sciences come emphases on generality. From Christian tradition comes the emphasis of wisdom (or its agency) present in materiality and its factors, proportioning and reproportioning them, known through being proportioned or reproportioned by it, while from the sciences come emphases of substantiality and regularity ascertainable through a detached knowledge. From Christian tradition comes the emphasis on the rich dynamism by which wisdom is present for humankind in the world, a dynamic in which humankind may participate through praise; and from this rich dynamism comes the "attractive" character of wisdom for the Christian, where for the sciences the tendency is to hypostatize the object sought for, and the means of seeking for it. For Christian tradition, too, history is a time of incompletion and contingency in which wisdom is present in the dark places as well as the light, where for the sciences, history is a regularity and in that sense fixed in its meaning. Each, as we have said, draws on the other.

As we said much earlier, however, both are now being judged for their adequacy by reference to a new situation. While presented as in many respects utterly new, the new situation combines many of the features of the scene which has been emerging for the past two hundred years. What is this new "postmodern" situation? It defies generalization, and in actuality resists any synthetic picture. But even at the risk of generalizing, it is above all a picture of plenitude, consisting of an endless complexity and dynamism of meaning at every level. Imagine any connection that appears in the history of knowledge, and then imagine that connection being seen as a complexity of interrelations; the picture thus obtained would not be inappropriate. Hence, so-called "correspondence" notions of knowledge and rational agency, in which a simple one-to-one relation is drawn between words or concepts and realities, are vastly oversimple; all such relations are multiple and complex. The same argument affects all supposed affinities, emphasizing their "difference", "deconstructing" the simplicities on which they are founded. The consequence is that all that gives a solid foundation for knowledge and rationality, particularly the "onto-theology" of the Western tradition, and its "logocentrism", are dissolved. And with them go conventional notions of knowledge and rationality.[43]

A further indication of the immensity of the changes implicit in these suggestions can be given by referring to a problem in topology. If one cuts a hole in the inner tube of a bicycle tire where the valve is and begins to pull the rest of the tube through the hole, what happens? The issue with modern understanding—though hardly fully appreciated yet—is that one can repeat the exercise at an infinite number of points on the tube, drawing the tube through *after* it has been drawn through at an infinite number of other points. That is a fascinating prospect, not only a testimony to the amazing creativity of human understanding but an indication of the possibility of an endlessly multiplying complexity in knowledge. If such major endeavors as those which have to do with the factors of materiality we discussed earlier provide more and more holes through which other endeavours—and even their own—can be drawn, then knowledge becomes fuller and fuller, with no limit in sight. It is, as we said, an indefinite plenitude.

Perhaps it is because Nietzsche is so influential in it that this postmodernism has been taken both as a "reduction of meaning to mere nothingness" and as antichristian, suggesting that all Christianity is a sacrifice of the intellect to maintain a "theological construct" called the Word of God. But what should be clear by now is that those characteristics of "Christian tradition" which are thus accused are in fact not Christian tradition at all but the product of various kinds of rationalism imposed on Christian faith.

It would be far too much to claim that Christian faith has refounded the possibility of knowledge and rationality in this new situation. But precisely because by its faith in Jesus Christ it is prepared for the presence of the Wisdom of God in particularity, in the factors of materiality and in the reproportioning of all "things" and relations as their maker and redeemer is praised in them, Christian faith at least has the means by which to rediscover the possibility of knowledge and rationality in the new situation.

NOTES

1. The most obvious example is the opposition offered by Christians to the teaching of evolution in schools in the United States, accompanied by a claim for equal time for the teaching of creation science. See Michael Ruse, *Darwinism Defended* (Reading, Mass.: Addison-Wesley, 1982).

2. The legitimacy of the notion of secularization, as employed for example by Karl Löwith (*From Hegel to Nietzsche: The Revolution in Nineteenth Century Thought* [London: Constable & Co., 1964]), is persuasively contradicted by Hans Blumenberg (*The Legitimacy of the Modern Age* [Cambridge: MIT Press, 1985]).

3. T. F. Torrance, *Divine and Contingent Order* (Oxford: Oxford University Press, 1981), 1.

4. From two different directions, historical and epistemological, the work of Wolfhart Pannenberg in *Theology and the Philosophy of Science* (London: Darton, Longman & Todd, 1976) and T. F. Torrance in *Theological Science* (Oxford: Oxford University Press, 1969) has been of considerable importance in this respect.

5. Cf. Basil Mitchell, *The Justification of Religious Belief* (London: Macmillan & Co., 1973).

6. Arthur R. Peacocke, *Creation and the World of Science* (Oxford: Oxford University Press, 1979), 47.

7. John Hick, *God and the Universe of Faiths: Essays in the Philosophy of Religion* (London: Macmillan & Co., 1973), chap. 3; cf. Ian Barbour, *Myths, Models and Paradigms: A Comparative Study in Science and Religion* (London: SCM Press, 1973).

8. Cf. Nicholas Rescher, *Scientific Progress* (Oxford: Basil Blackwell, 1978), 194ff.

9. As quoted in John Watkins, *Science and Scepticism* (London: Hutchinson & Co., 1984), 137.

10. See Ronald F. Thiemann, *Revelation and Theology: The Gospel as Narrated Promise* (London: University of Notre Dame Press, 1985); and George Lindbeck, *The Nature of Doctrine* (Philadelphia: Fortress Press, 1984), respectively.

11. See Nicholas Rescher, *Cognitive Systematization* (Oxford: Basil Blackwell, 1979); and Thiemann, *Revelation and Theology.*

12. Cf. Paul Feyerabend, *Beyond Method: Outline of an Anarchistic Theory of Knowledge* (London: New Left Books, 1975).

13. See Ilya Prigogine, *From Being to Becoming: Time and Complexity in the Physical Sciences* (San Francisco: W. H. Freeman & Co., 1980); and Daniel W. Hardy and David F. Ford, *Jubilate: Theology in Praise* (London: Darton, Longman & Todd, 1984); in the U.S.A., *Praising and Knowing God* (Philadelphia: Westminster Press, 1985), 96–99.

14. Thomas F. Torrance, *Reality and Scientific Theology* (Edinburgh: Scottish Academic Press, 1985), xi.

15. See Elliott Sober, *Simplicity* (Oxford: Clarendon Press, 1975).

16. Interesting examples of this "inner proportioning" are found in Augustine, Calvin and Schleiermacher, for all of whom the agency of knowing is to be proportioned to that which is known, while the notion of a simple correspondence is to be found, e.g., in Descartes and Kant.

17. Cf. Augustine, *Confessions* 1.7: "For if he is happy, as indeed he is, who lives in accordance with that part of the soul which appropriately governs the rest, and this part is called reason, does he not, I ask, live in accordance with reason who seeks after truth in an exemplary way?" (G. O'Daly, *Augustine's Philosophy of Mind* [London: Gerald Duckworth & Co., 1987], chap. 7).

18. Wolfhart Pannenberg suggests that "modern philosophy is totally dominated by the Augustinian idea that man cannot understand himself in his relation to the world without presupposing God as both his own origin and the origin of his world. . . . The starting-point is Augustine's idea of *veritas* as presupposed in all human consciousness" (Pannenberg, *Theology and the Philosophy of Science,* 306). It is, however, the reference of knowledge to what is supposed as its own positive content that is central to the history of philosophy, not the presupposition of God; referring it to the supposition of God would mistake the history of philosophy's ultimate reference for the history of religion.

19. Harold Bloom, *Agon: Towards a Theory of Revisionism* (New York: Oxford University Press, 1982), 5.

20. See O'Daly, *Augustine's Philosophy of Mind,* 92.

21. Modern examples of such a thing occur in the writings of D. H. Lawrence, who finds a false dichotomy in the sexual act, where the bodily act of intercourse is not itself pure love when the mind "observes from above".

22. Augustine, *De diversis quaestionibus octoginta tribus* 9, quoted in O'Daly, *Augustine's Philosophy of Mind,* 92.

23. On this view of history and the importance of context, see Amos Funkenstein, *Theology and the Scientific Imagination from the Middle Ages to the Seventeenth Century* (Princeton: Princeton University Press, 1986), chap. 4.

24. It is noticeable that the notion of "paradigm-shifts", as seen in the writings of Thomas Kuhn for example, is constructed on the supposition that all knowledge in a given time is formed through the assimilation of theory and practice to a particular "positive content", which may collapse when new theory and practice can no longer be assimilated to it. In our terms, it collapses when it is overcome by the contaminants it would formerly have been able to exclude. See Thomas S. Kuhn, *The Structure of Scientific Revolutions,* 2d ed. (Chicago: University of Chicago Press, 1970).

25. Stanley L. Jaki, *Science and Creation* (Edinburgh: Scottish Academic Press, 1974), viii. See also idem, *The Road of Science and the Ways to God* (Edinburgh: Scottish Academic Press, 1978).

26. Cf. Harold Nebelsick, *Circles of God: Theology and Science from the Greeks to Copernicus* (Edinburgh: Scottish Academic Press, 1985), xiii.

27. Ex. 3:14–15, translation by Martin Buber and Franz Rosenzweig, quoted in Pamela Vermes, *Buber on God and the Perfect Man* (Chico, Calif.: Scholars Press, 1980), 85–86.

28. See Richard Sorabji, *Time, Creation and the Continuum* (London: Gerald Duckworth & Co., 1983), 230–31, who claims that the same is true of Thomas Aquinas.

29. See Jürgen Moltmann, *Theology of Hope* (London: SCM Press, 1967), 254–55.

30. "And in nothing is Scriptural history more strongly contrasted with the histories of note in the present age than in its freedom from the hollowness of abstractions. . . . The histories and political economy of the present and preceding century partake in the general contagion of its mechanic philosophy, and are the *product* of an unenlivened generalizing Understanding. In the Scriptures they are the living *educts* of the Imagination. . . . These are the Wheels which Ezekiel beheld, when the hand of the Lord was upon him, and he saw visions as he sat among the captives by the river of Chebar. *Whithersoever the Spirit was to go, the wheels went, and thither was their spirit to go: for the spirit of the living creature was in the wheels also*" (Samuel Taylor Coleridge, *The Statesman's Manual,* in *Lay Sermons,* ed. R. J. White [London: Routledge & Kegan Paul, 1972], 28–29).

31. Hardy and Ford, *Jubilate,* 173–75.

32. See Kornelis H. Miskotte, *When the Gods Are Silent* (London: William Collins Sons, 1967), 141.

33. See George Herbert's hymn:

> Seven whole days, not one in seven, I will praise thee;
> In my heart, though not in heaven, I can raise thee.
> Small it is, in this poor sort to enrol thee:
> E'en eternity's too short to extol thee.

But Herbert's piety has caused him to interiorize the raising ("In my heart, though not in heaven . . .") rather than to treat it as a matter of raising wisdom through knowledge of the world.

34. This accounts for the striking concern for particular places and histories which one finds in the Old Testament, which are interwoven in a master narrative of the history of the Jewish people.

35. Despite some limitations, Dietrich Bonhoeffer's *Cost of Discipleship* (London: SCM Press, 1948) and *Ethics* (London: SCM Press, 1955) are valuable expositions of the person and work of Christ as the presence of God for those who respond to the call of Christ which constitutes their relation to their neighbour. The limitations arise from the dualisms implicit in the exposition, with individuals set apart and related only through response to being called, and the church called out of the world to respond to the world.

36. These have become common accusations. See Maurice Wiles, *The Making of Christian Doctrine* (Cambridge: Cambridge University Press, 1967), 157–

58, who sees early doctrine as the imposition of interpretations, particularly of a Platonic kind, on the figure of Jesus. In different vein, Bernard Lonergan, in *The Way to Nicea* (London: Darton, Longman & Todd, 1976), sees doctrine as the product of "differentiated consciousness", as distinct from the "undifferentiated consciousness" which prevails in the New Testament. He does not suppose that it is an alien intrusion, but the result of the characteristically human tendency to reflect rationally. He fails to recognize that it is required by response to Jesus as agent of wisdom.

37. Elie Wiesel, *Night* (New York: Bantam Books, 1982), 63–65.

38. Ibid.

39. See Rowan Williams, *The Wound of Knowledge* (London: Darton, Longman & Todd, 1979); in the U.S.A., *Christian Spirituality: A Theological History from the New Testament to Luther and St. John of the Cross* (Atlanta: John Knox Press, 1980).

40. Compare the more limited statement, largely based on a communicational view of the relationship of God and humankind: "The Trinity of the economy of salvation is the immanent Trinity" (Karl Rahner, *Theological Investigations* [London: Darton, Longman & Todd, 1966], 4:87).

41. See Daniel W. Hardy, "Christian Affirmation and the Structure of Personal Life", in *Belief in Science and in Christian Life: The Relevance of Michael Polanyi's Thought for Christian Faith and Life,* ed. T. F. Torrance (Edinburgh: Handsel Press, 1980), chap. 4.

42. A particularly interesting example of such a reconstruction is to be found in P. W. Atkins, *The Creation* (London: W. H. Freeman & Co., 1981), in which the first stages of spatiotemporal existence are explained through a series of abstractions artificially connected. But scientific literature abounds with examples; the search for ways to "unify" science provides many examples.

43. See Joseph O'Leary, *Questioning Back: The Overcoming of Metaphysics in Christian Tradition* (Minneapolis: Winston Press, 1985).

13

THE CHRISTIAN FAITH
AND THE WORLD
RELIGIONS

LESSLIE NEWBIGIN

I. THE CHANGED SITUATION

Charles Gore and his colleagues were concerned "to put the Catholic faith into its right relation to modern intellectual and moral problems". They were concerned to vindicate a genuine "development" of Christian theology that would neither lose its firm moorings in the age-long creed of the church nor retreat into a narrower and harder dogmatism, but rather "enter into the apprehension of the new intellectual and social movements of each age" and so enable the church to "throw herself into the sanctification of each new social order" and to show "under changed conditions the catholic capacity of her faith" (*Lux Mundi,* preface).

While the discussions that gave birth to *Lux Mundi* were going on in Oxford, things were happening elsewhere in which these dons were not involved. In what we now see as the greatest period of their activity, missionaries were busy in Asia, Africa and the Pacific, preaching, arguing, teaching and healing—laying the foundations for what would be hailed sixty years later, in William Temple's Canterbury enthronement sermon, as "the great new fact of our time", the presence of the church in every part of the world, a global society made up of peoples from many cultures and drawn from many religious traditions.

The meeting of the Western religious tradition with the great religions of the East was indeed already under way. Max Müller's publication of the fifty volumes of Sacred Books of the East had begun. The mutual interpenetration of Eastern and Western cultures and religions was beginning, but—for these Oxford scholars—it was not yet visible

310

as one of the major new realities with which Christianity would have to come to terms and which would test the meaning of its claim to catholicity. The other world religions presented no immediate challenge to English Christianity. Rather, the new challenges came from within the Western tradition.

The situation a hundred years later is very different. The explosive power of Western ideas, politics, commerce, technology and religion, penetrating into the ancient cultures of Asia, Africa and the Pacific, has not only set in motion revolutionary movements within those cultures. It has also triggered a corresponding movement in the opposite direction. Ideas and people can now move so quickly that the distances which for centuries separated the great cultures of humankind have almost been abolished. We are now acutely aware of living in a single global society. In the photographs beamed back to us from outer space we have seen what no previous generation could ever see—our planet as one fragile spacecraft, one vessel moving through the vast ocean of space, a vessel in which all who travel must learn to live together as one family if they are not to perish together in one catastrophe.

And those of us who inhabit that part of the planet which used to be called Christendom have to acknowledge our responsibility for these vast changes in the total human situation. We cannot step out of our place in history. Hendrick Kraemer's words, written thirty years ago, are still apt:

> This eastern invasion, which has been set in motion and will constantly increase in strength, is ultimately the West's own doing. The most significant point is that the West, by its contacts and by its efforts of understanding, has by its invasion of the East made the eastern cultures and religions an event of great purport in its own quest, and an important part of its own native crisis in religion and culture. So this involvement in the eastern cultural and religious values and achievements has provided the West with ample material for its own cultural and religious doubts and self-criticism. The least that can be said about it is that the inescapable fact of the plurality of cultures and religions has not only become a weighty practical and social problem, but in the spiritual realm of either creates a spirit of relativistic indifferentism, a leaning towards the plausibility of a synthetic common denominator as the evident solution, or a propensity towards regarding the Christian heritage as irrelevant. De Lubac's words: "Si l'Europe ne retrouve pas sa foi, alors elle est mûre pour une colonisation spirituelle", are not inappropriate.[1]

311

That "spiritual colonisation" is already a reality. I am not referring to the vigorous missionary outreach of Islam in Europe, financed by the oil-rich states of the Middle East, nor to the more modest enterprises of Hindus and Buddhists in winning European converts to their faiths. I am thinking rather of the way in which that attitude to religion which is characteristic of India has (with obvious modifications) become widespread among Western Christians. It is an attitude that no longer sees religion as providing the intellectual framework within which public life is understood, but rather sees "religions" as alternative paths to personal salvation, offering a range of options within which each person is free to choose and between which one does not argue about conflicting truth-claims.

For many centuries, and especially since the rise of Islam, the Christian West was isolated from the great religions of Asia. After that event, it was confronted by an aggressive power in which religious faith was fused with political and military organisation to create a mighty imperial power. Western Christendom and Islam faced each other as rival military powers, while Eastern Christendom, except in Russia, survived only as isolated enclaves within a much more powerful empire.

After Western Christendom broke up in the religious wars of the seventeenth century, the intellectual leadership of the European nations turned from the vision of a Christian society to a new vision of a society ordered by the principles of the Enlightenment. Religious belief became more and more a matter for personal choice rather than being the generally accepted way of understanding and ordering public life. It was no longer an intrinsic element in belonging to European society. At the same time, the opening up of communications with the rest of the world vastly extended the mental horizon of the European peoples, reinforcing the tendency to see Christian belief as only one among a wide variety of options. For the savants of the late eighteenth century, China exercised a special fascination as exemplifying a high culture which owed nothing to Christianity.

Until the end of the Second World War these ideas were probably those of a minority of intellectuals in most of the European nations. For most people, Christianity in one form or another was accepted as the religion to which one naturally adhered, even if the adherence was tenuous. It was normal to be baptised, married and buried with Christian rites. "Religious education" in the schools was based on the Bible. Since 1945 several factors have combined to change the situation: the end of the colonial empires, the migration of millions of people from the former colonies to the old metropolitan countries, the enormous increase in intercontinental air travel, and the development of radio and television networks reaching into every part of the globe. The result today is that, not for a few intellectuals but for the majority of ordinary people, Christianity is seen as only one among many religions, all worthy of respect. At the same time, the general acceptance of the idea of a secular society, of a secular style of public education, of a public life that is ordered without explicit reference to any religious beliefs, has—as its counterpart—the general relegation of religious belief to the area of private and personal choice, an area sharply distinguished from the public sphere. It is true that there are movements on what is called the "new religious right", principally but not exclusively in the United States, to make an identification of Christian belief with certain public policies. And it is also true that there are substantial vestiges of a tribalism which conflates religious belief with ethnic allegiance (for example, in Ulster). But these are exceptions to the general rule. For most people in contemporary Western society, it would be safe to say that the following assumptions are not usually called into question: *(a)* Christianity is one religion among the many world religions, all of which are to be treated with respect because they are concerned with God and with the immortal soul; *(b)* religious belief is a matter of personal choice and everyone is entitled to have "a faith of his or her own"; *(c)* the proper way in which religious people should behave towards one another is to be described in terms of coexistence, cooperation and dialogue, not in terms such as proselytism, evangelism, conversion or mission.

What, exactly, is new in this situation? It is not the fact that there is a plurality of religions in the world. That, apparently, has always been so. Nor is it an entirely new fact that Christians have become conscious of this plurality. From the churches of the early centuries living in the religiously plural world of the eastern Mediterranean, to the churches living and witnessing among the ancient religions of Asia today, there have always been Christians who were well aware of this plurality. What is new, at least for the churches of the old Christendom, is the widespread acceptance of religious pluralism as an ideology. Indians have traditionally seen the *dharma* as universal and eternal. Muslims have affirmed that the Qur'ān is God's final and decisive word to the whole of humankind. And Christians have affirmed that Jesus is Lord of all, the light of the whole world. Today such confidence is widely regarded among British and North American Christians as a mark of ignorance or naivety. Religious pluralism, the view that in principle and for always humankind will be religiously divided and that this is not to be deplored but to be welcomed, is something relatively new. At least the authors of *Lux Mundi* did not feel bound to consider it among the new things with which the Catholic faith must reckon. Today we can hardly avoid facing it.

II. THE CONTEMPORARY DEBATE

The contemporary debate about religious pluralism is vigorous and shows no sign of faltering. During the early part of the present century the debate was mainly among missionaries, for it was they who were in direct contact with people of other faiths. Indeed, it was largely (though by no means entirely) through the writings of missionaries that Christians in the West came to know something of Eastern religions. The Jesuits at the imperial court in China, Ziegenbalg and Plutschau in Tranquebar, and Carey in Bengal were among those who by their writings awakened European interest in Asian religions. The first two decades of the present century saw the publication of an immense amount of scholarly work, mostly written by missionaries, on the non-Christian religions. The world missionary conference at Edinburgh in 1910 gathered together and focussed much of this discussion, and its volume on "The Christian Message" gives evidence of its high quality. What triggered the most passionate debate was the publication in 1932 of the report of the Laymen's Foreign Missionary Enquiry entitled "Re-thinking Missions". This report, theologically directed by W. E. Hocking, looked towards the convergence of all the religions in a common way of life which could be described as the "kingdom of God" and which Christians found exemplified in Jesus Christ. The major response to this report came in the book of Hendrick Kraemer commissioned for the world missionary conference at Tambaram in 1938—"The Christian Message in a Non-Christian World". This book, published exactly half a century after *Lux Mundi,* provided the main focus of debate for the next twenty-five years, and it was still largely a debate among missionaries and leaders in the Indian churches.

With the merger of the International Missionary Council and the World Council of Churches in 1961, the debate moved naturally into the larger context of a council of churches. It was no longer a debate conducted in the context of explicit missionary activity; rather, it was a debate about the way in which different religious communities can live and work together in the interest of the human community as a whole. The churches in the newly emancipated nations were facing the colossal task of helping their peoples to achieve national unity across the lines dividing the different religious and tribal groups that had been held together by the colonial power but must now find a new basis for unity. The debate about the relation of Christianity to the other religions had to be carried on in the new context of an urgent search for human unity. The first occasion on which the issue of religious pluralism was given a full discussion in an assembly of the World Council of Churches was in 1975 at Nairobi. The document, prepared by the section on "Seeking Community: The Common Search of People of Various Faiths, Cultures and Ideologies",[2] was not accepted by the whole Assembly, and it was clear that there was no common mind among the churches. Subsequent years have seen, both in the World Council of Churches and in its member churches, a struggle to articulate the nature of the relation that ought to exist between Christians and people of other faiths and ideologies, the proper role of dialogue, and its relation to the dominical commission to "make disciples of all nations". The debate continues, and there is little sign of consensus. A brief survey of some of the positions taken will help to introduce the theme, even though it cannot do justice to the full variety of views expressed in the debate.

III. THE EXCLUSIVIST POSITION

There are those who affirm that faithfulness to the revelation in Christ as attested in Scripture requires us to believe that all those who have not made an explicit commitment of faith in Christ are eternally lost. It is indeed not difficult to point to biblical texts that support—or seem to support—this view. Plainly, if this is the real situation of those who are outside the Christian church, then the question of dialogue simply does not arise. If a house is on fire and there are people trapped inside, one does not propose a dialogue about the different experiences of those inside and those outside. The only proper response is to rush in and rescue the victims by any means possible. If all non-Christians are in fact destined for eternal fire, then any method, however violent, that has the possibility of converting them is not only permitted but required.

315

The difficulties in this view are obvious. The question whether this is in fact the view that Scripture requires us to take will be considered later. The view under discussion is sometimes condemned on the ground that it would be unjust on the part of God thus to condemn those millions who, through no fault of their own, have never heard the gospel. But the argument from justice cannot stand. If it is the case (as it is) that all human beings have sinned and do sin grievously against the love of God, then punishment is not unjust. Nevertheless, if God's response to human sin is that which was revealed and effected in the ministry, death and resurrection of Jesus, it is difficult to accept this scenario. And if it is true that the faith which sets a person right with God is ultimately a matter of the heart and conscience (however necessary it may also be that the faith is outwardly confessed), can anyone other than God pronounce final judgment on whether or not this faith exists in any particular case?

Moreover, every proposal to deny all knowledge of God outside explicit Christian confession breaks down in actual missionary practise. No one can communicate the gospel without using the word "God". If one is talking to people of a non-Christian religion, one is bound to use one of the words that the language of that people provides to denote "God". Plainly the content of the word as heard by the non-Christian will have been furnished by religious experience outside the Christian faith. By using the word, the missionary is taking non-Christian experience as the starting point. Without doing this, there is no way of communicating. This fact does not by itself refute the position we are considering, but it makes it impossible to assert a total discontinuity between the gospel and the religions.

IV. THE AFFIRMATION OF PLURALISM

At the other end of the spectrum of opinions, there are those views which in one way or another affirm religious pluralism. Within this cluster of views there are differing answers to the question about the relation between mission and dialogue. John Hick is one of the most influential of those who disclaim any uniqueness or centrality for Christianity among the religions. Using his well-known analogy of the Copernican revolution in astronomy, he has argued that we require "a shift from the dogma that Christ is at the centre to the realisation that it is God who is at the centre, and that all religions of mankind, including our own serve and revolve around him".[3]

316

There are logical difficulties in this position. The different religions are the social embodiments of different ways of apprehending the ultimate reality, the source and goal of our being—whether or not the word "God" is used to designate that reality. In this sense, the Copernican model has a measure of aptitude. But, with all their differences, the religions make truth-claims about what that reality is. Insofar as these claims differ, one is bound to ask which of them is true or nearest to the truth. If that question is disallowed, if one refuses to ask the question about truth, one is subverting religion at its heart. Moreover, if one refuses to make judgments between the different truth-claims, one is still under the necessity of justifying that refusal, for it is itself a claim to know something about what is really the case. There can be no absolute validity about the claim that no truth-claim is absolutely valid. We have no independent standpoint from which we can compare all the different apprehensions of truth, *including our own,* with the truth itself.

In the case of Hick, however, it is clear that we are not dealing with a total relativism; far from it. The God of whom he speaks, who is the centre of his Copernican system, is not unknown. He is known as infinite and inexhaustible love. Without question, this understanding of God is part of Hick's profoundly Christian faith. "God" who is at the centre of Hick's Copernican system is God as Hick has come to know him through the Christian tradition.

A not dissimilar position is taken by Wilfred Cantwell Smith in his "Meaning and End of Religion".[4] Smith distinguishes between the experience of God which is the living heart of all religion and the cumulative tradition of credal statement, ritual, ethical behaviour and corporate life which develops through history around this central core. It is axiomatic for him that the central experience—"religion" properly so called—is always and everywhere one. There is one reality with which the religious experience brings people into contact, whatever the "religion" to which they adhere. It follows, for example, that condemnation of idolatry rests on a misunderstanding. No one has ever worshipped an idol. People have worshipped and do worship God—the one God—under different forms and images. The forms are many: the reality worshipped is one.

Plainly, this position is vulnerable to the same kind of criticism as that which we have applied to Hick's. To affirm that all the different names and forms under which men and women have worshipped the Source of their being refer in fact to the same reality implies either that that reality is unknowable or else that one has access to information about it which authorises the affirmation. In the second case, one is under the obligation to disclose the source of the information, and this will involve making truth-claims. The apostolic author who affirms that God has spoken in many and various ways through numerous messengers is in a position to make that affirmation because he relies explicitly on a claim that he believes to be true—namely, that God has spoken through his Son (Heb. 1:1–2).

The other alternative is that we conclude that God (or ultimate reality) is unknowable. The Christian tradition has always affirmed both that God's being is a reality beyond human comprehension and, at the same time, that God has so revealed his true nature that we know how to walk through this world in such a way that we are led towards the place where we shall see God as God is. This "Way" has been disclosed, even though the end of the journey is beyond our sight (John 14:1–6). Thus, although God is not to be fully known in this life, we are given enough to know the direction of our seeking. And the seeking is both intellectual and practical. We walk by faith, not by sight; but faith is a cognitive faculty which enables us to know in which direction to walk. Walking by faith is not wandering about in a twilight where all cats are grey.

In its contemporary phase, Western culture makes a sharp distinction between knowledge and faith. Faith, since John Locke, has been understood as what we must rely on when certain knowledge is not available. Since Descartes, our culture has been fascinated by the ideal of a kind of knowledge that would be invulnerable to doubt, that would be true "objectively" not merely in the sense of being really true but in the sense of relieving the knowing subject of any personal responsibility or commitment. In this cultural context it is easy to relegate the truth-claims of religion to the sphere of "subjectivity", to treat them as matters on which individuals make their own personal choice while leaving others free to make theirs. Here, as a result, one does not merely acknowledge the plurality of religions as a fact; one applauds religious pluralism as a principle. But this principle is not accepted in the public world of "facts" which are true "objectively" and can be known to be so by the methods of modern science. Here pluralism is not accepted. Statements of "fact" are either true or false. Of course there are differences of opinion about the facts, but these are not applauded as evidence of pluralism. They are regarded as temporary, challenging scientists to a vigorous program of experiment and argument until agreement is reached.

Yet upon reflection we are bound to reject this bifurcation of the universe into two separate parts and of our attempts to understand and deal with it into two quite different kinds of mental activity. Philosophers and historians of science have no difficulty in showing that the entire edifice of modern scientific knowledge rests upon faith commitments whose truth cannot be demonstrated from any more fundamental certainties; and—on the other hand—the religious person in the activity of prayer, worship and practical obedience certainly believes that his or her faith is directed to a reality that is not merely "subjective". It is not just faith in faith. It is faith in something or someone, a cognitive faculty that is seeking contact with a reality beyond the self.[5]

Religious pluralism as it is popular in the West today is one manifestation of this split through the heart of contemporary Western culture. It is a split, a wound, which cannot remain forever unhealed. The scientific method treated in isolation is unable to give answers to the deepest human questions about the source and the goal, the why and the wherefore of human existence. It cannot do so for the very simple reason that the enormous fruitfulness of the scientific method has depended upon the elimination of these questions from its working. The elimination is a methodological decision which has been abundantly justified, but it does not mean that the matters eliminated from consideration do not exist. It is the great world religions, the poets and the philosophers that have sought answers to these questions. Religious pluralism as an ideology implies that these questions are unanswerable. The truth-claims of the religions are taken to be merely different expressions of human subjectivity, devoid of "objective" truth.

If C. P. Snow is right in speaking of the "two cultures"[6] in our society, and if W. G. Pollard[7] is also right in saying that while the contemporary scientific culture is in the full vigour of health, the other "culture" is merely the fragmented remains of an older culture that was once coherent but has lost its vitality, then we can understand why pluralism is rejected in the first and accepted in the second. Its acceptance is precisely the sign of intellectual exhaustion. The arduous search for reality sustains the immense labours of scientists but (it would appear) is widely abandoned in that area of human culture which is concerned with ultimate meanings.

It is illuminating to compare our present situation in respect of religious pluralism with the situation of the church in its first four centuries, making its way through the syncretistic medley of religions that was characteristic of the last days of the Greco-Roman world. The quest for ultimate truth had been widely given up as hopeless. Reality is, in the end, beyond human comprehension. The sensible person settles for the situation tartly described by Gibbon in which all religions are for the people equally true, for the philosophers equally false, and for the government equally useful. There were powerful forces tending to suck the church into this syncretistic broth.[8] But in resisting these, the great theologians of the church devoted their intellectual energies to the task of making clear and intelligible the fact that that ultimate reality, God himself, had in fact disclosed himself, his nature and purpose, in the career of a human being whose life and work were accessible for critical study. And they did not hesitate to use this divine self-disclosure as the touchstone by which the philosophies and religions of their time were to be tested. The shape of the Christian faith was hammered out by people of brilliant intellect, living in a religiously plural world but refusing to accept religious pluralism; affirming the supremacy of reason *(logos)* over all the religious "superstitions" of their time, but bearing witness that the divine reason had taken human form in the life and ministry of Jesus Christ.

V. "PROVISIONAL PLURALISM"

A third position must be distinguished from that of total religious pluralism—namely, one that accepts a provisional pluralism in the context of an explicit criterion of ultimate religious truth. It is largely in this form that the religious "colonisation" of western Europe has been most effective. From the dramatic appearance of Swami Vivekananda at the World Parliament of Religions in Chicago in 1893, through the influential work of Dr. Sarvepalli Radhakrishnan during the years when he was teaching in Oxford, and down to the present day, the philosophy of the Vedanta has been attractive to Western intellectuals as providing the ultimate criterion of religious truth. The word "vedanta"—literally the end of the Vedas—points to that in which all religion reaches its true goal. That goal is the point at which all duality between subject and object disappears and one is enabled to realise the identity of the individual soul with the world soul. This realisation can come only at the end of a long and hard road of spiritual discipline, and few reach the end. But this road defines the religious quest.

Scholars of the strictest school of the Vedanta usually distinguish three stages in the journey, or three circles in the inward spiral. The first is the way of duty, of good works—the *karma marga*. Beyond this is the way of faith and devotion, the *bhakti marga*, the stage at which one relies on no good works but wholly on the grace and mercy of a loving personal God, to whom one clings with total devotion. But even this does not take one to the end of the journey. That is reached only by following the way of wisdom, the *gnana marga*, a way of total renunciation, a "journey inwards" to the still centre of the soul where all duality disappears and the soul is at one with the ultimate reality.

From this perspective it is clear that the various religions of the world, and the various religious experiences of men and women, are understood and evaluated according to the progress they have made along this path. Evangelical Christianity, for example, will be seen as an example of the *bhakti* stage in the journey. It will not be condemned as false. It will be accepted as a genuine and valid expression of a certain stage in growth towards the truth. The Christian will be gently encouraged to move beyond the place he or she has reached towards the centre point where all are one because the All is One. Here the names and forms and events that belong to the various world religions disappear in the white light of truth, for indeed they were only shadows. Here any claim for final validity on behalf of one of these names or forms is ruled out. An assertion by the Christian that Jesus is the truth by which all else is to be tested must necessarily be uncompromisingly rejected. All forms of religion, from the most "primitive" to the most sophisticated, can be accepted and welcomed. In that sense one can speak here of religious pluralism. But it is not an absolute pluralism. There is one criterion by which all truth-claims in the field of religion can be and must be tested.

There is another, and quite different, kind of "provisional pluralism" which comes not from an Eastern but from a Western source. It was influentially represented in the famous "Laymen's Report"[9] to which reference has already been made. Here also religious plurality is accepted as a fact and the variety of religions is welcomed, but there is a criterion by which they are judged. This is implicit in the fact that the report looks toward a convergence of the religions in the idea and practice of the way of life that is described as the kingdom of God and that is defined by the example of Jesus. Unlike most of those who have discussed the problem of religious pluralism, the Laymen's Report does not concern itself mainly with the question, "Who can be saved?" It is concerned, rather, with the question, "How can the nations move towards a tolerable world order?" It sees Western science and technology as being, in spite of their Western provenance, essentially universal. There is no cultural imperialism involved in their worldwide spread. But as far as religion is concerned, Christianity will not make its contribution to the coming world order by trying to displace the other religions by its missionary effort. Rather, it must join with them in a common quest which will require all the religions, including Christianity, to "reconceive" themselves in a single world faith capable of obtaining a beneficent world order. The character of this world order, however, will be determined by Jesus' teaching about and manifestation of the kingdom of God.

There is thus a provisional religious pluralism which (as in the case of the Vedanta) precludes the attempt to convert people from one religious allegiance to another. But it is not an absolute pluralism, for there is a criterion by which the religions are evaluated and a goal towards which they must all be summoned to strive.

These two varieties of "provisional religious pluralism" face different kinds of difficulty. Certainly the position of the Vedantin cannot be logically faulted. Much of human history testifies to its enduring power. Even though the number of those who have the spiritual stamina to win through to the deepest levels of "realisation" is small, the idea that a pure mysticism of this kind is the real heart of religion is widespread. Moreover, it fits well with the dominant scientific culture of the West, since it eliminates the idea of a personal God, creator and sustainer of the cosmos, whose will determines what is right and what is wrong in human conduct. Mystical experience is a very widely attested fact in many cultures, and there are no grounds on which the truth of this testimony can be questioned, however it may be explained. But the claim that mystical experience is the central clue for understanding the whole human situation is a claim of faith. Its truth cannot be demonstrated. It must take its place along with the other faith commitments that lie at the root of the other world religions and ideologies. There are no grounds upon which this claim can assert priority over the others.

It is often remarked that in interreligious discussions Western thinkers tend to argue disjunctively in terms of "either-or", whereas Eastern thinkers are more inclined to say "both-and". This difference is sometimes treated as though it was merely a matter of cultural conditioning in which questions of truth are not involved. But profound issues of truth are involved. It is indeed true that, as a result of honest dialogue, two opposed positions are seen in a new light to be different aspects of one truth. But that larger truth must itself be open to critical question in the light of other apprehensions of reality. The Vedantin who tends to take the "both–and" position to its greatest lengths does so on the basis of his belief in the ultimate identity of all things, as expressed in the slogan *tat tvam asi.* That is itself a truth-claim that can be questioned. In pure monism there is no room for "either–or", but (in spite of John A. T. Robinson)[10] one must make up one's mind as to whether or not monism gives a true account of reality.

The view that is exemplified in the Laymen's Report has considerably less credibility than has the Vedanta as a way of dealing with religious pluralism. No doubt there is a natural tendency to judge a religion by the kind of life (personal and social) that it engenders, and there is dominical authority for this. But there are two obvious difficulties. The first is that one has to ask for the source of the criterion by which a certain kind of society is judged to be desirable. The source will be found in one or other of the great religions or ideologies. One has to ask, "Why should we desire the kind of society that the report looks forward to?" The reader of its pages fifty years after they were written can easily see that its vision of the "kingdom of God" was remarkably similar to the generally accepted goals of progressive capitalism at that point in history.

The second difficulty is that it is not in the nature of genuine religion to accept a merely instrumental role in relation to social goals. The devout worshipper seeks to give praise and honour to God *because he is God,* not because it is a way of securing a better society. At a later stage I shall have to criticise a type of argument that concentrates exclusively on the question of individual salvation. The Laymen's Report escapes this criticism. But it is also necessary to say that a view which considers only the role of religion in shaping society cannot be finally acceptable.

VI. "ANONYMOUS CHRISTIANITY"

Another way of dealing with the plurality of religions has been that taken by a number of Roman Catholic scholars, of whom Karl Rahner has been the most influential. He has set out his views in four theses,[11] which may be summarised as follows: (1) Christianity understands itself as the absolute religion, being founded on the unique event of the incarnation of God in Jesus Christ. But since this event occurred at a certain point in history, we have to ask about God's relationship to people who lived before that event or before that event was brought to their notice. Moreover, this question will not just be about individuals considered without reference to their religious affiliations but about the religions themselves. "Man, who is commanded to have a religion, is also commanded to seek and accept a social form of religion" (p. 120). (2) It follows that non-Christian religions, even if they contain error (as they do), are lawful and salvific up to the time at which the gospel is brought to the attention of their adherents. The gospel requires us to assume that God's grace is offered to all, and that "in a great many cases at least" it is accepted (p. 124). But after the point at which the gospel has been preached, the non-Christian religion is no longer lawful. (3) The faithful adherent of a non-Christian religion may and must therefore be regarded as an "anonymous Christian". He or she can be saved through the faithful practice of the other religion. But the one who accepts the gospel "has a greater chance of salvation than the anonymous Christian" (p. 132). (4) The other religions will not be displaced by Christianity. Religious plurality will be a continuing fact, and conflict will become sharper with the passage of time.

This way of dealing with religious pluralism is of course unacceptable to devout non-Christians. Hindus, Buddhists and Muslims are not impressed by the information that they are already Christians without having made a decision to that effect, any more than a Christian is persuaded to the view that he or she is a Hindu on the way towards the truth. But what is to be said from the standpoint of Christian theology about this proposal? At this stage in the discussion perhaps six points may be made.

1. We must surely believe that God, who has revealed himself in Jesus Christ, is indeed gracious to all, that his love is always directed to all that he has made, that in truth every human being exists from moment to moment by God's grace, and that we must expect to find evidence of this fact in all of human life. God, who is the Word, is the light that illumines every human life (John 1:9).

2. We need not, however, and we should not accept Rahner's assertion that it is human religion that is the sphere of God's gracious dealing with all people. This is simply taken for granted in his writing, but it

must surely be rejected. There is much in the Gospels to suggest that it is not in religion but in the ordinary human relationships of loyalty, trust and kindness that the light of God is to be discerned. In the final judgment the sheep and the goats are separated on grounds that have nothing to do with religion (Matt. 25:31ff.). And in the Fourth Gospel, from which I have just quoted, it is made clear not only that the light of God's truth shines on every human being but also that the light shines in the darkness and that it is among the men and women of religion that the darkness is at its most profound. That God deals graciously with every human soul is something that (in the light of Christ) we must affirm. But that this dealing is primarily or exclusively by way of the person's religion is something that we have good grounds for denying. Here we follow the example of one of the earliest theologians to make use of the thought of the Johannine Prologue in expounding the gospel for a world of religious pluralism. Justin Martyr in his *Apology* claims the great philosophers such as Socrates and Plato as among those who walked in the light of God's Word but condemns the religions of his time as irrational superstitions or as the work of demons.[12]

3. Rahner affirms that religions are necessarily social and that we must therefore trace the salvific work of grace not only in the lives of individual adherents of these religions (a work which some have thought to be in spite of rather than by means of this adherence) but in the religions themselves. The religions as such, he argues, are salvific, or rather are the unwitting bearers of the saving work of Christ. On this we must make both a positive and a negative comment. Positively, we must affirm in the light of Scripture that salvation is a making whole and therefore a corporate affair. It is not only the reconciliation of women and men with God and with one another; it is also the reconciliation of the whole cosmos ("all things, whether on earth or in heaven", Col. 1:20) in Christ. To think of salvation purely in terms of the destiny of the individual soul is therefore to violate the basic meaning of the word. But, having fully accepted that salvation is necessarily social, we have to ask why the social element is to be identified with social organisations of religion. There are other societies that can become bearers of the grace of God—families, guilds and societies of all kinds, schools and universities and, of course, the state which is (according to Paul) a servant of God for our good (Rom. 13:4).

4. The fourth point can be introduced here but must be developed

later after other positions are reviewed. It is characteristic of Rahner, as of many other participants in this discussion, that they fix attention almost exclusively on the fate of the individual soul. They ask, "Can the individual non-Christian be saved?" and answer (in Rahner's case), "Yes, through faithful adherence to his or her religion." At this point in the discussion the individual is abstracted from the whole society and the whole history without which no human life can be understood. Salvation is now treated in terms of an atomic individualism. The biblical vision of the consummation of the whole human and cosmic story has been lost. It would be helpful to refer here to the main concern of the Laymen's Report about the role of the religion in the future development of the human story. With all its defects, to which we have drawn attention, this is an attempt to do justice to the biblical truth that salvation is to be understood in terms of the human story as a whole and can not be rightly conceived in terms of the destiny of each soul considered as a separate individual. Rahner, Hans Küng[13] and others are critical of Protestant theologians who are reluctant to pronounce firm judgments on the fate of individual non-Christians. We shall look at this criticism later. But it is reasonable at least to formulate another question: Ought we to concentrate on the question, "Can the individual non-Christian be saved?" or on the question, "Where can we find the revelation of God's nature and purpose which can guide the human race as a whole in its shared journey?" We are obviously touching here very difficult questions about the relation of the individual story to the total human story and about the relation of the kingdom of God to history. At this stage it is enough to point out that Rahner's way of putting the question is not the only possible one.

5. Rahner sees the non-Christian religions as salvific up to, but only up to, the point at which the gospel is presented. Once the reality of God's incarnation in Christ has been clearly presented, no other religion is lawful. Salvation now depends absolutely on acceptance of the gospel (p. 120). The one who rejects it has rejected salvation. If this is so, it would almost seem better that the missionary should not go, since his or her going precipitates such a terrible crisis. It is indeed true that, according to the Fourth Gospel, the coming of Jesus does precipitate this crisis: "If I had not come and spoken to them, they would not have sin; but now they have no excuse for their sin" (John 15:22). Does every preaching of the gospel where it has not been preached before precipitate such a crisis? Rahner says that one who has accepted the

gospel has, "other things being equal, a still greater chance of salvation than someone who is merely an anonymous Christian" (p. 132), but the one who has rejected it has no chance at all. How does Rahner reconcile this with Paul's argument in Romans 9—11 that the Jews who have most emphatically rejected the gospel are, nevertheless, destined for salvation? It seems clear that the picture is more complicated than the one that Rahner has drawn.

6. Finally, and very briefly, if the devout adherents of non-Christian religions are already on the way to salvation as anonymous Christians, it is very hard to see why it is precisely they who are generally most hostile to the preaching of the gospel, while those who profess no religion are often those most open to it. Why is it that the most devout and zealous upholders of the religion of Israel were those who were most determined to destroy Jesus? If, as we have argued, there can be no total discontinuity between non-Christian religion and the gospel, equally there can be no simple continuity. The situation is more paradoxical.

VII. "THE CHRIST PRINCIPLE"

We may look briefly at two scholars who, while unambiguously affirming the centrality and decisiveness of the Christ-event, also take a generous view of the world's religions but are not preoccupied with the question, "Can the individual non-Christian be saved?". Kenneth Cragg has been for many years an outstanding interpreter of Islam to Christians and of the gospel to Muslims. In his recent book *The Christ and the Faiths*,[14] he widens his field of study to include Judaism, Buddhism and Indian religion. He is concerned primarily with the conditions for fruitful coexistence, cooperation and mutual understanding between the great world religions. While clearly affirming the unique responsibility of the church to live by and to bear witness to the saving revelation of God in Jesus Christ, and while delineating sharply the areas of incompatibility between each of the other four religions and Christianity, he is eager also to explore the areas where mutual hospitality is possible, where Christians can accept and acknowledge insights from the other religions and vice versa. Basing his thought on the Gospel incident in which Jesus rebuked his disciples because they had rejected those who healed in Jesus' name but were not part of their company (Luke 9:49–50), Cragg argues that there are many who, outside the church, do the works of Jesus, and that we must believe that they are accepted by him. As a missionary with a lifelong commitment to the task of commending the gospel to Muslims, Cragg has no doubt about the unique and inescapable responsibility of the church to bear witness to Jesus. But he would wish the church so to extend its vision of God's universally gracious work as to include in Christian worship acceptable passages from the scriptures of the world religions.

With regard to this proposal, I think that the question has to be asked whether this does not confuse the issues between the "Christ-principle" and the "Christ-event". If at the heart of the Christian testimony there is the affirmation that God has chosen a certain people and a certain history to be the bearers of the divine purpose and therefore the clue to all human history, it must be asked whether the church's witness will not be radically confused by the substitution of something else than the Old Testament in its liturgy. Will it mean that the story that continues from the Old Testament through the present experience of the church becomes merely the narrative representation of a body of ideas rather than the actual history which is the clue to all history? If it is true that this history is the clue to all history, then it is understandable that there are reflections of it in all the strands that make up the human story as a whole. But these reflections cannot replace the central story. Obviously, to raise this question is not to pass any judgment on the truth value of the religious literature which might be proposed for inclusion in place of the Old Testament in the church's liturgy.

M. M. Thomas of India is, like Kenneth Cragg, clear and unambiguous about the centrality and decisiveness of Jesus and at the same time generous in his approach to the other religions. His major concern in his many writings has been with the problem of maintaining a free and open secular society which can cope with religious plurality and moderate interreligious conflict. He differs from the writers so far considered in that it is fundamental to his position that secular ideologies are included along with religions in his effort to understand the scope of the gospel and the role of the church. He is clear that the ultimate truth is in Jesus Christ. But he is concerned to deal responsibly with the penultimate issues that statesmen have to wrestle with, especially in a vast country like India where the struggle for human community is made more difficult by the rivalry of religions and ideologies. In his most recent book[15] he affirms the central role of the eucharistic community which binds together those totally committed to Christ, but he wants to keep its frontiers open to other communities, both religious and secular, in which the "Christ-principle" is honoured even though the name of Jesus is not acknowledged. Here, in welcome contrast to the over individualism of much of the literature on religious pluralism, salvation is seen in terms of the healing of the entire human community and not merely in terms of the destiny of the individual soul after death.

The difficulty with the position of M. M. Thomas, attractive as it is, lies (I think) in the relation of the penultimate to the ultimate. It is right to recognise that ultimate religious commitments can negate the proper (if penultimate) concern to secure human unity in a religiously plural society. But the commitment to a society in which all are free to practise their religion and yet are bound together in a common commitment to human values must, in the last resort, rest upon some ultimate belief about human nature and destiny. We have seen in contemporary Western societies how quickly the secular society can become the pagan society in which the ultimate commitment is to a hedonistic and destructive individualism. People of different ultimate commitments can and should cooperate in securing penultimate objectives (such as national unity), but, by definition, the ultimate commitment must govern everything.

VIII. "BIBLICAL REALISM"

The name that dominated discussion of this topic in Protestant circles for almost a quarter of a century from the Tambaram conference of 1938 was that of Hendrik Kraemer. His famous book *The Christian Message in a Non-Christian World*, written for that conference, was a sustained rebuttal of the theology represented by the Laymen's Report. Kraemer was deeply influenced by, but not uncritical of, the theology of Karl Barth. He followed Barth in refusing to regard the Christian faith as merely one example of the larger phenomenon called "religion". It must, of course, be remembered that when Barth made his famous equation "Religion is unbelief",[16] he was not thinking primarily, if at all, of the world religions, with which he had little direct contact. He was speaking about the religion that he knew all around him and in which he had been nurtured, the religion of Protestant Europe. He was rejecting Schleiermacher's understanding of religion (including Christianity) as essentially an aspect of human experience. He was affirming the gospel as news about a unique action of the sovereign lord God.

Kraemer followed Barth in this, but declined to follow the latter's refusal to discuss the ways in which God works outside the unique revelation in Christ (p. 120). However, Kraemer was clear that the work of God in human experience outside the direct range of the gospel is to be evaluated in the light of the unique revelation in Christ, not the other way around.

Kraemer used the phrase "biblical realism" to describe his approach. He insisted that while religion is a very widespread feature of human experience, and while Christianity as it exists in history shares many of the characteristics of a religion, the gospel is the announcement of a unique event, something (to use his favourite phrase) *sui generis,* something that cannot be put in a class along with other events. It cannot be treated as one example of a class of things called "religion". That God, the source of all that is, was incarnate in the human being Jesus, suffered, died and rose again, is an event, a fact of history, which is—quite simply—unique. There are, of course, in many cultures myths of dying and rising gods; but in respect of none of these can one speak of a date in history. There is no place in such myths for words like those which affirm that the death of Jesus happened "under Pontius Pilate". In this unique event, Kraemer affirmed, God "opened a way of reconciliation where there was no way before" (p. 76). This event, therefore, calls for a response from every human being.

The well-nigh universal fact of human religion represents the human seeking for God, and God's grace is certainly at work in this seeking. Kraemer had no desire to deny the universal graciousness of God towards all people. But what was important for him was the fact that the church had been charged with the unique and unsharable responsibility of making known to all peoples the mighty event in which reconciliation is offered to the whole world. Kraemer was a profound and loving student of the religious life of humankind. He gave much time to deep-going dialogue with devout representatives of other faiths. But, with all this, Kraemer insisted in all of his writings that the gospel is the announcement of that one, unique and decisive event in which a holy God has reconciled a sinful world to himself, and that it is the duty of the church to bear witness among all the nations to that event.

The earlier discussions of Kraemer's position centred on the question of continuity or discontinuity between the gospel and the world's religions. Recent discussion has been dominated by the question to which Rahner devotes his main attention—namely, the question of the salvation of the non-Christian. In a recent survey of the whole debate, Gavin

D'Costa[17] divides the possible positions into three: "pluralist" (represented by Hick), "exclusivist" (represented by Kraemer), and "inclusivist" (represented by Rahner). In classing Kraemer as exclusivist, D'Costa—like many others before him—assumes that Kraemer regards all who have not accepted the gospel as lost. Kraemer nowhere says this; it is assumed to follow from his affirmation of the uniqueness of the gospel event. It is certainly true that Kraemer refused to recognise any of the world religions as ways of salvation alternative to Christ. He did not, however, draw the conclusion that all non-Christians are eternally lost. Is this merely a failure of logical rigour? I do not think so. The assumption that this is the only possible conclusion arises (I think) from the fact that the whole discussion is dominated by the question about the salvation of the individual soul. As always, everything depends upon how we formulate the question. If we insist that the Bible must answer our questions in the way we formulate them (whether about the destiny of the soul or about the future of our society), we shall find ourselves faced either with silence or with contradiction. If, on the other hand, we suspend our questions and try to listen to the way in which the Bible puts the issue, I think we may find that we are not shut up to what seem like impossibilities. We must suspend the argument for a moment and try to attend to the way the Bible portrays the human situation.

IX. THE DRAMA OF SALVATION

At the risk of distortion, let me try to suggest in five affirmations the main lines of the biblical picture, the central plot in the drama of salvation.

1. The whole cosmos and the whole human family is the creation of a wise and loving God, held in being from moment to moment by God's overflowing goodness. God's grace is without limit. God's tender mercies are over all God's works. God has never left himself without witness. There is no human being in whose consciousness there is not some trace of God's presence and goodness.

2. There runs through all being a dark mystery, a perversion, an apostasy, which results in the alienation of human being from its source. The depth of this alienation is crucially and decisively exposed in the events that are recorded in the New Testament. In the events of the ministry and death of Jesus it is seen that humankind, even in the highest of its achievements, is at enmity with the source of being. The

depth and the horror of this mystery are shown in the fact that those human achievements which reflect the universal goodness of God—the religion and morality, the law and the political order, which claim to represent God's purpose of righteousness—are the weapons turned against the incarnate Lord to destroy him.

3. This apostasy, this rejection of the truth of human being, is carried through in actual historical events at particular times and places. God's dealing with it is also, necessarily, a matter of particular events in history. It is a matter of names, times and places. It is a matter of one people among all the peoples—Israel. Eventually it is a matter of one human being among all that people—Jesus. It goes, necessarily, by the way of election—of one chosen and called for the sake of the many. It has the necessary particularity which is the stuff of human history. And as the story unfolds, it becomes more and more clear that the purpose of election is fulfilled in the suffering of the elect. One people is called to bear the sin of many. Finally one man dies, the Elect, to bear and bear away the sin of the world.

4. The crucified is raised from the dead. To chosen witnesses (election again!) he reveals himself as the one who has finally overcome the dark power that holds the world in thrall. He sends them out to be his witnesses and tells them that they will be authentic witnesses as they share his conflict. In sending them, "he showed them his hands and his side" (John 20:20). The victory over sin and death which they are to proclaim and to embody is one that lies on the other side of death and the grave. It is a consummation that will gather into one glorious event both the story of every human soul and the story of all the nations. Living in the world where the power of sin and death is still at work, they will be corporately a sign, because a first fruit, of that consummation. They will not become a new imperial power bringing the world under their control; as the suffering servant of God, they will be the sign of a kingdom which is God's alone and which is to come. They will also be a learning community, not pretending to possess all the truth, but having the promise that, as they bear witness among all the nations, the Spirit will lead them into all the truth.

5. This community is therefore no triumphant company of the saved surrounded by the multitude of the lost. It is the sign and first fruit of God's purpose to save all. Does that eliminate judgment? Are all in the end necessarily saved? There is no such assurance. The New Testament, in many different strands of its teaching, affirms that there is a

final judgment, that it is indeed possible to miss the way and to be lost, that God's judgment is a reality which will have to be faced. Three things are clear in the New Testament teaching about this judgment: *(a)* The judgment will be in accordance with what each one has done. Not those who say "Lord, Lord", but those who do the will of God will be accepted; *(b)* the main thrust of the warnings about judgment is directed against those who are confident that they are safe; *(c)* the one thing that can certainly be said is that there will be surprises. The first will be last and the last first. Those who thought they were safely inside will find that they are left out, and the outsiders will find to their surprise that they are accepted. The warning is therefore clear: "Do not pronounce judgment before the time, before the Lord comes" (1 Cor. 4:5). To the very natural question, "Lord, will those who are saved be few?" Jesus answers with a sharp switch from speculation about other people to the urgent challenge facing the self: "Strive to enter by the narrow door."

X. HOPE FOR A DIVINE CONSUMMATION

This very brief reminder of the main lines of the biblical teaching is given simply to put into its right context the question that has dominated recent discussion about religious pluralism. That question has been about the possibility of salvation for the non-Christian. That question has to be put alongside the other one that has played a much smaller role in the discussion, the question, "What belief holds out hope for the future of the human race?" We have noticed that this question appears in the Laymen's Report and in the work of M. M. Thomas. It is surely an equally legitimate question if one is looking at the matter from a biblical perspective. The centre of attention in the Bible is not the destiny of the human soul considered as an atomic entity; it is the completion of God's whole purpose in a consummation which gathers up the story both of the human soul and of the cosmos. To think only in terms of one or the other of these questions is to be headed for an impasse. Human being cannot be understood except in terms of sharing in a story along with other human beings and in the context of the created world. If everything is subordinated to the question of the destiny of the individual soul, the story of the race and of the cosmos becomes a tale without meaning. But if everything is concentrated on a vision of the future within history, the individual (who will be dead before it is realised) is marginalised. To those who affirm, like Kraemer, the unique and decisive character of the Christ-event, the question is always asked: "What, then, is the fate of those who lived and died before that event, or before they had the opportunity to know of it?" If one is thinking entirely in terms of the salvation of the individual soul, then the question seems to lead inevitably to an exclusivist position. How, then, does it come about that Paul is sure that Israel, who has emphatically rejected the Christ, will nevertheless be saved (Rom. 11:26)? The answer is that he is not thinking in these terms. Nor, of course, is he thinking in terms of an intrahistorical utopia. He is thinking of an event that is beyond history, an event of which the resurrection of Jesus from the dead is the sign and pledge, an event in the light of which both the long story of Israel and the nations, and also the story of each human soul, will find its meaning.

There is, of course, an immensely strong and ancient religious tradition, most typically represented in the religious life of India, which affirms that the ultimate meaning of human life will be found by looking away from the events of history to that inner "cave of the heart" where the immortal self knows itself to be one with the universal self. From this point of view it is absurd to suggest that an event at one particular time and place could be decisive for salvation. In that case, one will not look to religion for the vision and the motive power to create a just and peaceful human society. One will not expect human history to contain the clues to eternal reality. There is indeed a massive logic and an enduring attraction in this position, and there are many who affirm that this is the real essence of the religious truth.

The Christian gospel is not an answer to the problems of the meaning of human life formulated in either of the two ways we have been looking at. It is the witness of a community to the fact that in specific ways at particular times and places God, the author of all being, has so acted as to break the power that binds us in sin and death and opened for us a path that leads to the glorious consummation of all human and cosmic being. For those who have been called to be part of this community and commissioned to be bearers of this witness, it is simply unthinkable that one should keep silent about it, and unthinkable that one should be willing to allow this witness to be listed as merely an expression in story form of one of the varieties of human religious experience. It must be shared as the clue both to the whole human story and therefore to every person's story. It *can* be told, because every human language contains words that bear witness to the fact that every human being already has—however deeply buried or however gravely distorted—some witness in heart and conscience to the reality of God. If this were not so, the story could not be told. The story invites that radical conversion, that U-turn of the whole being, which is called repentance. It invites belief and a response of grateful obedience. It does not propose a masterful programme of world domination. It does not promise that, within history, the followers of Christ will be the masters and teachers of the human race. It is not an invitation to a theocratic imperialism as the clue to the human story. Nor does it offer to the individual a guarantee of personal salvation apart from continued participation with Jesus in the warfare of the kingdom of God against the powers of evil. There is no private salvation apart from active involvement in the ongoing work of Christ in the world. The apostle who is sure that nothing can separate him from the love of Christ also knows that he must accept the discipline of a Christian soldier, lest having preached to others he himself should be disqualified (Rom. 8:38–39 and 1 Cor. 9:24ff.).

The gospel is not an answer to the question which we put either in terms of personal salvation or in terms of the human future. It is the announcement of a sovereign work of God which sets aside these self-centred questions and directs attention to God and his glory. It invites us to a life of worship and obedience that is wholly directed to God, a life that finds its central direction in the prayer that Jesus taught his disciples: "Our Father in heaven, your name be hallowed, your kingdom come, your will be done on earth as in heaven." With its central point of reference in the crucified and risen Jesus, it promises a continuing share in the tribulations which are the experience of those who stand with him at the frontier between the reign of God and the power of Satan. In those tribulations they have his peace. And if it is asked, "What motive is there for the work of missions if in the end the non-Christian may be saved and the Christian may be lost?" the answer is simple. It is that we want to be where Jesus is, and he himself said on his way to the cross, "Where I am, there shall my servant be" (John 12:26). As we share with him in his warfare, we share also in the foretaste of his victory.

Here lies the possibility of a kind of life that makes sense both of one's personal story and of the story of the human race. Indeed the one cannot be meaningful except as part of the other. And when it is objected (as repeatedly happens) that to propose one name, the name

335

of a human being who happened to live at a particular time and place and as part of one particular culture, as the name in and through which all human being is to find fulfilment is arrogant imperialism, we must put the counterquestion: "If not this name, then what other?". And if the reply is, "We must give equal honor to many names," the next question must be: "Is the human story a unity or not? Are there many conflicting stories? Is there in the end no unifying meaning which makes sense of the human story as a whole? Or are we left finally in a twilight where there is no sure landmark and we must all go our separate ways?"

The gospel of God's free and sovereign grace carries with it the invitation to believe that there is in truth one story, not the story of the triumph of modern civilisation with its science and technology (as the Laymen's Report suggested), nor the story of religion. It is a real story which looks towards a real ending at which it will all make sense. Because it is the real story, it contains the names of people and places and the dates of crucial events. But that does not entail the exclusion of those who lived without knowledge of it. According to the New Testament, the whole human race from its beginning is involved. The men and women of faith in all ages were looking to Christ. They are not lost. With us they still look forward to his coming in victory, for it was God's purpose that they without us "should not be made perfect" (Heb. 11:40). Equally we shall not be made perfect without the generations yet to come. It is one story with one goal. While we are on the way, we do not see the end: we walk in the faith that at the end we shall see and understand. But we do not abandon the faith that there is one story and that we have the clue to our journey when we take our bearings from that story which has its centre in Jesus Christ.

XI. AN ECUMENICAL FAITH

The century since the writing of *Lux Mundi* has seen the rise of the ecumenical movement. The fact that the present volume brings together contributions from beyond the Anglican communion is as natural for us in 1988 as it would have been questionable to the original authors in 1888. A way of thinking that is popular today suggests that the time has come to extend the ecumenical movement beyond the confines of the Christian churches to include all the religions. We are often urged to accept this "wider ecumenism". Certainly if "ecumenism" is only a matter of interchurch relations, then it has no right to the name. The *oikoumené* is the whole inhabited earth and embraces all peoples. That is why it is important not to forget that the origins of the modern ecumenical movement were in the missionary enthusiasm which dared to claim the whole world for Christ and dared to use the slogan "The Evangelisation of the World in This Generation". It is plain, therefore, that to accept religious pluralism as a principle of action—to propose that theology must henceforth be centred not in Christ but in the general religious experience of the human race—would not be an extension of the ecumenical movement but a reversal of it. A movement of mere theological relativism would never have developed the power that this one has done. This one was born out of a fresh conviction about the absolute supremacy of Jesus Christ. It was born at the missionary frontiers where Christians met those who did not know Christ, at the point where the stark realisation of the difference between Christ and no-Christ made all the differences between Christians seem small. The greatness, the finality, the absoluteness of what God had done in Jesus Christ for the salvation of the whole world radically relativised the differences between the Christian confessions of him. The World Council of Churches could not have come into existence and could not have survived without its christological basis. The churches that constitute it, divided as they are in their conceptions of what is essential to the being of the church, could accept common membership only because these differences—great as they are—are displaced from the centre of attention by the absolute claim of Jesus Christ.

To accept religious pluralism would be to reverse this movement. It would be to relativise that which alone has enabled the churches to relativise their own differences—namely, the absolute Lordship of Jesus Christ. One must therefore ask: "What is the absolute in relation to which Jesus is relativised? Is it 'religion' in general?". If that is the answer, the further question has to be pressed: "What, in the medley of human religious ideas, is the criterion of truth?". Or is the absolute the absolute necessity for human unity? Then one has to ask: "Where is the centre around which the conflicting wills of people and nations are to find reconciliation?". As André Dumas has pointed out, every proposal for human unity that does not point explicitly to the centre around which this unity is to be created has as its hidden centre the beliefs and interests of the one who proposes it. The word "imperialism" is the word we normally use to describe proposals for human unity that do not originate with ourselves. The Christian church points unambiguously to Jesus Christ as the one whom God has set forth to be the given centre of human unity, the one who "through the blood of his cross" can reconcile all people and all things. One can, of course, reject this. One can treat this as a mythological way of describing one of the varieties of religious experience and give it a place in a syllabus for the comparative study of religions. But one certainly cannot claim that to do so is to extend the ecumenical movement.

To deny religious pluralism and to affirm the centrality, the decisiveness, the absoluteness of this one name, is to affirm that—in the last analysis—the human story is one story, not a medley of different stories. It is to affirm that we belong together in one history and that this history has a shape, a meaning, a goal. But that affirmation can be made without incurring the accusation of imperialism only because it is made, not in the name of the Christian church, but in the name of the one who reigns from the tree, the one who has made peace by the blood of the cross, the one who alone has broken the power of sin and death and pierced the barrier that divides the time of our human history from the eternal of God in whom is our home.

The "cash value" of these theological statements is only to be realised in the actual mission of the church as it refuses to be domesticated within any one culture but presses beyond every frontier to the ends of the earth and the end of time. To affirm the centrality of Christ, the cruciality of his incarnation, ministry, death and resurrection for the entire human story, is now an act of faith. Faith will vanish into sight only at the end when he is confessed in every tongue and in the idiom of every culture, when all the nations bring their distinctive treasures into the city where he reigns. The church *in via* does not possess the fulness of the truth (John 16:12ff.). That is why, as the writers of *Lux Mundi* affirmed, there must be development in the church's doctrine. But (as the Johannine text just referred to reminds us) authentic development takes place in a missionary context. Every translation of the gospel into a new language involves necessarily some development. Jesus' promise to lead the church into the fulness of the truth is part of the missionary commission. The church is not led into the fulness of the truth simply by theological reflection. It is led as it allows the Holy Spirit to challenge the world's assumptions about sin and righteousness and judgment as it moves into one human culture after another.

The biblical paradigm for this development is provided (as has often been pointed out) in the story of the conversion of Cornelius and its sequel (Acts 10:1—11:18). That event was not only the conversion of Cornelius—the recruitment of a pagan household into the church. It was also the conversion of the church to a much fuller understanding of its nature and mission. But this was not the result of some kind of synthesis between the religious experiences of Peter and Cornelius. It was not that, by sharing their different religious insights and experiences, they arrived at a fuller apprehension of the truth. It was that, by a sovereign action of the Holy Spirit, two things happened: Cornelius and his household became part of Christ's ongoing mission, and the church was led to a fuller understanding of the nature of that mission. The *occasion* was Peter's faithful word of witness to the gospel (Acts 10:36–43). The active agent was the Holy Spirit leading the church one step along the road to the fulness of the truth, which is not something that happens apart from the gathering of the fulness of the nations. Once again we are reminded that we, the church at any one time and place, cannot be made perfect without them, all the nations. The uniqueness and universality of what God has done in Christ is to find its expression through mission to all the nations. Christ, who is the light of the world ("Lux Mundi"), leads us into the fulness of the truth as we follow him in his mission to all the nations and so learn that he is "Lumen Gentium", the light whose one glory is to be reflected in the manifold richness of a multicultural world, the world of all the nations. The true pluralism will not look for a plurality of divergent human stories but to the plurality of many different gifts in the one body of him "in whom all the fulness of God was pleased to dwell" and through whom God is pleased "to reconcile to himself all things, whether on earth or in heaven, making peace by the blood of his cross" (Col. 1:19–20).

NOTES

1. Hendrik Kraemer, *World Cultures and World Religions* (Philadelphia: Westminster Press, 1960), 322.

2. David M. Paton, ed., *Breaking Barriers: Nairobi* (Grand Rapids: Wm. B. Eerdmans, 1976), 70–84.

3. John Hick, *God and the Universe of Faiths* (London: Macmillan & Co., 1973), 131.

4. W. Cantwell Smith, *The Meaning and End of Religion: A New Approach to the Religious Traditions of Mankind* (New York: Macmillan Co., 1963).

5. See, for a recent discussion, Alexander Thomson, *Tradition and Authority in Science and Theology* (Edinburgh: Scottish Academic Press, 1985).

6. C. P. Snow, *Two Cultures and the Scientific Revolution* (Cambridge: Cambridge University Press, 1959).

7. W. G. Pollard, *Transcendence and Providence: Reflections of a Physicist and Priest* (Edinburgh: Scottish Academic Press, 1986), 54ff.

8. Cf. the vivid phrase of G. K. Chesterton: "If the Christians had accepted (sc. religious pluralism) they and the whole world would certainly, in a grotesque but exact metaphor, have gone to pot" (*The Everlasting Man* [New York: Dodd, Mead & Co., 1925], 202).

9. *Re-Thinking Missions: A Laymen's Enquiry After a Hundred Years* (1932).

10. John A. T. Robinson, *Truth Is Two-Eyed* (London: SCM Press, 1979).

11. Karl Rahner, *Later Writings,* vol. 5 of *Theological Investigations,* trans. H. H. Kruger (Darton, Longman & Todd, 1966), 118ff.

12. Justin Martyr, *Apology* 1. 5–6, 46.

13. Hans Küng, *On Being a Christian* (London: William Collins & Co., 1977), 99.

14. Kenneth Cragg, *The Christ and the Faiths: Theology in Cross-Reference* (Philadelphia: Westminster Press, 1987).

15. M. M. Thomas, *Risking Christ for Christ's Sake: Towards an Ecumenical Theology of Pluralism* (1987).

16. Karl Barth, *Church Dogmatics,* G. W. Bromiley and T. F. Torrance, gen. eds. (Edinburgh: T. & T. Clark, 1956), I/2, 297.

17. Gavin D'Costa, *Theology and Religious Pluralism: The Challenge of Other Religions* (London: Basil Blackwell, 1986).

14

THE LAST THINGS

GEOFFREY WAINWRIGHT

I. *LUX MUNDI* 1889

To those of us who have lived through the greater part of the twentieth century, in which eschatology has been one of the most fashionable words in academic theology and the events of world history have brought to many minds the thought of "apocalypse now", it comes as a surprise that the contributors to *Lux Mundi* should have been so lacking in prescience as to devote such little attention to "the last things". Even the evolutionary theory in which many were already beginning to discover radically historicist and immanentist implications did not find its challenge integrated into the transcendental scheme of traditional Christian eschatology. Nor were our authors preoccupied with the question of the final emptiness or otherwise of hell which had bothered so many Victorians. Yet the volume contains some scattered hints that are of value to discussion of the perennial issues in eschatology and therefore also to our particular situation.

1. In the opening chapter on faith, Henry Scott Holland wrote that "faith anticipates the future". It can do so, in the first place, because faith is a personal act, and "a person is a consistent and integral whole". Twentieth-century anthropology has come to emphasize consciousness of a future dimension, including its opportunities and threats, as a fundamental constituent in human being. In his essay on "The Hermeneutics of Eschatological Assertions", Karl Rahner summarizes thus:

> If man is a being involved in history, which means more than a merely external temporal succession such as holds good for physical objects, he cannot understand himself in any given present moment without looking

backwards for origins in a genuinely temporal past, and without looking forwards towards a genuinely temporal future. His self-understanding refers him to the beginning and the end of his temporal history, both as an individual and in the life of humanity. Anamnesis and prognosis are among the necessary existentials of man. . . . If the presentness of man's being includes his reference to the future, then the future, while remaining truly future, is not simply something spoken of in advance. It is an inner moment of man and of his actual being as it is present to him now. And so knowledge of the future, just in so far as it is still to come, is an inner moment of the self-understanding of man in his present hour of existence—and indeed grows out of it.[1]

Such constitutive orientation to the future at the level of creation is the basis for a fully eschatological prospect for humankind in the realm of redemption. In matters of salvation, Holland, like Rahner after him, held that faith anticipates the future not only through a subjective anthropological capacity (itself an endowment from God) but—and this is a sine qua non—in virtue of the graciousness of its object, "Jesus Christ, the same yesterday, today, and for ever":

In His personality, in His character, we are in possession of the ultimate principle, under which the final estimate of all things will be taken. We have given us, in His sacrifice and mission, the absolute rule, standard, test, right to the end. Nothing can fall outside it. In Him, God has summed up creation. We have touched in Him the "last days".

This christological locus and norm of "the end", of ultimate reality, has been decisively impressed on twentieth-century theology by Karl Barth, who saw in the eternal election of the Son as the head of the human race the ground of God's covenant of salvation with creation. The rootage of this all-embracing vision in primitive Christianity is at least as early as the Letter to the Ephesians. Thus within the Scriptures we have warrant for such a speculative translation of what appears in other parts of the New Testament under the more dramatic imagery of the return of Christ on the clouds of heaven for the general resurrection and the final judgment. "Blessed is He who has come and who is to come" sings the Syrian liturgy. Walter Kreck deftly entitled his eschatological treatise *Die Zukunft des Gekommenen* (1961). The incontestable triumph of God's universal purpose in Christ is hymned in Phil. 2:5–11, where it is envisaged that at the name of Jesus every knee will bow and every tongue confess that Jesus Christ is Lord, to the glory of God the Father. The christological reference will have to be kept

central when we later discuss the content and scope of God's kingdom.
2. In his *Lux Mundi* chapter on the church, Walter Lock was still confident enough to uphold the historic faith in a department about which Ernst Troeltsch was soon to declare that it was "closed for repairs". According to Lock, the church expectant and triumphant "strengthen[s] and complete[s] each aspect of the Church's work". The company of departed Christians witness to the faith, encourage us by their moral example, and even now by their pure worship inspire us to "a wider, more spiritual adoration". While Protestants have been unwilling to pry into how the saints help us by their prayers and have doubted, given the decisiveness of this earthly life, whether the further purification of the departed may be affected by the prayers of survivors (cf. Calvin, *Institutes* III. v. 10; III. xx. 21–27), classical Protestantism has nevertheless believed the earthly and the heavenly church to be united in a fellowship of praise. Charles Wesley, who invites believers to "join [their] friends above", in another hymn rejoices:

Happy the souls to Jesus joined,
And saved by grace alone;
Walking in all his ways, we find
Our heaven on earth begun.

The church triumphant in thy love,
Their mighty joys we know;
They sing the Lamb in hymns above,
And we in hymns below.

Thee in thy glorious realm they praise,
And bow before thy throne;
We in the kingdom of thy grace,
The kingdoms are but one.

The holy to the holiest leads,
From hence our spirits rise,
And he that in thy statutes treads
Shall meet thee in the skies.

In investigating the "conditions of possibility" for "meaning in human existence", Helmut Gollwitzer, in *Krummes Holz, aufrechter Gang* (1970), posited on the one hand against liberal individualism and on the other against Marxist or scientific materialism the need for a *social* life that *transcends death*. According to Thomas Aquinas, the final fruit of the eucharist is precisely the *pax* of the heavenly city. Whether such a hope is or will be justified, and what effect it has or should have on life here and now, are of course matters of difference and debate between unbelievers and traditional Christians and, as to the details, even among the latter. It is, however, certain that an eschatological expectation of that kind belongs to the historic Christian faith. We shall reflect further on it later.

3. In his chapter on the sacraments in *Lux Mundi*, Francis Paget held that they "forecast", and perhaps even begin, the transfiguration of our bodies as well as our souls: "Alike in us and in the Sacrament the powers of the world to come invade the present, and already move towards the victory which shall be hereafter." As a "perpetual prophecy of the glory that shall be revealed in us, the glory that shall pervade and transfigure our whole being", the sacraments declare "the mysteriousness of our present being". They "offer to guide" the occasionally experienced "flashes", "pulses", "shoots of everlastingness" into "an ordered, hallowed, course of loving service and of steady growth"— "till, in this world and beyond it, He has made a perfect work; till we are wholly ruled and gladdened by His presence, and wholly wrought into His image." That accords very well with the finest description of sacrament I know by a twentieth-century theologian, namely, that of the Neuchâtel Reformed scholar Jean-Jacques von Allmen in his *Prophétisme sacramentel* (1964):

Sacrament takes place when the age to come chooses, touches, exorcises (or pardons), occupies and consecrates an element in this age and thereby makes itself present. The sacrament is an echo of the first coming of Jesus Christ and an earnest of his second, he himself being the sacrament *par excellence*. The sacrament is prophetic in that it is for the present age both a threat and a promise, signifying its end and its future, calling it to repentance and hope.

Certainly the age-long sacramental experience teaches that, to be Christian, an eschatology must have God as the power of the future, must treat humankind as responsible and holistic beings called to a high destiny that it appears possible to forfeit, and must find a place for the materiality of creation and the concreteness of history. To these we shall, again, return.

4. "Christian Ethics" is the chapter under which R. L. Ottley, in the most sustained eschatological passage of *Lux Mundi,* deals with "the consummation of God's kingdom". God is "the highest Good", and

God's kingdom is both "the goal of the movement of the entire universe" and "a Good to be appropriated by man, through conscious and disciplined moral effort": "The history of mankind is the record of a Divinely directed movement carried on through free human agency." "The visible order of the universe and the history of mankind are verging towards a consummation, a catastrophe, which relatively to us must be regarded as an end." In an "intermediate stage", "there is to be a supreme manifestation of moral evil, a culmination of those tendencies and an outburst of those forces which already seem to threaten not the framework merely, but the foundations of society. The decay of Christian Churches, the profound corruption of social life, the tyranny of materialistic lawlessness—these seem to be plainly foretold in Scripture, and with a purpose: that of shielding men from a moral despair which might paralyze their efforts, or undermine their patience, as they witness the 'birth-pangs' of a new order. The Christian will ever guard against such a temper of alienation, or self-isolation, from the world, as will lead him to depreciate the national, political or civil movements of his time. For civilization is appointed to reach, through whatever convulsions, an ethical consummation, the prospect of which must inspire strength to labour, and patience to endure." After a purification through judgment, "the last stage of the kingdom of God is one of glory, to be exhibited in the perfection of the moral community." The perfection of human personality implies harmony between body and spirit; moral law and freedom; liberty, holiness and love. Perfection is consummated by blessedness, "a living relation to God" enjoyed by "a society of renewed personal beings".

Ottley thus already gave an eschatological sharpness to those perennial relations that H. Richard Niebuhr, in his *Christ and Culture* (1951), was to treat rather under the "providential" rubric that the "the relative history of men and movements is under the governance of the absolute God". The relations between "History and Eschatology", to borrow the title of Rudolf Bultmann's Gifford Lectures of 1953, have been constantly debated in twentieth-century theology. Among the questions that such debates raise, as we shall see, is that of the human and the divine contributions to God's kingdom and the salvation of our race. Ottley, we saw, held firmly to the ethical character of the divine kingdom and human salvation on account of their personal nature; and that is far from being in contradiction to their traditional description as worship and communion.

II. FROM 1889 TO 1989

Three years after *Lux Mundi* came Johannes Weiss's *Die Predigt Jesu vom Reich Gottes* (1892), soon to be followed by the early works of Albert Schweitzer. According to this then revolutionary reading of the Gospels, Jesus stood in the tradition of Jewish apocalyptic and proclaimed the imminent irruption of the mighty kingly rule of God into history from beyond. Jesus expected the event to take place before his disciples had finished the preaching tour on which he sent them (Schweitzer makes recurrent reference to Matt. 10:23); but when this hope failed, Jesus tried to force God's hand by his own voluntary death, expecting that he would be immediately vindicated and would himself return on the clouds of heaven to bring in the kingdom. Jesus' own eschatological expectations were directed to the immediate future, and they were disappointed. The tendency to portray Jesus as a deluded fanatic militated against the ready acceptance of what have since been recognized as irreversible acquisitions in the exegesis of Weiss and Schweitzer, namely, that the Gospels see the kingdom of God as a final and decisive act of God entering history and that Jesus, whether in his first coming or a second or both, is there presented as playing a critical role in ushering in the divine kingdom.

H. von Campenhausen called attention to a key saying that is found in multiple attestation in the Gospels: Matt. 10:32–33 = Luke 12:8–9; Mark 8:38 = Luke 9:26. When people are confronted by Jesus, it is by their response to him—their confession of him and their discipleship to him—that their place in God's kingdom is decided.[2] By his words (parables, sayings), his mighty deeds (exorcisms, healings), and his behaviour (table fellowship, forgiveness of sins), Jesus announces the kingdom, so that his presence signals its dawn (Bultmann) or even its realization (C. H. Dodd). Jesus appears in the Gospels as the inaugurator of God's rule and even as its bearer. Origen was to call him "the kingdom itself", "the kingdom in person" *(autobasileia)*. His role in the history of salvation provoked his followers to the ontological confession that here was the Word made flesh, the divine Son in human measures. The way was then open again, in the manner of the sapiential and even of the legal tradition, to appreciate the perennial and permanent values in his teaching, example and empowering presence.

While twentieth-century exegesis eventually reached this broad historical reconstruction, hermeneutics has found the greatest difficulty—illustrated by widely divergent proposals—in discerning the abiding and current significance of the first-century eschatology that has Jesus at its centre. Not even the "fin de siècle" could assimilate the rediscovery of the apocalyptic Jesus. Schweitzer himself managed to salvage only the notion and praxis of "reverence for life". For a time it seemed that the Great War and its aftermath would supply a latter-day pole to the hermeneutical ellipse. Karl Barth's *Römerbrief* (1918; 1921[2]) proclaimed an eschatological version of the Christian message with great pathos to people living "between the times". The "collapse of Western civilization"—the two volumes of Oswald Spengler's *Der Untergang des Abendlandes* appeared in 1918 and 1922—provided the context and backdrop for a message of judgment and hope grounded in Jesus Christ as the Yes/No/Yes of God to the world who comes "directly from above" at each proclamation of the Word. Something of the excitement continued into the Barmen Declaration of 1934. But the "wildness" of Barth's "critical theology" was tamed by Barth himself in his *Church Dogmatics;* and although the theologian continued to comment in an occasional manner on political matters, the urgent tone of his earlier writings became rather dulled as present events became absorbed in an immensely longer story now conceived as stretching from eternity to eternity.

Some of the European "dialectical theologians" turned to existentialism, so that a Bultmann could now locate the eschaton in the consciousness of the individual believer poised between an imprisoning past and the freedom of the future:

> Do not look around yourself into universal history, you must look into your own personal history. Always in your present lies the meaning in history, and you cannot see it as a spectator, but only in your responsible decisions. In every moment slumbers the possibility of being the eschatological moment. You must awaken it.[3]

From the 1930s through the 1960s, British New Testament interpretation became dominated by Dodd, for whom a certain Platonic eternism helped to link the kingdom's presence in the ministry of Jesus with its presence to all subsequent times in such a way as to avoid the discomfort of the particularities and sequential character of history. In isolated North America, the mainstream of academic theology and church life was largely able to stay with the immanentism of a "social gospel" that continued from the nineteenth century the Ritschlian notion of the kingdom of God as the moral and spiritual society gradually being built up over the years by the followers of Jesus in accordance with the task bequeathed to them by their master. It is questionable how far even Reinhold Niebuhr was able to introduce a transcendent dimension into eschatological thinking.

For a while, the Second World War, accompanied by the Holocaust and culminating in Hiroshima, raised the eschatological awareness of ecumenical Christianity regarding world history. The First Assembly of the World Council of Churches took place in 1948 under the theme "Man's Disorder and God's Design". The Second Assembly convened in 1954, at the height of the cold war, under the title "Jesus Christ the Hope of the World"; but, as with later "hope" studies, strong tensions manifested themselves concerning the relation between this-worldly and transcendent hopes. Both in Jürgen Moltmann's *Theologie der Hoffnung* (1964) and in the liberation theologies of Latin America the emphasis falls upon hope in history, yet Gustavo Gutiérrez will insist that this is not to the detriment of an ultimate hope, since there is but one history and one reality, which is (in a phrase reminiscent of Pierre Teilhard de Chardin) "christo-finalized".

The academic theologian who has done most to keep the apocalyptic dimension in scholarly reflection on eschatology is probably Wolfhart Pannenberg. Following up on his youthful programme in favour of "universal history", Pannenberg wrote a christological treatise in which a central place is occupied by the resurrection of Jesus as God's vindication of him in history and from beyond, "the beginning of the end". It is argued a posteriori that Jewish apocalyptic expectations provided an indispensable framework for the reality of God's act and its interpretation. The final consummation has now reached by prolepsis into the ongoing history of the world. The as-yet-unrepeated act of resurrection causes great difficulties for Pannenberg's thesis with Christian scholars of Humean and Troeltschian inclinations. Pannenberg is right to see the need—which he has not yet supplied in detail—for a revolutionary "eschatological ontology" whereby what is most real is that which "will be". That is what gives faith and theology their "hypothetical" character; so far we have only "signs".

While most of academic theology has been at a loss to integrate apocalyptic features into its current interpretation of New Testament eschatology, the apocalyptic vision has been maintained by an undercurrent in popular Christianity, particularly in North America. This can be traced back at least to the Great Awakening of the eighteenth century: Jonathan Edwards saw the revivals as evidence of the dawning millennium that would precede the return of Christ. The modern Protestant missionary movement pursued an optimistic thrust, aiming—by 1900—at "the evangelization of the world in this generation", whereby the "spread of civilization" (an Enlightenment inheritance) was linked with the diffusion of the gospel. More drastic had been the Millerites (Adventists) and the Darbyites. Dispensationalism, which finally achieved dominance among the apocalyptically-minded, declines to set the day or the hour but nevertheless holds to the imminence of Christ's secret advent to set up a millennial rule which will be followed in open glory by the general resurrection and judgment.

Sophisticated Christians ignore such apocalypticism on account of the "naivety" of its "literal" reading of the Scriptures, and even go so far as to deride it when its proponents find in the descriptions of Armageddon precise predictions of modern geopolitical constellations and events. Nevertheless the popular temper has at least the merit of raising in acute form several issues that have to be taken seriously by any who wish to maintain a faith recognizably isomorphic with original Christianity. As we seek to come to terms with the apocalyptic versions of primitive Christianity, and with the apocalyptic features that stud even variant scriptural formulations of the eschatological project, we shall keep an eye on the way in which other New Testament schemes already handle by reinterpretation the "delay of the parousia" (Parusieverzögerung) or, less precisely, the failure of God's kingdom to be immediately established. I am thinking, for instance, of Luke's recognition to the church of a continuing role in a "history of salvation" of indefinite duration (H. Conzelmann, Die Mitte der Zeit [1954]); of the way in which, in the Pauline writings, the detailed scenario of the Thessalonian letters can gradually give way to the generalized cosmic vision of Ephesians (C. H. Dodd, "The Mind of Paul: II," in his New Testament Studies [1953], in particular pp. 109–28); and of the manner in which "existential" themes do already figure in Paul and become dominant in the Fourth Gospel (R. Bultmann, Theologie des Neuen Testaments [1953]). In this way we may be able to penetrate to a "second naivety" in which even apocalyptic comes into its own again.

One thing must be made clear about the ensuing discussion. I am rejecting as historically false and interpretatively misleading the opposition made by Karl Rahner and adopted by Edward Schillebeeckx:

"Biblical eschatology must always be read as an assertion based on the revealed present and pointing to a genuine future, but not as an assertion pointing back from an anticipated future into the present. To extrapolate from the present into the future is eschatology, to interpolate from the future into the present is apocalyptic. . . . The apocalyptic suggestion is either fantasy or gnosticism."[4] Substantially, this seems to me to underplay the extent to which New Testament and later Christian belief considers the end already present in Christ and the Holy Spirit. Formally, it appears better to look on apocalyptic as a mode, or at least a feature, of Christian eschatology, from the start and recurrently.

III. CHARACTERISTICS OF APOCALYPTIC

From later writings in the Old Testament, texts in the intertestamental period, and the New Testament itself, it is possible to discern an apocalyptic expectation which, however weird and wonderful the details of its various manifestations, shares several broad characteristics:

1. *The universalization of horizons.* As Israel interacts with the nations, it becomes clear that human history is a single process under the one God, the Lord, and headed towards a climax. "On that day," says Zech. 14:8–9, "the Lord will become king over all the earth; on that day the Lord will be one and his name one." Or again:

> On this mountain the Lord of hosts will make for all peoples a feast of fat things, a feast of wine on the lees, of fat things full of marrow, of wine on the lees well refined. And he will destroy on this mountain the covering that is cast over all peoples, the veil that is spread over all nations. He will swallow up death for ever [cf. 26:19], and the Lord God will wipe away tears from all faces, and the reproach of his people he will take away from all the earth; for the Lord has spoken. It will be said on that day, "Lo, this is our God; we have waited for him, that he might save us. This is the Lord; we have waited for him; let us be glad and rejoice in his salvation." (Isa. 25:6–9)

The universal judgment reappears in the parable of Matt. 25:31–46, when "all nations" are gathered before the Son of man upon his throne of glory. The scope becomes cosmic, when "things in heaven, and things in earth, and things under the earth" acknowledge the sovereignty of Christ (Phil. 2:10, King James Version), and all things are put in subjection under his feet (1 Cor. 15:24–28).

2. *Conflict.* In the face of present battles, Jewish apocalyptic, perhaps under the influence of Persian dualism, sees good meeting evil in a

terrible final battle. God defeats the adversaries, and the victory is complete. Christ's cross and resurrection are presented in those terms in Col. 2:15: "Having spoiled the principalities and powers, he made a show of them openly, triumphing over them in it" (King James Version). In the Book of Revelation, the beast finally loses out to the Lamb. The theme of the believer's fight with evil, found for instance in Eph. 6:10–20, is maintained above all in the ancient liturgies, as C. Vagaggini has emphasized.[5]

3. *Crisis*. Inherited from the great prophetic tradition stretching from Amos to Ezekiel is the idea that divine judgment can be averted or survived only through repentance. "The day of the Lord is darkness, and not light": "Seek me and live. . . . Seek good, and not evil, that you may live" (Amos 5:4, 14). "The day of the Lord of hosts shall be upon every one that is proud and lofty, and upon every one that is lifted up; and he shall be brought low" (Isa. 2:12, King James Version). "Blow the trumpet in Zion, and sound an alarm in my holy mountain; let all the inhabitants of the land tremble; for the day of the Lord is coming, it is near at hand. . . . Turn to me with all your heart" (Joel 2:1, 12, New King James Version). "Repent," say both John the Baptist and Jesus, "for the kingdom of God is at hand" (Matt. 3:2; 4:17).

4. *The vindication of God and the salvation of the elect*. The most intrinsic purpose of apocalyptic is to comfort the believer in the face of adversity. Jewish apocalyptic arose in times of distress, whether under Assyrian attack, under the threat of Babylonian captivity or in its aftermath, or under Greek occupation or Roman. In vindicating the elect, God will be vindicated. Suffering will be turned to joy in an age of plenty, a condition of plenitude:

> The earth also shall yield its fruit tenthousandfold, and on each vine there shall be a thousand branches, and each branch shall produce a thousand clusters, and each cluster shall produce a thousand grapes, and each grape shall produce a cor of wine. And those who have hungered shall rejoice.
> (Apocalypse of Baruch 29:5)

What makes the new age "final", a *ne plus ultra,* is that death will be swallowed up in a fulness of life, to which the faithful departed will also be raised (already Dan. 12:2). According to the Book of Revelation, every tear will be wiped dry, the marriage supper of the Lamb enjoyed, and God praised and adored.

5. *Determinism*. The confidence of the apocalyptists resides in the fact

351

that the outcome is already "written". To the visionary, "heaven is open," to use the phrase of Christopher Rowland.[6] Knowledge of what is to come reveals the final triumph of God's cause according to a predetermined plan. In full-blown apocalyptic, future events and their results are described in such detail that they appear "fixed". It is this last feature which has caused the profoundest difficulty for modern interpreters who fear that human freedom—and even God's freedom in interaction with personal creatures—is thereby denied. We shall need to discuss this question in the section devoted to responsibility and action, human and divine.

Meanwhile we shall make an attempt to grasp the essence of apocalyptic. Is apocalyptic not simply a bizarre symbol system but rather myth in some more drastic sense? Let me confess that I consider Christianity finished when theology is reduced to anthropology in the manner of Ludwig Feuerbach. Unless God acts towards, in and for the world, the game is not worth the candle. We must try therefore to interpret the projects and features of biblical and Christian apocalyptic for what they confess concerning the engagement between God and the world. This engagement, and therefore the message of the apocalyptic, is both perennial and yet particular, given the sequential and concrete character of history. We shall not look to ancient apocalyptic for one-on-one predictions of contemporary events; but nor must we ignore either its perennial truths or, more particularly, its more subtle application to a here-and-now that—unless significant consequence in history is rejected—is nearer to the end than when Christians first believed. Hermeneutically, we shall be seeking correspondences. Let us look for hints of the first four characteristics of biblical apocalyptic in the present situation, so that we may find our place between the biblical expectation (however strangely expressed) and the coming fulfilment (in whatever form it may turn out). The hermeneutical fusion of horizons is possible because in fact upon all since Christ "the end of the ages has come" (1 Cor. 10:11). Like his historical contemporaries, we also who live in the overlap of the ages are summoned to read "the signs of the times":

1. *Universalization of horizons.* The "one world" is coming into being. It is seen in the network of communications (the global village); in economic interdependence (oil, grain, multinationals, financial systems); in the universal threat residing in the military capacity of competing powers for total destruction. Our earthly destinies as individuals

and peoples are more than ever directly interwoven with that of the entire human race. Space technology extends man's reach into the cosmos. What, in a sense that shows itself increasingly ultimate, is to *become* of the whole human project and the corner of creation we inhabit?

2. *Conflict.* Morally weighted conflicts receive conflicting interpretations: Communists foment class war; President Reagan calls the USSR the evil empire; the South accuses the North of oppression; medical technology raises acutely questions of the nature and value of human life. How are people to discern the spirits in conflicts whose transcendent character is at least refractively recognized in the "science fiction" of current literary, cinematographic and popular imagination?

3. *Crisis.* There is a widespread sense of impending doom among reflective people. What is to be repented of, and what forms might repentance take? Or if it should come to judgment, what hope is there of renewal? Again: there are multiple calls for "justice". Whence do people draw their concept, standard and practice of justice? Where is the righteousness of God's kingdom to be sought and found?

4. *The vindication of God and the salvation of the elect.* While suffering is hard to measure, many would say that there is today at least a greater awareness of suffering, which of course compounds the phenomenon, the distress, and the problem traditionally designated "theodicy". Suffering is of many kinds. Who are the sufferers in today's world? Do they call out for God or against God? Is suffering a sign of election? Or of rejection? Or is it quite without meaning? Are there signs of deliverance? Or should it be redemption? How is what Schillebeeckx calls humanity's "history of suffering" *(Leidensgeschichte)* related to what others have called "the history of salvation" *(Heilsgeschichte)?* Or, since suffering is inescapably individual, how is the suffering *(Leiden)* of particular persons related to their salvation *(Heil)?*

Far from being merely rhetorical, the questions in the preceding paragraphs are profoundly human and theological. In their present intensity and breadth, they are the contemporary form of the questions that both "provoked" the rise of biblical apocalyptic and to which biblical apocalyptic—and the action of God to which it testifies—are the divine "response". Our attention to the apocalyptic mode should at least have the benefit of recapturing the note of urgency that is struck in much of the New Testament and which yet has sometimes been lacking in theological discussions of eschatology and in the preaching of the church. With that in mind, let us now turn to the theological discussion of eschatological issues.

IV. RESPONSIBILITY AND ACTION: DIVINE AND HUMAN

In several ways already—most obviously in the mention of determinism—the question has been broached of the relation between God's responsibility and action, on the one hand, and human responsibility and action, on the other. For all except the sheerly deterministic and the deistically inclined among Christian theologians, questions arise concerning God's providence and grace and, correspondingly, concerning human freedom and cooperation in respect of the divine purpose. These "general" questions regarding the interactive relations between God and the (human) world take on a sharper focus in an eschatological perspective.

The more the absolute, ultimate end is assimilated to the absolute, primordial beginning (according to Gunkel's formula of "Urzeit gleicht Endzeit"), the greater will be the emphasis on the sheerly creative power of God in the production of new heavens and a new earth: God "calls into being that which is not" (cf. Rom. 4:17). This vision becomes existentially problematic for inhabitants of the old earth under the old heavens when it is asked whether an entirely new population will be created for the new world, to replace the old. Fortunately it is theologically possible to attach greater significance to what has existed, exists, and will have existed in the "old" creation. According to 2 Cor. 5:17 it is possible "in Christ" for one to make the transition from the old to the new creation. What, then, would be the continuities between the old creation and the new? How ultimately real is human responsibility in particular? How finally decisive is what each "has done in the body" (cf. 2 Cor. 5:10)? Perhaps a dialectical answer is to be found in the *other* notion of Rom. 4:17, namely, that God "gives life to the dead". What is raised will be what God has already sanctified in this life: "To set the mind on the flesh is death, but to set the mind on the Spirit is life and peace. . . . If the Spirit of him who raised Jesus from the dead dwells in you, he who raised Christ Jesus from the dead will give life to your mortal bodies also through his Spirit which dwells in you. . . . If you live according to the flesh you will die, but if by the Spirit you put to death the deeds of the body you will live" (Rom.

8:1–13). The moral agency of the human person seems clearly recognized. "He who made us without ourselves," said St. Augustine in a phrase that John Wesley liked to quote, "will not save us without ourselves."

If the "new creation" is begun by incorporation into Christ, how is life in the present related to the advent of God's definitive kingdom? Enough has been given in advance for Christians to live "as though". To meet the dawning day, they are to "cast off the works of darkness and put on the armor of light" (Rom. 13:11–14; cf. the Anglican collect of Advent). The thought is already present in St. Matthew's Gospel that to take upon oneself the yoke of the kingdom meant in some sense the arrival of the kingdom (Matt. 11:25–30).[7] Positively, it may be expected that "lives of holiness and godliness" will somehow "hasten" (if that is the meaning of *speudontas* in 2 Pet. 3:11–13) "the coming of the day of God". Negatively, it may be wondered whether human wickedness can so tire God's "patience" that the opportunity for repentance (2 Pet. 3:9) is finally lost—and the world's *self*-destruction executes the judgment of God. There is a poem by Kurt Marti:

> und führe uns nicht
> wohin wir blind
> uns drängen
> in die do-it-yourself apokalypse
> sondern erlöse uns
> von fatalität and sachzwang
> damit das leben
> das du geschaffen
> bleibe auf diesem kleinen
> bisher unbegreiflich erwählten
> planeten
> im schweigenden all.

The echo to the Lord's Prayer is a reminder that all things are *finally* in the hands of God—who has shown favour through the very act of creation and still calls for responsible living. Yet perhaps *this* world does have to end before the next can fully come. Will God intervene for the sake of the elect? To save them *from* or *through* the end? But since the saints of God have graced every generation, we are thereby approaching questions to do with the relations between individual and corporate eschatology.

GEOFFREY WAINWRIGHT

V. INDIVIDUAL AND CORPORATE
ESCHATOLOGY

Progressivist views of history, whether evolutionary or revolutionary, Darwinian or Marxist, sacrifice the past and present generations for
the sake of the future. Even assuming the immanent ameliorability of
the human race, the problem of individual death would remain. This
suggests that the human predicament will not be solved "in time". If
there is no reason to privilege a particular generation (and it remains
in fact possible to view history as internally consequential without
positing such a privilege), then the question of the ultimate significance, if any, of *every* human life has to be faced. Put in terms of the
"history of salvation", it is the question asked of Paul concerning
believers who die before the final advent of Christ (1 Thess. 4:13–18;
1 Cor. 15:[12]18–19).

Paul there speaks of an intervening "sleep", but in Phil. 1:23 he
apparently has a more "active" expectation of "departing and being
with Christ" (cf. the word of Jesus to the penitent thief on the cross at
Luke 23:43: "Today you will be with me in Paradise"). At this point,
traditional Christian eschatology, in both East and West, invokes the
notion of "soul". A mid-century generation of "biblical theologians"
defamed this idea in the name of an alleged "Hebrew view of man".
Except on a sheerly materialist view, we *are* more than our bodies; and
"soul" is as good a term as any for our transcendent aspect. If "the
Greeks" were wrong, it was in affirming an alleged "natural" immortality, the inadmissibility of a "divine spark" in humankind. As *creatures,*
we always depend on the good pleasure of God.

Christian scholasticism thought of the soul as the "form" of the body.
The difficulty of conceiving, or at least imagining, the soul without a
material expression has led some contemporary theologians to posit a
"resurrection *in* death". In their *Resurrectio Mortuorum: Zum theologischen Verständnis der leiblichen Auferstehung* (1986), G. Greshake and J.
Kremer speculate that the dying person immediately receives a
"spiritual body". Interesting issues thereby arise concerning the connexions between such general anthropological considerations and the
resurrection of Jesus. To put the point gently, several New Testament
writers view the emptiness of Jesus' tomb as significant; but if Jesus
were "raised in death", it seems more likely that his earthly body would
have remained behind. On the other hand, if Jesus' resurrection did

356

entail a tomb-emptying transformation of his earthly body for the heavenly realm, we have to wonder whether what was no doubt a "difficult" enough feat "on the third day" will not have become sheerly "impossible" by the time of "the last day" and the general resurrection from the dead, of which Jesus' resurrection is assumed to be the anticipation or prototype. It is not only moderns who, in trying to contemplate the possibility of the general resurrection, have found difficulty in the obsolescence and dissolution of the human body: patristic Christians already discussed such questions as the case of the mutilated and the age of one's body at the resurrection.

The answer to such puzzles obviously involves one's conception of God's sovereignty over time and space that are functions of creation. It would certainly be unwise for a scriptural Christianity to forget that St. Paul's introduction of the notion of a "spiritual body" occurs in the context of a still-future "end of history" (1 Cor. 15:12–57) and the expectation of a genuine transformation of *matter,* and indeed the matter that *has been* the physicality of persons who may in this context be said to "sleep". The treasuring of the remains of saints and martyrs by the earthly church—not to mention the care of cemeteries and the orientation of the body in Christian burial—is profoundly revealing of the content of eschatological faith and hope. In liturgies of burial, it is this very particular brother or sister who is commended, soul and body, to God. If one can swallow the camel of a transcendent consummation, it seems a little unnecessary to strain at the gnat of a bodily resurrection.

Between God's acceptance of the soul (or the gift of a "resurrection in death" to the individual) and the general resurrection (or a final and universal consummation) there is, in temporal terms, until now a "gap". It is the space in which succeeding generations live their earthly lives. Once given the fact that time is a function of creaturehood, the actual "length" of human history does not make any difference of principle. That is why the "delay" of the Parousia or the universal consummation is not strictly a problem. But as long as human history does in fact continue under present conditions, the solidarity of the human race in creation and redemption requires that the destiny of each member remains incomplete. Even the saints in heaven wait: "How long, O Lord?" (Rev. 6:10). Fellowship in the definitive kingdom will embrace all generations.

The hope of heaven, Marxist criticism has charged, is an illusion used by the rich to divert the poor from their misery. Beside the creditable story of charitable works and of efforts in favour of social change on the part of Christian persons and institutions, there is certainly also a history of heartlessness and acquiescence in the status quo in the church and among individual believers. But such failures stand in contradiction to the faith rather than flow from it as a consequence. It is precisely because their abiding character and eternal destiny are being shaped by their life and interaction here and now that human beings should be engaged in the building of a community of justice, peace and joy (cf. Rom. 14:17). No one should know that better than Christians. Moreover, a religion of the incarnation, the sacraments, and the resurrection—what William Temple called the most materialist of religions—has least cause to underestimate the importance of earthly blessings and the welfare of the total human being. Yet a certain detachment or ascesis is required by eschatological considerations regarding ultimate values: "Do not lay up for yourselves treasures on earth, where moth and rust consume and where thieves break in and steal, but lay up for yourselves treasures in heaven, where neither moth nor rust consumes and where thieves do not break in and steal. For where your treasure is, there will your heart be also" (Matt. 6:19–21). "What your heart clings and entrusts itself to is your god" (Luther, *Large Catechism*). Meanwhile Christian preachers would—directly or indirectly—be robbing the poor if they cut short either the challenge or the consolation that comes from a genuinely and comprehensively eschatological gospel.

What, finally, is to be made of death, the ultimate existential problem for the individual? It is idle to speculate on whether an unfallen humanity would still have known earthly death. "Sin," supposed Charles Gore in an appendix to *Lux Mundi,* "only introduced death in the sense in which Christ abolished it." A posteriori, it can only be recognized that sin constitutes the "sting" of death (1 Cor. 15:56). For the unredeemed or unrepentant sinner, physical death is the outward and visible sign of an inward and spiritual gracelessness. The sinless Christ, by his vicarious death and resurrection, has drawn the sting of death. To be in Christ is not to come under condemnation but to have "passed from death to life" (John 5:24). The Christian martyr is believed to have immediate access to heaven. Such a total self-gift as the martyr makes in faith, hope and love is paradigmatic for every Christian in the face of death. That is not to deny that beyond death, as we shall argue, there is need for purification and room for progress. How wide may the hope in Christ extend?

VI. THE SCOPE OF GOD'S KINGDOM

The Scriptures declare God's salutary purpose for the whole of creation: "And God saw everything that he had made, and behold, it was very good" (Gen. 1:31). To the extent that God has made a free creation, the divine sovereignty has been put at risk. Free creatures have fallen or, at the very least, have so far failed to reach God's intention for them (cf. Rom. 3:23). That raises questions as to *whether,* or at least *how,* God is God and Lord. Is eternal creaturely rebellion, or unrelenting refusal of pardoning grace, or a perpetual falling short of the goal: are these theologically conceivable without a finally unacceptable abridgment of the divine will and power? Or to put the question from the anthropological end: Are human beings so inalienably oriented by their Creator towards the good that all their most stubbornly mistaken perceptions of it will finally be corrected and they will come freely to rejoice in it? Or could the *cor inquietum* ultimately fail to find its peace in God, and the restlessness of the human heart described by Augustine prove to be an everlasting torment? It may be better to put these questions in terms of the *nature* of the freedom with which God endows us, and in terms of the *love* which marks God's will and the exercise of God's power. But we must not get there too quickly (indeed the discussion of freedom and love will flow over into the next two sections), for the original formulation of the questions captures well the gravity of certain problems.

Programmatic universalism—the belief that all will certainly be saved in the end—is attended by some of the same difficulties as double predestination, that is, the belief (to which we shall return in a moment) that the destiny of individuals, either to salvation or damnation, is determined by God from the beginning (the view that God "chooses" those who will be saved in the light of the faith which he foresees and foreknows in them is an attempt at mitigation which in fact only pushes the difficulty one step back, particularly if it is held that faith itself is a specially directed gift from God). While universalism appears more generous, it scarcely escapes the difficulty of a totalitarian overriding of created freedom and responsibility. Even a looser "universaler Heilsoptimismus", as formulated by Karl Rahner, may not take accountable evil seriously enough. Can Hitler ever be saved? Even the liberal Protestant thinker Peter Berger counted fundamental moral outrage at monstrous evil among the "signals of transcendence": "Deeds that cry out to heaven also cry out for hell."[8]

Will, then, the hell of the New Testament Scriptures and the Christian tradition be the *imposed*—and therefore unenjoyed—recognition of God's sovereignty? Again the question of created freedom arises: while the true use of creaturely freedom leads to the enjoyment of God, it is hard to see how, in any but the finally perfect (of which more later), we could be said to have freedom at all in regard to God, were we not able to refuse God; and one must correspondingly wonder whether a self-imposing God—even or especially in hell—were truly the God who made us. The moral question of a *punishing*—as distinct perhaps from a redemptively chastising—God is not far away. Since nobody asked to be born, why should anyone be punished? Certainly the subjective endurance of everlasting punishment makes little sense either theologically or anthropologically. Is it possible that hell may, in a special sense, be empty?

I come to that thought by way of a simple reflection on life and death. Physically and biologically, closure spells entropy and death. The "heart turned in upon itself"—the *cor in se incurvatum* was Luther's definition of sin—is moribund. May not the self-centred human person finally cut itself off from all life and so undergo the "second death" of total extinction? The attenuated existence of the hell brilliantly imagined in C. S. Lewis's *The Great Divorce* may perhaps reach the point of a complete fading away. The loss of a single soul would doubtless grieve God, and God's heart might remain wounded forever. The cross manifested God's vulnerability. God bears the final cost of the human experiment. The scars may remain in glory.

We must beware, if only for our own sake, of wanting God to give up too soon. In the scriptural picture, salvation and loss are not equally weighted. The creative purpose of God was a positive one. In describing the history of redemption, St. Paul in Romans 5 lets the plus outweigh the minus side of the account:

> But the free gift is not like the trespass. For if many died through one man's trespass, much more have the grace of God and the free gift in the grace of that one man Jesus Christ abounded for many. And the free gift is not like the effect of that one man's sin. For the judgment following one trespass brought condemnation, but the free gift following many tres-

passes brings justification. If, because of one man's trespass, death reigned through that one man, much more will those who receive the abundance of grace and the free gift of righteousness reign in life through the one man Jesus Christ. Then as one man's trespass led to condemnation for all men, so one man's act of righteousness leads to acquittal and life for all men. For as by one man's disobedience many were made sinners, so by one man's obedience many will be made righteous. Law came in, to increase the trespass; but where sin increased, grace abounded all the more, so that, as sin reigned in death, grace also might reign through righteousness to eternal life through Jesus Christ our Lord. (Rom. 5:15–21)

If God "desires *(thelei)* all men to be saved and to come to the knowledge of the truth" (1 Tim. 2:4), we must and may hope in the resourcefulness of God. A love that took self-giving to the point of suffering crucifixion is likely to be deep enough to persist while ever there is any chance of response. God's grace may be expected to assume and develop even the slightest human motion towards responsive love. And we may expect, from the evidence of Jesus' ministry, a particular divine care for those whose own capacities have been intolerably restricted by nature or society. And yet, when (nearly?) all is said and done, we may and must not underestimate the gravity of wilful refusal on the human side. In Romans 6, St. Paul scourges the supposition that we should "continue in sin that grace may abound" (v. 1), for "the wages of sin is death" (v. 23). But again: if that is the case, who would refuse, as "the free gift of God", "eternal life in Christ Jesus our Lord" (v. 23)?

But in what sense is receptive faith itself a gift from God? If it is a specially directed gift, then we are up against predestinationism in a strong sense. Unless understood universalistically, election means that others are "passed over", and that is tantamount to rejection from the start. With the atavistic Arminianism of my Methodist tradition, I am grateful for the revolution that Karl Barth operated within the Calvinist tradition. As is well known, Barth turned the notions of election (a word we have ourselves used) and reprobation from categories that fixed persons from the start and forever into the name rather of a dialectical process focussed on Christ—the eternal Son and inclusive head of a human race called to communion with God, redeemed after its fall, and having the gates of reconciliation open before it. Wesleyans would say that the universally prevenient grace of God—given in and on account of the universally sufficient death of Christ—is sufficient to enable all to accept the gospel freely when it is faithfully presented to them, and so enter into the salvation which God in love freely offers to penitent believers whose "faith works through love" (Gal. 5:6). Admitting that it is God who, in universal prevenience, grants us "to will and to do" (cf. Phil. 2:13), then "Whosoever will may come" has a better ring to it as a gospel call than "Whosoever may will come".

What of those who are prevented by historical circumstances of time and place from hearing the gospel? Without letting it undercut his missionary zeal, the apostle Paul apparently held that God has ways of informing, shaping and judging people who were outside the historical reach of the special revelation (Rom. 2:6–16). This may be ascribed to the Logos, who enlightens every human being (John 1:9). But the church is not thereby relieved of its historic commission to make disciples to Christ from all nations (Matt. 28:19; cf. Mark 16:15–16). The patristic and medieval picture of the harrowing of hell—based on a now questioned exegesis of 1 Pet. 3:19 and 4:6—shows Christ bringing the gospel to those who died before his time. That keeps the offer and work of salvation explicitly Christocentric and so respects the New Testament beliefs concerning the sole sufficiency of Christ (e.g., John 14:6; Acts 4:13). There is every reason to suppose that the "anonymous Christians" of this life will find their postmortem progress openly dependent on the one they did not here know by name.

Who knows how many will in the end "come and stay" (cf. John 1:39)? We may wonder about the number of saints with whom God wants to share the final kingdom. Predestinarians speak of a *numerus clausus*. A different view of human freedom may suggest that the answer is left to us—by individual choice for our own case and by collective decisions concerning the future history of the human race on earth. According to Mark 12:25, where Jesus says that "they neither marry nor are given in marriage", it appears that numbers will not be increased in heaven by that method. Whatever the numerical outcome, we may trust God that the community of the kingdom will constitute "the perfect society", satisfyingly proportioned and enjoying a qualitative fulness or catholicity.

A last question to be raised in this section concerns the *cosmic* scope of God's kingdom. What part does humanity play in the destiny of the whole creation? The New Testament, in particular the Pauline writings, sees the cosmos as in some sense dependent on the salvation of humanity.

The creation waits with eager longing for the revealing of the sons of God
. . . because the creation itself will be set free from its bondage to decay
and obtain the glorious liberty of the children of God. (Rom. 8:19–21)

All things were created through [Christ] and for him. . . . He is the head
of the body, the church; he is the beginning, the first-born from the dead,
that in everything he might be preeminent. For in him all the fulness of
God was pleased to dwell, and through him to reconcile to himself all
things, whether on earth or in heaven, making peace by the blood of his
cross. (Col. 1:16–20; cf. Eph. 1:10)

How does this look in the light of the loss of a geocentric, and hence
anthropocentric, world view? Will every star sing a carol? At this stage,
even speculation on the matter seems fruitless. But we may have a more
legitimate curiosity, at least on geocentric-anthropocentric terms, concerning the possible zoological, botanical and mineralogical dimensions
of salvation.

If water and oil have mediated the grace of the Holy Spirit, and bread
and wine the presence of Christ, then perhaps these material vehicles
of the divine—fruits of the earth and products of human labour—may
yet be destined for permanent glory. The inclusion of "sacramentals"
would further extend the range. And what of those works of art and
achievements of culture by which human beings have sought to glorify
God in the use of his gifts? If there is a sense in which the heavenly city
will have no temple (Rev. 21:22), is there another sense in which
Chartres cathedral will be brought in with the treasures of the nations
(cf. Rev. 21:26)? Drawing on a fine essay by W. A. Whitehouse on
"New Heavens and a New Earth",[9] Stephen Sykes writes that we
should not, as "aristocrats of the mind", scorn the suggestion that "new
heavens and a new earth will bear a relationship to the physical environment of our present life".[10] Heaven then becomes "the future of that
in us and in our interaction with the world which is of ultimate worth;
that, in other words, which has become part of the completion of the
will of God in time, and which may not, therefore, be allowed to slip
away from Him into futility or nothingness".[11]

Dogs may be expelled from the heavenly city (cf. Rev. 22:15), but
perhaps they will find a place in those outside pastures where the wolf
will dwell with the lamb and the leopard lie down with the kid (Isa.
11:6). The river of the water of life will flow through the street of the
city, nourishing the tree of life whose leaves are for the healing of the
nations (Rev. 22:1–2). The street of the city will be of pure gold,

transparent as glass (Rev. 21:21), and precious stones are laid into its walls (Rev. 21:19–20). The greater the range of creaturely being included in the final kingdom, the less troublesome becomes any attempt to decide at what stage of the evolutionary process "savable" existence emerged.

VII. THE LIFE OF GOD'S KINGDOM

In what will "eternal life"—a Johannine quasi-synonym for the kingdom of God—consist for human beings? Some process theologians have spoken of a purely objective storage in the memory of God; but this seems no more than a half concession to "scientifically" inspired doubts about "another life". It appears quite inadequate to the life of the risen Jesus, "the first of a large family" (cf. Rom. 8:29), and to the subjective implications of the biblical expectations concerning "seeing", "knowing", "feasting", "praising". In the words of the apostle: "Now we see in a mirror dimly, but then face to face. Now I know in part; then I shall understand fully, even as I have been fully understood" (1 Cor. 13:12). For St. Irenaeus, "the glory of God is man alive, and the life of man is the vision of God" *(Adversus haereses* IV.20.7). The eucharistic liturgies look forward to "participation at the heavenly table". According to the Westminster Catechism, "man's chief end is to glorify God and enjoy him for ever". To have others share in the divine glory must itself be *ad maiorem Dei gloriam*. The circulation of glory in the final kingdom is traditionally glossed as a circulation of God's *love* towards us and of ours towards God and our fellows. That echo of the great dual commandment (Matt. 22:37–40), itself rooted in the prior love of God for us (1 John 4), testifies that ethics are intrinsic to eschatology. The case of Jesus himself (cf. Heb. 10:5–10) shows that there is no dichotomy between everyday behaviour and true worship for others either: Rom. 12:1–2; 15:5–6; 1 Cor. 6:18–20; Heb. 13:15–16.

Having its source in God, the life of the kingdom will be inexhaustible:

> O the depth of the riches and wisdom and knowledge of God! . . . From him and through him and to him are all things. To him be glory for ever. Amen. (Rom. 11:33, 36)

Following Gregory of Nyssa, some contemporary theologians such as John Macquarrie[12] and Brian Hebblethwaite[13] have persuasively argued that there will be an endless progression in heavenly glory. The blessed will find their joy in exploring ever more deeply the unfathomable mystery of God, while the praise of God fitly requires more time than there is:

> When we've been there ten thousand years,
> Bright shining as the sun,
> We've no less days to sing God's praise
> Than when we first begun.
> (attr. John Newton)

> E'en eternity's too short
> To extol Thee.
> (George Herbert)

When the glorified worshippers are far enough sunk into the mystery of God, it will be morally impossible for them to backslide. The ancient collect spoke of God, "whom to serve is to reign" ("cui servire est regnare"). The Anglican Prayer Book rendered that as God "whose service is perfect *freedom*". When the creatures finally put their freedom to its truest use, they will sin no more; and the *non posse peccare* will not be restraint but liberation.

If there is to be progress in the heavenly service and enjoyment of God, there is no reason why the earlier stages may not be "purgatorial". Apart from some of us Methodists, few attain on earth even to that carefully limited perfection which Wesley preached. There will be room, therefore, for further purification and growth before the departed reach perfect love. At all stages we may expect God to respect the lineaments of a particular personality as these have taken shape in an earthly life that began, was lived, and ended at a particular time and place. To be forgiven and sanctified changes a person "beyond recognition", and yet *not* beyond recognition. To be purified and glorified will presumably not be otherwise. Christian eschatological talk presupposes, even in death and resurrection, an identity of the person. There is no reason to think this would be lost in purgatory or in glory. The identity of the person is necessary if heaven is not to be thought of as an extrinsic prize but rather as the enhanced continuance of those intrinsic "rewards" which are the fruit of the Spirit in believers: love, joy, peace, and all the rest (Gal. 5:22–23). If without "holiness . . . no one will see the Lord" (Heb. 12:14), the vision of God will be the intrinsic outcome of sanctification, the perfection of growth in grace.

With the Christian tradition I have spoken as though creatures will experience the final kingdom in a temporal way. That is because time seems to belong with creaturehood. But time in the kingdom will be "imperishable" time, not time for decay. Perhaps even God's "eternity" is to be seen as the creative ground and fulness of time rather than time's negation. Here two observations may be hazarded. First, we have already seen, anthropologically, how, even as creatures in time, human beings are able in some sense to integrate past and future into the present. Perhaps that is a reflection of the way in which God is able in himself to hold the times together. Second, God's decision, by an irreducible act of will, to create a temporally structured universe means that God must, in Hebblethwaite's words, "relate himself to it in a mode appropriate to its temporality. This is part of God's self-limitation, his *kenosis,* in creation".[14]

VIII. THE SHAPE OF GOD'S KINGDOM

The Eastern Orthodox consider the Christian liturgy to be "heaven on earth". A Western tradition from Cyprian to Calvin uses the eucharistic "Lift up your hearts" to make a similar point from the other direction. Following the principle of *Lex orandi, lex credendi,* an examination of the deep structures of the church's worship may therefore be expected to yield the dogmatic content of eschatological beliefs. This will now be the method used to summarize the Christian faith concerning the last things.

Worship is a human response to God's self-gift, the requital of God's love. According to the classical pattern expounded in St. Basil's treatise *On the Holy Spirit,* thanks and prayers are addressed in the Holy Spirit through Christ to God the Father. That corresponds to the fact that the Father's blessings reach us through Christ in the Holy Spirit. Nothing here is felt to contradict the ascription of equal glory to Father, Son and Holy Spirit, among whom there is mutual indwelling. The exchange of love between God and the worshippers according to this trinitarian pattern introduces the worshippers into the vital communion among the divine persons themselves, the very life of God. Salvation is finally to be made "partakers of the divine nature" (2 Pet. 1:4). The eucharist, which is the liturgy par excellence, appears as follows if we try to respect the eschatological reserve (the "not yet") while extrapolating from what is already given by anticipation.

By the sign of baptism, the Holy Spirit is already given, to those who accept the gospel, as the "first instalment" of their inheritance (cf. 2 Cor. 1:22; Eph. 1:13–14). It is the Holy Spirit who informs and enlivens the prayers of believers (cf. Rom. 8:15–17, 26–27) and opens them to the enjoyment and praise of God:

> Cleanse the thoughts of our hearts by the inspiration of thy Holy Spirit, that we may perfectly love thee and worthily magnify thy holy name; through Christ our Lord. Amen.
>
> *(Book of Common Prayer)*

In the eucharist, it is the Holy Spirit who sanctifies the bread and the wine, so that faithful partakers may receive through them the present and future benefits of Christ's redemption.

The coming of Christ at the eucharist anticipates his final Parousia and his perpetual open presence to his people in the final kingdom. In Schillebeeckx's striking expression, Christ is the original "sacrament of encounter with God". That is the ground on which the post-communion prayers of classical Western liturgies characteristically call the eucharist the "promise", "pledge", "taste", "image", "prefiguration" of a life in the final kingdom that will have feasting as one of its modes. As such, the eucharist is food for the journey meanwhile.

The "sacrifice of praise" is offered to the Father. It is not as though God needed flattery; rather, self-surrender is the mode of human response to the Creator and Redeemer. In Christ, the church is already included in the Son's eternal self-gift to the Father in the bond of the Holy Spirit. John Wesley concludes his sermon on "The New Creation" in a way that could well echo the endings of classical eucharistic anaphoras:

> And to crown all, there will be a deep, an intimate, an uninterrupted union with God; a constant communion with the Father and his Son Jesus Christ, through the Spirit; a continual enjoyment of the Three-One God, and of all the creatures in him!

The eucharist also carries an ecclesiological significance that is of eschatological import. For one thing, it enacts the communion of the saints. The departed are there commemorated, the fellowship of praise is joined, and the joys of friendship across the generations are anticipated. Second, the earthly church also, in the words of the Second Vatican Council, finds in the liturgy its "principal manifestation *(praecipua manifestatio Ecclesiae)*" *(Sacrosanctum Concilium,* 41). Perfection is

367

learned only in community. Third, as the Orthodox are well aware, there is in this earthly life also a "liturgy after the Liturgy". Life in Christ is to be lived in witness and charity amid the world, so that faith may be multiplied, and the eucharistic chorus augmented, and God further glorified (2 Cor. 4:13–15; cf. Matt. 5:16; 1 Pet. 2:9, 12). To preach the "gospel of the kingdom throughout the whole world, as a testimony to all nations": the church has a missionary task until—and in preparation of—"the end" (Matt. 24:14).

IX. THE LORD'S PRAYER

The aim of this chapter has been to outline the principal beliefs of the Christian tradition concerning the last things, and the terms in and on which they may be interpreted in the historical and cultural situation of today—or the conditions of their intelligibility, truth, and effectiveness as these now appear to those standing within the faith or open to it. Much of what has been written was in the interrogative mode. That lay in the nature of the case, since here, even more explicitly than with knowledge and belief in other areas, we are dealing in hypotheses that are based on fragmentary, though anticipatory, evidence and will remain incomplete until they are confirmed or otherwise in the future or at the end. Nevertheless, suggestions have been made concerning the limits within which our answers to difficult, controversial and open questions must fall, if they are to be recognizably isomorphic with the revelation to which the Scriptures bear witness, and therefore recognizably part of the Christian tradition.

Finally, I wish to pay tribute to the exegetical insights of Weiss and, especially, Schweitzer concerning one particular text which have, it seems to me, withstood the test of later scholarship. Such a leading contemporary as Raymond Brown continues to expound "The Pater Noster as an Eschatological Prayer".[15] Jesus announced the coming of the kingdom of God. His followers prayed for the definite establishment of God's eternal rule and intimated their own desire to be part of it. They requested a place at the messianic banquet and asked for forgiveness in the divine judgment as well as for preservation from, or deliverance in, the mighty struggle with evil that still stood between the community and the final realization of its prayer. As hopes for the imminent advent of the final kingdom faded, interpreters adapted the prayer to continuing life in the present age with the assurance that

368

God's kingdom had at least begun its entry into this world through the life, death and resurrection of Jesus and the gift of the Holy Spirit. As we still await the final transformation, we join in praying:

> Our Father in heaven,
> hallowed be your name,
> your kingdom come,
> your will be done,
> on earth as in heaven.
> Give us today our tomorrow's bread.
> Forgive us our sins,
> as we forgive our debtors.
> Save us from the time of trial,
> and deliver us from evil.
> For the kingdom, the power and the glory are yours
> now and for ever. Amen.

NOTES

1. Karl Rahner, "The Hermeneutics of Eschatological Assertions", in *More Recent Writings,* vol. 4 of *Theological Investigations* (London: Darton, Longman & Todd, 1966), 330–31; translation modified.

2. H. von Campenhausen, "Die Bekenntnis im Urchristentum", *Zeitschrift für die neutestamentliche Wissenschaft* 63 (1972):210–53; cf. 66 (1975):127–29.

3. Rudolf Bultmann, *History and Eschatology* (Edinburgh: Edinburgh University Press, 1957), 155.

4. Rahner, *Theological Investigations,* 4:337; cf. Edward Schillebeeckx, *The Understanding of Faith: Interpretation and Criticism* (New York: Seabury Press, 1974), 1–13.

5. C. Vagaggini, *Theological Dimensions of the Liturgy* (Collegeville, Minn.: Liturgical Press, 1976), 362–451: "The liturgy and the struggle against Satan."

6. Christopher Rowland, *The Open Heaven: A Study of Apocalyptic in Judaism and Early Christianity* (New York: Crossroad, 1982).

7. Cf. T. W. Manson, *The Sayings of Jesus* (London: SCM Press, 1949), 186–87.

8. Peter Berger, *A Rumor of Angels* (New York: Doubleday & Co., 1969), 87.

9. W. A. Whitehouse, "New Heavens and a New Earth", in *The Christian Hope,* by G. B. Caird and others (London: SPCK, 1970).

10. Stephen Sykes, "Life After Death", in *Creation, Christ and Culture,* ed. Richard M. McKinney (Edinburgh: T. & T. Clark, 1976), 271.

11. Ibid.

12. John Macquarrie, *Principles of Christian Theology,* 2d ed. (New York: Charles Scribner's Sons, 1977), 359–60.

13. Brian Hebblethwaite, *The Christian Hope* (Basingstoke, Eng.: Marshall, Morgan & Scott, 1984), 205–7.

14. Brian Hebblethwaite, in *The Heythrop Journal* 20 (1979):61–62.

15. Raymond E. Brown, *New Testament Essays* (Milwaukee: Bruce Publishing Co., 1965; 3d ed., 1982).

A BIBLIOGRAPHICAL EPILOGUE: BEFORE AND AFTER *LUX MUNDI*

DIKRAN Y. HADIDIAN

I. A BRIEF HISTORICAL SKETCH FROM THE OXFORD MOVEMENT TO THE OUTBREAK OF THE SECOND WORLD WAR

Eleven young Oxonian theologians "met between the years 1875 and 1885, engaged in the common work of University education; and compelled for their own sake, no less than that of others, to attempt to put the Catholic faith into its right relation to modern intellectual and moral problems".[1] The collection of essays *Lux Mundi* appeared in 1889, almost the end of the nineteenth century. Hence it will be proper to go back to the beginnings of the century and sketch briefly the developments in theological thought.

Francis Ernest Hutchinson was the Vicar of Leyland at the time he wrote the chapter on "The Growth of Liberal Theology" in the *Cambridge History of English Literature*. The opening paragraph reads as follows:

Religious thought has seldom been so stagnant in England as at the opening of the nineteenth century. The professional advocates of the Christian faith did not lack ability, but they had been traversing the same arid ground of external evidences for half a century. They continued to put the apostles into the witness box and acquit them according to the rules of the Old Bailey. They cross-examined saints for their attestation of miracle and prophecy, but omitted to discover the secret of their life. . . . A Paley or a Watson might display admirable commonsense, and be accounted by the faithful a match for Tom Paine; and yet the religious life remained starved. The methodist movement, with its evangelical

counterpart, had indeed given back to religious feeling its rightful place
and more, but had produced little or no theology except for the particularly acrid and unprofitable Calvinist controversy.[2]

Another Anglican, Leonard Elliott-Binns, fourteen years later wrote:

> The early years of the nineteenth century [were the] years of reviving life
> in the Church of England, and for this reviving life the Evangelicals, both
> directly by their own activities and indirectly by their example which they
> set to other schools of thought, were in the main responsible.[3]

It is quite obvious that "one is at the mercy of historians who have
a tendency to abstract from history only what they wish to emphasize",
so stated Professor Kitson-Clark[4].

We are perhaps closer to reality if we accept Roger Lloyd's verdict
that "the state of Anglican religion as a whole may have been at once
more vigorous than the Anglo-Catholic and more lethargic than the
Protestant historians are yet prepared to admit".[5]

We start with the Oxford Movement. The sesquicentennial celebration of the Oxford Movement during 1983 was the occasion of the
publication of a series of books under the editorship of David Nicholls.
The nine volumes appeared under the general title *Faith and the Future.*
Bishop Ramsey's foreword appeared in each volume. He reminded the
readers "that the renewal of the Church for today and tomorrow needs
a deep recovery of those themes of Catholic traditions and a vision of
their contemporary applications". Such is the case with what is called
"sacramental socialism". In his work entitled *The Christian Socialist
Revival, 1877–1914: Religion, Class, and Social Conscience in Late-Victorian
England* (Princeton, 1968), Peter d'A. Jones refers to sacramental socialism and states that "its roots . . . go back beyond Maurice to the
original Oxford Movement. If the social message of the earlier Oxford
Movement was minimal, its theology was obviously crucial to the development of sacramental socialism".[6] Geoffrey Wainwright, in his invitation to each of the participants to this present volume of essays, stated
that the centenary celebration volume of *Lux Mundi* "would engage a
team of theologians in the perennial duty of our profession", and
quoted Bishop Gore's prefatory words in *Lux Mundi:* "to attempt to
put the Catholic faith into its right relation to modern intellectual and
moral problems".

The thread that unites the Oxford Movement, the *Lux Mundi,* the
sesquicentennial celebration of the Oxford Movement, and now the

anticipation of the centenary of *Lux Mundi* is the deep concern for the recovery of the themes of Catholic tradition. Bishop Gore referred to a distinguished French writer and claimed that he often acted as an inspiration to many of them:

> Père Gratry felt painfully that the dogmas of the Church were but as an "unknown tongue" to many of his compatriots. "It is not enough," he said, "to utter the mysteries of the Spirit, the great mysteries of Christianity, in formulas, true before God, but not understood of the people. The apostle and the prophet are precisely those who have the gift of interpreting these obscure and profound formulas for each man and each age. To translate into common tongue the mysterious and sacred language . . . to speak the word of God afresh in each age, in accordance with both the novelty of the age and the eternal antiquity of the truth, this is what S. Paul means by interpreting the unknown tongue. But to do this, the first condition is that a man should appreciate the times he lives in. "Hoc autem tempus quare non probatis.'"[7]

The backdrop against which one has to look at *Lux Mundi* is the publication of *Essays and Reviews* in 1860. The reason the theologians in Oxford met for ten years (1875–85) was the currents of thought that *Essays and Reviews* surfaced in the church. According to Leonard Elliott-Binns, "The disputes which had followed the rise of the Oxford Movement and what men termed Papal Aggression, had been merely domestic quarrels; now (referring to the aftermath of the publication of *Essays and Reviews*) it seemed that religion itself was threatened."[8] This came about from two directions—a dual challenge to the authority of the Bible by historical studies and by science. The appearance of *Essays and Reviews* in 1860 by seven liberal and broad Anglican churchmen was a plea for the acceptance of modern critical views about the Bible. The critical work of J. W. Colenso, Bishop of Natal, on *The Pentateuch and the Book of Joshua* (1862) created more uproar in the church than the appearance of Charles Darwin's *On the Origin of Species* in 1859.

Owen Chadwick believes that "the unsettlement of faith about the Bible in 1861–65 was directly caused by historians, or those who posed as historians, in dealing with the texts of the Old and New Testaments. It was not caused by Darwin who published his *Origin of Species* in 1859. In one aspect the unsettlement was due not to the natural sciences but to the advance in historical study of ancient texts. In another aspect these students of ancient documents probably could not have written as they did unless they wrote in a climate of opinion already formed by natural scientists and by philosophers".[9]

Another current that surfaced with the publication of *Essays and Reviews* and for many churchmen confirmed it was the influence of German theology on British scholars. Margaret Anne Crowther summarizes the German scene in these words: "Most churchmen, ignorant of conditions in Germany, seem to have comforted themselves with the thought that rationalism prevailed there because of a feverish and unbalanced quality in the German mind which was alien to English common sense. Many thought of German universities as breeding grounds of atheism, and German scholars were considered among those who knew little of them as pedantic, over-erudite men, blinded by the conceit of their own speculations. The massive works of German scholars, often the products of several decades of research, seemed to prove only the barren and desiccated nature of German thought, divorced from true religious enthusiasm."[10]

In the Tractarian movement, the Latin fathers had dominated the thought of its leaders, with their emphasis on the allegorical method of interpretation, and in 1889 the publication of *Lux Mundi* under the leadership of Charles Gore brought a shift from Latin to Greek theology. Willis Glover, however, believes that "the significance of the book was not in the originality of its views but in that it marked the capitulation to higher criticism of the younger and abler members of the High Church".[11] John Henry Newman, already a long-time convert to Rome, was in the last year of his long life when *Lux Mundi* appeared, and it was his conviction that with its publication Tractarianism had come to an end.

The celebration of the one hundred and fiftieth anniversary of the Oxford Movement in 1983 indicated that Tractarianism was not dead. In a paper read at the Oxford Movement Conference, A. M. Allchin's concluding remarks serve to demonstrate this point. He writes: "We said . . . that changes in our situation had made it possible to see the Oxford Movement in a new perspective. We must now go further and say that what had seemed, thirty years ago, to be a closed episode in the past, rapidly receding into the distance, now appears to be a movement of new insights and new beginnings which we are only now coming to appreciate fully."[12] As for *Lux Mundi,* Bishop Ramsey believed "that a new era in Anglican thought began with [its publication]

374

in 1889 and it is no less certain that this era ended when the Second World War began in 1939".[13] There is much evidence that the *Lux Mundi* era did not end with the Second World War. A renewed extension is being given to its concerns by the fact that its centennial is being anticipated by a group of American and British theologians of various ecclesiastical traditions.

Two eras may be thought of in Anglican and Anglo-Saxon theology. S. C. Carpenter found it convenient to write a history of the Church of England from William Wilberforce to *Lux Mundi* and entitled it *Church and People, 1789–1889*. Bishop Ramsey's Hale Memorial Lectures at Seabury-Western brought the developments up to the Second World War. John Kenneth Mozley's book entitled *Some Tendencies in British Theology from the Publication of Lux Mundi to the Present Day* brought us to 1951. The post–Second World War decades will bring the second one hundred years to a close with its ecumenical interaction, as this endeavor demonstrates. The tracing of the developments in theology during these last five decades is done in the second part of this chapter.

Each attempt to "speak up" collectively assumes that the "time" demands such a statement. For example, Desmond Bowen looks at the Church of England in 1833 and states: "By 1833 it was clear that the slumber of the eighteenth century Church had come to an end. Parliament was dominated by reformers and the new industrial areas that they represented demanded a radical change in the Church so that it could satisfy the needs of a new society. . . . The Church had to find within itself spiritual strength to enable it to bargain with the State."[14] The Oxford Movement had begun in 1833 in the midst of a time when the Church of England was unpopular and the period in spiritual turmoil, so much so that Thomas Arnold believed "no human power could save the Church". John Henry Newman's very familiar hymn, "Lead, Kindly Light, Amid the Encircling Gloom", may be interpreted as an expression of restlessness or in the words of John Julian "the impassioned and pathetic prayer . . . one of the birthpangs . . . of the Oxford Movement".[15]

The rise of the Tractarian movement was due to what John Keble called "National Apostasy". Horton Davies reminds us that "it is a false stereotype that presents the Victorian Age as a period of unruffled calm, or even as a succession of mere storms in a teacup. It was rather a period of explosions—of political, social, moral, scientific, and religious revolutions. 'Change and decay in all around I see', is a Victorian expression for a Victorian experience".[16]

The Black Book or Corruption Unmasked (published in 1820) directed the attention of its readers to the corruption throughout society and especially to the fact that the clergy were acting as "ministers of the government rather than ministers of the Gospel". Lord Henley's *Plan of Church Reform* (published in 1832) demanded radical distribution of ecclesiastical wealth, the reassembling of Convocation, and the withdrawal of bishops from Parliament.

In spite of heavy opposition from the leadership, the reform movement became well established and a drastic change in the Church of England became inevitable. Keble said, "I suppose there can be no doubt that the die for a separation is now cast."

Church and state relationship needed to be reevaluated and reformed, and the bishop to do this was Charles Blomfield, Bishop of London. His was a reform from within the system. Putting the house in order required clergy, laity and the government to cooperate. Bishop Blomfield's leadership in the Ecclesiastical Commission made this possible. "Till Blomfield comes," said Archbishop York, "we will sit and mend our pens—and talk about the weather."[17]

Dr. Pusey was critical of Blomfield's policies. The Tractarians felt that the clergymen lacked spirituality and a sense of vocation. The Tractarian contribution "was their spiritual zeal, which inspired a whole generation of clergymen to renew their sense of vocation".[18] Sydney Smith, canon of St. Paul's, said to Gladstone in 1825, "Whenever you meet a clergyman of my age you may be quite sure he is a bad clergyman."[19] Bowen quotes the biographer of Bishop Blomfield, saying: "In character, habits, attainments, social position and general reputation the ordinary clergyman of 1860 is a very different being from the clergyman of 1810." Bowen adds, "That they were changed was in large measure due to the Oxford Movement."[20]

This did not mean, however, that the Tractarians had an easy time during this period. The appointment of R. D. Hampden to the chair of Regius Professor of Divinity at Oxford University in 1836 was preceded by several pro and con statements about Hampden and his Bampton lectures on "The Scholastic Philosophy Considered in Its Relation to Christian Theology". Tractarians were very critical not only of Hampden's appointment but also of Connop Thirlwall's being offered the bishopric of St. David's in 1840.

Newman's heart was no longer in the Anglican Church by the time he wrote Tract 90. In his *Apologia* he wrote: "From the end of 1841, I was on my death bed, as regards my membership with the Anglican Church."[21] His own colleagues—Pusey, Keble and William Palmer—were separating themselves from Newman, and this caused great anxiety to him.

Clergy-centered British history of the period depicts a gloomy picture, when Darwin's *On the Origin of Species* and the collection of *Essays and Reviews* were made public. "It is necessary to think of the years which followed 1859 not as years of an acute crisis of the mind but rather as the years of the great religious revivals among people who were probably little troubled by Darwinism and had certainly never read *Essays and Reviews.*"[22]

Who could surmise, reading *Essays and Reviews* (1860), that a revival movement led by Dwight L. Moody and Ira D. Sankey during 1858 and 1859 was drawing many Englishmen to their meetings? On the other hand, not all scholarly clergy were in favor of the project of preparing for the *Essays and Reviews*. The editor of the essays, Benjamin Jowett, wrote to A. P. Stanley about taking part in the project. Stanley refused, for he considered the project "inoperative". He went on to say: "We do not wish to do anything rash or irritating to the public or the University, but we are determined not to submit to this abominable system of terrorism which prevents the statement of the plainest facts and makes true theology or theological education impossible."[23]

It took a year after its publication for the public, the press and the pulpit to react and to respond. The denunciation came from the episcopal bench—Samuel Wilberforce, Connop Thirlwall and R. D. Hampden, and also from Carlyle. On a wider scale, the press and the pulpit denounced the authors as "Septem contra Christum". There was an attempt on the part of Samuel Wilberforce to have "a Synodical condemnation of the essayists in Convocation". The judgment was passed. Lord Chancellor Westbury in the House of Lords described it as "a well-lubricated set of words, a sentence so oily and saponaceous that no one can grasp it—like an eel it slips through your fingers, and is simply nothing".[24]

The period between the appearances of *Essays and Reviews* (1860) and *Lux Mundi* (1889) was a time of conflict between faith and reason, science and religion, geology and Genesis. By the end of the century, as is reflected in the work of Frederick Temple on *The Relation Between Religion and Science* (1896), evolution became a doctrine acceptable to educated Christians.

Textual criticism of the Bible, which had been carried on in the seventeenth and eighteenth centuries, became a concern for English scholars. The names of S. P. Tregelles, F. H. Scrivener, F. J. A. Hort, B. F. Westcott and J. B. Lightfoot were among the names of biblical scholars who made permanent contributions in the study of the Bible. Biblical criticism unsettled the faith of many in the church. But biblical criticism gained ground and acceptance among the educated clergy and laity. Resistance to biblical criticism was still very strong, so much so that even when, under Bishop Gore's editorship, the *Lux Mundi* essays were ready for publication, Oxford University Press refused to publish the book on the ground that it would "open the floodgates". The volume therefore was published by John Murray. The fact that the essay on "The Holy Spirit and Inspiration" was the most controversial one indicates that the majority in the church still were not reconciled with the conclusions derived from biblical criticism. Gore's chapter legitimized criticism: "But if we thus plead that theology may leave the field open for free discussion of these questions which Biblical criticism has recently been raising, we shall probably be bidden to 'Remember Tübingen', and not be over-trustful of a criticism which at least exhibits in some of its most prominent representatives a great deal of arbitrariness, of love of 'new views' for their own sake, and a great lack of that reverence and spiritual insight which is at least as much needed for understanding the books of the Bible, as accurate knowledge and fair investigation."

Church historians agree that the young scholars who contributed to the *Lux Mundi* volume were indebted to two different traditions in the church—one was Tractarianism through R. W. Church, Pusey and Liddon, and the other tradition was represented by F. D. Maurice, Coleridge, Westcott and Hort. The influence of Tractarianism was not so apparent, since in the case of Liddon, to use Archbishop Ramsey's words, *"Lux Mundi* grievously shocked the older theological generation and broke the heart of Liddon, who held that Gore had capitulated to German rationalism".[25] Archbishop Ramsey's own assessment needs to be quoted here: "It was not that *Lux Mundi* was near either to rationalism or to Pelagianism; rather was it that the writers put themselves alongside the standpoint of the contemporary inquirer after truth, and were faintly anticipating the method of William Temple which he described to Ronald Knox in the words: 'I am not asking what Jones will swallow: *I am Jones* asking what there is to eat!' "[26] The vitality of the Broad Churchmen, however, was directly related to Tractarian impetus even though Tractarians were not too pleased with the outcome. But there was also a "parting of the ways" because of the shift from Latin to Greek theology: the former placed a heavy emphasis on the doctrine of atonement, whereas *Lux Mundi* essayists found in the Greek fathers of Alexandria, as expressed by the Cambridge Platonists, the emphasis on "God's immanence in history rather than man's deliverance from sin".[27]

Lux Mundi was not as radical as *Essays and Reviews*. Owen Chadwick refers to the reverent nature of the volume, and if one would look for some explanation, the answer may be in its conciliatory nature, bringing together two movements, the Tractarian and the Broad Church outlook. *Lux Mundi* was a theological work expressing a synthesis, a converging of Tractarian piety, biblical criticism and Greek patristic thought.

S. C. Carpenter finds in the Broad Church and Tractarian movements two different attempts to solve the crisis, one by "buying up the opportunity" and the other by "redeeming the time". There was very little sympathy for each other's positions. But the life of the church in the ensuing decades proved that both attempts were needed. *Lux Mundi* infused a new and positive spirit among churchmen who looked more with hope than despair as the twentieth century drew near. The new and positive spirit of the churchmen led into the twentieth century with more hope than despair. Both the growing optimism and the "unsettlement of belief" were symbolized by the acceptance of evolution and the increased strength of the liberal wing of the church. The Modern Churchmen's Union was founded in 1898 within the Church of England, a successor of the Broad Churchman of early date, with strong emphasis on liberal Protestantism. *The Oxford Dictionary of the Christian Church* describes its aims as follows: "Among its aims are to uphold the comprehensiveness of the Church of England and to maintain the legitimacy of doctrinal adjustment to the forms of worship in accordance with the believed requirements of modern discovery."[28] In spite of the optimism resulting from the publication of *Lux Mundi,* Bishop Gore preached, on the eve of the twentieth century, "a most despondent sermon on the hollowness of modern progress". In the Oxford History of England series, R. C. K. Ensor, writing in the volume *England, 1870–1914,* spells out what Gore alluded to:

> The nineties were a period of unsettlement. It passed through a phase like an adolescent; its temper was explosive and quarrelsome; it boasted itself with the harshness of immaturity. Whole classes or strata of society were, in some degree, tasting power for the first time; and as they pushed their way out of the community, a kind of upstart arrogance became vocal to them. In religion, in social relations, in politics, in business, men grown contemptuous of the old ideals were stridently asserting new ones. The former clear objectives were gone, and as yet nothing took their place.[29]

With the death of Queen Victoria (January 22, 1901), a great epoch came to an end. "The sky of England had been clouding for years before: what with the collapse of the country-side, the new-born social unrest in the towns, the waning of religious faith, and above all the sense of an uncontrollable transition to the unknown—the feeling that the keys of power were blindly but swiftly transferring themselves to new classes, new types of men, new nations. The queen's death focussed it all."[30]

Optimism was eroding as the nineteenth century was coming to an end. Uncertainty and doubt led some people to search for substitutes in place of Christianity. The cult of Spiritualism attracted many. But what was constructive was the revival of interest in mysticism, which led W. R. Inge to deliver his Bampton Lectures on "Christian Mysticism" in 1899.

It was not a coincidence that the century was ushered in by the publication of William James's Gifford Lectures on *Varieties of Religious Experience* (1902). H. G. Wood refers to Frederick Temple's anticipation "that the center of interest in theology would shift in the twentieth century from metaphysics to psychology".[31] In February 1924, F. C. Burkitt in the last of a series of lectures on *Christian Beginnings* made the following closing remarks:

> I cannot help feeling that there will come a time in the not very distant future when the direct investigation of these early days of Christianity will have come to a standstill, when the task of rewriting the beginnings of the Christian Society will have been carried as far as the materials at our disposal will carry us. . . . It has been a wonderful century-and-a-half, since the beginnings of the historical criticism of the New Testament were laid

by Semler and Herder and Reimarus and Lessing, and we are not yet at the end. But the process will not go on forever, and this for two reasons. The first, of course, the supply of fresh material is not likely to continue indefinitely: the East has been ransacked, and much of its treasures used. But there is a more potent reason still. . . . From the scientific, academical, point of view, . . . Psychology gains and Historical Criticism loses. . . . Now one tends to take up the Philosophy of Religion with Psychology.[32]

A glance at the work of Alfred Caldecott on *The Philosophy of Religion in England and America* (1901) indicates that philosophy of religion, either as Natural Theology or Theism, was very much a lively discipline but as Caldecott states: "I have . . . foregone the scrutiny of Psychologists who have not come forward in some definite way to make some claim of the Empirical kind."[33]

The early decades of the twentieth century saw an increased activity in the study of psychology of religion, but this did not prevent theologians from pursuing their own studies. Hence we have another group of scholars from Oxford presenting a collection of essays in 1912 with the title *Foundations: A Statement of Christian Belief in Terms of Modern Thought.* Among the contributors were B. H. Streeter, A. E. J. Rawlinson, William Temple and W. H. Moberly. In 1925 a group of scholars presented the work entitled *Evolution in the Light of Modern Knowledge.* A companion to this work was published in 1929. *The History of Christianity in the Light of Modern Knowledge* had contributions by F. C. Burkitt, C. H. Dodd, John Garstand, Sir Frederick G. Kenyon, James Moffatt, Gilbert Murray, William Temple, and others. A further development was expressed in yet another collection of essays entitled *Essays Catholic and Critical* (1926). In all these, the provocation did not go unheeded by the conservatives. Two names, R. A. Knox and Frank Weston, the Bishop of Zanzibar, responded to the liberalizing of theology. Credit is given to the efforts of Archbishop Davidson of Canterbury for averting many crises in the church. A commission was appointed in 1922 representing Anglo-Catholics, Modern Churchmen and Evangelicals, which was presided over by William Temple, and the report was published in 1938 under the title of *Doctrine in the Church of England.* "Discerning readers will see that the contributors to *Foundations* and *Essays Catholic and Critical,* who were strongly represented on the Commission, must have exercised a good deal of influence on its findings, which were found equally acceptable to Liberal Evangelicals. This was indeed the high tide of liberal theology in England."[34] One more collective work, *Mysterium Christi* (1930), this time the results of the second British-German Theological Conference held in 1928 under the auspices of the then Dean of Chichester, G. K. A. Bell, and Adolf Deissmann, brought to the public the essays on the question, "What think ye of Christ?" Of the twelve participants, seven were from the United Kingdom and five from Germany—a remarkable evidence of the close interaction of German and British theologians. But the tide was to change and this was the result of the Second World War and the development of dialectical theology. To this we shall return in the second half of this essay.

Once more we turn to the England of the early decades of the twentieth century. The influence of Harnack was quite obvious in the development of what became known as "New Theology". Harnack's *Wesen des Christentums* appeared in 1901 in English under the title of *What Is Christianity?* setting the foundation for many decades to come for a liberal Protestant interpretation of Christianity. We have referred already to the Modern Churchmen's Union. Among their leaders were H. Rashdall, W. R. Inge, E. W. Barnes and K. Lake. One of their main objectives was to have churchmen "honestly and loyally endeavoring to vindicate the truths of Christianity by the light of scholarship and research". It was, however, in a very particular way that the "New Theology" expressed Harnack's imprint. R. J. Campbell, minister of London's City Temple (1903–15) who later was ordained as an Anglican priest, was its chief exponent. John Kenneth Mozley describes "New Theology" as a "reinterpretation of Christian theology under the influence of the idea of divine immanence".[35] This is the period in British history known as the Edwardian years [1901–10], which was the decade of "calm and contentment, of pomp and luxury, of assured wealth and unchallenged order".[36]

If one nonconformist led the liberal theological development, another nonconformist, P. T. Forsyth, began the "reconstruction of evangelical theology . . . anticipated by many years the best insights of the neo-evangelical theologians of later generations".[37] The attempt to anticipate and fulfill the need for a new statement on Christian belief came through the seven Oxford men in the collection of essays referred to above, namely, *Foundations.* Since the "new theology" repudiated the deity of Christ, both Forsyth and the Oxford men addressed themselves to the interpretation of the person of Christ.

Each decade or so it became desirable on the part of scholars to issue collective works summarizing the results of their research and scholarship in one area of interest or in various fields. So we have the *Cambridge Companion to the Bible,* published in 1892, which also appeared in revised form in 1916. In 1902 six Oxford tutors brought out a volume entitled *Contentio Veritatis: Essays in Constructive Theology.* The opening words of the preface read as follows:

> The beginning of the twentieth century finds the Church of England face to face with some very urgent problems. Of these the most clamorous, and perhaps the least important, is the controversy which rages round the Ornaments Rubric, and kindred topics—the problem which the daily press has dignified by the title of "Crisis in the Church". Those who take a wider view of the course of religious thought during the past century will not be disposed to treat these disputes about ritual quite so seriously. . . . The acrimonious dispute between Natural Science and the old orthodoxy, which agitated the last generation, is happily a thing of the past. . . . Meanwhile, especially among our younger men and women of fair education, there is widespread unsettlement and uneasiness. There is a vague feeling that the Old Orthodoxy is impossible; people suspect that much that was once commonly believed is no longer tenable, but they do not know how much, nor by what it is to be replaced.[38]

The shift from Oxford to Cambridge with the appearances of *Cambridge Theological Essays* (1905) and the *Cambridge Biblical Essays* (1909) did not bring the expected controversial discussion. John Kenneth Mozley believed that this was due "to greater individualism of Cambridge Theological tendencies as compared with that of Oxford. . . . Moreover, there was no such intensive influence upon Church life as a whole flowing out of Cambridge as was characteristic of Oxford".[39]

The decade before the Second World War is described by Horton Davies as "the return to Biblical Orthodoxy": "The date given for the beginning of the demise of liberal theology and for its replacement by Biblical theology is 1933. This may seem the less arbitrary, when it is remembered that Karl Barth's *Commentary on the Epistle to the Romans* appeared in English translation by Sir Edwyn C. Hoskyns in 1933. That event signalizes the impact on British theology of both Europe's greatest twentieth century theologian and a great English Biblical scholar."[40]

The main impact came with the works of Sir Edwyn C. Hoskyns, an Anglican High Churchman, with his contribution on "The Christ of the

Synoptic Gospels" in *Essays Catholic and Critical* (1926) and especially with the appearance of *The Riddle of the New Testament* (1931), with his pupil F. N. Davey collaborating. Hoskyns in his *Cambridge Sermons* spoke these words: "Once again, my brothers in Christ, may I warn you that, as Christians and as men, you are moving along a path narrow and sharp as the edge of a razor, for on one side of you lies the blasphemy of human idolatry, and on the other side of you the chasm of detachment and cynical aloofness. Between the two walked the Christ."[41] Hoskyn's early death (1937) at the age of forty-nine cut short his influence. It was the works of C. H. Dodd and especially his *Apostolic Preaching and Its Development* (London 1936) that gave to his generation and after the concept of "realized eschatology". "The primitive church, in proclaiming its Gospel to the world, offered its own fellowship and experience as the realization of the Gospel. This is the essence of the matter."[42]

Other New Testament scholars and theologians joined in the development of biblical theology in Great Britain: Nathaniel Micklem, T. W. Manson, Vincent Taylor, R. Newton Flew, A. G. Hebert, Lionel S. Thornton, Lovell Cocks, J. S. Whale, Archbishop A. M. Ramsey and others. Most of their works began in the period under study, but their major contributions appeared after 1940.

The decade of the 1930s ended with the outbreak of the Second World War. The war, though it turned out to be "the finest hour" of the British people, also meant the end of the lingering Victorian period.

In summary, then, of the period between 1830 and 1940, we reflect as follows:

Basil Willey, in his chapter on "Septem contra Christum" (as the authors of the *Essays and Reviews* were called by the critics), discusses the article by Mark Pattison on "Tendencies of Religious Thought in England, 1688–1750". Here he points out Pattison's estimate of the eighteenth century, with Newman and Carlyle agreeing with him, "as an age of decay in religion, licentiousness of morals, public corruption, profaneness of language . . . an age whose poetry was without romance, whose philosophy was without insight, and whose public men were without character".[43] Obviously many Anglicans preferred to forget that period. Willey states: "But one cannot write or think history in this way; today is today in virtue of yesterday."[44] We have referred already to Bishop Gore's words on the eve of the twentieth century concerning

384

"the hollowness of modern progress". This brief survey has been interspersed with phrases such as "the nineties were a period of unsettlement", "unsettlement of religious belief", "growing optimism and erosion of it", "an age of uncertainty and doubt", and "unsettlement of faith in the Bible".

A recent study of the period 1850–1960 by Susan Budd under the title *Varieties of Unbelief: Atheists and Agnostics in English Society, 1850–1960* (London, 1977), attempts to show what drove British intellectuals away from religion and belief to secularism, unbelief and atheism. The foremost of the causes of unbelief was the critical reading and studying of the Bible, and Susan Budd states that Thomas Paine's *The Age of Reason* (1793) became the most influential book for the nineteenth-century intellectuals; the reading of Robert Blatchford's *God and My Neighbour* (1903), for the early-twentieth-century intellectuals. The Bible was no longer regarded as divinely inspired, hence intellectually and morally no longer authoritative.

In spite of all these expressions and experiences of the Victorian Age and its extension into the first four decades of the twentieth century, there are other assessments and perceptions of equal value and veracity. Here we find Victorians themselves (John Stuart Mill, Matthew Arnold, Thomas Carlyle, Disraeli, Herbert Spencer, Tennyson and many others) referring to their respective periods as "an age of transition".[45] The transition was not necessarily from the eighteenth to the nineteenth century but from the Middle Ages to a period yet unknown. They were leaving behind feudalism and an agrarian society and entering into the age of steam and industrial society. Houghton refers to Thomas Arnold who, "on seeing the first train pass through the Rugby countryside, said, 'feudality is gone forever' ".[46] The industrial revolution brought the democratic revolution. It also meant expansion in manufacturing and the distribution of the manufactured goods to the four corners of the earth. Speed, pressure of work and more crowded living took the "joy" out of living. The literature of the period abounds in disgruntlement about what the transitional period was bringing about. But it was not an age of despair. "The Victorians might be, and often were, uncertain about what theory to accept, or what faculty of the mind to rely on; but it never occurred to them to doubt their capacity to arrive at truth."[47]

A glance at Houghton's work and its chapter headings will give the reader the "attitudes" present during the greater part of the nineteenth century: optimism, anxiety, the critical spirit and the will to believe, anti-intellectualism, dogmatism, rigidity, commercial spirit, the worship of force, earnestness, enthusiasm, hero worship, love and hypocrisy.

The age of doubt was being replaced by the age of despair and anxiety. As the decade of the 1920s began to unroll, only to be followed by another worldwide conflict, it was also discovered that the world was no longer a "safe" place. It was a world entering a post-Christendom period where secularity and pluralism became the dominant trends.

II. FROM THE OUTBREAK OF THE SECOND WORLD WAR TO THE PRESENT TIME

The historical sketch from the Oxford Movement to the outbreak of the Second World War was confined to the theological scene in the United Kingdom with special focus on English theological developments.

From the outbreak of the Second World War to the present time the horizon widened. The commemoration of the centennial of *Lux Mundi* in 1989 finds us in a world changed by scientific, technological, social, cultural and political developments into a "global city." This, in turn, has ushered in a religious and a theological climate that no church historian could have predicted forty-five years ago. Even in 1966, it was stated that:

> The twentieth century could go down in history as one of the most lively periods in theology. Pitched battles have been fought as opponents have read each other out of the church. Dominant theological schools have risen to power and fallen. Theology has been pronounced dead but has risen to new life, and now there are theologians who tell us that it is not theology but God who has died. At the present moment theology seems to be in transit, and it would be a foolish man, who would try to forecast what its destination will be.[48]

Theology still seems to be in transit twenty years later, and what the destination will be is difficult to forecast. In sketching the highlights of the religious and theological developments since the outbreak of the Second World War to the present time, the focus toward the end will be on American theological voices.

Let us backtrack for a moment to the years of the First World War and start with Karl Barth, who at this period was pastor of Safenwil, Switzerland. We are told that the two editions of his commentary on *Romans* (1919, 1921) were the direct results of his "penetration into the Bible for the sake of his preaching". The commentary on *Romans* was called a "bomb-shell" in the German theological scene. As E. Thurneysen said, "Crisis theology" was born, but not in the context of pure academic and abstract concerns, for "Barth's word from the beginning was a 'political word' ".[49] The years between the two world wars, and Barth's own encounter with Hitler's Nazi regime, proved this. The "word" was also a judgment upon preaching in his day, not only by conservatives but also "by the liberal and culturally oriented educational preaching that has been so weakened by compromise".[50] The influence of Barth on the United Kingdom and North America was evidenced by the works translated into English: *The Word of God and the Word of Man* (Boston, 1928); *The Epistle to the Romans* (Cambridge, 1928); *Church and State* (London, 1939); *The Church and the Political Problem of Our Day* (London, 1939); and *The Doctrine of the Word of God* (Edinburgh, 1936).

The Second World War limited the full impact of the theological ferment to the European continent, but soon after the cessation of hostilities it spilled over to the shores of North America and brought to birth the "Biblical Theology Movement" and the American version of "Dialectical Theology" led by Reinhold Niebuhr. Niebuhr had delivered the first series of his Gifford Lectures in April and May 1939, "when the clouds of war were already hovering ominously over Europe; dark forebodings had become a dreadful reality before the second series was given in October, 1939".[51] Niebuhr wrote in his preface: "The study is based upon the conviction that there are resources in the Christian faith for an understanding of human nature which have been lost in modern culture."[52] There is no direct evidence that Niebuhr was influenced by Barth. But the Barth-Niebuhr influence together gave further impetus to the development of the Biblical Theology Movement.

If during the First World War it was Barth's *Romans* that came into being, during the Second World War it was an article by Rudolf Bultmann on "New Testament and Mythology" that triggered another major movement which came to overshadow the concerns of Barth and Niebuhr. American theology became primarily preoccupied with

Kerygma and Myth: A Theological Debate (1972). Bultmann's concern was the "original Schleiermacher concern to adapt the Gospel to a modern secular culture".[53] In the meantime, the current of theological thought initiated by Dietrich Bonhoeffer maintained that the world had "come of age" and we should look "beyond religion to worldly Christianity." In this discussion Paul Tillich became an active participant. He advocated dialogue with the world. With Bultmann, Bonhoeffer and Tillich currents in the air, "the Anglican Church's penchant for producing, at least every few decades, a 'turbulent priest' was illustrated when the then Bishop of Woolwich, John A. T. Robinson, published his critique of Christian orthodoxy which he entitled *Honest to God* (1963)".[54] Robinson stated in his preface: "I believe we are being called . . . to far more than a restating of traditional orthodoxy in modern terms. Indeed, if our defence of the Faith is limited to this, we shall find in all likelihood that we have lost out to all but a tiny religious remnant. A much more radical recasting . . . is demanded, in the process of which the most fundamental categories of our theology—of God, of the supernatural, and of religion itself—must go into melting."[55]

The scholarly consensus regarding Robinson's *Honest to God* may be stated in the words of Alasdair Heron: *"Honest to God* was not, in itself, a particularly profound (or clear) piece of writing, but it made an enormous impact and served to introduce to a far wider public in and around the churches some of the ideas, questions and answers circulating among theologians."[56] Moreover, Alan D. Gilbert writes: "In *Honest to God,* without being entirely fair to any of his sources, Robinson borrowed ideas from Bultmann, Bonhoeffer and Tillich to construct a single, coherent case for re-thinking the concept of God."[57] Finally, R. Manning quotes Max Warren, writing to the two archbishops (Michael Ramsey and Donald Coggan):

> What has so distressed so many in the past weeks of the controversy about the Bishop of Woolwich's book is that so few have sensed his deep missionary concern. . . . I know that his missionary concern to confront men with the Christ and so lead them to God is the very heart of his ministry.[58]

Rethinking of the concept of God ultimately led to what became known as the "death of God" movement. Two years prior to the publication of *Honest to God* and five years prior to Altizer and Hamilton's *Radical Theology and the Death of God* (1966), Gabriel Vahanian published his book entitled *The Death of God: The Culture of Our Post-Christian Era* (1961). As the subtitle indicated, Vahanian was looking at the Western culture and civilization built upon "the premise that God is dead".[59] His contention was that Western culture was shaped by Christianity but now "is weaning itself from the Christian spirit which has so far nurtured it".[60] His concern was the "corrosion and self-invalidation of Christianity".[61] "Our culture is no longer transcendentalist but immanentalist; no longer sacral or sacramental, but secularist or profane."[62] Vahanian decries the fact that we have lost the transcendentalist world view of Christianity. "Today only the reality of the world, in all its immediacy and imminence, provides man with a context for possible self-understanding. . . . Modern man lives in a world of immanence. . . . If anything characterizes the modern temper, it is a radical immanentism."[63] Altizer, on the other hand, argued that "the negation of Christendom, of the Christian God, can mean that the horizon of our present will open into a future epiphany of faith that will draw *all* things into itself".[64]

The "death of God" movement in America was in part stimulated by an observation of Karl Barth's:

> Observing that the waters of European theology are at present somewhat stagnant, Karl Barth recently said that what we need in Europe and America is not a renewal of an older form of theology but a "theology of freedom" that looks ahead and strives forward.
>
> If this indeed is the true task of theology today, then perhaps, at long last, the time has come for America to assume a theological vocation, a vocation previously denied her because America lacks deep roots in the past which have thus far been an essential presupposition for theological creativity.[65]

Altizer and Hamilton introduced their theological creativity in *Radical Theology and the Death of God*. Hamilton stated: "Radical theology [was moved] out of the realm of interior monologue" and the way was open for many other advocates to go public. Paul van Buren's *The Secular Meaning of the Gospel* (1963) antedated the Altizer and Hamilton volume. Van Buren does not discuss the phrase "death of God". He merely asks, "How may a Christian who is himself a secular man understand the Gospel in a secular way?"[66] By this, van Buren implied "that the meaning of the Gospel is to be focused in the areas of the historical and the ethical, not in the metaphysical or religious".[67]

"Secularization is and will remain a vital issue for Christian thought in the twentieth century": these are the opening words of the preface to *Secularization and the Protestant Prospect,* edited by James F. Childress and David B. Harned.[68] In the early 1960s, D. L. Munby gave the Riddell Memorial Lectures on *The Idea of a Secular Society* (London, 1963). "The secular society exists and flourishes in 'Western' societies, and is likely to develop in Communist societies as they grow to maturity and as Communist dogma becomes as irrelevant to the concerns of the common man as have theological pretensions of the Christian Church in the West."[69] In Munby, however, we find a gentle scholar who did not speak alarmingly. He contended that "[secular society] is framed more nearly in accordance with the Will of God as we can see it in Scripture, in the Incarnation, and in the way God actually treats men, than those societies which have attempted to impose on the mass of men what a small Christian group have believed to be in accordance with God's will".[70]

Secularization as discussed in the late 1960s and beyond has raised such questions as: What is the relationship between the church and the world? Is secularization a movement unfavorable to Christianity? In the church are we moving toward a "faith without religion"? Is secularization dechristianization? Or is it neutral? Does secularization enrich Christianity?

In 1971, a young Scottish thologian, Alistair Kee, educated at Union Theological Seminary in New York City under Daniel Day Williams, John Knox and John Macquarrie, had to explain his position for being "so different from their positions that it might be embarrassing for them to be identified as those most influential on my development".[71] "My primary concern", he wrote, "is not to attack belief in God, but to understand Christianity in such a way that in this age of faith, faith in Christ may be proclaimed as a real option, as I see it, *the* option."[72] Underlying all this restlessness was the desire and the attempt to "communicate" and "mediate" between our world views and the world view of the New Testament writers. Kee referred to the works of Robinson, Ogden and Macquarrie as "attempt[s] to make it possible for Christians to maintain their faith today in a way which is integrated with their secular view of the world".[73] The failure in all these efforts, according to Kee, resulted from their attempts to maintain a "religious belief [which] means belief in God, and this theology has not brought belief in God any nearer to nonbelievers".[74] Kee's position was clearly that "the future of Christianity is not viable unless we can find a way of presenting it which includes the old doctrine of God, but does not demand belief in God as a prior condition of becoming a Christian".[75] How did Kee propose to do this? Not through "reduction but escalation," and this meant "that a new basis had to be found for human judgments".[76] As the title of his book suggests, "choosing the way of transcendence, we make a value judgment that things are not as they seem. . . . We make an act of faith. . . . Faith involves commitment to a decision. . . . Secular faith in Christ involves asking men to risk themselves on the way to transcendence".[77]

Remembering that *Lux Mundi* was a series of studies in the religion of the incarnation, we note that the 1970s was a decade when the doctrine of incarnation became the target for radical criticism in the work edited by John Hick entitled *The Myth of God Incarnate* (London, 1973). The contributors, including Dennis Nineham and Maurice Wiles of Oxford, and Don Cupitt of Cambridge, claimed that in England "the traditional doctrine of the incarnation has long been something of a shibboleth, exempt from reasoned scrutiny and treated with unquestioning literalness".[78] A critical response came with *The Truth of God Incarnate,* edited by Michael Green (London, 1977). Theologians who participated in this debate were John Macquarrie, Brian Hebblethwaite and Stephen Neill. A year later (1978), the papers of a symposium were published under the title of *Incarnation and Myth: The Debate Continued.* Three of our present contributors, Stephen Sykes, Brian Hebblethwaite and Lesslie Newbigin were among the participants in the symposium.

As we approach the celebration of the centennial of *Lux Mundi,* which tried to interpret the faith as the religion of the incarnation, one is reminded of Archbishop Temple's declaration in his Gifford Lectures (1932–34): "It may safely be said that one ground for the hope of Christianity that it may make good its claim to be the true faith lies in the fact that it is the most avowedly materialist of all the great religions. . . . By the very nature of its central doctrine Christianity is committed to a belief in the ultimate significance of the historical process, and in the reality of matter and its place in the divine scheme."[79]

Among many voices in the post–Second World War period, one that was not heard long enough, was the voice of an American Methodist theologian, Carl Michalson, who taught at Drew University in Madison, New Jersey. He was killed in an airplane crash on November 8,

1965. John D. Godsey of Drew University claimed that "probably no American theologian was more effective in interpreting the meaning of Christian faith to growing masses of searching and bewildered college students than Carl Michalson".[80] Michalson's volume *The Worldly Theology* was posthumously published. The subtitle expressed the focus of his thoughts: the hermeneutical focus of a historical faith.

Having died "with his boots on," as John D. Godsey describes it, there was no possibility of Carl Michalson cultivating a theology that had the promise of being a major voice on both sides of the Atlantic. It is proper, therefore, that a glimpse of his theological outlook be presented here in his own words. The last and twelfth chapter of the book was on "Theology and the Worldliness of Faith—The Prospect for a Theology as History":

> One of the significant points of arrival in contemporary theology is the almost general consensus that the reality of faith is historical. . . . The being of God-in-himself, his nature and attributes, the nature of the church, the nature of man, the preexistent nature of Christ—all these conjectural topics which have drawn theology into a realm of either physical or metaphysical speculation remote from the habitation of living men should be abandoned. . . . The task of an historical hermeneutic, an historical mode of interpretation, is to disengage the historical intention from the non-historical expression and to conserve and elaborate the intention. In the process, nothing meaningful is lost; but a good deal of meaningless discourse in theology may be terminated. . . . Theology as history is based on the supposition that the revelation which the Bible and Christian literature express is thoroughly historical and that the canonical text itself embodies the struggle of the early authors to interpret the faith historically, protecting it against non-historical vulgarization. . . . These, then, are the two most important methodological facets of theology as history. First, it is theology resolved to make no statements about reality which do not involve the question of the meaning of man's existence. Second, it is theology resolved to import no criteria into the interpretation of the Biblical faith which the Bible does not itself supply or confirm.

The major issue confronting the church remains secularization. If today's person is to "come of age," then this means, said Michalson, that "he is capable of handling his affairs without invoking a god".[81] The "state of theology" is not, however, as simple as that, for in the first place this is not just a recent development. It is customary to refer to Nietzsche. "To speak of the 'death of God' in its anti-Christian meaning is to invoke at once the name of Friedrich Nietzsche, the great genius in pain finally made mad by his perception into the inner meaning of Western culture. With him, still, we have to ask about the death of God".[82] Nietzsche not only announced the death of God but also declared "we have killed him".[83] Kierkegaard's attack upon Christendom, Bonhoeffer's call for "worldly holiness" and "non-religious theology," Bultmann's demythologization of the New Testament, Barth's criticism of the "preaching of the church in the light of the exegesis of the Scriptures"—all express in different ways "the feeling of desolation and futility which gripped the minds of thinking people".[84] Manwaring quotes from T. S. Eliot's *The Waste Land* (1922), stating that "the general climate of post-war Britain [and true of Christendom in general] soon changed to one of unease and disenchantment, leading to despair and depression".[85] This was only at the beginning of the century. The decades since then have shown more intensified trends toward nihilism. Mark C. Taylor of Williams College, Williamstown, Massachusetts, states:

> With the death of God a dark shadow falls over the light that for centuries illuminated the landscape of the West. Released from any fixed center, everything is left to wander through seemingly infinite space, erring "backward, sideward, forward—in all directions". Paradoxically, this eclipse begins during the period known as the "Enlightenment" and marks the dawn of what usually is labeled "the modern era". Modernism . . . involves the effort to overturn the hierarchical structures of domination upon which Western thought and society traditionally have rested. As such, it represents a contest both for and against mastery. Within the sphere of religion, the result of this struggle can be seen in the death of God.[86]

Taylor sees a "close tie between modern humanistic atheism and its apparent opposite, Reformation theology. Profoundly distressed by the abstraction and universality of medieval theology and deeply impressed by the concreteness and particularity of nominalist philosophy and theology, Luther started a religious and social revolution by directing his theological attention to the individual believer".[87] Luther's doctrine of *pro nobis* was closely tied to the scientist's point of view, namely, "the world is intended to respond to human probing and to serve man's purposes".[88] "When fully developed, the Cartesian philosophy of the *cogito* leads to the 'theory of the subject', which 'lies at the heart of humanism' and forms the basis of humanistic atheism."[89] Here Taylor quotes from J. Hillis Miller's *Poets of Reality:*

The ego has put everything in doubt, and has defined all outside itself as the object of its thinking power. *Cogito ergo sum:* the absolute certainty about the self reached by Descartes' hyperbolic doubt leads to the assumption that things exist, for me at least, only because I think them. When everything exists only as reflected in the ego, then man has drunk up the sea. If man is defined as subject, everything else turns into object. This includes God, who now becomes merely the highest object of man's knowledge. God, once the creative sun, the power establishing the horizon where heaven and earth come together, becomes an object of thought like any other. When man drinks up the sea he also drinks up God, the creator of the sea. In this way man is the murderer of God. . . . When God and the creation become objects of consciousness, man becomes a nihilist.[90]

Thus the survey comes to a close with a note of grave assessment of our times. If the church is to succeed in keeping the faith, it will also be bold enough to proclaim Jesus Christ as the "Light of the World".

NOTES

1. Charles Gore, ed., *Lux Mundi: A Series of Studies in the Religion of the Incarnation,* preface.

2. Francis Ernest Hutchinson, "The Growth of Liberal Theology," in *Cambridge History of English Literature,* ed. Adolphus W. Ward and A. R. Waller, 12:279.

3. Leonard Elliott-Binns, *The Evangelical Movement in the English Church,* 46.

4. Alluded to in Desmond Bowen, *The Idea of the Victorian Church,* 148.

5. Roger Lloyd, *The Church of England in the Twentieth Century,* 1:12.

6. Peter d'A. Jones, *The Christian Socialist Revival, 1877–1914: Religion, Class, and Social Conscience in Late-Victorian England,* 91, 92.

7. Gore, *Lux Mundi,* preface.

8. Leonard Elliott-Binns, *Development of English Theology in the Later Nineteenth Century,* 9–10.

9. Owen Chadwick, *The Victorian Church,* pt. 1, p. 3.

10. Margaret Anne Crowther, *Church Embattled: Religious Controversy in Mid-Victorian England,* 57.

11. Willis Glover, *Evangelical Nonconformists and Higher Criticism in the Nineteenth Century,* 194.

12. A. M. Allchin, "The Understanding of Unity in Tractarian Theology and Spirituality", in *Tradition Renewed,* Oxford Movement Conference Papers (1986), 236.

13. A. M. Ramsey, *From Gore to Temple: The Development of Anglican Theology Between Lux Mundi and the Second World War, 1889–1939,* 1.

14. Bowen, *The Idea of the Victorian Church*, 15.

15. John Julian, ed., *Dictionary of Hymnology*, 1:668.

16. Horton Davies, *Worship and Theology in England: From Newman to Martineau, 1850–1900*, 173.

17. S. C. Carpenter, *Church and People, 1789–1889: A History of the Church of England from William Wilberforce to Lux Mundi*, 98.

18. Bowen, *The Idea of the Victorian Church*, 54.

19. Ibid., 53.

20. Ibid., 54.

21. John Henry Newman, *Apologia* (Oxford: Oxford University Press, 1967), 137.

22. G. Kitson-Clark, *The Making of Victorian England*, 148.

23. In Sidney Leslie Ollard, ed., *Dictionary of English Church History*, 208.

24. In A. O. J. Cockshut, *Anglican Attitudes: A Study of Victorian Religious Controversies*, 79–80, quoted in Bowen, *The Idea of the Victorian Church*, 171.

25. A. M. Ramsey, *From Gore to Temple*, 7.

26. Ibid.

27. Bowen, *The Idea of the Victorian Church*, 175.

28. F. L. Cross, ed., *The Oxford Dictionary of the Christian Church*, 26.

29. R. C. K. Ensor, *England, 1870–1914*, 304.

30. Ibid., 268.

31. H. G. Wood, *Belief and Unbelief Since 1850*, 82.

32. F. C. Burkitt, *Christian Beginnings*, 140–42.

33. Alfred Caldecott, *The Philosophy of Religion in England and America*, 427–28.

34. Alec R. Vidler, *The Church in an Age of Revolution, 1789 to the Present Day*, 200.

35. John Kenneth Mozley, *Some Tendencies in British Theology from the Publication of Lux Mundi to the Present Day*, 34.

36. Ensor, *England, 1870–1914*, 241.

37. Glover, *Evangelical Nonconformity*, 224.

38. *Contentio Veritatis: Essays in Constructive Theology*, v, vi.

39. Mozley, *Some Tendencies in British Theology*, 27.

40. Horton Davies, *Worship and Theology in England: The Ecumenical Century, 1900–1965*, 177.

41. Edwyn C. Hoskyns, *Cambridge Sermons*, 149.

42. C. H. Dodd, *The Apostolic Preaching and Its Development*, 135.

43. Basil Willey, *More Nineteenth Century Studies: A Group of Honest Doubters*, 151.

44. Ibid.

45. Walter E. Houghton, *The Victorian Frame of Mind, 1836–1870*.

46. Ibid., 4.

47. Ibid., 14.

48. William Hordern, ed., *New Directions in Theology Today,* 13.

49. E. Thurneysen, *Revolutionary Theology in the Making: Barth–Thurneysen Correspondence, 1914–1925,* 14.

50. Ibid., 20.

51. Reinhold Niebuhr, *The Nature and Destiny of Man,* 1:viii.

52. Ibid., vii.

53. Alan D. Gilbert, *The Making of Post-Christian Britain,* 121.

54. Randle Manwaring, *From Controversy to Co-Existence: Evangelicals in the Church of England, 1914–1980,* 134.

55. John A. T. Robinson, *Honest to God,* 7.

56. Alasdair Heron, *A Century of Protestant Theology,* 152.

57. Gilbert, *The Making of Post-Christian Britain,* 121.

58. Manwaring, *From Controversy to Co-Existence,* 136.

59. Gabriel Vahanian, *The Death of God: The Culture of Our Post-Christian Era,* xiii.

60. Ibid., xxxii.

61. Ibid.

62. Ibid.

63. Ibid., 147, 188.

64. Thomas J. J. Altizer and William Hamilton, *Radical Theology and the Death of God,* 20.

65. Ibid., 9.

66. Paul M. van Buren, *The Secular Meaning of the Gospel, Based on an Analysis of Its Language,* xiv.

67. Ibid., 197.

68. James F. Childress and David B. Harned, eds., *Secularization and the Protestant Prospect,* 11.

69. D. L. Munby, *The Idea of a Secular Society and Its Significance for Christianity,* 12.

70. Ibid., 34.

71. Alistair Kee, *The Way of Transcendence: Christian Faith Without Belief in God,* x.

72. Ibid.

73. Ibid., 72.

74. Ibid.

75. Ibid., 188.

76. Ibid., 225.

77. Ibid., 229.

78. John Hick, ed., *The Myth of God Incarnate,* xi.

79. William Temple, *Nature, Man and God* (1935; reprint, New York: AMS Press, 1979), 478.

80. Carl Michalson, *Worldly Theology: The Hermeneutical Focus of an Historical Faith,* vii.

81. Ibid., 11.

EPILOGUE

82. Paul Ramsey, in Vahanian, *The Death of God,* xiii.
83. Friedrich Nietzsche, *The Gay Science* (New York: Random House, Vintage Books), 181.
84. Manwaring, *From Controversy to Co-Existence,* 23.
85. Ibid.
86. Mark C. Taylor, *Erring: A Postmodern a/Theology/,* 20.
87. Ibid., 20–21.
88. Ibid., 21.
89. Ibid., 22.
90. Ibid., 3.

BIBLIOGRAPHY: PART ONE

Bowen, Desmond. *The Idea of the Victorian Church.* Montreal: McGill University Press, 1968.

Budd, Susan. *Varieties of Unbelief: Atheists and Agnostics in English Society, 1850–1960.* London: William Heinemann, 1977.

Burkitt, F. C. *Christian Beginnings.* London: University of London, 1924.

Caldecott, Alfred. *The Philosophy of Religion in England and America.* London: Methuen, 1901.

Carpenter, S. C. *Church and People, 1789–1889: A History of the Church of England from William Wilberforce to Lux Mundi.* London: SPCK, 1933.

Chadwick, Owen. *The Victorian Church.* Part I. New York: Oxford University Press, 1960.

Cockshut, A. O. J. *Anglican Attitudes: A Study of Victorian Religious Controversies.* London: William Collins Sons, 1959.

———. *The Unbelievers: English Agnostic Thought.* New York: New York University Press, 1966.

Colenso, J. W. *The Pentateuch and the Book of Joshua.* 7 pts. London: Longmans, Green, 1862–79.

Contentio Veritatis: Essays in Constructive Theology. By Six Tutors. New York: E. P. Dutton, 1902.

Cross, F. L., ed. *The Oxford Dictionary of the Christian Church.* London: Oxford University Press, 1957.

Crowther, Margaret Anne. *Church Embattled: Religious Controversy in Mid-Victorian England.* Hamden, Conn.: Archon Books, 1970.

Davies, Horton. *Worship and Theology in England: From Newman to Martineau, 1850–1900.* Princeton: Princeton University Press, 1960.

———. *Worship and Theology in England: The Ecumenical Century, 1900–1965.* Princeton: Princeton University Press, 1965.

Dodd, C. H. *The Apostolic Preaching and Its Development.* London: Hodder & Stoughton, 1936.

Elliott-Binns, Leonard. *Development of English Theology in the Later Nineteenth Century.* London: Longmans, Green & Co., 1952.

————. *The Evangelical Movement in the English Church.* London: Methuen & Co., 1928.

Ensor, R. C. K. *England, 1870–1914.* Oxford History of England. Oxford: Clarendon Press, 1936.

Foundations, A Statement of Christian Beliefs in Terms of Modern Thought; by Seven Oxford Men. London: Macmillan & Co., 1929.

Glover, Willis. *Evangelical Nonconformists and Higher Criticism in the Nineteenth Century.* London: Independent Press, 1954.

Gore, Charles, ed. *Lux Mundi: A Series of Studies in the Religion of the Incarnation.* London: John Murray, 1889 and often.

Hoskyns, Sir Edwyn C. *Cambridge Sermons.* London: SPCK, 1970.

Houghton, Walter E. *The Victorian Frame of Mind, 1836–1870.* New Haven: Yale University Press, 1978.

Jones, Peter d'A. *The Christian Socialist Revival, 1877–1914: Religion, Class, and Social Conscience in Late-Victorian England.* Princeton: Princeton University Press, 1968.

Julian, John, ed. *Dictionary of Hymnology, Setting Forth the Origin and History of Christian Hymns of All Ages and Nations.* Vol. 1. London: John Murray, 1957.

Kitson-Clark, G. *The Making of Victorian England.* New York: Atheneum, 1971.

Lloyd, Roger. *The Church of England in the Twentieth Century.* Vol. 1. London: Longmans, Green & Co., 1946.

Mozley, John Kenneth. *Some Tendencies in British Theology from the Publication of Lux Mundi to the Present Day.* London: SPCK, 1952.

Ollard, Sidney Leslie, ed. *Dictionary of English Church History.* London: A. R. Mowbray, 1912.

Ramsey, A. M. *From Gore to Temple: The Development of Anglican Theology Between Lux Mundi and the Second World War, 1889–1939.* New York: Charles Scribner's Sons, 1960.

Vidler, Alec R. *The Church in an Age of Revolution: 1789 to the Present Day.* London: Hodder & Stoughton, 1962.

Ward, Sir Adolphus W., and A. R. Waller, eds. *Cambridge History of English Literature.* Vol. 12. Cambridge: Cambridge University Press, 1914.

Welch, Claude. *Protestant Thought in the Nineteenth Century.* Vol. 1, 1799–1870; Vol. 2, 1870–1914. New Haven: Yale University Press, 1972–1985.

Willey, Basil. *More Nineteenth Century Studies: A Group of Honest Doubters.* New York: Columbia University Press, 1956.

Wood, H. G. *Belief and Unbelief Since 1850.* Cambridge: Cambridge University Press, 1955.

BIBLIOGRAPHY: PART TWO

Altizer, Thomas J. J., and William Hamilton. *Radical Theology and the Death of God.* Indianapolis: Bobbs-Merrill, 1966.

Bartsch, Hans Werner. *Kerygma and Myth: A Theological Debate.* London: SPCK, 1972.

Childress, James F., and David B. Harned, eds. *Secularization and the Protestant Prospect.* Philadelphia: Westminster Press, 1970.

Gilbert, Alan D. *The Making of Post-Christian Britain.* London: Longmans, Green & Co., 1980.

Heron, Alasdair. *A Century of Protestant Theology.* Philadelphia: Westminster Press, 1980.

Hick, John, ed. *The Myth of God Incarnate.* London: SCM Press, 1977.

Hordern, William, ed. *New Directions in Theology Today.* Introduction. Philadelphia: Westminster Press, 1966.

Kee, Alistair. *The Way of Transcendence: Christian Faith Without Belief in God.* London: SCM Press, 1971.

Manwaring, Randle. *From Controversy to Co-Existence: Evangelicals in the Church of England, 1914–1980.* New York: Cambridge University Press, 1985.

Mascall, E. L. *The Secularization of Christianity: An Analysis and a Critique.* London: Darton, Longman & Todd, 1965.

Michalson, Carl. *Worldly Theology: The Hermeneutical Focus of an Historical Faith.* New York: Charles Scribner's Sons, 1967.

Miller, J. Hillis. *Poets of Reality.* Cambridge, Mass.: Harvard University Press, Belknap Press, 1965.

Munby, D. L. *The Idea of a Secular Society and Its Significance for Christianity.* London: Oxford University Press, 1963.

Niebuhr, Reinhold. *The Nature and Destiny of Man.* Vol. 1. New York: Charles Scribner's Sons, 1943.

Robinson, John A. T. *Honest to God.* Philadelphia: Westminster Press, 1963.

Taylor, Mark C. *Erring: A Postmodern a/Theology/.* Chicago: University of Chicago Press, 1984.

Thurneysen, E. *Revolutionary Theology in the Making: Barth–Thurneysen Correspondence, 1914–1925.* Richmond: John Knox Press, 1964.

Vahanian, Gabriel. *The Death of God: The Culture of Our Post-Christian Era.* New York: George Braziller, 1961.

van Buren, Paul M. *The Secular Meaning of the Gospel, Based on an Analysis of Its Language.* New York: Macmillan Co., 1963.